A Brief Guide to Arguing about Literature

A Brief Guide to Arguing about Literature

SECOND EDITION

John Schilb
Indiana University

John Clifford
University of North Carolina at Wilmington

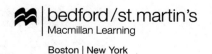

bedford/st.martin's
Macmillan Learning

Boston | New York

For Bedford/St. Martin's
Vice President, Editorial, Macmillan Learning Humanities: Edwin Hill
Editorial Director, English, and Publisher for Literature: Karen S. Henry
Senior Executive and Developmental Editor: Stephen A. Scipione
Executive Editor, Literature: Vivian Garcia
Editorial Assistant: Julia Domenicucci
Production Editor: Louis C. Bruno Jr.
Senior Media Producer: Allison Hart
Publishing Services Manager: Andrea Cava
Marketing Manager: Sophia Latorre-Zengierski
Project Management: Jouve
Senior Photo Editor: Martha Friedman
Photo Researcher: Angela Boehler
Permissions Manager: Kalina Ingham
Senior Art Director: Anna Palchik
Text Design: Jean Hammond
Cover Design: William Boardman
Cover Art: A-Digit / Getty Images
Composition: Jouve
Printing and Binding: Edwards Brothers Malloy, Inc.

Manufactured in the United States of America.

1   0   9   8   7   6

f   e   d   c   b   a

For information, write: Bedford/St. Martin's, 75 Arlington Street, Boston, MA 02116
(617-399-4000)

ISBN 978-1-319-03530-3

Acknowledgments

Text acknowledgments and copyrights appear at the back of the book on pages 297–98, which constitute an extension of the copyright page. Art acknowledgments and copyrights appear on the same page as the art selections they cover.

Preface for Instructors

A Brief Guide to Arguing about Literature, Second Edition, is the first part of *Arguing about Literature: A Guide and Reader*, Second Edition, which combines two books: a guide to skills of writing, especially means of argument; and a collection of literature, organized by themes. Both versions of *Arguing about Literature* connect the teaching of literature with the teaching of composition, and offer substantial advice about writing as well as numerous sample papers. In particular, we give students much aid in writing *arguments* on various topics. We emphasize that an argument is ideally not a form of combat but instead a civilized effort that people make to show their ideas are reasonable.

To be clear: although this brief guide does include a sampling of fiction, poetry, drama, and argumentative writing, its intention is to allow instructors to use our pedagogy with their own choice of literary or argumentative readings rather than the selection in our thematic anthology.

Both brief and full versions of *Arguing about Literature* are designed for two common kinds of courses. The first is a composition course where students learn techniques of argument by practicing them through essays they write, principally about literature. The second is a literature course that is nevertheless concerned to help students craft good arguments about their readings.

In this second edition, *A Brief Guide to Arguing about Literature* has been strengthened for both kinds of courses where it is assigned. For the composition course, we provide more suggestions for analyzing and writing arguments and more arguments for analysis. For the literature course, we offer more advice about reading literature closely and more literature to read. For both kinds of courses, we present more instruction on writing researched arguments and update our discussion of documentation to conform with the 2016 eighth edition of the *MLA Handbook*.

What's in This Guide

As in the first edition, the book focuses on effective ways of writing and reading. In Chapter 1, we introduce elements of argument with an analysis of Paul Goldberger's "Disconnected Urbanism" that elaborates such terms as issues, claims, audience, evidence, and ethos. Chapter 2 explains how to develop an effective style of argument, with ways to move beyond the formulaic five-paragraph essay. Chapter 3 concentrates on teaching strategies for arguing about literature, then Chapter 4 offers strategies for the close reading of literature. Chapter 5 returns to the writing process, familiarizing students with other moves that foster good argument essays. Chapter 6 shows students how to write arguments about the main literary genres: short stories, poems, and plays. Chapter 7 on how to write researched arguments treats this subject at length, and includes three student annotated papers. These examples that show students how they can address various common types of research-based assignments such as entering a critical conversation, developing an argument that places a literary work in cultural context, and using a literary work to examine contemporary social issues. All of the papers are about Charlotte Perkins Gilman's feminist classic, "The Yellow Wallpaper," which we reprint along with several documents that put the story in historical context. The book concludes with "Writing with Critical Approaches to Literature," a chapter that identifies and demonstrates contemporary critical approaches to literature, ranging from reader-response and feminist criticism to postcolonialism and queer theory; it uses these approaches to analyze a particular short story, in part by presenting a sample student paper on it.

New to the Second Edition

The revisions in the second edition reflect the many useful suggestions of our users and reviewers as well as our own attempts to integrate new developments in literature and composition studies.

More advice on understanding and composing arguments.   Chapter 1 now includes diagrams and flowcharts that illustrate how the elements of argument work together. We have also prepared a new second chapter on writing effective arguments that details strategies for doing just that and explains how students can get beyond the constricting five-paragraph essay-writing formula many of them have learned to rely on.

More strategies for critical reading and opportunities to practice it.   Chapter 4 on the reading process now includes a section on how to get ideas for writing by tracing characters' emotions, using as an example Edward Hirsch's poem "Execution," and concludes with additional literary selections on which students can attempt the array of close-reading strategies they have learned in the chapter.

Necessary additions and updates to the chapter on research and documentation.   In Chapter 7, treatment of research includes more information about using sources and avoiding plagiarism, as well as citation and documentation coverage that reflects the new 2016 MLA guidelines.

New literature and new arguments.   We have added stories by Rivka Galchen, Alison Alsup, and James Joyce, a poem by Edward Hirsch, and arguments on topics of great interest to students (such as defaulting on student loans and public shaming on social media) by Regina Rini, Lee Siegel, Sophia McDougall, Jon Ronson, and Jennifer Jacquet.

Acknowledgments

The terrific staff at Bedford/St. Martin's of Macmillan Learning continue to be wise and generous collaborators in our efforts. Once again, we have relied on our wonderful guides and longtime friends, senior executive editor Steve Scipione and editorial director and literature publisher Karen Henry. To their company, we welcome executive editor Vivian Garcia. We are grateful for the careful work editorial assistant Julia Domenicucci performed in assembling the manuscript and the instructor's manual and in carrying out the numberless tasks it took to make a second edition out of *Arguing about Literature*. We want to express thanks to Edwin Hill, vice president of the Humanities division of Macmillan Learning, for his support of the project. In production, we are grateful to managing editor Elise Kaise, and especially to Andrea Cava, Louis Bruno, and Andrea Stefanowicz, who turned a manuscript into a book. In the permissions department, text permissions were effectively negotiated by manager Kalina Ingham and editor Elaine Kosta, and the photo permissions were capably handled by Angela Boehler. In marketing, we are most grateful to Joy Fisher Williams and Sophia Latorre-Zengierski.

We thank Janet E. Gardner, formerly of the University of Massachusetts–Dartmouth, for her contributions to the chapter on research as well as Joyce Hollingsworth of the University of North Carolina at Wilmington and Laura Sparks of California State University–Chico for their ample and timely work on the instructor's manual.

As always, John Schilb is indebted to his former University of Maryland colleague Jeanne Fahnestock and his colleagues at Indiana University, especially Christine Farris, Kathy Smith, and Lisa Ottum. John Clifford thanks Sheri Malman for her expert editorial assistance.

Of course, we remain grateful as well to the instructors whose comments on various editions of *Making Literature Matter* honed our thinking on literature and argument, and many of whom urged us to consider a shorter, more argument-intensive version of the book. But the most trenchant suggestions for the second edition of *A Brief Guide to Arguing about Literature* came from those who taught from and reviewed the first edition: Katherine Baker, College of Southern Nevada; Rebecca Brothers, Jefferson Community and Technical College; Elizabeth Carlyle, College of the Redwoods; Jacob Crane, Bentley University; Mildred Duprey, College of Southern Nevada; Mildred Espree, San Jacinto College; Donna Gordon, Houston Community College; Jacquelyn Harrah, Lone Star College–Montgomery; Barbara Jones, Sam Houston State University; Andrew Logemann, Gordon College; Kenneth McNamara, Georgia Perimeter College; Kimberly Moen, Lone Star College; Catherine Olson, Lone Star College–Tomball; Christopher Perkins, College of Southern Nevada; John Rollins, Lone Star College–Tomball; Stuart Rosenberg, Cypress College; Tannie Shannon, Sam Houston State University; Alice Thomas, Lone Star College–Montgomery; Lisa Tucker, Raritan Valley Community College; and Ronald Tyson, Raritan Valley Community College.

We dedicate this book to our wives, Wendy Elliot and Janet Ellerby. May our relationships with them never be compact, always expanding.

John Schilb, *Indiana University*
John Clifford, *University of North Carolina at Wilmington*

GET THE MOST OUT OF YOUR COURSE WITH ADDITIONAL RESOURCES FOR TEACHING AND LEARNING WITH *A BRIEF GUIDE TO ARGUING ABOUT LITERATURE*, SECOND EDITION

Consider an e-Book Option

A Brief Guide to Arguing about Literature, Second Edition, is also available as a PDF-style e-book. You can find further information about the PDF-style e-book via the online catalog page; visit **macmillanlearning.com/ebooks**.

Want More Literature and Arguments? Choose the Version with an Anthology

As we mentioned, this guide is also included in a longer book, *Arguing about Literature: A Guide and Reader,* Second Edition, which features additional chapters on the themes of family, love, freedom and confinement, justice, and journeys. Each thematic chapter includes fiction, poetry, drama, and arguments, all of which are grouped in clusters that focus on particular issues—for example, stories about mothers and daughters, poems about racial injustice, plays about constraining marriages, arguments about immigrant experience—so that students can gain insights by comparing texts. Throughout are special clusters that focus on literary criticism, contexts for research, or the connection of literature to current issues. Please note that the *Guide and Reader* version is not available as an e-book. To view a full table of contents and order an evaluation copy, visit **macmillanlearning.com/arguingaboutlit/catalog**.

Gain Access to Your Instructor's Manual

A print-only evaluation copy of *A Brief Guide to Arguing about Literature,* Second Edition, comes with teaching advice bound into it. Written by John Schilb, John Clifford, Joyce Hollingsworth, and Laura Sparks, this manual includes sample syllabi; suggestions for teaching argumentation, composition, and literature; and an annotated bibliography for further research. Use ISBN 978-1-319-07059-5 to order an evaluation copy or visit the Bedford/St. Martin's catalog (**macmillanlearning.com**) for further information.

Join Our Community

The Macmillan English Community is home to Bedford/St. Martin's professional resources, featuring content to support the teaching of literature—including our popular blog, *LitBits*, as well as articles, research studies, and testimonials on the importance of literature in our classrooms and in our lives. Community members may also review projects and ideas in the pipeline. Join at **community.macmillan.com**.

Engage Your Students with Digital Assignments

Teaching Literature with Digital Technology is a collection of digital assignments, each created by a contributor in the fields of literature and composition. Edited by Seattle-based scholar and teacher Tim Hetland and available as a print text or PDF e-book, this resource for instructors invites students to become knowledge-makers as it introduces creative uses of social media, digital tools, podcasts, multimodal assignments, and digital archives to learn about literature. Sample assignments can be viewed in the Professional Resources folder on the Macmillan English Community site. To order the print text, use ISBN: 978-1-4576-2948-8; to order the PDF e-book, use ISBN: 978-1-319-07643-6.

Assign *LaunchPad Solo for Literature* — the Online, Interactive Guide to Close Reading

To get the most out of *A Brief Guide to Arguing about Literature*, Second Edition, assign it with *LaunchPad Solo for Literature*, which can be packaged at **a significant discount**. With easy-to-use and easy-to-assign modules, reading comprehension quizzes, and engaging author videos, *LaunchPad Solo for Literature* guides students through four common assignment types: responding to a reading, drawing connections between two or more texts, listening to a reading, and instructor-led collaborative close reading. Get all of our great resources and activities in one fully customizable space online; then use our tools with your own content. To learn more about how you can use *LaunchPad Solo for Literature* in your course, please see the last pages of this preface.

Package One of Our Best-Selling Brief Handbooks at a Discount

Do you need a pocket-sized handbook for your course? Package *EasyWriter* by Andrea Lunsford or *A Pocket Style Manual* by Diana Hacker and Nancy Sommers with this text at a twenty percent discount. For more information, go to **macmillanlearning.com/easywriter/catalog** or **macmillanlearning.com/pocket/catalog**.

Teach Longer Works at a Nice Price

Volumes from our *Literary Reprint* series — the *Case Studies in Contemporary Criticism* series, the *Bedford Cultural Edition* series, the *Bedford Shakespeare* series, and the *Bedford College Editions* — can be shrinkwrapped with *A Brief Guide to Arguing about Literature* at a discount. For a complete list of available titles, visit **macmillanlearning.com/literaryreprints/catalog**.

Trade Up and Save Fifty Percent

Add more value and choice to your students' learning experiences by packaging their Macmillan textbook with one of a thousand titles from our sister publishers, including Farrar, Straus & Giroux and St. Martin's Press — at a discount of **fifty percent** off the regular prices. Visit **macmillanlearning.com/tradeup** for details.

LaunchPad Solo
macmillan learning

Pairing *A Brief Guide to Arguing about Literature* with *LaunchPad Solo for Literature* helps students succeed.

Available for free when packaged with *A Brief Guide to Arguing about Literature*, *LaunchPad Solo for Literature* gets to the heart of close reading. It offers a set of online materials that help beginning literature students learn and practice close reading and critical thinking skills in an interactive environment.

To package *LaunchPad Solo for Literature*, use ISBN 978-1-319-07189-9.

How can *LaunchPad Solo for Literature* enhance your course?

It helps students come prepared to class. Assign one of almost 500 reading comprehension quizzes on commonly taught stories, poems, plays, and essays to ensure that your students complete and understand their reading. For homework assignments, have students work through close reading modules that will prepare them for lively, informed classroom discussions.

It gives students hands-on practice in close reading. Easy-to-use and easy-to-assign modules based on widely taught literary selections guide students through three common assignment types:

- *Respond to a Reading*
  Marginal questions that refer to specific passages in a publisher-provided literary work prompt students to read carefully and think critically about key issues raised by the text.

- *Draw Connections*
  Students read and compare two or more publisher-provided texts that illuminate each other. Students can download these texts, which have been annotated to highlight key moments and contextual information, and respond in writing to a series of questions that highlight important similarities and differences between and among the texts.

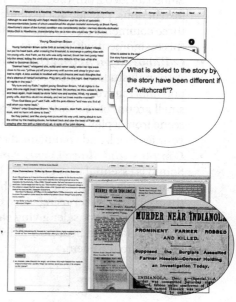

To explore *LaunchPad Solo for Literature*, visit **launchpadworks.com**.

- *Collaborate on a Reading*
  Instructors can upload their favorite text
  or choose from over 200 publisher-provided
  texts to create a customized lesson on close
  reading. Using the highlighting tools and
  notes feature in *LaunchPad*, the instructor
  can post notes or questions about specific
  passages or issues in a text, prompting
  students to respond with their own comments,
  questions, or observations. Students can also
  respond to each other, further collaborating
  and deepening their understanding of a text.

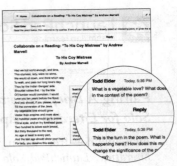

It lets you create multimedia assignments about literature. *LaunchPad Solo for Literature* enables you to embed videos, including favorite selections from YouTube, directly into your digital course. Whether you want students to analyze a Shakespearean scene, listen to W. B. Yeats reading his poems, or compare *The Great Gatsby* in print and on film, the tools are at your fingertips. You can annotate these videos for your students, or ask them to leave their own comments directly on the video content itself. Consider some of these assignment suggestions:

- *Create a Dialogue around an Assignment*
  Some projects are complicated because they involve many choices and stages. Record yourself explaining the project, and upload the video to the Video Assignment tool. Require students to comment by asking a question or by proposing a topic.
- *Critique a Video as a Group*
  Embed a video from YouTube or from another source. In your assignment instructions, provide discussion questions. Require students to add two or three comments on the video that respond to the prompt. You may grade this assignment with a rubric.
- *Collaborate on Acting Out a Scene from a Play*
  Although students most often study plays as written texts, it can be fun and informative to have them act out scenes for their classmates. Assign small groups of students to record themselves acting out their favorite scene from a play and upload the video for the class to watch. You can add your feedback and comments directly on the video.
- *Compare and Share Poems Your Students Read Aloud*
  Sound is essential in poetry, and how a poem is read can be as important to understanding as the words themselves. Invite students to record themselves—either using video or audio only—and share the results with the class. Consider giving each student a "mood" for their reading, so that the class can hear how different tones and interpretations affect their response to the poem.

Brief Contents

Contents

8. Writing with Critical Approaches to Literature   270

Contents by Genre

Stories

Poems

Plays

Arguments about Current Issues

Contexts for Research

CHAPTER 1

What Is Argument?

The first word in our book's title may puzzle you. Why would we want you to argue? Are we really inviting you to yell or sneer? The word *arguing* may remind you of spats you regret. Almost everyone has suffered arguments like these. They arise in the media all the time. Talk radio hosts and their callers mix strong opinion with insult. Television's political panels routinely lapse into squabbles; guests feel required to clash. Quarrels explode on daytime talkfests; couples fight over who's cheated on whom. Online forums are plagued by "trolls," writers who crudely mock others' posts. No wonder many people define *arguing* as combat. It often seems like war.

But our book is about arguing in a positive sense. We define it as a calm, courteous process in which you

- identify a subject of current or possible debate;
- analyze why you view the subject the way you do;
- address others who may not share your view; and
- try to persuade them that your view is worth accepting or at least makes sense.

This better kind of arguing occurs at various times and places. You may try to coax friends who dread horror films into joining you at *Saw 12*. In class, you may need to explain the logic of your stand on climate change. Beyond campus, you may advocate for social causes. For instance, you might petition your city to launch recycling sites.

Let's face it: to argue is to disagree, or to air views that not all may hold. Still, at its best, argument is an alternative to war. It's not a contest you try to "win" by insisting you're right. Ideally, argument is a form of **inquiry**, a process in which you test your beliefs, consider other views, and stay open to changing your mind. Rather than immediately attack your critics, you note principles you share with them. When their thinking differs from yours, you treat their positions fairly. If any of their ideas strike you as wise, you adjust your thinking. In the meantime, you recognize the limits of your knowledge and understanding. You admit, too, your inner conflicts: how your thoughts are divided, your values in conflict, your feelings mixed. Indeed, essayist Phillip Lopate observes that "the real argument should be with yourself." Columnist David

Brooks goes even further: "If you write in a way that suggests combative certitude," he warns, "you may gradually smother the inner chaos that will be the source of lifelong freshness and creativity." In their own fashion, these writers point to something important about argument: at its best, it teaches you about yourself and your world, while alerting you to what you still must learn.

Students regularly encounter this kind of arguing in college. Academic subjects aren't just pools of information. They go beyond proven facts. Disciplines grapple with uncertainties: problems, questions, and conflicts they haven't yet solved. Physicists disagree about the origins of the universe. Historians write conflicting accounts of Hitler's Germany; they debate how much his extreme anti-Semitism was traditional there. Two sociologists may scan the same figures on poverty and make different inferences from them. Typically, scholars draw conclusions that are open to challenge. They must explain why their judgments are sound. They expect to engage in reasoned debate with their colleagues. They see this as their field's best chance for truth.

In your classes, expect disagreements. They're crucial to learning in college. Often classmates will voice ideas you don't immediately accept. Just as often, they'll hesitate to adopt some opinion of yours. Authors you read will deal with controversies from their own points of view. As a writer yourself, you will enter debates and have to defend your stands.

No one naturally excels at this type of arguing. It takes practice. Our book is a series of opportunities to become skilled in this art. Our book's chief springboard for argument is works of literature. Those we include don't deliver simple, straightforward messages. They offer puzzles, complications, metaphors, symbols, and mysteries. In short, they stress life's complexity. They especially encourage you to ponder multiple dimensions of language: how, for example, shifts of context can change a word's meaning. Each of our literary works calls for you to interpret. As you read the text, you must figure out various features of it. Other readers may not see the text as you do. So next you'll *argue* for your view. Often you'll do this by composing essays and perhaps online posts. From Chapter 2 on, we offer strategies for you to argue about literature as a writer.

This chapter is a general introduction to arguing. Let's start with an example: an article titled "Disconnected Urbanism" by noted architecture critic Paul Goldberger (b. 1950). He wrote it for the February 22, 2003, issue of *Metropolis* magazine. Goldberger worries about cell phones. He believes they lead cities to lose a sense of community and place. At the time he wrote, these phones weren't yet packed with apps, nor could they connect to the Internet. Still, they were a big development, which pained Goldberger. As you read, note his key points and his efforts to sway his readers to them. Afterward, we raise questions to help you study his text. Then we refer to it as we explain the basic elements of argument.

PAUL GOLDBERGER
Disconnected Urbanism

There is a connection between the idea of place and the reality of cellular telephones. It is not encouraging. Places are unique — or at least we like to believe they are — and we strive to experience them as a kind of engagement with particulars. Cell phones are precisely the opposite. When a piece of geography is doing what it is supposed to do, it encourages you to feel a connection to it that, as in marriage, forsakes all others. When you are in Paris you expect to wallow in its Parisness, to feel that everyone walking up the Boulevard Montparnasse is as totally and completely there as the lampposts, the kiosks, the facade of the Brasserie Lipp — and that they could be no place else. So we want it to be in every city, in every kind of place. When you are in a forest, you want to experience its woodsiness; when you are on the beach, you want to feel connected to sand and surf.

This is getting harder to do, not because these special places don't exist or because urban places have come to look increasingly alike. They have, but this is not another rant about the monoculture and sameness of cities and the suburban landscape. Even when you are in a place that retains its intensity, its specialness, and its ability to confer a defining context on your life, it doesn't have the all-consuming effect these places used to. You no longer feel that being in one place cuts you off from other places. Technology has been doing this for a long time, of course — remember when people communicated with Europe by letter and it took a couple of weeks to get a reply? Now we're upset if we have to send a fax because it takes so much longer than e-mail.

But the cell phone has changed our sense of place more than faxes and computers and e-mail because of its ability to intrude into every moment in every possible place. When you walk along the street and talk on a cell phone, you are not on the street sharing the communal experience of urban life. You are in some other place — someplace at the other end of your phone conversation. You are there, but you are not there. It reminds me of the title of Lillian Ross's memoir of her life with William Shawn, *Here But Not Here*. Now that is increasingly true of almost every person on almost every street in almost every city. You are either on the phone or carrying one, and the moment it rings you will be transported out of real space into a virtual realm.

This matters because the street is the ultimate public space and walking along it is the defining urban experience. It is all of us — different people who lead different lives — coming together in the urban mixing chamber. But what if half of them are elsewhere, there in body but not in any other way? You are not on Madison Avenue if you are holding a little object to your ear that pulls you toward a person in Omaha.

The great offense of the cell phone in public is not the intrusion of its ring, although that can be infuriating when it interrupts a tranquil moment. It is the fact that even when the phone does not ring at all, and is being used quietly and discreetly, it renders a public place less public. It turns the boulevardier

5

into a sequestered individual, the flaneur into a figure of privacy. And suddenly the meaning of the street as a public place has been hugely diminished.

I don't know which is worse—the loss of the sense that walking along a great urban street is a glorious shared experience or the blurring of distinctions between different kinds of places. But these cultural losses are related, and the cell phone has played a major role in both. The other day I returned a phone call from a friend who lives in Hartford. He had left a voice-mail message saying he was visiting his son in New Orleans, and when I called him back on his cell phone—area code 860, Hartford—he picked up the call in Tallahassee. Once the area code actually meant something in terms of geography: it outlined a clearly defined piece of the earth; it became a form of identity. Your telephone number was a badge of place. Now the area code is really not much more than three digits; and if it has any connection to a place, it's just the telephone's home base. An area code today is more like a car's license plate. The downward spiral that began with the end of the old telephone exchanges that truly did connect to a place—RHinelander 4 and BUtterfield 8 for the Upper East Side, or CHelsea 3 downtown, or UNiversity 4 in Morningside Heights—surely culminates in the placeless area codes such as 917 and 347 that could be anywhere in New York—or anywhere at all.

It's increasingly common for cell-phone conversations to begin with the question, "Where are you?" and for the answer to be anything from "out by the pool" to "Madagascar." I don't miss the age when phone charges were based on distance, but that did have the beneficial effect of reinforcing a sense that places were distinguishable from one another. Now calling across the street and calling from New York to California or even Europe are precisely the same thing. They cost the same because to the phone they are the same. Every place is exactly the same as every other place. They are all just nodes on a network—and so, increasingly, are we.   [2003]

≡ THINKING ABOUT THE TEXT

1. Imagine that Goldberger could observe how people now use cell phones in places you ordinarily go, such as a college campus. To what extent would he see the kind of behavior that he worried about in his 2003 piece? How much evidence could he find for his argument that cell phones are diminishing people's sense of place and *dis*connecting them from one another?

2. Goldberger does not say much about the advantages of a cell phone. Which, if any, do you think he should have mentioned, and why? How, if at all, could he have said more about the advantages while still getting his readers to worry about these phones?

3. Goldberger wrote before smartphones came along, enabling use of apps and the Internet. In what ways, if any, does this newer technology affect your view of his argument?

4. As he indicates by including the word *urbanism* in his title, Goldberger is chiefly concerned with how cell phones affect their users' experiences of cities. If he had written about cell-phone use in suburbs or in rural areas, do you think he would have changed his argument in some way? If so, in what respect?

5. It seems quite possible that Goldberger himself uses a cell phone. If this is the case, does it make his concern less valid? Why, or why not? Moreover, he does not end his piece by proposing that humanity abandon the technology. Why, conceivably, does he avoid making this recommendation? What might he want his readers to do instead?

Understanding Rhetoric

Goldberger's article is an example of **rhetoric**. This is a term from ancient Greek. It means writing, speech, and visual images used for a certain purpose: to affect how people think and act. Rhetorical texts don't just convey a message. They aim to shape beliefs and conduct. Often they're efforts to alter these things. Probably several of Goldberger's readers are joyously addicted to cell phones; he nudges them to reconsider their overattachment.

A related term is the **rhetorical situation**. It's the specific context you have in mind when you engage in rhetoric. As Figure 1.1 shows, this context includes three major elements: your topic, your audience, and possible "channels."

1. **The particular *topic* you choose.** This subject may already interest the public. Any school shootings in the United States immediately provoke disputes over gun control, school safety, mental illness, and screen violence. But the topic needn't be a calamity.

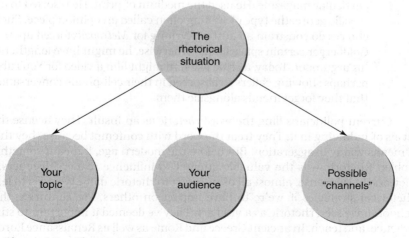

Figure 1.1   Elements of the rhetorical situation

When Goldberger wrote, cell phones were booming as a trend, so their effects were debated a lot. He didn't have to alert his readers to this subject or remind them of it. Other writers must do one or the other. This was the situation for legal scholars Woodrow Hartzog and Evan Zelinger in 2013, when they posted an online argument about Facebook. At the time, people worried that Facebook's privacy protocols wouldn't securely protect users' personal data. Hartzog and Zelinger deliberately shift to another subject. They recommend thinking less about *privacy* and more about *obscurity*, which they note is a word "rarely used" in debates about Facebook's risks. To them, *privacy* is so vague a concept that brooding about how the site guards it is futile. They call for pushing Facebook to keep personal facts *obscure*: "hard to obtain or understand" when cyberstalkers hunt them.

2. **The main readers, listeners, or viewers you decide to address; your *audience*.** Goldberger wrote for readers of the city-oriented magazine *Metropolis*. Its mission statement declares that it "examines contemporary life through design," publishing articles that "range from the sprawling urban environment to intimate living spaces to small objects of everyday lives." This magazine also seeks to put design in "economic, environmental, social, cultural, political, and technological contexts." Readers of *Metropolis* would expect it to probe cell phones' impact on cities. Perhaps Goldberger hoped his piece would someday circulate more widely, as it now does on the Web. But surely his target group loomed in his mind as he decided on content, form, and words.

3. **Possible "channels" for the text.** These include available institutions, media, and genres. Goldberger composed his article for a particular magazine. He used the medium of print. He resorted to a specific genre: the type of writing often called an opinion piece. Such choices do constrain an author. Writing for *Metropolis* forced upon Goldberger certain space limits; otherwise, he might have lengthened his argument. Today, a critic like him might film a video for YouTube, perhaps showing callers so absorbed in their cell-phone conversations that they forget friends alongside them.

Current politicians fling the word *rhetoric* as an insult. They accuse their rivals of indulging in it. They treat the word with contempt because they think it means windy exaggeration. But before the modern age, it meant something nobler. Rhetoric was the valuable attempt to influence readers, listeners, or viewers. In this sense, almost all of us resort to rhetoric daily. We need to learn rhetorical strategies if we're to have impact on others. For centuries, then, schools have seen rhetoric as a vital art. They've deemed it important to study, practice, and teach. In ancient Greece and Rome as well as Renaissance Europe, it was a core academic subject. American colleges of the nineteenth century also made it central. This focus survives in many courses today, especially ones about writing or speech. Our book reflects their commitment to rhetoric, especially through our advice about writing.

The Elements of Argument

Within the field of rhetoric, arguments are a more specific category. When you argue, you attempt to **persuade** an **audience** to accept your **claims** regarding an issue. To achieve this aim, you present **evidence**, explain your **reasoning**, rely on **assumptions**, and make other kinds of **appeals**.

The boldfaced words play key roles in this book; we mention them often. These eight basic elements are also identified in Figure 1.2, which suggests visually how the elements work together.

Below we briefly explain the elements, using them to make suggestions for writing an argument. Taking Goldberger's piece as a sample, we begin with

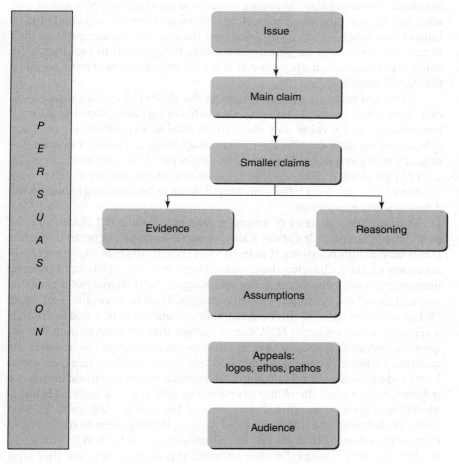

Figure 1.2   Elements of argument

issue and then move to *claims, persuasion, audience, evidence, reasoning, assumptions,* and *appeals.* We'll return to these elements in Chapter 3, where we explain their role in arguments about literature.

ISSUES

An **issue** is a question not yet settled. People have disagreed—or might disagree—over how to answer it. Goldberger's question seems to be this: How are cell phones transforming culture? But he doesn't state his question flat out. He presumes his readers will guess it. Other writers of arguments put their questions plainly. They want to ensure their readers know them. This seems to be Jeremy Rozansky's goal in an argument he wrote for the January 19, 2013, issue of *The New Atlantis.* His article's topic is steroid-using athletes. To him, debates about men like Barry Bonds and Roger Clemens focus too much on whether they played "fair" or are naturally talented. Rozansky calls for thinking about something else: "What are athletes doing when they play sports, and what are we watching when we watch?" His own answer is "a certain kind of human excellence." Then he explains how the men proved incapable of such virtue. But notice that he bluntly announces his question to begin with. By doing this, he stresses it. He signals that it's the most important issue raised by the steroid scandals.

When you write an argument, readers should find your main issue *significant.* It must be a question they believe is worth caring about. Sometimes they'll immediately see its value. But often you'll need to explain what's at stake. Scholars of rhetoric describe the task as establishing the issue's **exigence**, the urgency or importance of the situation. Goldberger brings up exigence at the start of paragraph 4. There he states that on city streets, the use of cell phones "matters," for "the street is the ultimate public space and walking along it is the defining urban experience."

For another statement of exigence, let's turn to a 2013 piece from the online magazine *Slate.* It's about a strange topic: animals put on trial. Author James McWilliams points out that in 1457, a French village brought a sow and six piglets to court, charging them with killing a boy. The piglets were declared innocent; the sow was found guilty and hanged. McWilliams notes that this was just one of many animal trials in past ages. Then he states his chief issue: "What are we to make of this evidence that our ancestors imputed to animals a sense of moral agency?" McWilliams realizes that his readers may find his question trivial. They may not see its relevance to the present. So he states the question's stakes: "These seemingly odd trials have much to teach us about how fundamentally our relationship with animals has changed and how, more poignantly, we've lost the ability to empathize with them as sentient beings." McWilliams goes on to praise how courts of the past treated animals. Even guilty verdicts respected these creatures, he says. Putting them on trial credited them with powers of thought and the potential to act well. McWilliams wants modern humans to adopt the same attitude. At present, he believes, they treat animals as objects. Whether or not you agree with McWilliams, he resembles Goldberger in stating why his issue matters.

CLAIMS

Perhaps you associate the word *claims* with insurance companies. It's familiar as a term for the forms you fill out when someone bashes your car. You may not be used to calling other things you say or write *claims*. But even when you utter a simple observation about the weather—for instance, "It's beginning to rain"—you make a claim. A **claim** is a statement that is spoken or written so that people will think it true. With this definition in mind, you may spot claims everywhere. Most of us make them every day. Most claims *are* accepted as true by the people to whom we make them. Imagine how difficult life would be if the opposite were so. Human beings would constantly fret if they distrusted everything told them.

But claims may conflict with other claims. We've defined an *issue* as a question with various debatable answers. *Claims*, as we use the term, are the debatable answers. In this sense, most of Goldberger's statements are claims, for readers might resist them. Take his main claim, which he identifies at the start of paragraph 6. There he argues that cell phones are prime forces in a pair of "cultural losses." These are "the loss of the sense that walking along a great urban street is a glorious shared experience" and "the blurring of distinctions between different kinds of places." Readers might object to Goldberger's view in various ways. Some might argue that neither of these losses has occurred. Others might say that these losses have happened but that cell phones didn't cause them. So Goldberger has more work to do. Like all debatable statements, his requires support.

When you write a college paper, typically you'll raise an issue. Then you'll make one main claim about it. This can also be called your **thesis**, a term you may know from high school. It won't be your *only* point. You'll make smaller claims as your essay continues. But stating your main claim, and remaining focused on it, will be important.

PERSUASION

It's commonly assumed that if two people argue, they are dogmatic. Each insists on being proclaimed correct. But at its best, argument involves efforts to **persuade**. You argue in the first place because you want others to accept your claims. Yet you can't expect them to applaud at once. To attempt **persuasion** is to concede that your claims need defense. Goldberger knew that much of his readership adored the phones that disturb him. He'd have to justify his stance.

Most likely he figured that he couldn't turn all the fans into critics. Such conversions can be hard to pull off. But he could pursue a more modest goal: showing that his claims merit study. Whether or not they gained approval from everyone, he could make them seem reasonable. Probably he'd be happy if a reader said, "I'm fonder of cell phones than Goldberger is, but I can't dismiss his criticisms. I'm willing to keep reflecting on them." A response like this can be your aim, too. Realistically, *persuasion* doesn't mean everyone eventually agrees with you. An argument you write may leave some readers maintaining another view. But you've done much if they conclude that your ideas are credible—worth their bearing in mind.

AUDIENCE

The word **audience** may first make you think of people at plays, concerts, movies, or lectures. Yet it also describes readers. Not everything you write is for other human eyes; in college courses, you may produce notes, journal entries, blog posts, and essays for yourself alone. But in most any course, you'll also do public writing. You'll try to persuade audiences to accept claims you make.

This task requires you to consider more than your subject. You must take your readers into account. McWilliams realized that his audience wouldn't know about animal trials. He'd have to begin with anecdotes explaining what these hearings were like. By contrast, Goldberger's average readers would be aware of cell phones. Also, he supposed that they had a certain vocabulary—that they knew "boulevardier" and "flaneur" meant someone who likes to explore city streets. Evidently he saw his audience, too, as holding two beliefs about cell phones. One is that they help people connect. The other is that they make private life more public, for chatter on them is often overheard. Deliberately, Goldberger challenges both ideas. He argues that because cell phones distract people from their surroundings, they lead to "*disconnected urbanism*" and turn "a public place less public." Unfortunately, sometimes your audience will have a vaguer profile than his. You may have to guess what your target group knows, assumes, and values.

EVIDENCE

Evidence is support you give your claims so others will accept them. What sort of evidence must it be? That depends on what your audience expects. Disciplines differ in this respect. In literary studies, claims about a text seem more plausible if they're backed by quotations from it. (We discuss this standard more in Chapter 2.) Scientists must not only conduct experiments but also describe them so that others can repeat them and see if the results are the same. Anthropologists feel pressured to base their conclusions on field research. Not that your audience will always be academic scholars. It can easily be more diverse. Goldberger's audience included experts in design but also nonprofessionals with interests like theirs. In short, his readership was mixed.

To persuade this group, Goldberger offered two kinds of evidence. His climax is a personal tale about a Hartford-based friend of his who called him from New Orleans and then from Tallahassee. Clearly, Goldberger wanted his audience to find this story typical of modern life. He hoped it would serve as what rhetorical theorist Kenneth Burke calls a *representative anecdote*. Its effect would be to reinforce his claim that cell phones ruin callers' sense of place. In addition, Goldberger presses his readers to consult their own experiences. He bids them recall how they've used cell phones on city strolls. At such moments, he seeks to remind them they "are not on the street sharing the communal experience of urban life." Similarly, he prods them to remember how "increasingly common" it is "for cell-phone conversations to begin with the question, 'Where are you?' and for the answer to be anything from 'out by the pool' to 'Madagascar.' "

As a writer, you might have to guess your audience's standards of proof. You'll be influenced by experiences you've had with such readers. Perhaps you'll also have opportunities to review drafts with them.

REASONING

Philosopher Gary Gutting observes that "facts alone are necessary but not sufficient for a good argument. As important as getting the facts right is putting the facts into a comprehensible logical structure that supports your conclusion." This advice can help you as you strive to persuade others through writing. Besides evidence, your readers will expect you to show careful **reasoning**. Ideally, they'll come away feeling that your ideas truly connect. They should sense that your main claim derives from your other ones. Goldberger's logic seems to follow the flow of the chart in Figure 1.3.

Goldberger doesn't arrange these ideas as a list. He might bore readers if he did! Still, ideally readers will see his claims as a methodical sequence. When you write an argument, guide your audience step by step through your

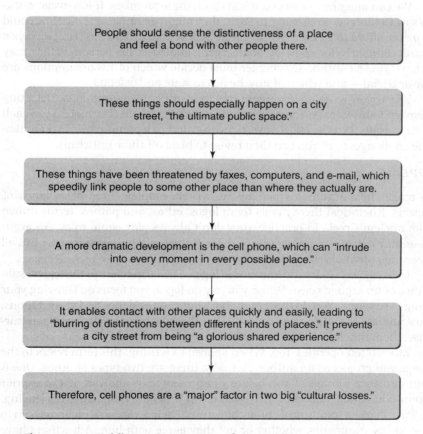

People should sense the distinctiveness of a place and feel a bond with other people there.

These things should especially happen on a city street, "the ultimate public space."

These things have been threatened by faxes, computers, and e-mail, which speedily link people to some other place than where they actually are.

A more dramatic development is the cell phone, which can "intrude into every moment in every possible place."

It enables contact with other places quickly and easily, leading to "blurring of distinctions between different kinds of places." It prevents a city street from being "a glorious shared experience."

Therefore, cell phones are a "major" factor in two big "cultural losses."

Figure 1.3   Goldberger's sequence of reasoning

reasoning. Help them follow your logic. Make your essay seem an orderly train of thought.

ASSUMPTIONS

Already we've mentioned certain **assumptions** of Goldberger's. But other beliefs appear to have steered him. They include some that readers may reject. Assumptions behind an argument may be numerous and debatable. That's why we single them out as an element here.

One category is beliefs about the audience's experiences. As Goldberger asks his readers to imagine "When you are in Paris," he supposes that all of them have visited Paris or might go there some day. Another type of assumption concerns the writer's values. When Goldberger laments cities' loss of uniqueness, he assumes that uniqueness is good. A third type is what rhetorical theory calls *warrants*. This term refers to the writer's beliefs about what can serve as evidence. Recall that Goldberger climaxes his argument with a personal story. He relies on a warrant when he offers this tale. It's the assumption that the story is evidence for his argument's main claim.

We can imagine readers skeptical about these premises. If low-wage workers saw Goldberger's reference to Paris, they might grumble or scoff. How could *they* ever afford to go there? Others may believe that uniqueness isn't always a benefit. Similarly, for some of Goldberger's audience, his personal story may lack weight. As author, Goldberger must decide which of his assumptions are safe or trivial—and which, if any, he has to state and defend.

When you write an argument, try to identify its assumptions. Detecting them isn't always easy. You may need to have friends and classmates read each of your drafts. But the effort pays. Growing alert to a premise helps you anticipate challenges to it. You can then revise to head off these criticisms.

APPEALS

To make their arguments persuasive, writers employ three basic kinds of appeals. Rhetorical theory calls them **logos**, **ethos**, and **pathos**, terms drawn from ancient Greek. In practice, they don't always play equal roles. An argument may depend on one or two of these strategies, not the entire trio. But all three are potential resources.

In a way, we've already introduced **logos**. The term refers to the logical substance of an arguer's case. When you rely on logos, you focus on showing your claims are sound. You do this by emphasizing your evidence and your reasons. Most audiences will demand anyway that these features be strong. It's no surprise, then, that logos is the most common type of appeal.

Ethos often operates, too. When applied to writing, this term refers to the image you project as an author. Actually, there are two types of ethos. One is your audience's image of you before you present your analysis. It's your prior reputation. Many readers of *Metropolis* know that Paul Goldberger is a leading, Pulitzer Prize–winning critic of architecture. Their awareness inclines them to respect his arguments, whether or not they agree with him. Advertisers have reputational ethos in mind when they hire celebrities for endorsements. The hope is that you'll join Weight Watchers because Jennifer Hudson did. This ethos also comes into play with self-help manuals. Often their covers boast that the writer is an academic. You're supposed to buy *How to Find Lovers by Loving Yourself* because its author has a Ph.D.

Most of us, however, aren't famous or highly credentialed. There remains a second kind of ethos: the picture of you that people form as they read your text. To gain their trust, you should patiently lay out your claims, reasons, and evidence. This is what Goldberger does. True, cell phones bother him enough that he uses the word *offense* and points out that their ring "can be infuriating." But he doesn't lash out against them. He avoids harsh, righteous anger. He signals that his argument won't become a "rant." He declares the phones' impact "not encouraging" — a fairly mild criticism. He doesn't demand they be smashed to bits. He simply mourns "losses" they cause.

When arguers are scornful, some of their audience may object. John Burt points out a problem that Stephen Douglas's ethos created in his famous debates with Abraham Lincoln. When the two men competed for a U.S. Senate seat in 1858, the main issue was slavery. On this topic, Douglas planned to come across as a seeker of compromise. But on stage, he fiercely insulted Lincoln, showing nastiness and not tact. As Burt observes, "Douglas's own management of his case was so intemperate, so inflammatory, and so personal that whatever case one could make for his position, he himself was the last person who could plausibly carry the day for that case." Sometimes anger *is* right, especially when injustice must be noticed and stopped. But for much of your writing, especially in college, Goldberger's tone will serve better.

Writers enhance their ethos through **concessions** and **qualifications**. Concessions are civil (or even kind or admiring) acknowledgments of views or experiences other than yours. One appears in Goldberger's piece. Largely he claims that cell phones wreck people's sense of place. But he does admit that unique geography survives to some extent. In paragraph 2, he notes that here and there you can find "a place that retains its intensity, its specialness, and its ability to confer a defining context on your life." He's quick to add that these settings fall short of an "all-consuming effect." Nevertheless, he grants that they've somehow remained distinct. Most readers will like his recognizing this fact.

In rhetorical theory, qualifications aren't credentials for a job. They are two kinds of words. One kind helps writers strengthen their claims. A common example is the word *very*, as in a sentence like "Cell phones are very bad for cities' sense of community." Yet many readers think terms of this sort are unnecessary. "Bad" is already emphatic; why stick "very" before it? The second kind of qualification has the opposite effect. Words in this category weaken a claim. They help writers sound cautious, often an attractive trait. Goldberger uses words of this type:

- In paragraph 1, where a more reckless writer might have simply declared, "Places are unique," he adds, "or at least we like to believe they are."

- In paragraph 3, he doesn't just proclaim that *all* city dwellers have lost a sense of place. He makes use of the word *almost*, saying this is becoming the experience of "almost every person on almost every street in almost every city."
- In paragraph 4, he resists generalizing about *every* inhabitant of a city. Instead, he asks "what if half of them are elsewhere, there in body but not in any other way?"
- In the next paragraph, he doesn't claim that a cell phone's ring *is* infuriating. Rather, he more softly notes that it "can be."
- In paragraph 6, he doesn't simply announce that an area code has become *just* a set of numbers. Rather, he laments that it "is really not much more than" them.

Such language makes Goldberger look careful. Similar terms include *probably*, *maybe*, *perhaps*, and *possibly*. These words suggest that the writer isn't self-righteously certain. Take this claim from Hartzog and Zelinger's article about Facebook: "Many contemporary privacy disputes are probably better classified as concern over losing obscurity." With "probably," the authors identify their claim as a hypothesis. They grant that it isn't sure fact. Like Goldberger, they project restraint.

Pathos is an appeal to the heart. You find it in charities' ads. Many show photos of suffering children—kids hungry, injured, or poor. These pictures are meant to rouse pity. If they succeed, viewers sob and donate. At other times, pathos stirs fear. Activists warn that if society ignores them, apocalypse will come. Pathos-filled arguments aren't dry in tone. Their language expresses moods. Pathos targets its audience's emotions. When you write such arguments, you push readers to feel the stakes of your issue. You hope they'll passionately favor your claims. Sure, you risk sounding excessive: too sad, too mad, too scared, or too hurt. But pathos can be a respectable tool, as well as a powerful one. Plenty of subjects even demand an emotional tone. Readers expect essays on genocide to anguish over its victims. Further, pathos can join logos and ethos. Arguments that move readers may also awe them with logic; the author's image may impress them, too.

Goldberger's piece oozes despair and sorrow. He deeply regrets cell phones' impact on cities and prods his audience to share his grief. He saves his most notable pathos for the end. There he claims that cell technology is turning all of us into "nodes on a network." It's a chilling final image. He wants to leave readers worried that cell phones will destroy their souls.

Sample Argument for Analysis

We've specified elements of argument and style. Now try to spot their presence in the following opinion piece. "A New Moral Compact" was originally published in November 2012, right around Veterans' Day. The author, David W. Barno (b. 1954), is a retired lieutenant general. He served the U.S. Army in key leadership roles, his experiences including combat campaigns in Afghanistan,

Grenada, and Panama. Barno is now senior advisor and senior fellow at the Center for a New American Security, a group whose mission is "to develop strong, pragmatic, and principled national security and defense policies." His article appeared simultaneously on the Center's Web site and in the digital edition of *Foreign Policy* magazine. Anyone might come upon his piece through a search engine. But probably he took his main audience to be elected officials, their staffs, other policy experts, military professionals, and academic scholars who study national defense.

As you read, consider the following questions:

- What is Barno's main *issue*, and what is his main *claim* about it?
- What smaller claims does he make as he develops his main one?
- Where in his article are you especially conscious of Barno's attempting *persuasion*?
- Where are you especially conscious of how Barno views his *audience*?
- What *evidence* does Barno offer?
- What are the steps in his *reasoning*?
- What are his major *assumptions*?
- To what extent does his argument rely on *logos*?
- To what extent might his *reputational ethos* matter to his readers?
- What sort of *ethos* does he create through his words?
- How much, and where, does his argument use *pathos*?

DAVID W. BARNO

A New Moral Compact

As our nation enters its second decade of armed conflict overseas, it is appropriate to reflect on the moral compact between our government, our people, and our soldiers. Eleven years of conflict in Afghanistan and Iraq, combined with the prospect for open-ended global warfare against terrorists, has blurred the lines between peace and war, perhaps forever. It has also effectively lowered our national threshold for decisions to conduct military operations or go to war. The reasons have as much to do with our declining personal stake in these conflicts as with the dangerous state of the world.

I recently attended an event honoring former Pennsylvania governor Tom Ridge for his public service. Ridge came from a working class family, won a scholarship to Harvard, and went on to law school. Upon completing his first year, he unexpectedly received his draft notice from Uncle Sam.

Tom Ridge did not seek to dodge his unwelcome summons. In his family, when you were called, you dropped whatever you were doing in your life and you went, as his father did in World War II. But as a Harvard grad and law student, he clearly had other options.

The Army decided to make Tom Ridge an infantryman. He soon became a sergeant and shipped out to Vietnam, where he joined the 101st Airborne for a year in combat from 1969 to 1970. None of the handful of young men he led in his small infantry rifle squad was a graduate of Harvard or any other college, but they were draftees from all social strata across the United States. Ridge observed: "The military is a great leveler. Nobody cares who you are, where you went to school, who your parents were. None of that mattered."

The only reason Ridge was in the Army and ultimately fought for a year in   5
Vietnam was the draft lottery system. The Selective Service system randomly assigned numbers to each draft age male by birth date in an annual "lottery"; depending on the needs of the war that year, if your number came up, you were called. Theoretically, your chances of being drafted as a college grad under the lottery system were equal to those of a high school drop-out born on the same date. In the real world, however, both college deferments (see: Dick Cheney, Bill Clinton) and clever manipulation of the system allowed many of the well-off and well-educated to avoid service altogether. And for each of those who sidestepped the call, some other, less fortunate young man was called up to take his place. Some of whom, of course, never came back—a sharp point little noted in discussions about the complex national legacy of the Vietnam War.

In the Vietnam era, draftees were called up for a maximum of two years of service, with one of those almost inevitably spent in Vietnam. And unlike in today's "all-volunteer" military, no draftee was ever sent back to Vietnam for another tour unless he volunteered—probably with a voluntary re-enlistment for longer service. With draftees serving only two years in uniform, it would have been nearly impossible to send a soldier for a second 12-month combat tour within the scope of his two-year service obligation. It simply wasn't done. If you were unfortunate enough to be drafted, you at least knew that the nation drew the line at one year of combat.

Contrast Tom Ridge's world of 1969 with that of America's combat soldiers today. In 2012, there is no draft, and our all-volunteer force has spent the last eleven years in prolonged, bloody ground wars in Iraq and Afghanistan. The Army of this era fields about 560,000 troops on active duty, in comparison to 1.2 million at the height of the Vietnam war. Nearly 3 million Americans are veterans of the post-9/11 wars, with large numbers having served multiple combat tours. It seems obvious that some of the stress on the force—manifested by unprecedented rates of suicide and creeping indiscipline—has come from these widespread repeat deployments, the likes of which no soldier of the Vietnam era ever involuntarily faced. In fact, even career officers and sergeants in the Vietnam-era force—distinct from the two-year draftees—rarely served more than two one-year tours in Vietnam over the entire course of that ten-year war.

In today's military, it is not uncommon to see Army lieutenant colonels and senior sergeants deployed three or four times for 12- to 15-month combat tours over the past decade—a back-breaking, family-stressing commitment the likes of which we have never before asked of our men and women in uniform. Even in World War II, only a small fraction of our nearly 16 million uniformed men and women served more than three years in a combat zone, and the entire war was finished for the United States in 45 months. Our war in

Afghanistan has lasted 134 months. It now has eclipsed the American Revolution and Vietnam as the longest war in U.S. history. Stunningly, sizable numbers of the very same sergeants and officers fighting the war today are the men and women that led the way into the earliest campaigns in Afghanistan and Iraq. If you are a career officer or NCO in today's Army and Marines, by and large you either continue to deploy—or you leave the service. There are few other options. Across our volunteer force, over 6,500 have been killed and more than 50,000 wounded since 2001. Consider the burden of that stark reality upon career military families.

Both of my sons have served one-year combat tours in Afghanistan. When our youngest son, an Army pilot, was called to go back after completing his first tour, I was suddenly angry. Not an anger that derived from misunderstanding our rotation system, nor from seeing the war as somehow unjust. My anger was visceral, unbidden, reflexive. And as I examined my unexpected reaction, it came down to this: my son was going back, yet 99 percent of his military age contemporaries were not—and never would, no matter how long the war lasted. Neither his civilian peers, their parents, nor their spouses or siblings would ever be exposed in any way to the gut-wrenching dangers of being in the middle of a lethal national enterprise. It simply wasn't important enough for our nation to insist that all of us shared the sacrifice of unlimited liability that war demands from those who fight it. Having a cadre of admirably willing volunteers simply has made it too easy for us to go to war.

For we Americans as a people, that's just wrong. There must be some limit to what we will ask of our men and women in uniform before the rest of us feel some moral obligation to step in. Tom Ridge—representing all of the people of the United States in 1969—got the telegram, put his life on hold, stepped forward and served in combat alongside a broad cross-section of America's youth. Today, we call on no one to make this kind of sacrifice. We have even made that a matter of some pride, a nation that has moved beyond the dark days of "conscription."

Yet at what point are we morally compelled to in some way expose every American family to our fights abroad, to invest some moral equity as a nation and a society into fighting our wars? Absent any prospect whatsoever for our current or future wars to touch any of us personally, where is the moral hazard—the personal "equity stake"—that shapes our collective judgment, giving us pause when we decide to send our remarkable volunteer military off to war? They are fully prepared to go—but they trust the rest of us to place sufficient weight and seriousness into that decision to ensure that their inevitable sacrifices of life and limb will be for a worthy and essential cause.

Throughout our history, American decisions on going to war have been closely connected to our people because they remain matters of life and death. And they were always seen as matters of deep import to the nation as a whole, since all could be called upon to fight. Today such profound decisions are all but free of consequences for the American people. When the lives and the deaths of our soldiers no longer personally impact the population at large, have we compromised our moral authority on war? How can our elites and our broader populace make wartime decisions in good conscience when those paying the price are someone else's kids — but assuredly never their own?

The past ten years suggest that relying on a professional military comprised only of willing volunteers has eroded the core societal seriousness that we have always accorded to national decisions of war and peace. One wonders if we would have entered our recent conflicts as quickly — or let them drag on so long — if our Army was filled with draftees, drawn from a random swath of families across all segments of America.

One policy to better connect our wars to our people might be to determine that every use of military force over 60 days would automatically trigger an annual draft lottery to call up 10,000 men and women. They would serve in every branch of service for the duration of the conflict, replaced by future draft tranches in limited, like-sized numbers. Ten thousand draftees would comprise only about 5 percent of the number of new recruits the military takes in each year, but they would signify a symbolic commitment of the entire nation. Every family in the country would now be exposed to the potential consequences of our wars and come to recognize in a personal way that they had a stake in the outcome. The national calculus on go-to-war decisions subtly changes when all families can be called upon to answer the call to arms.

In the last decade, war has become something done by "the 1 percent" — our rightly acclaimed force of volunteers — with 99 percent of America uninvolved, and sometimes seemingly uninterested. But with war becoming this easy, our historic caution in committing our troops abroad has frayed dramatically. Partly as a result, "America at war" is slowly becoming a permanent condition. We have gradually, almost imperceptibly, eroded the bonds of responsibility linking our soldiers, our people, and our government. It's time to reestablish that moral compact between our people and our wars.   *[2012]*   15

Writing a Response to an Argument

Often, a college course will require you to read arguments. Just as often, you will respond to them by writing an argument yourself. As you compose your reactions to these texts, you will make, develop, and support claims. Here are some tips to help you:

- Before you write about the text, be sure you understand it in its entirety. Identify its main claim, its other claims, and how they all relate. In your essay, don't treat these claims one by one in isolated fragments, stating your opinion of each. Instead, put in context any claim you discuss. Explain its role in the author's overall reasoning process. You can begin to establish this larger framework in your introduction by summarizing what the author basically argues.
- Perhaps you'll disagree with the argument. Even then, show respect for its author. Avoid snarky remarks like, "What planet is this guy on?" Audiences tend to prefer a more civil ethos. Calling the author stupid, evil, or crazy may drive your readers away. Let your tone suggest that you're reflective, not mean.

- When you first read the argument, you may strongly approve or object. But don't settle for extreme verdicts. Let your written response include concessions and qualifications, not just big evaluative claims. Your readers will appreciate learning what's complex about the argument and how reactions to it can be mixed. Whatever your attitude toward it, show the reasoning and evidence behind your view.
- When writing about the argument, refer to its author. Make this person the subject of several active verbs: for example, "Barno claims," "Barno argues," "Barno proposes," "Barno calls for." After all, the argument isn't an orphan. Nor is it a random series of free-floating ideas. You're studying an entire case put forth by a particular human being. Take opportunities to remind your readers—and yourself—of this fact. Start doing so with your introduction.
- For each sentence you write, make clear whose view it expresses. Are you conveying an idea brought up in the argument you're analyzing, or is this your own idea? Help your readers distinguish between the two. If you write about Barno's argument, for example, let them know when you're reporting *his* claims and when you're stating *yours*.
- Give your response a title that previews what you'll say.

Further Strategies for Analyzing an Argument So You Can Write a Response to It

In the college courses that require you to read and write about arguments, you'll be asked to analyze not only the claims they make but also the issues they raise and the support they give their stances. To write about an argument thoughtfully, read it several times. You may need to study it at length before you detect its points. Below, using David Barno's essay as an example, we suggest some strategies for analyzing and getting ideas to respond to arguments.

1. Identify *all* of the argument's basic elements.   After you've examined the argument thoroughly, pinpoint not just its main claim and smaller claims but also, its evidence, its reasoning, its assumptions, its appeals, and the audience it seems to address.

2. Map the argument's path.   By this, we mean you should try to outline the argument's stages, noting points made at each. Just as important, recognize choices the arguer faced. For each stage, identify issues he or she *doesn't* pursue.

To construct your map, you might use only words. The map may prove more thought provoking, though, if it's a flowchart. See how we've mapped Barno's argument below. For each stage, we've drawn a box. Within it, we summarize what Barno says at that stage. Beneath each box we name one or more issues that he *doesn't* address.

An argument that avoids certain questions may still prove persuasive. But tracing routes it *doesn't* take helps you understand and judge it. You'll have a better sense of what to say in your written response.

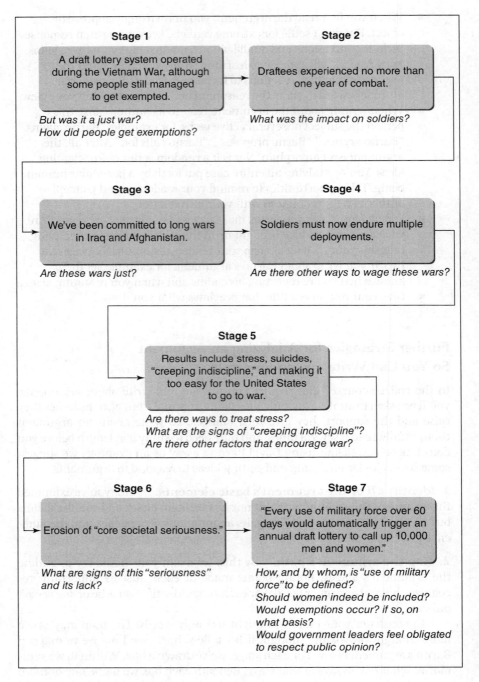

Stage 1

A draft lottery system operated during the Vietnam War, although some people still managed to get exempted.

But was it a just war?
How did people get exemptions?

Stage 2

Draftees experienced no more than one year of combat.

What was the impact on soldiers?

Stage 3

We've been committed to long wars in Iraq and Afghanistan.

Are these wars just?

Stage 4

Soldiers must now endure multiple deployments.

Are there other ways to wage these wars?

Stage 5

Results include stress, suicides, "creeping indiscipline," and making it too easy for the United States to go to war.

Are there ways to treat stress?
What are the signs of "creeping indiscipline"?
Are there other factors that encourage war?

Stage 6

Erosion of "core societal seriousness."

What are signs of this "seriousness" and its lack?

Stage 7

"Every use of military force over 60 days would automatically trigger an annual draft lottery to call up 10,000 men and women."

How, and by whom, is "use of military force" to be defined?
Should women indeed be included?
Would exemptions occur? if so, on what basis?
Would government leaders feel obligated to respect public opinion?

Figure 1.4   The stages of Barno's argument

3. Identify the values the argument honors.   Often arguers support a claim by tying it to common values. These are principles they assume their audience already holds. Here are examples of values that Barno emphasizes as he argues for a draft lottery:

- **Morality.**   Barno uses the word *moral* several times. Not only does it appear in the title of his essay, it also pops up in paragraphs 10, 11, and 15. In paragraph 11, it even appears twice, along with the related word *morally*. Most, perhaps all, of his readers see worth in a moral life.

- **Realism.**   Most people find it crucial to remain in touch with reality. To support his proposal for a lottery, Barno points out deaths and woundings suffered by current volunteers. He hopes his audience will want to do something about "the burden of that stark reality upon career military families" (para. 8).

- **Shared sacrifice.**   When Barno reports the suffering that military families alone endure, he expects his readers will feel guilt. After all, *shared* sacrifice is a common ideal.

- **Family.**   Barno's audience surely believes that the family unit is valuable. The author joins his readers in seeking to protect it from needless risk. As he develops his argument, Barno laments the "family-stressing commitment" demanded by current wars (para. 8). He refers to his own family as suffering from this plight (para. 9). When he proposes a lottery that would reach "families across all segments of America" (para. 13), he's hardly out to harm them. Rather, he wants the country to hesitate more before waging war. If war affects more families, he suggests, they won't rush to endorse it. Family is something he *and* the nation prize.

- **Bonds of responsibility.**   Barno resorts to this phrase in his final paragraph. With it, he links his proposal to Americans' sense of community. He has faith that his readers still deem social ties important. He affirms the principle of looking out for one another. It's a tradition he wishes to sustain.

- **Prudence.**   Ancient teachers of rhetoric and ethics emphasized the virtue of prudence. It's the exercise of careful, cautious judgment. Today, it remains a value many arguers bring up. Barno concludes by emphasizing "our historic caution in committing our troops abroad" (para. 15).

- **Seriousness.**   Related to realism and prudence is the attitude of *seriousness*. Barno uses the word twice, in paragraphs 11 and 13. By it, he means intense concern. He assumes his readers regard this as the approach anyone should take to "matters of deep import" (para. 12). These include the costs of war.

Consider what values an argument gives *priority* to. Often arguers press their audience to choose *between* values it holds. Barno emphasizes community spirit as an American ideal, but many people in the United States cherish personal freedom as well. On plenty of occasions, the American public has debated which of these principles to favor. Someone who prefers individual liberty might protest a military draft. Barno, however, favors one, asking his readers to put community ties over freedom of self.

4. Identify words in the argument that can have more than one definition. You can also grasp an argument better if you pinpoint words in it that can have more than one definition. Not everyone, that is, would give these words the meanings that the arguer does. Examples include a number of Barno's values. Take, for instance, *morality* and *seriousness*. For him, both terms mean a willingness to share the risks of war. For other people, *morality* might mean sparing citizens from a draft, and *seriousness* might mean recognizing that the American public won't agree to the lottery that Barno wants. A similar difference of opinion may occur with the word *caution*. Barno believes a country that exercises caution would be reluctant to launch wars. Others might think that a policy of caution involves attacking potential foes before they can ever strike.

Note, too, that not everyone would join Barno in thinking the American government expresses the public's will. At the very end of his essay, he refers to "our wars," as if all Americans are responsible when their leaders send troops into combat. Someone might argue that the president and Congress rarely do what the public wants. Consider the various possible definitions of additional terms Barno uses, such as these:

- *indiscipline* (para. 9)
- *expose* (para. 11)
- *consequences* (para. 12)

An Argument for Analysis

We've identified several ways to study arguments. We close this chapter by inviting you to practice these methods. Try applying them to the following opinion piece. After it, we'll pose questions to aid your analysis.

This essay's author, Regina Rini, has held research fellowships at Oxford University and earned a doctorate in philosophy at New York University. Currently, she is an assistant professor and faculty fellow at the New York University (NYU) Center for Bioethics, as well as an affiliate faculty member in the Medical Ethics division of the NYU Department of Population Health. In addition to her academic articles, she has contributed to the op-ed pages of the *Los Angeles Times* and to two philosophy blogs, *Practical Ethics* and *The Splintered Mind*. Rini first published the following argument on December 8, 2015, in *Aeon*, an online magazine that deals with topics in philosophy, science, psychology, health, technology, and culture at large. Note Rini's title. It's a question that was sparking debate at many American colleges when she wrote.

REGINA RINI

Should We Rename Institutions that Honor Dead Racists?

We all know what Juliet says about a rose: by any other name, it would smell as sweet. But we probably don't remember why she says this, or what happens next. Juliet is lamenting that a certain young man happens to be called "Romeo Montague," a name associated with her family's dire enemies. Romeo then emerges from the shadows and insists that the name is "hateful to myself, because it is an enemy to thee." He declares his moniker dispensable, under one condition: "Call me but love, and I'll be new baptized; henceforth I never will be Romeo."

What altered scent might emanate from a renamed Woodrow Wilson School of Public and International Affairs? The Princeton institution faces calls to drop its nominal affiliation with America's 28th president, who was also governor of New Jersey, president of the university, and a horrible racist. Similarly, students at Yale have demanded a rebranding of Calhoun College, named after John Calhoun, who championed "Indian removal" and told the Senate that slavery was a "positive good." And Georgetown University, my own alma mater, has agreed to strip the names of two Jesuit slave-sellers from campus buildings. Across the country, student Juliets are asking their administrator Romeos to be newly baptized.

And why not? It is reasonable to prefer not to live in a quadrangle named after a man who extolled the "positive good" of your great-great-grandparents' forced labor. It is reasonable to wish not to study in a place that honors a man who would have you keep to your own, segregated end of the lecture hall. For students of color, living in a United States that preaches equality and practices something else, it is reasonable to expect an honest reckoning with our damaged patriarchs.

But the problem is consistency. Once we've started rescinding honors from besmirched heroes, where should we stop? On any reasonable scale of evil, the segregationist Wilson cannot be as bad as George Washington, who owned hundreds of slaves. So must we also rename several universities, a northwestern state, and the District of Columbia? The last, in fact, seems to require double renaming, as Christopher Columbus is now seen as a genocidal monster. Perhaps "America" itself ought to go: Amerigo Vespucci wrapped up his first voyage to the New World by setting a native village on fire and "thereon made sail for Spain with 222 captive slaves."

This, say opponents, is the absurdity to which we will be reduced. Where   5
does the bonfire end? Surely we can't consider renaming every legacy of a moral scofflaw. Who has the time?

But, in fact, we regularly give things new names. In 2005, a man in California petitioned to rename Mount Diablo, because federal rules prohibit naming a geographic formation after "a living person" such as Satan. The man's preferred alternative, "Mount Reagan," was unsuccessful, but this has not stopped the Mount Reagan Project from questing after another peak to rechristen. Ronald Reagan's name, incidentally, already adorns National Airport in Virginia — which was previously named for none other than the sacrosanct Washington. It would be worrisome if this *reductio* of name-changing was deemed absurd only when racism is the issue. Still, it is worth pausing to consider just what it takes to give something a name.

The British philosopher J L Austin gave naming as a prime example of a "performative utterance," the kind of speech act whereby merely saying something makes it so. But not all attempted naming is felicitous. In *How to Do Things with Words* (1962), Austin offered the following delightful demonstration:

> Suppose, for example, I see a vessel on the stocks, walk up and smash the bottle hung at the stern, proclaim: "I name this ship the *Mr Stalin*" and for good measure kick away the chocks: but the trouble is, I was not the person chosen to name it . . . We can all agree (1) that the ship was not thereby named; (2) that it is an infernal shame.

Austin's point was that the giving of a name requires a certain social authority. But unlike the Royal Navy, in schools and cities the authority to name does not entirely belong to a single person. Students (and faculty, staff, and alumni) have an interest in not seeing their college linguistically cavort with blackguards. The citizens of a democratic state have a right to call themselves as they wish. And the procedure by which we determine how to (re)name our collective institutions has its own name — it is called debate. Why not have this debate, openly and honestly, rather than dismiss the entire project?

The US philosopher Saul Kripke is known for his causal theory of reference. According to Kripke, proper names pick out their objects via a causal chain going back to the object's "baptism." Once upon a time, someone (probably his parents) pointed at Romeo and said: "That one will be called Romeo," and this caused other people to call the child Romeo, onward until the night under Juliet's balcony. But there is nothing in this story to prevent a re-baptism, or a displacement of the old name by the same causal channels. Suppose the young lovers decide that the man formerly known as Romeo Montague is now Keyser Söze. If they can cause enough fair Veronese to refer to him thus, then so shall he be (though this is unlikely to solve Keyser's trouble with his in-laws).

We are links in a causal chain of reference, stretching back to institutional   10
baptisms in 1931 and 1948, when university administrators pointed to a college and called it Calhoun, or pointed to a school and called it Wilson. These were performative utterances, issued with full authority, and part of their aim was to honor the legacies of dead racists. We do not have to be unthinking links in the chain. We, collectively, have the authority to pass on these names, or to replace them. Whatever we do — continue the chain or disrupt it — we are making a choice about whether to uphold the honor intended by those baptisms.

In fact, the students at Princeton are not asking us to make a comprehensive judgment: Wilson, good man or bad? The idea is to ask: does continuing to apply the name of such a person express *our* values, rather than the values of a gone generation? We are not deciding the fate of Wilson's eternal soul. We are asking whether we, who are the only ones with the authority to keep or change the name, have good reason to pass the name on to the next generation.

We know that renaming tends to follow political revolution. Famously, Byzantium turned to Constantinople, which turned to Istanbul. Saint Petersburg was Leningrad was Petrograd was Saint Petersburg. Decolonization brought a mass shedding of imposed titles, from Mumbai (Bombay) to Zimbabwe (Rhodesia) to Jakarta (Batavia). We are ready to accept that names change with the times and with the politics. Or would you insist that I am writing in New Amsterdam?

So if renaming can follow political revolution, then why not moral revolution? Why are we not free to ask ourselves whether to uphold the values that led our ancestors to name in honor of slaveholders and segregationists?

Perhaps we will decide, together, that on balance the good done by Washington or Wilson outweighs the evil. Perhaps. But I think we should seriously listen to those whose histories are most in the weighing. It can be hard, for some whose ancestors were not enslaved or segregated, to fully appreciate the pain caused by honoring these names. Yet even if you cannot understand it yourself, you can see it in others. And perhaps this will move you to agree, as an act of civic love, to accede to their requests. Like Romeo, listening in the night, we might find our collective name hateful to ourselves, "because it is an enemy to thee."   [2015]

≡ THINKING ABOUT THE TEXT

1. The title of Rini's essay is "Should We Rename Institutions that Honor Dead Racists?" It's a question that indicates the issue she addresses. What do you consider her main claim to be? Is it a simple yes or no answer to the question, or is it something else? Rini could have left the word *dead* out of her title. Why do you think she includes it?

2. Try to map Rini's argument. What are its main stages? For example, what is it doing in paragraph 2? In paragraph 4? Identify passages where she could have pursued certain issues but didn't. What are these issues?

3. The magazine in which Rini published her piece gives this advice to its contributors: "Steer clear of technical language or jargon—explain your idea as you would to someone without any expertise in the area. *Aeon* wants to make big ideas accessible to a wide audience." To what extent does Rini follow this advice? In paragraph 10, she refers to Keyser Söze, the villain in the movie *The Usual Suspects*. How would you respond to someone who says that not all of Rini's readers would get this reference?

4. Not everyone addressing Rini's title question would start with a paragraph about William Shakespeare's play *Romeo and Juliet*. Why, conceivably, does Rini choose to begin this way?

5. Where does Rini bring in evidence for her position? What kind of evidence is it? What does it consist of?

6. In paragraphs 12 and 13, Rini uses the word *values*. What specific values does she promote in her essay?

7. In paragraphs 9, 11, and 12, Rini uses the word *authority*. How does she seem to define this word? To whom is she willing to give authority?

8. Notice Rini's use of the pronoun *we*. Where, specifically, does she employ it? For what purpose, do you think? Apply the same questions to her use of *you*.

9. In addition to her title, Rini poses several other questions in her essay. A different writer might have only made statements. What is the effect of Rini's frequent question raising?

10. What, if any, renaming events and controversies can you think of? To what extent does Rini's essay help you make sense of them? The following are some examples we've come across recently:

   • At Clemson University in South Carolina, students demanded a new name for Tillman Hall, named after segregationist politician Ben Tillman.

   • At Duke University and East Carolina University, the name of North Carolina governor Charles Brantley Aycock was removed from dormitories because of his support for Jim Crow–era discrimination policies.

   • In Texas, the name of Robert E. Lee High School was challenged.

   • Also in Texas, the Board of the Houston Independent School District stirred debate when it expressed interest in renaming six of its schools that bore the names of Confederate leaders.

   • For the past several years, the owner of the Washington Redskins football team has been pressured to change the team's name because many consider the word *redskin* derogatory toward Native Americans.

   • Central State University in Ohio, which had received more than two million dollars from Bill Cosby and his wife, decided to change the name of a communications building named after them. The decision came after Cosby was accused by multiple women of drugging, sexually assaulting, and/or raping them.

CHAPTER 2

Writing Effective Arguments

In Chapter 1, we defined rhetoric and argumentation, presented the elements of argument in the context of arguments by Paul Goldberger and David Barno, and suggested several strategies to analyze arguments. In this chapter, we refer back to those elements and to the arguments by Goldberger and Barno as we suggest ways to develop your own effective arguments.

Strategies for Developing an Effective Style of Argument

When you write an argument, including one that responds to someone else's, try to incorporate the elements we discussed in the first chapter. Also good to study are features of an effective **style**. Try the following methods and techniques.

Mark transitions. Readers want to know how each of your sentences relates to the ones immediately before it and after it. Usually a word or two can show this. Barno's third sentence begins with the word *It*, a pronoun that refers to the state of war mentioned in the previous sentence. Especially crucial is the language of shifts from one paragraph to the next. For example, Barno begins paragraph 10 by declaring "that's just wrong." With the word "that," he looks back to the situation he described at the end of the previous paragraph: how having a volunteer military encourages the United States to engage in war.

Create coherence by repeating words and by using similar words. Readers appreciate signs that you have carefully focused and structured your argument. Through repeating its key words, you can show that it follows a coherent line of thought. Barno notably repeats the word *national*. It appears in paragraphs 1, 5, 9, 12, and 14. He also uses the closely related word *nation* in paragraphs 10, 12, and 14. These repetitions provide his argument with a unifying thread. They emphasize that his readers should think about how to serve their country, not just how to satisfy themselves.

Use patterns of sounds to give your sentences force. As you write a draft, read its sentences aloud. Listen to the sounds of each. Perhaps, by changing certain words in a sentence, you can create more compelling rhythmic patterns. A good example is the opening sentence of Barno's paragraph 3:

Tom Ridge did not seek to dodge his unwelcome summons.

This isn't an especially flashy statement, but it's well crafted. It uses these stylistic techniques:

- **Alliteration.** The repetition of consonant sounds at the beginnings of words. Both *did* and *dodge* begin with the letter *d*. Both *seek* and *summons* begin with the letter *s*.
- **Assonance.** The repetition of vowel sounds. *Tom*, *not*, and *dodge* feature the same vowel. So do *Ridge*, *did*, and *his*. So do parts of the last two words: *un*, *come*, *sum*, and *mons*.
- **Other consonant patterns.** An *m* sound links the words *Tom*, *unwelcome*, and *summons*. A *dg* sound connects *Ridge* with *dodge*.
- **One-syllable words.** Words that consist of just one syllable can have a punchy impact, especially if several such words appear in a row. In Barno's sentence, the first eight words are each a single syllable long. The last two words of the sentence, "unwelcome summons," have an unwelcome sound, for they break the powerful pattern set up by the previous words.

Balance the parts of a sentence.   Look at the following two sentences. The first comes from Paul Goldberger's "Disconnected Urbanism" (p. 3). The second comes from Barno's essay:

> When you are in a forest, you want to experience its woodsiness; when you are on a beach, you want to feel connected to sand and surf. (para. 1)

> Contrast Tom Ridge's world of 1969 with that of America's combat soldiers today. (para. 7)

In each sentence, the parts balance. It's an engaging feat. Readers like rhythmic symmetry. They won't demand it of every sentence you write, but they'll appreciate it when they see it.

Vary the lengths of sentences.   A series of long sentences may confuse your readers while also losing their attention. On the other hand, a series of short sentences may come across as choppy, obscuring how ideas connect. Try to mix sentence length, as Barno does in paragraph 8:

> Even in World War II, only a small fraction of our nearly 16 million uniformed men and women served more than three years in a combat zone, and the entire war was finished for the United States in 45 months. Our war in Afghanistan has lasted 134 months. It now has eclipsed the American Revolution and Vietnam as the longest war in U.S. history. Stunningly, sizable numbers of the very same sergeants and officers fighting the war today are the men and women that led the way into the earliest campaigns in Afghanistan and Iraq.

Even in long sentences, be as concise as possible. Don't use more words than necessary; make each one count.

Use active verbs, not just passive ones.   *Active* and *passive* are terms of grammar. When a verb is in active voice, the subject of that verb performs an action. When a verb is in passive voice, its subject is acted upon. The active tends to make a sentence more dramatic and concise. Also, it better identifies who or what is doing something. Here are examples from Barno's essay:

> The Army decided to make Tom Ridge an infantryman. (para. 4)
>
> The Selective Service system randomly assigned numbers . . ." (para. 5)
>
> The Army of this era fields about 560,000 troops on active duty . . . (para. 7)
>
> We have gradually, almost imperceptibly eroded the bonds of responsibility . . . (para. 15)

At times, Barno does resort to passive voice. For instance, he repeatedly uses the passive form of the verb *to call* when he refers to the demands of military service:

> In his family, when you were called . . . (para. 3)
>
> . . . draftees were called up for a maximum of two years of service . . . (para. 6)
>
> . . . our youngest son, an Army pilot, was called to go back . . . (para. 9)
>
> . . . when all families can be called upon to answer the call of arms. (para. 14)

Barno's practice suggests that both kinds of voice, active and passive, are resources for arguers. Neither is automatically preferable. But of the two, active voice is more dynamic. And again, it identifies the action's performer more clearly.

Use precise verbs to identify an arguer's acts.   When responding to an argument, use verbs that pinpoint what the arguer does. Avoid vague verbs such as *talks about*. You're not conveying much if you write a sentence like this:

> Barno talks about having a draft lottery to stir concern about war.

A more exact alternative would be this:

> Barno calls for a draft lottery to stir concern about war.

The verb *calls* will give your readers a sharper sense of what Barno is doing when he brings up the lottery as a topic. Here are some other verbs you might use to convey an arguer's actions:

argues	criticizes	proposes	analyzes
claims	questions	recommends	examines
contends	challenges	urges	studies
asserts	complains	demands	probes
submits	protests	requests	focuses on

declares	regrets	emphasizes	detects
confirms	doubts	insists	finds
implies	objects to	underscores	reveals

Use figurative language.   Arguments may register more strongly with their audience if they explain ideas through figurative language. Such phrases can make concepts more vivid. Three main types are analogies, metaphors, and similes.

An **analogy** calls attention to a similarity between two things while still regarding them as largely distinct. Barno uses this technique in paragraph 11. There he urges his readers to "invest moral equity as a nation and a society into fighting our wars." His analogy is financial. Just as Americans take chances with money by investing in stocks, so should they morally consent to the possibility of being drafted. Of course, moral codes can differ a lot from activities of the stock market. But Barno emphasizes that both require a willingness to take risks.

A **metaphor**, on the other hand, implies that two things are the same. An example appears in Barno's paragraph 10. There he says that when Tom Ridge received his draft notice, he "put his life on hold." Commonly, the term *on hold* refers to phone calls. To put a call on hold is to keep the caller waiting. Barno uses the term to suggest that when Ridge agreed to military service, he had to postpone the kind of living he actually preferred.

A **simile** also equates two things but uses the word *like* or *as* to connect them. No similes appear in Barno's text, but here's one that might have:

> For soldiers assigned to repeated tours of combat zones, war is like a recurring nightmare. Every time they come back home, they feel as if they've finally been able to wake from a horrible dream. Yet soon they find themselves having to experience its terrors again.

Create *perspective by incongruity*.   This term, coined by Kenneth Burke, refers to the move that arguers perform when they give language a strikingly unconventional meaning or application. At the end of paragraph 10, Barno acknowledges that many Americans view the previous military draft as "dark days." But by putting the term in quotation marks, he prods his readers to question this particular use of it. Throughout his essay, he suggests that the term better fits the present age. To him, our current era is the real "dark days," for the absence of a draft has caused military families much suffering.

Structuring Your Argument: Beyond the Five-Paragraph Essay

When writing an argument, you may feel tempted to follow an age-old format: the five-paragraph essay. It works like this: Your first paragraph introduces three points. Each of your next three paragraphs develops one of these points. You conclude with a paragraph that repeats these points, reminding your reader of them. Done! It's a simple, easy recipe. No wonder that, for generations, students have relied on it. Many learn this stock procedure in junior high or earlier. Then they expect it to serve them forever after. But rarely does such writing delight teachers of college courses. For most of them, it reeks of formula. They don't find it truly fresh, developed, or complex. It's not the kind of prose they crave and reward.

To see what we mean by the five-paragraph model, take a look at the following essay. It's an argument we've written in response to Barno's text.

The Three Flaws in Barno's Proposal

David W. Barno's essay "A New Moral Compact" criticizes how the United States depends on volunteers to staff its military. He worries that this policy allows the rest of the country to overlook the sacrifices that soldiers make. Barno wants the United States to be more cautious about committing itself to wars. He thinks that we will be more restrained if more of us might have to serve in the military. Therefore, he proposes "that every use of military force over 60 days would automatically trigger an annual draft lottery to call up 10,000 men and women" (x). But Barno's proposal has three flaws. First, the American people will probably never agree to it. Second, our political leaders will probably get bogged down in debates about how to define "use of military force." Third, some people selected by the lottery will find ways of getting exempted from service, so the process will not really be fair.

One big problem with Barno's proposal is that a draft lottery is bound to be unpopular. Much of the country will object to it and demand that legislators fight against any effort to establish it. Barno admits that our ability to end the military draft after the Vietnam War was "a matter of some pride" (x). Ever since the United States declared its independence from Great Britain, our society has valued individual liberty. Many Americans are happy and grateful that our nation's youths are now free from having to serve in the military. They would oppose a new draft.

Another major flaw in Barno's proposal has to do with his phrase "use of military force." His draft lottery is supposed to take place when this "use" has continued for more than sixty days. Barno assumes that the president and Congress will have a common understanding of when such "use" has occurred. But he is too optimistic. In recent years, the federal government has been plagued by intense disputes. The president, the Senate, and the House of Representatives seem unable to agree on *any* issue. Even if American soldiers are fighting in a war that has gone on for years, various politicians will probably claim that this activity does not amount to "use of military force." They will quarrel over what this term means.

A third problem with Barno's proposal is that some people who are selected in the draft lottery will still manage to escape military service. Barno mentions that when there was such a lottery during the Vietnam War, "clever manipulation of the system allowed many of the well-off and well-educated to avoid service altogether" (x). The same thing is likely to happen now. Even if they wind up with a high lottery number, rich people will use all sorts of excuses to beat the system. Everyone else will notice this and point out that the lottery is not fair.

In conclusion, there are three reasons why Barno's proposal will not work. One is that the public will not appreciate it. Also, the president and other elected officials will disagree about the definition of "use of military force." Finally, people will find ways to evade service even if the draft selects them. Given all these problems, we should not adopt Barno's plan.

We think our essay makes some good observations. But its five-paragraph scheme harms it. Organizationally, it's just a loose string of points. At the outset, the overall claim about Barno's argument is merely a number: "Barno's proposal has three flaws." Then, one by one, each flaw gets a single paragraph. Such limited treatment seems superficial; readers will want greater depth. And the paragraphs don't appear linked. Each seems a mini-essay set apart. You could even rearrange their sequence; there's no logic to the order they're in. The final paragraph seems wasteful, for it echoes points already made.

So focus your essay on one main claim. Take several paragraphs to develop and support it. Link these paragraphs to one another. Put them in an order that makes sense. Let your conclusion go beyond what you've already said. You might identify your argument's further implications. You might note issues you've left unresolved.

Look again at our essay that criticizes Barno's proposal. We could have spent an entire text on any of the flaws we found. Imagine a whole essay on the second flaw: Barno's not realizing politicians will clash over how to define "use of military force." An essay could say much in claiming this flaw to exist. Think of the various questions we might have addressed. For example, what are some past governmental debates over the meanings of words? What euphemisms might leaders substitute for "use of military force"? What meanings might this term have? Such questions can't be handled in one paragraph alone. They call for abundant explanation, reasoning, and evidence.

A Student Response to an Argument

The following essay demonstrates several of the strategies we've discussed in this chapter. The author, Justin Korzack, composed it for a course on debating social issues. Basically, he wrote an argument that reacts to Barno's. To support his response, he investigated presidential history. Still, his essay isn't a full-blown research paper, a genre we discuss in Chapter 6. Nor, probably, is it the finest response ever written. But it does perform moves worth adding to your rhetorical repertoire.

Justin Korzack
Professor Hartfield
English 111
10 April - - - -

How to Slow Down the Rush to War

In "A New Moral Compact," David W. Barno worries about
the United States' current reliance on an all-volunteer military. He claims that this policy allows civilians to feel too
complacent about the country's committing itself to major
hostilities. Barno is a retired lieutenant general with a substantial combat record. Therefore, you might assume that he
himself is comfortable with war. But this is not so, at least
with respect to our recent long-term conflicts. He feels that
these engagements have had serious consequences for the
professional soldiers required to carry them out. In his view,
the public at large needs to become more aware of war's
human costs. To make all citizens more alert to these, he
proposes "that every use of military force over 60 days would
automatically trigger an annual draft lottery to call up 10,000
men and women" (20). Obviously this measure would disrupt
the lives of many people. Whether or not they ever planned
to become soldiers, they might now be forced to serve.
Nevertheless, Barno believes, this threat would be worthwhile,
for it would function as a brake. He expects that it would make
Americans more reluctant to send troops into extensive and
deadly combat campaigns.

Summarizes Barno's argument so that readers understand his overall reasoning. Also points out which claims are his. Makes him the subject of several active verbs.

Is Barno's solution useful enough to justify the widespread
anxiety it might cause? Not really, because Barno misdiagnoses
the problem in the first place. What needs more attention and
criticism is not public apathy. Rather, it's the institution of the
Presidency. For the last several decades, the nation's Chief
Executive has sought to initiate military action without
interference from public opinion and even the U.S. Congress.
The President should consult more widely and thoroughly before
dispatching Americans to the battlefield.

Identifies main issue by phrasing it as a question.

The paragraph varies the lengths of sentences and ends with the student's own main claim.

Barno makes a valuable contribution when he reminds his
readers of how terrible war can be. Moreover, he raises a legitimate concern when he points out that our nation's current
military commitments have imposed awful burdens on
recruits. Using the appeal of pathos, he stresses the suffering
undergone by soldiers who have had to serve several tours of
duty in deadly, traumatic places like Iraq and Afghanistan. He
contrasts their experience with that of people like former governor Tom Ridge. Even though Ridge was, after being drafted
into the army, sent to fight in Vietnam, at least his time there

The first of several concessions in this paragraph.

lasted only one year. Barno emphasizes that many members of today's military are repeatedly assigned to combat. These soldiers include one of Barno's own sons, a fact that he reports while admitting that he's angry about it. Some readers may feel that because of his personal connection, Barno's complaint about repeated rounds of service is nothing but self-interest. But his use of his son's situation as a representative anecdote seems appropriate, for numerous other people in the military have been required lately to return to war. In light of this unfortunate trend, it would be understandable if Barno called for reviving the draft as a gesture of fairness. He could argue that exempting civilians from military service is morally wrong, given that the professional defenders of our nation have had to fight so much. Not everyone would agree with him, but his position would be credible.

A somewhat different motive, however, leads Barno to suggest that a draft lottery be held every year if a military action extends beyond two months. He makes this proposal because he feels that Americans outside the military have grown indifferent to the challenges it faces. In his view, the lottery would make civilians more conscious of combat deployments. At the same time, they would question more the necessity of going to war, for they might be drawn into combat themselves. This skepticism is something that Barno would welcome. To him, the government has grown too inclined to hurl troops into conflicts. He wants our leaders to make such decisions more slowly and carefully. He expects the lottery would achieve this goal, by raising public awareness and concern.

Clear transition from previous paragraph.

Probably Barno is right to sense that exposing significant numbers of Americans to a draft lottery would make the country uneasier about entering into war. Some greater unrest would most likely occur. Yet he provides no evidence for his claim that dependence on an all-volunteer force "has eroded the core societal seriousness that we have always accorded to national decisions of war and peace" (19). Why must his readers assume that the public is, at present, absolutely indifferent to the ordeals faced by our soldiers in Iraq and Afghanistan? Contrary to what he suggests, many civilians do seem to show "sufficient weight and seriousness" about the U.S.'s current military ventures (19). For instance, numerous cars display "Support our Troops" signs, and supportive crowds regularly turn out for ceremonies welcoming reservists as well as National Guard members home from combat. Barno might respond that these are rituals of cheerful robots, propaganda that hardly shows deep thinking about the government's

Another concession, just before criticisms begin.

Provides supporting examples.

Figurative language.

choices. But civilians are perhaps able to appreciate soldiers' service while being thoughtful about the policies that demanded it. Barno appears to forget that when the invasion of Iraq was beginning, thousands of people marched in several cities to protest it. Moreover, critical attitudes toward current American wars have certainly mounted in the last few years. President Obama's decision to pull our military out of Afghanistan soon, along with his earlier decision to withdraw us from Iraq, stems in part from his awareness that much of our country has already grown tired of these commitments. He knows that we have woken up to how fatigued we are.

Perspective by incongruity.

Yet even if our nation adopted Barno's proposal and became considerably more skeptical about war, chances seem slight that these developments would inhibit our leaders. Beginning with Harry S. Truman's "police action" in Korea during the early 1950s, no U.S. President has asked Congress for an official declaration of war. Instead, each President has essentially used the military as he has seen fit, seeking Congressional permission only at times and only in thin ways. The procedure has been to "consult" Congress in a superficial manner but not in a profound one. Lyndon Johnson took Congress's Gulf of Tonkin Resolution as a pretext for dramatically escalating the U.S. troop presence in Vietnam. Richard Nixon ignored massive antiwar protests and continued to bomb the same region. Ronald Reagan felt free to send soldiers to Grenada; Bill Clinton felt able to put them in Kosovo. George W. Bush had fairly minimal Congressional authorization to attack Iraq, on the basis of what turned out to be false information about Saddam Hussein's weapons stockpile. Similarly, after 9/11, Congress authorized Bush to pursue terrorists in Afghanistan. But that campaign was never officially declared as a war, even though it has managed to become the longest war in American history. Moreover, the current president is similarly determined to act independently. For all the sensitivity that Barack Obama has shown to the country's war fatigue, he has tried as much as possible to keep his policies on drone attacks secret from Congress and from Americans at large.

Begins another set of examples.

Identifies two possible meanings of the same word.

Balances the two halves of the sentence.

Therefore, devoting energy to Barno's proposed policy may be counterproductive. His recommendation is thought-provoking and based on vast military experience, but probably his readers would do better to focus on Presidential power. In military matters, the head of the country has tended to act on his instincts rather than seek meaningful advice from others. Figuring out ways to change or curb this habit seems an agenda more worthwhile than implementing the threat of a draft.

Concession; use of qualifications ("may be," "probably," "has tended").

Arguing in the First Person: Can You Use *I*?

More than ever, people engage in personal writing. As we text our friends, contribute to blogs, or post on social media, millions of us update the world about our daily lives. Perhaps you regularly report on your experiences in these ways. If so, your writing often relies on the first person. Over and over, it features the pronoun *I*. Some of your teachers, however, may have warned you against this pronoun. Many of us recall being told to ban it from our writing. In particular, its use was forbidden in essays meant for school. It's always good to find out what your current teachers' policies are about use of the first person in student essays. But nowadays, you might find your instructors more flexible about using *I* in essays. After all, it appears in countless online messages. Also, autobiography can prove to be a resource. References to yourself can help arguments you write for a course. They can inspire, support, and enliven the cases you make for your claims.

For an example, look again at Barno's paragraph 9. It reports the anger he felt when his son faced another combat tour. Barno's personal story carries larger implications. It makes a point about lots of people, not just the story's teller. With his account, Barno identifies hardships imposed on many enlistees and their families. He draws on his own experience to convey war's human costs.

Not always will the first person benefit an argument. Using *I* may bother your readers if you merely express your feelings. Here's a hypothetical example of what we mean:

> I definitely believe that Barno is too harsh in calling for a draft lottery. I very much feel that his proposal would put many people in needless danger. I worry that it won't stop our country from going to war. I fear that his plan will just send more civilians into combat. I also dislike the idea that his draft would require people to give up their freedom. I really value individual liberty. This constitutional right is very important to me.

A passage like this dwells too much on its author's emotions. Readers may lose sight of the argument the writer seeks to make. They may also suspect a lack of actual evidence. *Why* would Barno's draft lottery not keep the United States from war? The passage fails to offer real support for this claim. Instead, it stresses the "I's" own state of mind.

First-person arguments can backfire in another way. It's when they give the arguer's experiences too much authority. We're thinking of passages like this:

> Military families are more content than Barno admits. My brother Bob has done two tours of duty in Afghanistan. They have been rough for him, and he was even slightly wounded in a battle. But he has always been willing to perform his required service. I've never heard him complain that the army has mistreated him. My parents, my sister, and I are also true patriots. We're happy and proud that Bob

has turned out to be such a brave warrior. I've sent him many e-mails saying so. Everyone I know has regularly thanked him for his service instead of protesting America's decision to send our troops abroad in our defense. Bob and the rest of our family prove that the enemies of our country will never defeat the American spirit.

Personal anecdotes may indeed prove relevant to a claim you're making. They can be appropriate for an argument essay you write. Some version of the story above might play a useful role. It could nicely complicate Barno's emphasis on despair. But in its present form, the story doesn't "prove" anything. Bob's family may not be typical of military clans. The claim that they're representative needs much more support. In general, remember that not everyone's life resembles yours. Readers will want you to recognize the limits of your knowledge, as well as possible ways your history differs from others'.

Arguments for Analysis

We end this chapter by offering two additional arguments. Both of them conspicuously use the first person. We tend to think that their reliance on *I* is justifiable. Even so, the claims they make call for debate. We include these essays to invite your response. You might write an argument of your own about one or both of these texts. In any case, consider their main ideas, and study their techniques of persuasion. To help, we pose questions after each piece.

The first originally appeared as an op-ed column in the *New York Times* on June 6, 2015. Author Lee Siegel (b. 1957) is a veteran editor and cultural critic. Besides writing five books, he has contributed essays to many newspapers and periodicals. In 2002, he won the National Magazine Award for Reviews and Criticism. Siegel earned undergraduate and graduate degrees from Columbia University. As you'll see, he makes an argument about college students' debt.

LEE SIEGEL

Why I Defaulted on My Student Loans

One late summer afternoon when I was 17, I went with my mother to the local bank, a long-defunct institution whose name I cannot remember, to apply for my first student loan. My mother co-signed. When we finished, the banker, a balding man in his late 50s, congratulated us, as if I had just won some kind of award rather than signed away my young life.

By the end of my sophomore year at a small private liberal arts college, my mother and I had taken out a second loan, my father had declared bankruptcy and my parents had divorced. My mother could no longer afford the tuition that the student loans weren't covering. I transferred to a state college in New Jersey, closer to home.

Years later, I found myself confronted with a choice that too many people have had to and will have to face. I could give up what had become my vocation (in my case, being a writer) and take a job that I didn't want in order to repay the huge debt I had accumulated in college and graduate school. Or I could take what I had been led to believe was both the morally and legally reprehensible step of defaulting on my student loans, which was the only way I could survive without wasting my life in a job that had nothing to do with my particular usefulness to society.

I chose life. That is to say, I defaulted on my student loans.

As difficult as it has been, I've never looked back. The millions of young people today, who collectively owe over $1 trillion in loans, may want to consider my example.   5

It struck me as absurd that one could amass crippling debt as a result, not of drug addiction or reckless borrowing and spending, but of going to college. Having opened a new life to me beyond my modest origins, the education system was now going to call in its chits and prevent me from pursuing that new life, simply because I had the misfortune of coming from modest origins.

Am I a deadbeat? In the eyes of the law I am. Indifferent to the claim that repaying student loans is the road to character? Yes. Blind to the reality of countless numbers of people struggling to repay their debts, no matter their circumstances, many worse than mine? My heart goes out to them. To my mind, they have learned to live with a social arrangement that is legal, but not moral.

Maybe the problem was that I had reached beyond my lower-middle-class origins and taken out loans to attend a small private college to begin with. Maybe I should have stayed at a store called The Wild Pair, where I once had a nice stable job selling shoes after dropping out of the state college because I thought I deserved better, and naïvely tried to turn myself into a professional reader and writer on my own, without a college degree. I'd probably be district manager by now.

Or maybe, after going back to school, I should have gone into finance, or some other lucrative career. Self-disgust and lifelong unhappiness, destroying a precious young life—all this is a small price to pay for meeting your student loan obligations.

Some people will maintain that a bankrupt father, an impecunious background and impractical dreams are just the luck of the draw. Someone with character would have paid off those loans and let the chips fall where they may. But I have found, after some decades on this earth, that the road to character is often paved with family money and family connections, not to mention 14 percent effective tax rates on seven-figure incomes.   10

Moneyed stumbles never seem to have much consequence. Tax fraud, insider trading, almost criminal nepotism—these won't knock you off the straight and narrow. But if you're poor and miss a child-support payment, or if you're middle class and default on your student loans, then God help you.

Forty years after I took out my first student loan, and 30 years after getting my last, the Department of Education is still pursuing the unpaid balance. My mother, who co-signed some of the loans, is dead. The banks that made them have all gone under. I doubt that anyone can even find the promissory notes. The accrued interest, combined with the collection agencies' opulent fees, is now several times the principal.

Even the Internal Revenue Service understands the irrationality of pursuing someone with an unmanageable economic burden. It has a program called Offer in Compromise that allows struggling people who have fallen behind in their taxes to settle their tax debt.

The Department of Education makes it hard for you, and ugly. But it is possible to survive the life of default. You might want to follow these steps: Get as many credit cards as you can before your credit is ruined. Find a stable housing situation. Pay your rent on time so that you have a good record in that area when you do have to move. Live with or marry someone with good credit (preferably someone who shares your desperate nihilism).

When the fateful day comes, and your credit looks like a war zone, don't be afraid. The reported consequences of having no credit are scare talk, to some extent. The reliably predatory nature of American life guarantees that there will always be somebody to help you, from credit card companies charging stratospheric interest rates to subprime loans for houses and cars. Our economic system ensures that so long as you are willing to sink deeper and deeper into debt, you will keep being enthusiastically invited to play the economic game.   15

I am sharply aware of the strongest objection to my lapse into default. If everyone acted as I did, chaos would result. The entire structure of American higher education would change.

The collection agencies retained by the Department of Education would be exposed as the greedy vultures that they are. The government would get out of the loan-making and the loan-enforcement business. Congress might even explore a special, universal education tax that would make higher education affordable.

There would be a national shaming of colleges and universities for charging soaring tuition rates that are reaching lunatic levels. The rapacity of American colleges and universities is turning social mobility, the keystone of American freedom, into a commodified farce.

If people groaning under the weight of student loans simply said, "Enough," then all the pieties about debt that have become absorbed into all the pieties about higher education might be brought into alignment with reality. Instead of guaranteeing loans, the government would have to guarantee a college education. There are a lot of people who could learn to live with that, too.

≡ THINKING ABOUT THE TEXT

1. What is your main response to Siegel's argument, and what is the main reason you would give in supporting your response?

2. What do you think is the strongest (best) point that Siegel makes? Identify and paraphrase the specific passage where this point appears.

3. Where does Siegel acknowledge readers who might disagree with his argument or challenge it? Refer to specific paragraphs.

4. Note places where Siegel uses the word *life*: for example, in paragraph 4. How, in each instance, does he seem to define this word? Do his definitions seem logical to you? Why, or why not?

5. How would you describe Siegel's ethos: that is, the image of himself he creates as a writer?

6. In paragraphs 14 and 15, Siegel uses the pronoun *you*. Why, do you think? How is this choice of pronoun strategic?

7. Is it possible for readers to criticize Siegel for defaulting and yet still agree with certain parts of his essay? Explain.

8. Even if you agree with Siegel's position on the issue of student debt, what is something additional that he could have said or done in his essay to make his argument more persuasive?

9. In an article he wrote about Siegel's essay, *Slate* magazine correspondent Jordan Weissmann accused Siegel of "dispatching criminally negligent financial advice." Weissmann even said that the *New York Times* "should consider apologizing for publishing this deeply irresponsible op-ed." Do you agree with Weissmann that the essay shouldn't have been published at all? Why, or why not?

10. How sincere does Siegel seem when he encourages his readers to default on their student loans? Do you believe that a significant portion of his readers would see him as indeed calling for them to break the law? Why, or why not?

The second selection originally appeared in the August 23–29, 2013, issue of the *New Statesman*, a long-established weekly British news and opinion magazine. The author, Sophia McDougall (b. 1979), has contributed numerous pieces to this periodical. She is, however, chiefly a novelist. She has gained particular attention for her *Romanitas* trilogy, the first volume of which was published in 2005. These novels offer an alternate history in which the Roman Empire has lasted up to the present. In 2014, McDougall also produced a children's book titled *Mars Evacuees.*

You'll see that in paragraph 5 of her essay, McDougall refers to "George from the Famous Five." This reference may puzzle many American readers. But McDougall's main audience, living in Great Britain, would know it well. She has in mind a set of children's novels by Enid Blyton, an English writer. Begun in 1942, this multivolume series depicts the adventures of four children and their dog. The one girl in the group is Georgina, more commonly known as George.

SOPHIA McDOUGALL

All Princesses Know Kung Fu

I hate strong female characters. This might seem an odd thing to say, because I love many female characters in popular culture who exhibit resilience and courage. In *Crouching Tiger, Hidden Dragon*, I love Jen (Zhang Ziyi) sneering, "He is my defeated foe," when asked if she's related to Li Mu Bai (Chow Yun-Fat). I love Jane Eyre declaring, "I care for myself," despite the world's protracted assault on her self-esteem.

But the phrase "strong female character" has always set my teeth on edge and so have many of the characters—the princess in *Shrek* who knows kung fu; Angelina Jolie in the 2010 thriller *Salt*—who plainly have been written to fit the bill. No one ever asks if a male character is "strong." Nor if he's "feisty" or "kick-ass," come to that.

The patronizing premise of the strong female character is that she's anomalous. "Of course, normal women are weak and boring and can't do anything worthwhile," goes the logic. "But this one is different. She is strong! See, she kicks people in the face."

Are our best-loved male heroes "strong male characters"? Is, say, Sherlock Holmes strong? In one sense, yes: he faces danger and death in order to pursue justice. Yet he is often unreliable—and as an addict and a depressive he even claims his crime-fighting is a form of self-medication. So is Sherlock Holmes strong? The answer is not just "yes," but "he's far more than that."

The strong female character, by contrast, has something to prove. She's on the defensive even before she starts. She's George from the Famous Five, all grown up and still bleating with the same desperate lack of conviction that she's "every bit as good as a boy." 5

Nowadays the princesses all know kung fu and yet they are still the same princesses. They're still love interests, still the one girl in a team of five boys, and they're all kind of the same. They march on screen, punch someone to show how tough they are, throw around a couple of one-liners or forcibly kiss someone because getting consent is for wimps—and then, with ladylike discretion, they back out of the narrative's way. Their strength lets them, briefly, dominate bystanders but never dominate the plot. It's anodyne, a sop, a Trojan horse—it's there to distract and confuse you, so you forget to ask for more.

What do I want instead? I want a male-to-female character ratio of 1:1 instead of 3:1 on our screens. I want a wealth of complex female protagonists who can be either strong or weak or both or neither, because they are more than strength or weakness. Gunslingers and martial artists, sure, but also interesting women who are shy and quiet and do sometimes put up with things, because often in real life there's no alternative.

And besides heroines, I want to see women in as many and as varied secondary roles as men: female sidekicks, mentors, comic relief, rivals, villains. In other words, equality.

≣ THINKING ABOUT THE TEXT

1. McDougall begins with a statement that she quickly acknowledges "might be an odd thing to say." Why start with such a sentence, therefore?

2. In your own words, why does McDougall "hate strong female characters"?

3. How accurate does McDougall strike you as she refers to specific characters (or types of characters) in popular culture? What examples can you think of that support or challenge her argument?

4. In her first paragraph, McDougall says "I hate" and "I love." What "I + verb" expression does she repeatedly use in her last two paragraphs? What's the effect of this final strategy?

5. McDougall is good at paragraph transitions. After her introduction, she connects the start of each paragraph to the paragraph that comes before it. What are the specific ways she does this?

6. We've felt obliged to explain McDougall's reference to "George from the Famous Five." Perhaps only a British audience would understand this reference. Should she have dropped it, then? Why, or why not?

7. The last word in McDougall's essay is *equality*. What, basically, does she mean by it? How realistic is she when she calls for popular culture to practice equality in her sense of the term?

CHAPTER 3

How to Argue about Literature

What Is Literature?

Most people would say that *literature* consists of fiction (novels as well as short stories), poetry, and drama. It's a reasonable definition. But limiting the term to these genres can be misleading. After all, they connect to everyday life. Often they employ ordinary forms of talk and blend them with less common ones. Also, things that function as symbols in stories, poems, and plays may do so in daily conversation. As we speak with one another, we may associate fire with passion, water with life, evening with death. Throughout the day, actually, people put literary genres into practice. Perhaps you have commented on situations by quoting a song lyric or citing a line of verse. No doubt you are often theatrical, following scripts and performing roles. Certainly you tell stories. Imagine this scenario: a traffic jam has made you late for a class; now, you must explain your delay. You may relate a tale of suspense, with you the hero struggling to escape the bumper-to-bumper horde. Almost all of us spin narratives day after day, because doing so helps us meaningfully frame our existence. As writer Joan Didion observes, "We tell ourselves stories in order to live."

You may admit that literature is grounded in real life and yet still tend to apply the term only to written texts of fiction, poetry, and drama. But this tendency is distinctly modern, for the term *literature* has not always been applied so restrictively. *Literature* was at first a characteristic of *readers*. From the term's emergence in the fourteenth century to the middle of the eighteenth, *literature* was more or less a synonym for *literacy*. People of literature were assumed to be well read.

In the late eighteenth century, however, the term's meaning changed. Increasingly it referred to books and other printed texts rather than to people who read them. At the beginning of this shift, the scope of literature was broad, encompassing nearly all public writing. But as the nineteenth century proceeded, the term's range shrank. More and more people considered literature to be imaginative or creative writing, which they distinguished from nonfiction. This trend did take years to build; in the early 1900s, literature anthologies still featured nonfiction such as essays and excerpts from histories and biographies. By the mid-1900s, though, the narrower definition of literature prevailed.

This limited definition has become vulnerable. From the early 1970s, a number of literature faculty have called for widening it. In 1979, for instance, a National Endowment for the Humanities–Modern Language Association institute titled "Women's Nontraditional Literature" applied the term *literature* to genres that had not been thought of as such. Participants studied essays, letters, diaries, autobiographies, and oral testimonies. To each of these genres, women have contributed much; in fact, the institute's participants concluded that a literature curriculum slights many works by women if it focuses on fiction, poetry, and drama alone.

Of course, even within these three categories, the term *literature* has been selectively applied. Take the case of novelist and short-story writer Stephen King, whose books have sold millions of copies. Despite his commercial success, a lot of readers—including some of his fans—refuse to call King's writing literature. They assume that to call something literature is to say that it has artistic merit, and for them King's tales of horror fall short.

Yet people who use the term *literature* as a compliment may still disagree about whether a certain text deserves it. Plenty of readers do praise King's writing as literature, even as others deem it simply entertainment. In short, artistic standards differ. To be sure, some works have been constantly admired through the years; regarded as classics, they are frequently taught in literature classes. *Hamlet* and other plays by William Shakespeare are obvious examples. But in the last twenty years, much controversy has arisen over the *literary canon*, those works taught again and again. Are there good reasons why the canon has consisted mostly of works by white men? Or have the principles of selection been skewed by sexism and racism? Should the canon be changed to accommodate a greater range of authors? Or should literary studies resist having any canon at all? These questions have provoked various answers and continued debate.

Also in question are attempts to separate literature from nonfiction. Much nonfiction shows imagination and relies on devices found in novels, short stories, poems, and plays. The last few years have seen emerge the term *creative nonfiction* as a synonym for essays, histories, and journalistic accounts that use evocative language and strong narratives. Conversely, works of fiction, poetry, and drama may stem from real-life events. Charlotte Perkins Gilman based her 1892 short story "The Yellow Wallpaper" (see p. 244) on trauma she went through when her doctor, treating her for depression, made her stop work and vegetate. Gilman's heroine suffers torment similar to hers. A note of caution is in order, though. A literary text may seem autobiographical but not directly reflect the author's life. The situation of Gilman's heroine doesn't completely resemble her own. It differs in certain ways. Indeed, the character is too distressed to write a story as Gilman herself did. In short, Gilman didn't merely transmit her experience. Rather, she *transformed* it. So her artistic strategies merit study, especially since she could have tapped her experience in other ways. Keep in mind, too, that the author of a work isn't always the best guide to it. It may raise for its readers issues and ideas that the author didn't foresee. Besides, the author's comments about the text may leave aspects of it unexplained.

Some people argue that literature about real events is still literary because it inspires contemplation rather than action. This view of literature has traditionally been summed up as "art for art's sake." This notion brushes aside, however, all the novels, short stories, poems, and plays that encourage audiences to undertake certain acts. Famous examples are Harriet Beecher Stowe's antislavery novel *Uncle Tom's Cabin* (1852) and Upton Sinclair's *The Jungle* (1906) about the horrors of immigrant exploitation in the Chicago meat-packing industry. True, not every work of literature is so conspicuously action oriented. But even when a text seems more geared toward reflection, it may move readers to change their behavior.

In our book, we resist endorsing a single definition of *literature*. Rather, we encourage you to review and perhaps rethink what the term means to you. At the same time, to expand the realm of literature, we include several essays in addition to short stories, poems, and plays. We also present numerous critical commentaries as well as various historical documents. Throughout the book, we invite you to make connections among these different kinds of texts. You need not treat them as altogether separate species.

Why Study Literature in a College Writing Course?

We assume you are reading this book in a course aimed at helping you write. Quite likely the course is meant to prepare you for writing assignments throughout college, including papers in fields beyond English. It's natural to wonder how reading literature serves this purpose.

Much academic writing is, in fact, based on reading. You'll find the two interconnected in course after course. Many classes will ask you to produce essays that analyze published texts. To *analyze* means going beyond your first impressions, carefully noting a text's ideas, techniques, and effects. You'll also find yourself needing to *synthesize*: that is, to trace how the text is patterned, as well as how it relates to other works. Together, these acts of analysis and synthesis have been called reading *closely*, a process we explain and model in Chapter 4. We encourage you to practice this method with the selections in our book.

Often, college courses will ask you to write about some text that isn't easily understood. The purpose of your paper will be to help other readers of the text grasp its meanings and, perhaps, judge its worth. Literature is a good training ground for these skills of interpretation and evaluation. The poems, stories, plays, and essays in this book repeatedly invite inquiry. They don't settle for delivering simple, straightforward messages. Rather, they offer puzzles, complications, metaphors, symbols, and mysteries, thereby recognizing that life is complex. In particular, literary works encourage you to ponder the multiple dimensions of language: how, for example, a word's meaning can vary depending on context. Furthermore, much literature can help you understand your own life and conduct it better. In this capacity, literature serves as "equipment for living," Kenneth Burke's description of its function.

Some people *dislike* literature because they find it too vague and indirect. They resent that it often forces them to figure out symbols and implications when they would rather have ideas presented outright. Perhaps you'll wish that the narrator in Gilman's story had made clear why her observations prompted her to destroy her room's wallpaper. But in life, truth can be complicated and elusive. In many ways, literature is most realistic when it suggests the same. Besides, many readers—perhaps including you—appreciate literature most when it resists simple decoding, forcing them to adopt new assumptions and learn new methods of analysis. Indeed, throughout this book we suggest that the most interesting and profitable conversations about literature are those in which the issues are not easily resolved. One of the best things your course can provide you and your classmates is the chance to exchange insights about texts such as Gilman's.

We have been suggesting that one value of studying literature in a writing class is that it often engages not just thought but feeling. The two interweave so that readers find themselves engaging in interpretation and evaluation because they *care* about lives depicted in the text. Most of the works in this book appeal to your emotions, encouraging you to identify with certain characters, to be disturbed by others, and to wonder what happens next in the plot. Indeed, many readers of literature prize the moments when it makes them laugh or cry or gasp as well as think. To be sure, it can be argued that the most worthwhile literature gets us to comprehend and perhaps even appreciate, certain kinds of people who would normally confuse or disturb us. "When it's the real thing," critic Frank Lentricchia suggests, "literature enlarges us, strips the film of familiarity from the world; creates bonds of sympathy with all kinds, even with evil characters, who we learn are all in the family." This "enlargement" is both intellectual *and* emotional.

Finally, writing about literature is good training for other fields because literary analysis often involves taking an interdisciplinary perspective. A typical interpretation of "The Yellow Wallpaper" will bring in principles of psychology to explain the speaker's distressed state of mind. To evaluate the character's condition, readers also grapple with philosophical questions about what constitutes a "productive" or "good" or "free" life. Moreover, the heroine's entrapment in nineteenth-century gender roles has political, historical, and sociological significance.

Two Stories for Analysis

As we discuss the process of arguing about literature, we mention arguments that might be made about the following pair of stories. Each features a speaker who is introducing someone else to certain kinds of work. It is useful to compare these texts. Indeed, we emphasize comparison throughout this book. As you read each story, take a few moments to reflect on the questions we ask after each one, perhaps jotting down your responses to keep them in your mind as you read the rest of the chapter.

The first story, "Orientation," originally appeared in a 1994 issue of *Seattle Review* and was subsequently selected for *The Best American Short Stories 1995*.

DANIEL OROZCO

Orientation

The son of Nicaraguan immigrants, California-born Daniel Orozco (b. 1957) currently teaches at the University of Idaho. His award-winning short fiction has appeared in a variety of magazines, including Harper's *and* Zoetrope, *and has been collected in* Orientation and Other Stories *(2011). He received a B.A. from Stanford University, an M.A. from San Francisco State University, and an M.F.A. from the University of Washington. He has also held a writing fellowship at Stanford.*

Those are the offices and these are the cubicles. That's my cubicle there, and this is your cubicle. This is your phone. Never answer your phone. Let the Voicemail System answer it. This is your Voicemail System Manual. There are no personal phone calls allowed. We do, however, allow for emergencies. If you must make an emergency phone call, ask your supervisor first. If you can't find your supervisor, ask Phillip Spiers, who sits over there. He'll check with Clarissa Nicks, who sits over there. If you make an emergency phone call without asking, you may be let go.

These are your IN and OUT boxes. All the forms in your IN box must be logged in by the date shown in the upper left-hand corner, initialed by you in the upper right-hand corner, and distributed to the Processing Analyst whose name is numerically coded in the lower left-hand corner. The lower right-hand corner is left blank. Here's your Processing Analyst Numerical Code Index. And here's your Forms Processing Procedures Manual.

You must pace your work. What do I mean? I'm glad you asked that. We pace our work according to the eight-hour workday. If you have twelve hours of work in your IN box, for example, you must compress that work into the eight-hour day. If you have one hour of work in your IN box, you must expand that work to fill the eight-hour day. That was a good question. Feel free to ask questions. Ask too many questions, however, and you may be let go.

That is our receptionist. She is a temp. We go through receptionists here. They quit with alarming frequency. Be polite and civil to the temps. Learn their names, and invite them to lunch occasionally. But don't get close to them, as it only makes it more difficult when they leave. And they always leave. You can be sure of that.

The men's room is over there. The women's room is over there. John LaFountaine, who sits over there, uses the women's room occasionally. He says it is accidental. We know better, but we let it pass. John LaFountaine is harmless, his forays into the forbidden territory of the women's room simply a benign thrill, a faint blip on the dull flat line of his life.

Russell Nash, who sits in the cubicle to your left, is in love with Amanda Pierce, who sits in the cubicle to your right. They ride the same bus together after work. For Amanda Pierce, it is just a tedious bus ride made less tedious by the idle nattering of Russell Nash. But for Russell Nash, it is the highlight of his day. It is the highlight of his life. Russell Nash has put on forty pounds, and

5

grows fatter with each passing month, nibbling on chips and cookies while peeking glumly over the partitions at Amanda Pierce, and gorging himself at home on cold pizza and ice cream while watching adult videos on TV.

Amanda Pierce, in the cubicle to your right, has a six-year-old son named Jamie, who is autistic. Her cubicle is plastered from top to bottom with the boy's crayon artwork—sheet after sheet of precisely drawn concentric circles and ellipses, in black and yellow. She rotates them every other Friday. Be sure to comment on them. Amanda Pierce also has a husband, who is a lawyer. He subjects her to an escalating array of painful and humiliating sex games, to which Amanda Pierce reluctantly submits. She comes to work exhausted and freshly wounded each morning, wincing from the abrasions on her breasts, or the bruises on her abdomen, or the second-degree burns on the backs of her thighs.

But we're not supposed to know any of this. Do not let on. If you let on, you may be let go.

Amanda Pierce, who tolerates Russell Nash, is in love with Albert Bosch, whose office is over there. Albert Bosch, who only dimly registers Amanda Pierce's existence, has eyes only for Ellie Tapper, who sits over there. Ellie Tapper, who hates Albert Bosch, would walk through fire for Curtis Lance. But Curtis Lance hates Ellie Tapper. Isn't the world a funny place? Not in the ha-ha sense, of course.

Anika Bloom sits in that cubicle. Last year, while reviewing quarterly reports in a meeting with Barry Hacker, Anika Bloom's left palm began to bleed. She fell into a trance, stared into her hand, and told Barry Hacker when and how his wife would die. We laughed it off. She was, after all, a new employee. But Barry Hacker's wife is dead. So unless you want to know exactly when and how you'll die, never talk to Anika Bloom.   10

Colin Heavey sits in that cubicle over there. He was new once, just like you. We warned him about Anika Bloom. But at last year's Christmas Potluck, he felt sorry for her when he saw that no one was talking to her. Colin Heavey brought her a drink. He hasn't been himself since. Colin Heavey is doomed. There's nothing he can do about it, and we are powerless to help him. Stay away from Colin Heavey. Never give any of your work to him. If he asks to do something, tell him you have to check with me. If he asks again, tell him I haven't gotten back to you.

This is the Fire Exit. There are several on this floor, and they are marked accordingly. We have a Floor Evacuation Review every three months, and an Escape Route Quiz once a month. We have our Biannual Fire Drill twice a year, and our Annual Earthquake Drill once a year. These are precautions only. These things never happen.

For your information, we have a comprehensive health plan. Any catastrophic illness, any unforeseen tragedy is completely covered. All dependents are completely covered. Larry Bagdikian, who sits over there, has six daughters. If anything were to happen to any of his girls, or to all of them, if all six were to simultaneously fall victim to illness or injury—stricken with a hideous degenerative muscle disease or some rare toxic blood disorder, sprayed with semiautomatic gunfire while on a class field trip, or attacked in their bunk beds by some prowling nocturnal lunatic—if any of this were to pass, Larry's girls would all be taken care of. Larry Bagdikian would not have to pay one dime. He would have nothing to worry about.

We also have a generous vacation and sick leave policy. We have an excellent disability insurance plan. We have a stable and profitable pension fund. We get group discounts for the symphony, and block seating at the ballpark. We get commuter ticket books for the bridge. We have Direct Deposit. We are all members of Costco.

This is our kitchenette. And this, this is our Mr. Coffee. We have a coffee pool, into which we each pay two dollars a week for coffee, filters, sugar, and CoffeeMate. If you prefer Cremora or half-and-half to CoffeeMate, there is a special pool for three dollars a week. If you prefer Sweet 'n Low to sugar, there is a special pool for two-fifty a week. We do not do decaf. You are allowed to join the coffee pool of your choice, but you are not allowed to touch the Mr. Coffee. 15

This is the microwave oven. You are allowed to *heat* food in the microwave oven. You are not, however, allowed to *cook* food in the microwave oven.

We get one hour for lunch. We also get one fifteen-minute break in the morning, and one fifteen-minute break in the afternoon. Always take your breaks. If you skip a break, it is gone forever. For your information, your break is a privilege, not a right. If you abuse the break policy, we are authorized to rescind your breaks. Lunch, however, is a right, not a privilege. If you abuse the lunch policy, our hands will be tied, and we will be forced to look the other way. We will not enjoy that.

This is the refrigerator. You may put your lunch in it. Barry Hacker, who sits over there, steals food from this refrigerator. His petty theft is an outlet for his grief. Last New Year's Eve, while kissing his wife, a blood vessel burst in her brain. Barry Hacker's wife was two months pregnant at the time, and lingered in a coma for half a year before dying. It was a tragic loss for Barry Hacker. He hasn't been himself since. Barry Hacker's wife was a beautiful woman. She was also completely covered. Barry Hacker did not have to pay one dime. But his dead wife haunts him. She haunts all of us. We have seen her, reflected in the monitors of our computers, moving past our cubicles. We have seen the dim shadow of her face in our photocopies. She pencils herself in in the receptionist's appointment book, with the notation: To see Barry Hacker. She has left messages in the receptionist's Voicemail box, messages garbled by the electronic chirrups and buzzes in the phone line, her voice echoing from an immense distance within the ambient hum. But the voice is hers. And beneath her voice, beneath the tidal *whoosh* of static and hiss, the gurgling and crying of a baby can be heard.

In any case, if you bring a lunch, put a little something extra in the bag for Barry Hacker. We have four Barrys in this office. Isn't that a coincidence?

This is Matthew Payne's office. He is our Unit Manager, and his door is always closed. We have never seen him, and you will never see him. But he is here. You can be sure of that. He is all around us. 20

This is the Custodian's Closet. You have no business in the Custodian's Closet.

And this, this is our Supplies Cabinet. If you need supplies, see Curtis Lance. He will log you in on the Supplies Cabinet Authorization Log, then give you a Supplies Authorization Slip. Present your pink copy of the Supplies Authorization Slip to Ellie Tapper. She will log you in on the Supplies Cabinet Key Log, then give you the key. Because the Supplies Cabinet is located outside the Unit Manager's office, you must be very quiet. Gather your supplies quietly. The Supplies Cabinet is divided into four sections. Section One contains letter-head stationery, blank paper and envelopes, memo and note pads, and so on. Section Two contains pens and pencils and typewriter and printer ribbons, and the like. In Section Three we have erasers, correction fluids, transparent tapes, glue sticks, et cetera. And in Section Four we have paper clips and push pins and scissors and razor blades. And here are the spare blades for the shredder. Do not touch the shredder, which is located over there. The shredder is of no concern to you.

Gwendolyn Stich sits in that office there. She is crazy about penguins, and collects penguin knickknacks: penguin posters and coffee mugs and statio-nery, penguin stuffed animals, penguin jewelry, penguin sweaters and T-shirts and socks. She has a pair of penguin fuzzy slippers she wears when working late at the office. She has a tape cassette of penguin sounds which she listens to for relaxation. Her favorite colors are black and white. She has personalized license plates that read PEN GWEN. Every morning, she passes through all the cubicles to wish each of us a *good* morning. She brings Danish on Wednesdays for Hump Day morning break, and doughnuts on Fridays for TGIF afternoon break. She organizes the Annual Christmas Potluck, and is in charge of the Birthday List. Gwendolyn Stich's door is always open to all of us. She will always lend an ear, and put in a good word for you; she will always give you a hand, or the shirt off her back, or a shoulder to cry on. Because her door is always open, she hides and cries in a stall in the women's room. And John LaFountaine—who, enthralled when a woman enters, sits quietly in his stall with his knees to his chest—John LaFountaine has heard her vomiting in there. We have come upon Gwendolyn Stich huddled in the stairwell, shiver-ing in the updraft, sipping a Diet Mr. Pibb and hugging her knees. She does not let any of this interfere with her work. If it interfered with her work, she might have to be let go.

Kevin Howard sits in that cubicle over there. He is a serial killer, the one they call the Carpet Cutter, responsible for the mutilations across town. We're not supposed to know that, so do not let on. Don't worry. His compulsion inflicts itself on strangers only, and the routine established is elaborate and unwaver-ing. The victim must be a white male, a young adult no older than thirty, heavyset, with dark hair and eyes, and the like. The victim must be chosen at random, before sunset, from a public place; the victim is followed home, and must put up a struggle; et cetera. The carnage inflicted is precise: the angle and direction of the incisions; the layering of skin and muscle tissue; the rearrange-ment of the visceral organs; and so on. Kevin Howard does not let any of this interfere with his work. He is, in fact, our fastest typist. He types as if he were on fire. He has a secret crush on Gwendolyn Stich, and leaves a red-foil-wrapped Hershey's Kiss on her desk every afternoon. But he hates Anika Bloom, and keeps well away from her. In his presence, she has uncontrollable fits of shaking and trembling. Her left palm does not stop bleeding.

In any case, when Kevin Howard gets caught, act surprised. Say that he   25
seemed like a nice person, a bit of a loner, perhaps, but always quiet and polite.

This is the photocopier room. And this, this is our view. It faces southwest. West is down there, toward the water. North is back there. Because we are on the seventeenth floor, we are afforded a magnificent view. Isn't it beautiful? It overlooks the park, where the tops of those trees are. You can see a segment of the bay between those two buildings there. You can see the sun set in the gap between those two buildings over there. You can see this building reflected in the glass panels of that building across the way. There. See? That's you, waving. And look there. There's Anika Bloom in the kitchenette, waving back.

Enjoy this view while photocopying. If you have problems with the photocopier, see Russell Nash. If you have any questions, ask your supervisor. If you can't find your supervisor, ask Phillip Spiers. He sits over there. He'll check with Clarissa Nicks. She sits over there. If you can't find them, feel free to ask me. That's my cubicle. I sit in there.   *[1994]*

≡ **THINKING ABOUT THE TEXT**

1. Orozco reports that since his story was published, "it has even been included in an employee orientation manual, which is either very funny or very disturbing." What is *your* reaction to this news? Does this orientation resemble other orientations with which you are familiar? In what ways? Consider the kinds of advice given and language used.

2. Does the office described here resemble other offices with which you are familiar? In what ways? At what points in the story does this office seem unusual?

3. List at least three adjectives that describe Orozco's narrator. What influences your evaluation of this narrator? What would you say to someone who claims that the story is more about the narrator than about the office?

4. What assumptions do you make about the narrator's audience, that is, the listener being oriented? Write a page or two from this person's point of view, stating his or her response to the orientation.

5. Does the order of the narrator's statements matter? Explain.

The next story, Jamaica Kincaid's "Girl," first appeared in *The New Yorker* in 1978 and was later reprinted in her first book, a 1984 collection of short stories titled *At the Bottom of the River.*

JAMAICA KINCAID
Girl

Originally named Elaine Potter Richardson, Jamaica Kincaid (b. 1949) was born on the island of Antigua in the West Indies. At the time, Antigua was a British colony. Kincaid lived there until she was seventeen, when she emigrated to the United States. Soon she became a nanny for the family of Michael Arlen, television critic for The New Yorker. *Eventually, the magazine published her own short stories and during the early 1990s her gardening columns. Although she continues to live in the United States, almost all of her writing deals with her native land. In particular, she has written about Antiguan women growing up under British domination. She has published the novels* Annie John *(1985),* Lucy *(1990),* Autobiography of My Mother *(1996), and* Mr. Potter *(2002). Her books of nonfiction include* A Small Place, *an analysis of Antigua (1988); a memoir,* My Brother *(1997);* My Garden (Book) *(1999); and* Talk Stories *(2001), a collection of brief observations that she originally wrote for* The New Yorker. *In 2009, she was inducted into the American Academy of Arts and Sciences and is currently a professor of literature at Claremont McKenna College in California. Her latest novel is* See Now Then *(2013).*

Wash the white clothes on Monday and put them on the stone heap; wash the color clothes on Tuesday and put them on the clothesline to dry; don't walk barehead in the hot sun; cook pumpkin fritters in very hot sweet oil; soak your little clothes right after you take them off; when buying cotton to make yourself a nice blouse, be sure that it doesn't have gum on it, because that way it won't hold up well after a wash; soak salt fish overnight before you cook it; is it   5
true that you sing benna° in Sunday school?; always eat your food in such a way that it won't turn someone else's stomach; on Sundays try to walk like a lady and not like the slut you are so bent on becoming; don't sing benna in Sunday school; you mustn't speak to wharf-rat boys, not even to give direc-   10
tions; don't eat fruits on the street—flies will follow you; *but I don't sing benna on Sundays at all and never in Sunday school*; this is how to sew on a button; this is how to make a button-hole for the button you have just sewed on; this is how to hem a dress when you see the hem coming down and so to prevent yourself from looking like the slut I know you are so bent on becoming; this is how   15
you iron your father's khaki shirt so that it doesn't have a crease; this is how you iron your father's khaki pants so that they don't have a crease; this is how you grow okra—far from the house, because okra tree harbors red ants; when you are growing dasheen, make sure it gets plenty of water or else it makes your throat itch when you are eating it; this is how you sweep a corner; this is   20
how you sweep a whole house; this is how you sweep a yard; this is how you smile to someone you don't like too much; this is how you smile to someone you don't like at all; this is how you smile to someone you like completely; this is how you set a table for tea; this is how you set a table for dinner; this is how you set a table for dinner with an important guest; this is how you set a table for   25

---

7 benna: Calypso music.

lunch; this is how you set a table for breakfast; this is how to behave in the presence of men who don't know you very well, and this way they won't recognize immediately the slut I have warned you against becoming; be sure to wash every day, even if it is with your own spit; don't squat down to play marbles— you are not a boy, you know; don't pick people's flowers—you might catch something; don't throw stones at blackbirds, because it might not be a blackbird at all; this is how to make a bread pudding; this is how to make doukona;° this is how to make pepper pot; this is how to make a good medicine for a cold; this is how to make a good medicine to throw away a child before it even becomes a child; this is how to catch a fish; this is how to throw back a fish you don't like, and that way something bad won't fall on you; this is how to bully a man; this is how a man bullies you; this is how to love a man, and if this doesn't work there are other ways, and if they don't work don't feel too bad about giving up; this is how to spit up in the air if you feel like it, and this is how to move quick so that it doesn't fall on you; this is how to make ends meet; always squeeze bread to make sure it's fresh; *but what if the baker won't let me feel the bread?*; you mean to say that after all you are really going to be the kind of woman who the baker won't let near the bread? [1978]

32 doukona: A spicy plantain pudding.

≡ THINKING ABOUT THE TEXT

1. Is "Girl" really a story? What characteristics of a story come to mind as you consider this issue?

2. Describe the culture depicted in "Girl" as well as the role of females in that culture. Is either the culture or the role of females in it different from what you are familiar with? Explain.

3. Do you think that the instructions to this girl are all given on the same occasion? Why, or why not? Who do you suppose is giving the instructions? Would you say that the instructor is oppressive or domineering? Identify some of the assumptions behind your position.

4. What effect does Kincaid achieve by making this text a single long sentence? By having the girl speak at only two brief moments?

5. At one point, the girl is shown "how to make a good medicine to throw away a child before it even becomes a child" (lines 33–34). What do you think of the instructor's willingness to give such advice? What do you conclude from its position in the text between "how to make a good medicine for a cold" (line 33) and "how to catch a fish" (line 35)? Does the order of the various pieces of advice matter? Could Kincaid have presented them in a different order without changing their effects?

≡ A WRITING EXERCISE

Once you have read both stories, write brief responses to each. You might jot down things you especially notice about them, feelings they evoke in you, and questions you have about them. You might also note your own work experiences that they lead you to recall. With each story, freewrite for ten minutes without stopping.

Strategies for Arguing about Literature

We return now to the specific elements of argument we discussed in Chapter 1. Remember that when you argue, you try to **persuade** an **audience** to accept your **claims** about an **issue**, working toward this aim by offering **evidence**, showing your **reasoning**, making **assumptions**, and employing other kinds of **appeals**. Here, with Orozco's and Kincaid's stories as our sample texts, we show how you can turn these elements into strategies for writing arguments about literature.

IDENTIFY ISSUES

Recall that an **issue** is something about which people have disagreed or might disagree. Even as you read a text, you can try to guess what features of it will lead to disagreements in class. You may sense that your own reaction to certain aspects of the text is heavily influenced by your background and values, which other students may not share. Some parts of the text may leave you with con-flicting ideas or mixed feelings, as if half of you disagrees with the other half. At moments like these, you come to realize what topics are issues for you, and next you can urge the rest of your class to see these topics as issues, too.

An issue is best defined as a question with no obvious, immediate answer. Thus you can start identifying issues by noting questions that occur to you as you read. Perhaps this question-posing approach to texts is new for you. Often readers demand that a text be clear, and they get annoyed if it leaves them puzzled. Certain writing ought to be immediately clear in meaning; think of operating instructions on a plane's emergency doors. But the value of a liter-ary work often lies in the work's complexities, which can lead readers to reexamine their own ways of perceiving the world. Also, your discussions and papers about literature are likely to be most useful when they go beyond the obvious to deal with more challenging matters. When your class begins talk-ing about a work, you may feel obliged to stay quiet if you have no firm state-ments to make. But you can contribute a lot by bringing up questions that occurred to you as you read. Especially worth raising are questions that con-tinue to haunt you.

In the case of Daniel Orozco's "Orientation," one possible issue concerns the reliability of the narrator. Should we accept as true everything the narrator says, or should we be suspicious of the orientation this person gives? A possible issue with Jamaica Kincaid's "Girl" concerns how much affection the main speaker has for the girl she addresses. A logical hypothesis is that these two are mother and daughter, but to what degree is the speaker showing motherly love? In fact, people may disagree over how to define this term. What does it mean to *you*?

You may feel unable to answer questions like these. But again, you achieve much when you simply formulate questions and bring them up in class. As other students help you ponder them, you will grow better able to explore issues through writing as well as through conversation.

You are more likely to come up with questions about a text if you assume that for every decision the writer made, alternatives existed. In "Orientation," Orozco might have had the many characters speak, but instead he chose to write the story as a mostly uninterrupted monologue. Similarly, Kincaid might have given the girl of her title more of a speaking voice. When you begin to explore why authors made the choices they did, you also begin to examine the effects of those choices.

You will recognize writers' options more easily if you compare their texts with others. For instance, with "Orientation" you cannot be sure how old the narrator and new employee are, but Kincaid's story is pointedly titled "Girl," and its speaker is clearly a female adult. Although both stories are about education, Kincaid's is concerned with the transition from youth to adulthood. She shows how a girl's transition to womanhood involves learning certain gender "rules" of her sex. Thinking of Kincaid's focus can strengthen your awareness that Orozco has chosen not to reveal whether his story's two characters are male or female.

Next, we identify ten kinds of issues that arise in literature courses. Our list will help you detect the issues that come up in your class and discover others to bring up in discussions or in your writing. The list does not include every kind of issue; you may think of others. Moreover, you may find that an issue can fit into more than one of the categories we name. But when you do have an issue that seems hard to classify, try to assign it to a single category, if only for the time being. You will then have some initial guidance for your reading, class discussions, and writing. If you later feel that the issue belongs to another category, you can shift your focus.

1. Issues of fact.   Rarely does a work of literature provide complete information about its characters and events. Rather, literature is usually marked by what literary theorist Wolfgang Iser calls "gaps," moments when certain facts are omitted or obscured. At such times, readers may give various answers to the question, What is happening in this text? Readers tackle questions of fact only if they suspect that the answers will affect their overall view of a text. It may not matter, for example, that we fail to learn the exact product or service of the company described in Orozco's "Orientation." More consequential seems the question of whether Barry Hacker's dead wife is really sending messages to the office. Imagine a reader who believes that Orozco's narrator is merely fantasizing a ghost. Imagine a second reader who thinks the wife is truly haunting the office. How might these two readers see the whole story differently because of their different assumptions?

2. Issues of theme.   You may be familiar with the term **theme** from other literature courses. By *theme* critics usually mean the main claim that an author seems to be making with his or her text. Sometimes a theme is defined in terms of a single word—for example, *work* or *love*. But such words are really mere topics. Identifying the topics addressed by a text can be a useful way of starting to analyze that text (see pp. 102–109). A text's theme, however, is best seen as an assertion that you need at least one whole sentence to express.

With many texts, an issue of theme arises because readers can easily disagree about the text's main idea. In literature classes, such disagreements often occur, in part because literary works tend to express their themes indirectly. This is especially the case with stories like "Orientation" and "Girl," in which the main speaker's views are not necessarily the same as the author's. Readers of these two stories may give various answers to the question, What is the author ultimately saying? Perhaps some readers will take Kincaid to imply that mothers always know best. Other readers may conclude that Kincaid thinks that excessively controlling mothers are damaging to children.

If you try to express a text's theme, avoid making a statement that is so general that it could apply to many other works. Arguing that Kincaid's theme is "Girls are pressured to fit stereotyped roles" does not get at her story's details. On the other hand, do not let a text's details restrict you so much that you make the theme seem relevant only to a small group. If you argue that Kincaid's theme is "Antiguan women are domineering," then the many readers who are *not* from Antigua will wonder why they should care. In short, try to express themes as *midlevel generalizations*. With Kincaid's story, one possible theme is "In some cultures, women prepare girls for adulthood by teaching them to follow conventions *and* to assert themselves." A statement like this seems both attentive to Kincaid's specific text and applicable to a large portion of humanity. You are free to challenge this version of Kincaid's theme by proposing an alternative. Moreover, even if you do accept this statement as her theme, you are then free to decide whether it is a sound observation. Identifying a theme is one thing; evaluating it is another.

Keep in mind that a theme ties together various parts of a text. Focusing on a single passage, even if it seems thematic, may lead you to ignore other passages that a statement of theme should encompass. For instance, the last words of "Girl" may tempt you to believe that its theme is "be the kind of woman who feels the bread." Yet in other parts of the story, the main speaker seems to be calling for a compliant attitude. You need to take these moments into account as well.

Often you will sense a work's theme but still have to decide whether to state it as an **observation** or as a **recommendation**. You would be doing the first, for example, if you expressed Kincaid's theme as we did above: "In some cultures, women prepare girls for adulthood by teaching them to follow conventions *and* to assert themselves." You would be doing the second if you said Kincaid's theme is "Women should teach girls to follow conventions *and* to assert themselves." Indeed, people who depict a theme as a recommendation often use a word like *should*. Neither way of expressing a theme is necessarily better than the other. But notice that each way conjures up a particular image of the author. Reporting Kincaid's theme as an observation suggests that she is writing as a psychologist, a philosopher, or some other analyst of human nature. Reporting her theme as a recommendation suggests that she is writing as a teacher, preacher, manager, or coach: someone who is telling her readers what to do. Your decision about how to phrase a theme will depend in part on which image of the author you think is appropriate.

You risk obscuring the intellectual, emotional, and stylistic richness of a text if you insist on reducing it to a single message. Try stating the text's theme as a problem for which there is no easy solution, which suggests that the text is complex. For instance, if you say that Kincaid's theme is "In some cultures, women who prepare girls for adulthood are caught in a contradiction between wanting to empower them and wanting to keep them safe," you position yourself to address various elements of the story.

Also weigh the possibility that a text is conveying more than one theme. If you plan to associate the text with any theme at all, you might refer to *a* theme of the text rather than *the* theme of the text. Your use of the term *theme* would still have implications. Above all, you would still be suggesting that you have identified one of the text's major points. Subsequently, you might have to defend this claim, showing how the point you have identified is indeed central to the text.

Issues of theme have loomed large in literary studies. We hope that you will find them useful to pursue. But because references to theme are so common in literary studies, students sometimes forget that there are other kinds of issues. As you move through this list, you may find some that interest you more.

3. Issues of definition.   In arguments about literature, issues of **definition** arise most often when readers try to decide what an author means by a particular word. The titles of Orozco's and Kincaid's stories are puzzling. In the first case, what does "orientation" mean, given that the narrator's description of life in this office might easily *dis*orient someone? In the second case, what does it mean to be a "girl" in this kind of culture? Notice that an issue of definition can arise even with ordinary language. Look at how the narrator of "Orientation" uses the word *free* in the story's third paragraph: "Feel free to ask questions. Ask too many questions, however, and you may be let go." To what extent, and in what sense, do the characters in the story seem "free"? Answering this question involves, we think, considering how much the office workers are able to assert themselves through their eccentric behavior.

4. Issues of symbolism.   In literary studies, an issue of **symbolism** usually centers on a particular image. In question are the image's meaning and purpose, including whether the image is more than just a detail. In "Orientation," the artwork of Amanda Pierce's autistic son is "sheet after sheet of precisely drawn concentric circles and ellipses, in black and yellow" (para. 7). Some readers may argue that the boy's art is one of many indications that life in this office is bizarre. Other readers may contend that the drawings have greater significance but may differ about what their significance is—that the narrator's thinking is circular, in the sense that the narrator is obsessed with describing the employees' eccentricities, or that the employees' actions are circular, in the sense that they are stuck repeating their strange conduct.

5. Issues of pattern.   With issues of **pattern**, you observe how a text is organized and try to determine how certain parts of the text relate to other parts. But think, too, about the meaning and purpose of any pattern you find, especially since readers may disagree about the pattern's significance. Also ponder the implications of any moment when a text *breaks* with a pattern it has been following. Disruptions of a pattern may be as important as the pattern itself.

A conspicuous pattern in "Girl" is the main speaker's series of commands, which includes repeated use of the words *this is how*. Indeed, **repetition** is a common pattern in literature. Yet at two points in Kincaid's story, the speaker is interrupted by italicized protests from the girl: *"but I don't sing benna on Sundays at all and never in Sunday school"* (lines 11–12) and *"but what if the baker won't let me feel the bread?"* (line 41). What should we conclude about the main speaker from her string of orders? What should we conclude about the girl from her two disruptions? Readers may have various answers to these questions.

A text's apparent oppositions are also patterns that may be debated. An example in "Orientation" is the distinction that the narrator makes between the majority of the office workers and those who should be avoided (Anika Bloom and Colin Heavey). Does this distinction make sense, or do the two groups seem more similar than the narrator admits? Again, different answers are possible.

6. Issues of evaluation.   Consciously or unconsciously, **evaluation** always plays a central role in reading. When you read a work of literature, you evaluate its ideas and the actions of its characters. You judge, too, the views you assume the author is promoting. Moreover, you gauge the artistic quality of the text.

Specifically, you engage in three kinds of evaluation as you read. One kind is *philosophical*: you decide whether a particular idea or action is wise. Another kind is *ethical*: you decide whether an idea or action is morally good. The third kind is *aesthetic*: you decide whether the work as a whole or parts of the text succeed as art. Another reader may disagree with your criteria for wisdom, morality, and art; people's standards often differ. It is not surprising, then, that in the study of literature issues of evaluation come up frequently.

Sometimes you may have trouble distinguishing the three types of judgment from each other. Philosophical evaluation, ethical evaluation, and aesthetic evaluation can overlap. Probably the first two operate in the mind of a reader who is judging the advice given by the main speaker in "Girl." This reader may, for instance, find the speaker insensitive: that is, neither smart nor humane. Moreover, if this reader thinks Kincaid sympathizes with the speaker, then he or she may consider "Girl" flawed as a work of art. Keep in mind, however, that you can admire many aspects of a literary work even if you disagree with the ideas you see the author promoting. Someone may relish Kincaid's colorful language regardless of the views presented in the story.

But whose works should be taught? Many scholars argue that literary studies have focused too much on white male authors, and some refuse to assume that the works of these authors are great and universally relevant.

They criticize the long neglect of female and minority writers like Kincaid, a black woman born and raised in the West Indies. In part because of these scholars' arguments, "Girl" now appears in many literature anthologies. Yet other people continue to prize "classics" by William Shakespeare, John Milton, and William Blake. This ongoing debate about the literature curriculum includes disagreements about the worth of recent texts. After all, contemporary literature has yet to pass a "test of time." Does Orozco's 1994 story deserve to be anthologized and taught? We think so and have included "Orientation" in our own book. What, though, is *your* evaluation of it? Also, what particular standards have you used to judge it?

7. Issues of historical and cultural context.   Plenty of literary works have engaged readers who are quite unlike their authors. These readers may include much-later generations and inhabitants of distant lands. Nevertheless, an author's own **historical and cultural context** may significantly shape his or her text. Although "Orientation" has elements that probably strike you as strange, many details of this story no doubt remind you of life in offices throughout the present-day United States. Still, readers may disagree over exactly which features of the story are typical of the contemporary American workplace. Consider as well Jamaica Kincaid's use of her past in "Girl." Though she has lived in the United States since she was seventeen, she evidently tapped memories of her childhood on Antigua to write this story and to represent the island's culture. Since many of the story's readers would be unfamiliar with Antigua, she had to decide what aspects of it to acquaint them with. What features of it does she emphasize, and what features does she downplay or omit? When Kincaid was born, Antiguans were under British control, and many labored hard for little money. Do these historical facts matter in "Girl"? If so, in what conceivable ways? Notice that answering such political and economic questions usually requires research. Even then, answers may be complicated. Indeed, rarely does a literary text straightforwardly reflect its author's background. Debate arises over how text and context relate.

We provide some background for each literary work we present to help you begin to situate it historically and culturally. In Chapter 7, we explain how to put literature in context, especially by doing research in the library and on the Internet. For now, we want to emphasize that contextualizing a work involves more than just piling up facts about its origin. In the study of literature, issues of historical and cultural context are often issues of *relevance*: which facts about a work's creation are important for readers to know, and how would awareness of these facts help readers better understand the work? Readers can inform themselves about a particular author's life, for instance, but they may disagree about the extent to which a given text is autobiographical.

Perhaps you like to connect a literary work with its author's own life. The authors of the two stories we have been discussing apparently drew to some extent on their personal experiences. Orozco has worked in an office, and Kincaid was a girl on Antigua. Of course, it is unlikely that Orozco's coworkers included a serial killer and a woman whose palms bled. You may be tempted, though, to think that "Girl" consists of advice Kincaid herself received. Yet when you assert that a work is thoroughly autobiographical, you risk over-looking aspects of the text that depart from the author's own experiences, impressions, and beliefs. We are not urging you to refrain from ever connecting the author's text to the author's life. Rather, we are pointing out that whatever links you forge may be the subject of debate.

Even the term *history* can be defined in various ways. When you refer to a work's historical context, you need to clarify whether you are examining (1) the life of the work's author; (2) the time period in which it was written; (3) any time period mentioned within the text; (4) its subsequent reception, including responses to it by later generations; or (5) the forms in which the work has been published, which may involve changes in its spelling, punctuation, wording, and overall appearance.

8. Issues of genre.   So far we have been identifying categories of issues. Issues of **genre** are *about* categorization, for they involve determining what *kind* of text a particular work is. You might categorize the works by Orozco and Kincaid as belonging to the short-story genre, but someone might disagree because they do not seem to have a conventional plot. This debate would involve deciding what the essential characteristics of a "short story" are. Even if you argue that Orozco's and Kincaid's texts belong to this genre, you could attempt to classify them more precisely by aiming for terms that better sum up their specific content and form. Issues of genre often arise with such further classification.

A literary text may relate in some way to a characteristic of ordinary, real-life interactions. Orozco's title—"Orientation"—signals that he is having fun with the guided tour that many offices give their new workers. Similarly, Kincaid's story "Girl" belongs to the parental-advice genre. Try, though, to dis-tinguish between text genre and real-life genre. Orozco's story can be labeled a *parody* (a comic imitation) or *satire* (an ironic critique) of an orientation, and Kincaid's story can be categorized as *an exploration of how gender roles are re-inforced.* In any case, you may find that two or more labels are appropriate for a particular text. For instance, perhaps you see Orozco's "Orientation" as both a *parody* and a *horror story.* If so, you must decide whether these labels are equally helpful. Much of the time, issues of genre are issues of priority. Readers debate not whether a certain label for a work is appropriate but whether that label is the best.

9. Issues of social policy.   In many works of literature, writers have at-tempted to instigate social reform by exposing defects in their cultures and encouraging specific cures. We earlier mentioned Upton Sinclair's 1906 novel *The Jungle*, which vividly depicts horrible conditions in Chicago's stockyards and thereby led the meat-processing plant owners to adopt more humane and hygienic practices. Even a work of literature that is not blatantly political or that seems rooted in the distant past may make you conscious of your own society's problems and possible solutions to them. Yet you and your classmates may propose different definitions of and solutions for cultural problems. The result is what we call issues of **social policy**.

Sometimes your position on a current issue of social policy will affect how you read a certain literary work. If you have worked in a highly regimented office, you may empathize with some of the employees described in Orozco's story. Similarly, your view on how girls and boys should be educated may affect your response to Kincaid's text. Even if current issues of social policy do not influence your original reading of a work, you can still use the work to raise such issues in your writing or in class discussion. Imagine discussing Orozco's story at a labor union's convention. What social policies might the story be used to promote there?

10. Issues of cause and effect.   Issues of **causality** are common in literary studies. Often they arise as readers present different explanations for a character's behavior. What causes Orozco's character Gwendolyn Stich to cry in the women's room? Why does the girl in Kincaid's story protest at two particular moments? Remember that even a work's narrator or main speaker is a character with motives worth analyzing. What personal reasons, for example, might lead Orozco's narrator to present the orientation in this way?

Such questions can be rephrased to center on the author. For instance, you can ask why Kincaid ends her story by having the characters speak about feeling the bread. If you look back at our discussion of these ten types of issues, you may see that most issues can be phrased as questions about the author's purposes. But remember your options. Focusing on authorial intent in a given case may not be as useful as sticking with another type of issue. Or you may turn a question about authorial intent into a question about authorial **effect**. How should readers react when Kincaid ends her story the way she does? You can address questions like this without sounding as if you know exactly what the author intended.

MAKE A CLAIM

A **claim** about a literary work is a position on it that not everyone would immediately accept as obvious truth. You have to argue for it. For examples of claims in literary studies, look at our explanations of ten kinds of issues. In that discussion, we mentioned a host of claims: that Orozco's narrator is merely fantasizing a ghost, that Kincaid's theme is "Women should teach girls to follow conventions *and* to assert themselves," that the autistic boy's circles symbolize the circular thinking of Orozco's narrator, that the main speaker in "Girl" is insensitive, and that "Orientation" is a horror story. These claims are debatable because in each case at least one other position is possible.

In literature classes, two types of claims are especially common. To criticize Kincaid's main speaker is to engage in **evaluation**. To identify themes of "Girl" is to engage in **interpretation**. Conventionally, interpretation is the kind of analysis that depends on hypotheses rather than simple observation of plain fact. Throughout this book, we refer to the practice of interpreting a work or certain aspects of it. Admittedly, sometimes you may have trouble distinguishing interpretation from evaluation. When you evaluate some feature of a work or make an overall judgment of that work, probably you are operating with a certain interpretation as well, even if you do not make that interpretation explicit. Similarly, when you interpret part of a work or the text as a whole, probably you have already decided whether the text is worth figuring out. Nevertheless, the two types of claims differ in their emphases. When you attempt to interpret a work, you are mostly analyzing it; when you attempt to evaluate the work, you are mostly judging it.

In class discussions, other students may resist a claim you make about a literary work. Naturally, you may choose to defend your view at length. But remain open to the possibility of changing your mind, either by modifying your claim somehow or by shifting completely to another one. Also entertain the possibility that a view different from yours is just as reasonable, even if you do not share it.

In much of your writing for your course, you will be identifying an issue and making one main claim about it, which can be called your **thesis**. As you attempt to support your main claim, you will make a number of smaller claims. In drafts of your paper, welcome opportunities to test the claims you make in it. Review your claims with classmates to help you determine how persuasive your thinking is. You will be left with a stronger sense of what you must do to make your paper credible.

AIM TO PERSUADE

As we noted in Chapter 1, persuasion involves defending your claims. But as we also observed, even the best argument essays may fail to convince all their readers. What you *can* do is motivate your audience to keep thinking about your ideas. This is a modest sense of persuasion but an achievement all the same. Suppose, in an essay on Kincaid's story, you claim that the speaker is loving despite her seeming stern. You may not induce all your readers to regard her as warm. Yet arguing for your idea can still be good, especially if you move people to mull it. Help them find your view worth pondering, whether or not everyone adopts it.

CONSIDER YOUR AUDIENCE

To argue effectively about a work of literature, you need to remember that not everyone will see it as you do. You have to explain and support your understanding of the work so that skeptics will come to find your view of it sound. Gear every step of your argument toward readers you have to persuade. Focus on what *they* will want you to clarify, elaborate, and defend. Forget about parts of the work irrelevant to your argument. If your main claim is about a certain character in "Orientation" — say, the serial killer — limit your remarks about others, no matter how colorful these figures seem.

Above all, you may wonder how familiar your readers already are with the text you are analyzing. Perhaps your teacher will resolve your uncertainty, telling you exactly how much your audience knows about the text. Then again, you may be left to guess. Should you presume that your audience is totally unfamiliar with the text? This approach is risky, for it may lead you to spend a lot of your paper merely summarizing the text rather than analyzing it. A better move is to write as if your audience is at least a bit more knowledgeable. Here is a good rule of thumb: *Assume that your audience has, in fact, read the text but that you need to recall for this group any features of the text that are crucial to your argument.* Although probably your paper will still include summary, the amount you provide will be limited, and your own ideas will be more prominent.

You can introduce your essay's main claim by referring to the audience of the literary text you're studying:

- **Readers you disagree with.** While some readers may feel that the speaker in "Orientation" gives a thoroughly objective tour of his office, what he chooses to emphasize suggests that his perspective on this workplace is not always trustworthy.
- **Hasty, superficial readers.** Because the physical abuse that Amanda Pierce's husband inflicts on her is so horrifying, readers may overlook the description of her son's artwork in the same paragraph. But his "concentric circles and ellipses" (para. 7) symbolize how life at this office is organized.
- **Puzzled readers.** Many readers may wonder whether Barry Hacker's dead wife has actually returned to haunt the office. Yet while she may indeed be a ghost, supernatural elements do not seem a major part of the story. Orozco evidently wants us to think more about real features of current office life.
- **Your own divided self.** While at first I thought Gwendolyn Stich is excessive in her devotion to penguin imagery, I have concluded that she deserves credit for striving to maintain a distinct identity in this bureaucratic setting.

GATHER AND PRESENT EVIDENCE

Evidence is the support that you give your claims so that others will accept them. What sort of evidence you must provide depends on what your audience requires to be persuaded. When you make claims during class discussions, your classmates and instructor might ask you follow-up questions, thereby suggesting what you must do to convince them. As a writer, you might often find yourself having to guess your readers' standards of evidence. Naturally, your guesses will be influenced by any prior experiences you have had with your audience. Moreover, you may have opportunities to review drafts with some of its members.

When you make an argument about literature, the evidence most valued by your audience is likely to be details from the work itself. Direct quotations from the text are powerful indications that your claims are well grounded. But when you quote, you need to avoid willful selectivity. If, when writing about Kincaid's story, you quote the girl's question *"but what if the baker won't let me feel the bread?"* without acknowledging the main speaker's response, you may come across as misrepresenting the text. In general, quoting from various parts of a text will help you give your readers the impression that you are being accurate.

If you make claims about the historical or cultural context of a work, your evidence may include facts about its original circumstances. You may be drawn to the author's own experiences and statements, believing these shed light on the text. But again, use such materials cautiously, for they are not always strong evidence for your claims. People are not obliged to accept the author's declaration of his or her intent as a guide to the finished work. Some people may feel that the author's statement of intention was deliberately misleading, while others may claim that the author failed to understand his or her own achievement.

EXPLAIN YOUR REASONING

As we pointed out in Chapter 1, your readers will expect more than evidence. They'll wish to see the process of reasoning behind your main claim. The steps in your logic should be clear in your essay's structure. This may need to differ from the structure of the literary text you analyze. Otherwise, you may confuse your readers—especially if you crawl through the literary work chronologi-cally, commenting on each of its lines. Perhaps your main claim is that although "Orientation" has supernatural touches, the story belongs more to the genre of satire. An essay that simply plods through the story won't help you develop this idea. Probably you should first identify for your audience the story's super-natural elements, whether or not the story itself starts with them. (In fact, Anika Bloom's bleeding palm doesn't show up until paragraph 10, and the ghost of Barry Hacker's wife isn't mentioned until paragraph 19.) You should then identify the story's satirical aspects. In addition, you'll have to define "the supernatural" and "satire" as genres, stating the typical features of each. In general, alert your audience to your stages of thought.

IDENTIFY YOUR ASSUMPTIONS

Writing arguments about literature involves making assumptions, some of which you may need to spell out. One common kind is *warrants*. These are assumptions that lead you to call certain things evidence. Consider in "Orientation" the narra-tor's remark that "you can see this building reflected in the glass panels of that building across the way" (para. 26). You might argue that through this state-ment, Orozco suggests that the office has closed in on itself and is not open enough to other kinds of living. As evidence for your claim, you might point out the following things: (1) at this moment in the story, a window acts as a mirror; (2) mirrors are sometimes associated with a fixation on the self; and (3) the narrator has already provided many examples of the employees' being stuck in their own routines. But then you may be asked for your warrants—your reasons for presenting this evidence as support for your claim. Some of your assumptions might be about literature: for instance, the transformation of an image (for example, a window into a mirror) is often symbolically significant, and images are often related to how characters in the text behave. Some of your assumptions might be about human nature: for example, if people are trapped in routines, they have trouble seeing how others live in the world at large. Some of your assumptions might be about historical periods and cultures: for instance, many contemporary American offices seem self-enclosed. Often literature classes are most enlightening when students discuss their assumptions about literature, about human nature, and about particular times and places. Your classmates may differ in their assumptions because they differ in the ways they grew up, the experiences they have had, the reading they have done, and the authorities that have influenced them.

Once you state your warrants for a claim you are making, your audience may go further, asking you to identify assumptions supporting the warrants themselves. But more frequently you will have to decide how much you should mention your warrants in the first place. In class discussion, usually your classmates' and instructor's responses to your claims will indicate how much you have to spell out your assumptions. When you write, you have to rely more on your own judgment of what your audience requires. If you suspect that your readers will find your evidence unusual, you should identify your warrants at length. If, however, your readers are bound to accept your evidence, then a presentation of warrants may simply distract them. Again, reviewing drafts of your paper with potential readers will help you determine what to do.

Another potentially significant set of assumptions has to do with your values, which often reflect your own life. You may want to condemn the speaker in "Girl" as a "bad" mother because your own is nicer. But this label requires more support than your personal experience. You'll need to explain why *various* people should apply it to the speaker—whatever particular mothers they've had. In general, be cautious with the terms you apply to literary figures. If you fling at them strong judgments—*bad, crazy, weird, normal, good*—some readers will suspect your mind is controlled by biases you grew up with. They'll prefer more precise, less extreme language, believing it better conveys a character's complexity.

MAKE USE OF APPEALS

As with other arguments, those about literature employ the appeals of **logos**, **ethos**, and **pathos**. You rely on logos when, to support your claims about texts, you stress your evidence and explain your process of thought. Ethos, the image you convey of yourself, often figures when you acknowledge interpretations other than yours. Your readers will appreciate your noting in the first place that these views can exist. You will look even better if you treat such alternatives with respect. Try making *concessions* to them, admitting they're not entirely wrong. For instance, you may want to argue that Kincaid's speaker holds men in contempt. Even so, consider granting that other readers of the story may see her differently. You might admit, for instance, that at moments she suggests her daughter should accept male power. Of course, you would still proceed to argue your own claim about her. But you'll have dealt admirably with a rival idea. In the same spirit, you might *qualify* your generalizations instead of stating them as absolute facts. Rather than declare that "the mother *is* scornful toward men," you might say that this is *probably* her attitude or that it *seems* to be her stance.

With the appeal known as pathos, you try to engage your readers' emotions. This move occurs to some degree in many arguments about literature, for literary works themselves often dramatize and arouse feelings. You can make your analysis compelling if you occasionally use emotional language yourself. You might refer to the "chilling" presence of the serial killer in Orozco's story or to the "intimidating" voice of the mother in Kincaid's. But keep such language limited. If you constantly vent your own passions, you may weaken your case. Take a look at this paragraph:

> Most of the employees in "Orientation" are creepy. They really bother me a lot, because they don't act in ways that strike me as normal. I definitely would not want to work in an office like that. I would fear being killed or interfered with somehow. Even the narrator disturbs me, because he acts like such a know-it-all and often points out what can get a staff member fired. I wouldn't care to have him be the person orienting me.

If you wrote a passage like this, it might annoy your readers. They might think it conveys far more about *you* than about Orozco's text. Probably they'd want more details of the story and fewer bursts of your feelings. Again, emotional words *can* play a role in your argument. They may well add to its force. But they're effective only when you supply them in small doses.

A Sample Student Argument about Literature

The following essay demonstrates several of the strategies we have discussed. Its student author had read Kincaid's "Girl" in a course on composition and literature. Her assignment was to write an argument paper about a specific element of the story. She chose to raise an issue and develop a claim about its ending.

Ann Schumwalt
English 102
Professor Peretti
3 February - - - -
            The Mother's Mixed Messages in "Girl"
    In Jamaica Kincaid's story "Girl," the speaker is evidently a mother trying to teach her daughter how to behave. The story is basically a single-paragraph speech in which the

mother gives various commands, instructions, and lessons, apparently in an effort at training her child to become what their culture considers a proper young woman. Only twice does the daughter herself interrupt the mother's monologue. It's interesting that the second break occurs near the end of the story. Right after the mother orders her to "always squeeze bread to make sure it's fresh," the daughter asks, *"but what if the baker won't let me feel the bread?"* (lines 40–41). There is only one more sentence before the story concludes: the mother responds by asking, "you mean to say that after all you are really going to be the kind of woman who the baker won't let near the bread?" (41–42). Faced with this final exchange, many readers may wonder why author Kincaid chooses to make it the story's conclusion. It could have appeared earlier in the text, and Kincaid might have ended with any of the mother's statements that now come before it. This ending also feels *in*conclusive, for the very last words are a question that does not receive an answer. What, therefore, is Kincaid trying to emphasize with this puzzling finish? A closer look at its language, as well as at other words of the text, suggest that Kincaid is deliberately making us uncertain about whether the mother's stern training will indeed help her daughter become strong enough to survive in their society. The mother may *believe* that she is providing sufficient survival skills, but Kincaid encourages readers to suspect that she is actually *dis*empowering her daughter, not letting her develop the willpower she needs to endure.

When the mother commands her daughter to squeeze the bread, probably she sees herself as pushing her to take charge of her life rather than meekly accept other people's treatment of her. To squeeze something is to perform a vigorous, self-assertive action, and in this case it would involve testing the baker's product instead of just accepting it. Earlier in the text, the mother offers a few other hints that she wishes the daughter to be aggressive, not passive. For example, she advises her on "how to make a good medicine to throw away a child before it even becomes a child" (33–34); on "how to bully a man" (36); and on "how to spit up in the air if you feel like it" (39). A number of readers may infer, too, that even when she is telling the daughter how to perform household chores like washing, ironing, setting meals, and sweeping, she is fostering her independence by enabling her to handle basic demands of daily existence.

But in crucial ways, the mother presses her daughter to play a subservient role in society. More specifically, she attempts to imprison her in a model of femininity that allows

Refers to puzzled readers, as a way of bringing up the main issue. The essay will help these readers with the "closer look" it proceeds to offer.

Introduces the essay's main issue (a cause-and-effect one) as a question.

The essay's main claim.

Because Ann is mainly concerned with the story's ending, she starts her paper with it rather than move chronologically through Kincaid's text.

Qualifies this statement rather than expressing it as an absolute fact.

Draws evidence from the text's actual words.

Acknowledges existence of another possible interpretation.

Pathos used with the negatively emotional words presses, subservient, imprison, and dominate. Evidence then offered to support such language.

for men to dominate. Emphasizing that "you are not a boy,
you know" (29–30), she demands that she "try to walk like
a lady" (8) and take care of her father's clothes. The various
chores that she expects her daughter to perform would make
life easier for the male head of the household. Moreover, they
seem duties that a boy would not be required to fulfill.   *A reasonable assumption.*
Similarly, the mother hopes to restrict the daughter's sexual
behavior. Repeatedly she warns her "to prevent yourself from
looking like the slut I know you are so bent on becoming"
(14–15). Again, it is doubtful that a boy would receive warn-   *An assumption, though*
ings like this. Like the United States, perhaps the culture   *qualified with the word*
reflected in this story even lacks a masculine equivalent of   *perhaps.*
the derogatory term "slut."

   At the end, I admit, the mother seems to associate her   *Concession.*
daughter with an image of power. She implies that the girl
should become "the kind of woman" whom the baker *does*
"let near the bread" so that she can test it by squeezing it
(41–42). But even here, actually, the mother does not envision
her daughter as actively taking charge. In the scenario she
sketches, the baker *allows* the girl to feel the bread. In order
to touch it, she must get his permission, rather than straightforwardly exert her own authority. Moreover, she first has to be
a certain sort of woman; otherwise, she has not earned the
right to examine his product. What type of woman is this?
While some readers may argue that the mother wants her
daughter to be an *assertive* female, many of the directions she
has already given her would greatly limit her sphere of action,
leaving her to be a relatively unadventurous housekeeping
"lady." Evidently the mother feels that the baker will give her
daughter access to the bread only if she is a basically tame
and polite version of womanhood.

   The mother may not realize that she is conveying mixed   *"May not" is a qualification,*
messages to her child. If we, as readers, take her to be hoping *indicating that Ann is less*
that her daughter becomes empowered *and* subservient, we   *than sure what the mother*
may be spotting a contradiction that the mother herself is not   *thinks.*
conscious of. But the daughter may be aware of it. Perhaps
the daughter is, in fact, now a grown-up woman who is trying
to make sense of the paradoxical pieces of advice her mother
gave her during her adolescence. The mother may have offered
these supposed bits of wisdom at various different times, but
the daughter is now remembering them all as one speech and
struggling to figure out their implications. Kincaid's decision
to conclude the story with a question mark may be her way of   *Even the text's punctuation*
indicating that even in adulthood, the daughter still has not *may be significant.*
determined whether her mother wanted to *liberate* her or
confine her. We can regard the daughter as someone who is
still attempting to "read" her mother's intentions. As actual

readers of this story, we would then be in the same position as she is, having to come up with our own interpretation of what her mother wanted her to do and be.

Looking at Literature as Argument

Much of this book concerns arguing *about* literature. But many works of literature can be said to present arguments themselves. Admittedly, not all of literature can be seen as containing or making arguments, but occasionally you will find that associating a literary text with argument opens up productive lines of inquiry. Moreover, as you argue about literature, arguments *within* literature can help you see how you might persuade others.

Some works lay out an argument that the author obviously approves of. For an example, let us turn to the following poem. It was written around 1652 by John Milton (1608–1674), a poet who played a leading role in England's Puritan revolution. Seeking to make dominant their own version of Christianity, the Puritans executed King Charles I and installed their leader, Oliver Cromwell, as head of state. Milton wrote "When I consider how my light is spent" while working as an official in Cromwell's government. This is an autobiographical poem and refers to Milton's growing blindness, which threatened to prevent him from serving both his political leader and his religious one, God.

JOHN MILTON

When I consider how my light is spent

When I consider how my light is spent,
   Ere half my days in this dark world and wide,
   And that one talent which is death to hide
Lodged with me useless, though my soul more bent
To serve therewith my Maker, and present   5
   My true account, lest He returning chide;
   "Doth God exact day-labor, light denied?"
I fondly ask. But Patience, to prevent
That murmur, soon replies, "God doth not need
   Either man's work or His own gifts. Who best   10
   Bear His mild yoke, they serve Him best. His state
Is kingly: thousands at His bidding speed,
   And post o'er land and ocean without rest;
   They also serve who only stand and wait."   *[c. 1652]*

The speaker does not actually spell out his warrants. Consider, however, his reference to Christ's parable of the talents (Luke 19:12–27). In the ancient Middle East, a *talent* was a unit of money. In the parable, a servant is scolded by his master for hoarding the one talent that his master had given him. By telling this story, Christ implies that people should make use of the gifts afforded them by God. For the speaker in Milton's poem, the parable has a lot of authority.

Evidently he feels that he should carry out its lesson. In effect, then, the parable has indeed become a warrant for him: that is, a basis for finding his blindness cause for lament.

Who, exactly, is the speaker's audience? Perhaps he is not addressing anyone in particular. Or perhaps the speaker's mind is divided and one side of it is addressing the other. Or perhaps the speaker is addressing God, even though he refers to God in the third person. Given that the speaker is answered by Patience, perhaps he means to address *that* figure, although Patience may actually be just a part of him rather than an altogether separate being.

At any rate, Patience takes the speaker for an audience in responding. And while Patience does not provide evidence, let alone warrants, Patience does make claims about God and his followers. Furthermore, Milton as author seems to endorse Patience's claims; apparently he is using the poem to advance them. Besides pointing out *how* God is served, Milton suggests that God *ought* to be served, even if God lets bad things happen to good people like Milton.

Every author can be considered an audience for his or her own writing, but some authors write expressly to engage in a dialogue with themselves. Perhaps Milton wrote his poem partly to convince himself that his religion was still valid and his life still worth living. Significantly, he did not publish the poem until about twenty years later. Yet because he did publish it eventually, at some point he must have contemplated a larger audience for it. The first readers of the poem would have been a relatively small segment of the English population: those literate and prosperous enough to have access to books of poetry. In addition, a number of the poem's first readers would have shared Milton's religious beliefs. Perhaps, however, Milton felt that even the faith of this band had to be bolstered. For one thing, not every Protestant of the time would have shared Milton's enthusiasm for the Puritan government. Recall that this regime executed the king, supposedly replacing him with the rule of God. Milton's words "His state / Is kingly" can be seen as an effort to persuade readers that the Puritans did put God on England's throne.

Certain arguments made in literary texts may or may not have the author's endorsement. Faced with a conflict of ideas, readers must engage in interpretation, forced to decide which position is apt to be the author's own view. A classic example is "Mending Wall," a famous poem by Robert Frost (1874–1963), from his 1914 book *North of Boston*. Troubled by his neighbor's desire to repair the wall between their farms, the poem's speaker argues against its necessity, but literary critics have long debated whether Frost agrees with the speaker's claims and reasons. How persuasive do you find them?

ROBERT FROST
Mending Wall

Something there is that doesn't love a wall,
That sends the frozen-ground-swell under it,
And spills the upper boulders in the sun;

And makes gaps even two can pass abreast.
The work of hunters is another thing: 5
I have come after them and made repair
Where they have left not one stone on a stone,
But they would have the rabbit out of hiding,
To please the yelping dogs. The gaps I mean,
No one has seen them made or heard them made,   10
But at spring mending-time we find them there.
I let my neighbor know beyond the hill;
And on a day we meet to walk the line
And set the wall between us once again.
We keep the wall between us as we go.   15
To each the boulders that have fallen to each.
And some are loaves and some so nearly balls
We have to use a spell to make them balance:
"Stay where you are until our backs are turned!"
We wear our fingers rough with handling them.   20
Oh, just another kind of outdoor game,
One on a side. It comes to little more:
There where it is we do not need the wall:
He is all pine and I am apple orchard.
My apple trees will never get across   25
And eat the cones under his pines, I tell him.
He only says, "Good fences make good neighbors."
Spring is the mischief in me, and I wonder
If I could put a notion in his head:
"*Why* do they make good neighbors? Isn't it   30
Where there are cows? But here there are no cows.
Before I built a wall I'd ask to know
What I was walling in or walling out,
And to whom I was like to give offense.
Something there is that doesn't love a wall,   35
That wants it down." I could say "Elves" to him,
But it's not elves exactly, and I'd rather
He said it for himself. I see him there
Bringing a stone grasped firmly by the top
In each hand, like an old-stone savage armed.   40
He moves in darkness as it seems to me,
Not of woods only and the shade of trees.
He will not go behind his father's saying,
And he likes having thought of it so well
He says again, "Good fences make good neighbors."   *[1914]* 45

Other literary works, though, present an argument that the author is unlikely
to endorse. In such cases, we might describe the work as *ironic* because we sense a
distance between the position being expressed and the author's own view.

Literature and Current Issues

When you read a literary work, you may find it doesn't make arguments. Nevertheless, it may help you grasp current issues. It may even help you form claims about them. To play this role, the work needn't be recent. Ancient tragedies can shed light on politics today. However old the text, literature may give you insights into contemporary debates. In turn, these debates may help you understand a work of literature better. They may lead you to notice aspects of it you'd otherwise neglect.

Here, we present a 2015 short story about a current practice: the public shaming of individuals and organizations. They suffer mass scorn for things they've said or done. These scoldings usually occur via social media like Twitter. Such denunciations are popular; each week, new ones erupt. Yet increasingly these assaults are criticized themselves. Not only do they provoke howls of protest from their targets, but they also elicit concerned warnings from a growing number of cultural commentators who point out that these attacks are often harmful, unfair, and mean. To give you a sense of this emerging debate, we follow the story with two nonfiction texts about public shaming today. By putting the story in "conversation" with these works, we suggest ways of connecting literature to real-life disputes.

The story's author, Rivka Galchen (b. 1976), was born in Toronto, Canada, but she has lived in the United States since she was a child. Although she holds an M.D. degree with a specialization in psychiatry, she has pursued a literary career. Besides earning an M.F.A. in creative writing at Columbia University, she has published a novel, *Atmospheric Disturbances* (2008), and a collection of short stories, *American Innovations* (2014). She has also written several pieces of journalism. "Usl at the Stadium" first appeared in the October 12, 2015, issue of *The New Yorker*. Galchen based the story on an actual series of events.

RIVKA GALCHEN

Usl at the Stadium

The game on Sunday had a 2 P.M. start, and Usl was featured on the Jumbotron intermittently from 4:02 to 4:09. By eight-thirty, his home phone was ringing. His home phone never rang. It was a holdover from another time. His mother had told him that it was essential, a matter of safety — for hurricanes, or blackouts, or terrorist attacks. You never knew what could happen until it happened. She had insisted on paying the bill so that Usl would keep the landline. She had pleaded, "Please grant me permission to protect my child," and so he had.

The landline was ringing because Usl had become an Internet sensation. Usl had been sleeping when he appeared on the Jumbotron at the Yankees game; the cameras and the commentators had turned on Usl numerous times, and at length, and he had slept through it all. It wasn't until the voices of strangers over that old-fashioned telephone alerted him that he understood how widely watched his sleep had been. Now a gentle feminine voice pitched him: "What we're thinking is that you come into the office and we'll take a top-quality, nice photo of you. We really love the idea that you get a chance to present yourself. You'll recapture control over your image."

Usl looked online to reconfirm who he was in the eyes of the world:

> Fatty cow that needs two seats at all time and represent symbol of failure

had been posted one minute earlier in the comments section under a YouTube clip. The clip had more than seventy thousand views. Wasn't it really just footage of a man dreaming? No one seemed to see it that way. Usl was only twenty-eight years old—could his life already be ruined? Could he save it? Usl told the woman on the phone that he needed to think about her idea, that he would call her back.

He called Gregory.

"People at a newspaper are not your allies," Gregory said. Gregory was Usl's friend but also his boss. Usl worked the buyback end of Gregory's store-front diamond-district place. Customers ascended the back stairs to consult with Usl about their old jewelry, and Usl weighed, assessed, proposed prices, bought. Gregory liked to say that it was a sultanate there on the second floor; the sultan was Usl. Now Gregory said, "These are people who demeaned Eliot Spitzer over private issues, who—"

"But people are saying untrue things about me—"

"You'll be extending the time that you're at the center of attention—"

"If you were me—"

"I'm not you. I'm not interested in fame. I am me. I'm interested in coming to work. I hope you're not thinking of not coming in to work tomorrow."

The angle of the camera in the footage was particularly unflattering—distorting, really. It wasn't a strong likeness.

Usl called the voice from the newspaper back. "I will come in."

The now slightly less kind-sounding woman informed Usl that if he made it in before 11 A.M. they would run the photo online the same day.

Usl trembled.

Or was the trembling elsewhere?

They had found his cell-phone number?

"I love you!" the text message read. It was his mother. "You are a great and successful and handsome and very good and nice man!!!" Even she had seen the footage? Usl's mother was very loving, had always been very loving. Good mothers are bad mothers, Usl thought. Only bad, mean mothers prepare you for what is to come. If Usl was ever a mother, whatever, a father, he wanted to be a bad one.

More calls came in, through the night, from television programs that had once seemed to occur in inaccessible lands but that turned out to be really less than thirty minutes away; they would send a car service. Usl couldn't sleep. When, as a child, he encountered characters six feet tall, fuzzy, offering hugs, or flyers, or hot dogs, he had been frightened. He unplugged the phone.

Then there was a knock at the door. Was he O. J. Simpson? They were pursuing him everywhere.

"It's me! It's Berge!"

Berge was Usl's neighbor. Usl let him in.   20

Berge said, "You've had a huge piece of luck. Huge. I know you may not see it, but this is the luckiest day of your life."

"I'm very tired," Usl said, and then felt ambushed by fresh shame—after all, why was he so tired? "People laugh, but I was sleeping because I haven't been getting my sleep. When you don't sleep, you're not yourself. When you don't sleep, you find yourself sleeping all the time."

"You're going to sue," Berge declared. Sue somebody. Berge would figure it out. He wouldn't charge—he would just take fifteen per cent upon collection. Did Usl feel damaged? Yes, Usl did feel damaged. Then there should be damages. Berge had recently passed the bar. He wasn't lying about that, Usl thought. Berge often shared his magazines with Usl; he was a nice guy, basically.

"But I can't sue thousands of people," Usl said. "It's thousands of people who have damaged me." He caught a glimpse of his screen:

He's dreaming of cupcakes.

"No, thousands wouldn't be sensible," Berge said. "We'll sue the Yankees."   25

"But I love the Yankees."

"We'll sue the Stadium."

"I love the Stadium. I've been happy there."

"You're very stressed. Let me figure it out for you."

By 1 A.M., Berge had prepared papers for Usl to sign—Berge was also a   30
notary, he said—naming a broadcasting corporation. "They won't take it personally," Berge assured him. "It's business."

By Tuesday, views of the YouTube footage had exceeded a million. Usl abandoned the Internet, turned on the radio for escape, and there learned that he, Usl, was a too sensitive behemoth who needed to be *#&$ed in his cookie-dough face; also, that he should eat celery. Normally, if you heard people talking about you on the radio it meant that you were crazy, since of course no one on the radio was talking about you, and if you thought that people on the radio were talking about you, as had happened to Usl's uncle, then you were supposed to go see somebody, a professional. Usl didn't want to see anybody.

"Gold resists attacks by almost all individual acids" appeared on his cell phone. A year earlier he had subscribed to GemFacts by text; at first it had bothered him, the repeated disappointment of thinking a person had contacted him and then discovering it was just an impersonal update.

Usl called Gregory again. "I can't come in today," he said.

"Take a joke," Gregory said. "They're talking things they don't know. Have those talkers ever handled gold rings like they were chickpeas? They're nobodies. So what if they say you're fat. You are fat. I'm also fat. It's not like it's not true."

Gregory was a cheerful man, and the son of a Holocaust survivor; he had   35
six children, and he sometimes wore a T-shirt that read, "I Have the Body of a
God: Buddha." "If you wanted to not be fat, you would be not fat," he said.

"It's not just that," Usl said. The two sports announcers, Mike and Mike—
voices Usl knew well, had thought of as friends of his, in a way—had said
of sleeping Usl the kinds of things that people say. Unpleasant things. But the
words of those false friends had then bloomed into much worse words, typed
up by viewers whose numbers were growing without perceptible limit. Usl was
reading:

> Please rid us of your nasty pimpled ass and put a shotgun in your mouth
> tonight, I'll buy the shells

Then:

> He is a waste of decent seats, he can sleep at the nachos stand and give a
> real fan a view, lol

Usl said to Gregory, "What really bothers me is that they think I don't
appreciate baseball. They think I don't understand what's at stake."

"Sure. It's suicide or sniper," Gregory said. "And you don't want to be a
sniper—I get it—so instead you feel really bad, you turn it on yourself. So as
not to kill people. But it's also not suicide or sniper: it's just get your pants on
and get on with your day. Do I have a chicken for an employee? I need a man.
It's man or pansy, it's—"

Usl hung up.   40

Usl had been unemployed for seventeen months when he got the job with
Gregory. When he started working, his mother gave him a polished blue stone
to keep in his pocket, to ward off evil. Mock if you want, but the stone had
worked. Usl had been enjoying his job for more than a year now. He had even
made a flyer on how to detect fake gold. The magnet test was overrated, the flyer
explained. In Usl's years of experience (even though it had been less than one
when he made the flyer), he had seen plenty of non-magnetic fake gold; recognizing real gold versus fake was about getting a feel for the weight of the thing
in your hands. That flyer of Usl's had been downloaded from his open Facebook
page a hundred and seventy-three times.

That had seemed like a big number. It had brought attention to Gregory's
shop. Gregory kept a poster of faces with various expressions on the office
wall—it was something the Chinese restaurant nearby had given them—and
Gregory had written Usl's name under the face labelled "Triumphant." He had
done this after an eighty-four-year-old woman, who had bought gold every
birthday of her life, brought it all in to sell after seeing a horoscope that read,
"Even a Gemini needs to slow down a bit once in a while, and with your ruler
Mercury still moving retrograde this is the ideal time." She explained to Usl that
she had visited several buyback places. She chose Usl. Because she trusted him,
because she could see his goodness in the way that his hands were not bossy or

deceptive. Usl had never before thought about his hands. But he did think, then, that it was true what she had said, that they were good hands.

By midday Tuesday, Usl had understood a few things. One was that he should have been in contact with his mother. Usl had not gone to the paper to be photographed; Usl had ceased to answer either of his phones. But his mother was in the papers; his mother had been photographed. In her own home, sitting in her armchair, with a red geranium plant at her side. In the caption, she was quoted: "He was very tired, because he had been working very hard. He is my son of gold." In the article, she was asked about Usl's name, which some people had said was short for "useless." She said that, no, that was not the case, that Usl had been the nickname of Usl's grandfather, Warhel, a beautiful soul who had died during a flu outbreak when he was only thirty-four. And, as for Usl himself, Usl was not a nickname, Usl was his full proper name, it was enough.

Usl called his mother.

"Someone had to tell them about the real you," she said. "Here you are— this celebrity—but the celebrity is this person who isn't you. They made me look very old in that picture, because of the green lighting, but I'm O.K. with that, because a mother has to fix what is said about her son, whatever the cost."   45

"Nothing's fixed," Usl said. He had the feeling, as he often did with his mother, that he was speaking to a ghost poorly educated about the present.

"They thought you were drunk," she went on. "Many people thought that. You can't let them think that—it will affect your future employment. I explained that you drink only Diet Coke."

That bit about the Diet Coke wasn't true, but Usl let it pass. "You're destroying me," he said, albeit softly.

The truth was, Usl knew, that the photograph of his mother was not as damaging as the papers that Berge had filed on his behalf.

Who gets paid 10 million to sleep there like a fat ass. FUCK YOU FATTY.

Berge had asked for nine million dollars in damages, not ten; of course the   50
commenters had the details wrong, had everything wrong. Usl should have followed his old rule: no decisions after midnight. It was said that the filing was full of misspellings and grammatical errors.

What a loser. And now he's suing? Double loser. His suit is the only thing that brought the world's attention to him. Triple loser. And if there is any justice on this earth, this case will be tossed out and he'll be ridiculed and humiliated all over. We're dealing with a quadruple loser at the very least, folks.

Berge was always full of ideas. One should stay away from people with ideas.

Americas pre-occupation with sports is obscene. Can't tell you how many kids I know can recite batting averages, game plays, but don't know the first 5 books of the Bible. Nor could they recite an account beyond Noah's Ark, and when they do its Hollywoodized to the point of recognizable gibberish. They Idolize these players, who in turn Idolize Money. Then these Sports-gods humiliate their fans, and their fans try to capitalize, and the lawyers capitalize. Who ends up loosing?

Ignominy was the only type of celebrity around. At least for Usl and everyone he knew.

"I love you," his mother texted again. "I love you very much. I love you very, very much. You are a strong man. They are trying to hunt down and destroy you. But you are a cheetah."

And then, automated delivery: "Gold is unaffected by oxygen at any temperature." If only.

Say what you will, Usl wanted to get a slice. Why not? He would leave his apartment. He could do it. Usl stepped into the elevator, which today smelled like urine; also there were bugs sun-printed in the case of the light fixture. He normally enjoyed his elevator; it had a mechanical floor-indicator arrow that still worked. It was classy. Just as he himself was classy. That was the truth. He worked with gold, which did not rust. 55

As he stepped out of the building, he saw three of his neighbors playing dominoes. One held up a newspaper and shook it at him, in fellowship or menace, he didn't know. He had more than once dreamed of everyone recognizing him, of extending a series of half waves to acknowledge his fellows with respect as he passed them on the street; now he walked by his neighbors quickly, panting slightly.

He ordered a slice of pepper-and-mushroom. The server put a slice of pepperoni on a paper plate. Usl re-stated what he wanted—pepper-and-mushroom. Mexican pop was playing loudly. The server had a red bandanna tied back over his thick black hair. Always Mexicans at the Italian places, Usl thought. The server squinted at Usl. A squint of recognition? "Pep-per-and-mush-room," Usl reënunciated. The guy gave him a second slice. "Just one slice," Usl said. "Just the pepper-and-mushroom. No pepperoni."

It was worked out. Nobody had shouted. A triumph.

"Yo, thanks," Usl said.

"Yo? It's not the barrio, man," the server said. "Be polite." 60

People were disgusting. You gave your heart, you tried to be considerate, and who cared? They thought Usl could be pushed around. Why did it seem so clear that he could be pushed around? How did they know? Other people slept at baseball games. The games were sometimes boring. There were commercials between innings, and also commercials mid-inning. The batters took their time getting to the box, as if nothing else in the world, no one else in the world, existed. It was selfish, really. There were millions and millions and millions of other people who were treated with more respect than Usl. Maybe billions. Some of them stupid, some fat, some ugly, whatever it was, but that was the truth, Usl didn't invent it. Who did they think they were—Brad Pitt? They couldn't all be Brad Pitt. If Brad Pitt had criticized him, that would be a different thing.

One day they weren't going to have Usl to kick around anymore. One day they'd be sorry. This was among the things that he hadn't said. That he kept not saying. He had not assumed another identity, or his own, and pursued the pursuers online. Oh, he had been tempted, but that was what the Others would do. He had not told the Others what he thought of them.

Usl was finishing his pizza when a man in an orange T-shirt and a hard hat, holding a large soda in one hand, made eye contact with him. Then he raised a fist in the air and shouted, "Yankees!"

Instinctively, Usl raised his fist in return. As if in the childishly imagined kingdom of fellowship and dignity.

"It's you, right?" the hard-hat man said.   65

Usl said, "No."

But already the man in the hard hat was signalling to others around him, shouting, calling things out. The hats were gathering.

Usl could find a small makeshift hut in the woods, not far from a beach. He had seen one once; he was going to go and live there. When the time seemed right, in maybe ten or fifteen years, he would return to civilization. He would be very fit, from living a life in nature. He would say his name was Dave. He would tell people how they should live. They would listen.

But he at least owed Gregory notice that he would be leaving, that he would be gone forever, sort of. Also, his paycheck would be useful. He was owed eight days. Truth be told, he wanted to run the idea by Gregory. Gregory, he realized, was like a dad to him. He would get his blessing.

Just in front of Gregory's, as Usl was staring at his phone—"You are my   70
star and my sunshine!"—someone tapped him on the shoulder.

By primal reflex, Usl nearly hit the man, shouted, defending his body. The man was saying, "Hey, hey, hey, sorry. I was just saying hello."

Usl looked up fully from his phone and realized it was Andre, the guy who regularly stood in front of Gregory's, handing out flyers for the business. Andre was a very slim and fairly straightforwardly good-looking black man; his appearance, today, seemed like a reproach. Usl said, "I apologize, I'm in such a high state of alert."

"A silver alert?" Andre asked.

"A what?" Usl said, his fear returning.   75

"Forget it, relax, forget it. I meant on your phone."

"What's silver, what's alert?" Usl said. Was he being asked about Google Alerts? About GemFacts? How was everyone allowed inside his head, his computer, his phone, his dreams.

"Like a silver alert, for when old people go missing," Andre said. "Amber alert for when a kid is missing, silver for old people. I think there's other colors, too. Sorry, I know you're under stress. It's just been on my mind. I was wondering how you get one of those alerts sent out. Like, once we found my mom

near where the buses are parked, between Ninth and Tenth Avenues. She had
no idea how to get home. She lives right near here, but she gets lost. And I'm
not in a total panic about her, but she's not answering my calls this morning,
so I was asking. Is your mom old? Is she right in the head?"

Andre had always seemed to Usl like a man with girlfriends, never
like a man with a mom. Usl still had the polished good-luck stone from his
mother. She was always trying, she was still trying. Usl said, "You could go
look for her."

"Tell Gregory I'm back in thirty minutes," Andre said.   80

"They're nobodies, Usl," Gregory said when he went inside. "They are small,
small people who can't find their own dicks because they are so small."

"You're a terrible man, Gregory. You're one of them."

"I'm just trying to cheer you up."

"By being a monster."

"Not nice."   85

"You're like a disease. For all I know, you started the comments about me.
What do I know? Evil isn't choosy. For all I know, you gave them my phone
number." Usl had yelled at no one yet; he was now yelling at Gregory. He found
that he had quite a lot to say. He said Gregory didn't even care about Andre's
mom.

"You know what, Usl? I'm going to tell you something that maybe you
don't want to hear."

Usl was ready for it.

Gregory said, "I'm going to tell you that I love you, and that I care for you."

Usl began to cry. He cried a little more. Eventually he said, "I'm just so tired.   90
When I'm tired, I make bad decisions."

"I understand," Gregory said. "You know, scientists used to ask, Why do
we sleep? What is the purpose of sleep? But then other scientists said that
these are the wrong questions. The question is, Why are we so often awake?
What is the purpose of being awake? I mean, besides for ten minutes of eating, a little bit of romance. Once that's over, why are we not immediately
again asleep?"

Gregory went on, "And so I said to myself one day, about this sleep question:
This is the answer to the problem of evil. The question isn't, Why is there evil?
The question is, Why is there good? I mean, it's not, Why is there the bubonic
plague and Putin? It's, Why is there spring and love and barbecue? Why is there
ever an unrequired kind act? Look, I'm just telling you how I go about my life,
because I am old and you are still young. There isn't supposed to be any gold in
the crust of the earth. It's a very heavy element. All the gold should be in the
molten core. Unreachable for us. So why do we keep finding gold in the crust?
How did it get there? Some people say it's meteorites that fell, that crashed, and
that this catastrophe splashed up gold. That's the only reason we come across
it. I don't subscribe to this theory. But I am sharing it with you."

Usl's sleep at the baseball game had been a sweet one. Sifting past and
beyond the ensuing terror, he found that he could remember that sleep, he

could remember his dream. He had been at a really nice desk, of a dark, well-polished wood. He recognized the desk; it had made an appearance in real life. When he was just a kid—a real kid, not a twenty-eight-year-old who felt like a kid but a twelve- or thirteen-year-old who really was that—he had been delivering something to a lawyer, to a proper lawyer. That lawyer had sat at such a desk. But before he saw it little Usl had waited outside the lawyer's office, outside but inside, inside the outer chamber, in the air-conditioning, and the secretary, a gentle-faced woman who looked a little bit like the pretty woman who drove a taxi in that old TV show, had asked him if he wanted some water. She had brought him some, in a cone-shaped paper cup, from the water cooler. This, Usl thought, must be real life. He must have been thirsty at the game. He must have been waiting.   [2015]

Galchen's story is fiction. But when she wrote about Usl, she had a real person in mind. In April 2014, Andrew Rector fell asleep while attending a Yankees/Red Sox game. Repeatedly, the stadium's jumbotron screen showed his sprawled, slumbering body. Countless viewers at home saw this spectacle as well, for the game was televised on ESPN. Soon, pictures of the snoozing man appeared online, receiving millions of hits. A similar number of messages about him swept through social media. Many of these messages mocked him. They ridiculed not only Rector's napping but also his considerable weight. He garnered even more scorn when he sued the ESPN commentators for damages. His suit was thrown out of court, however, just before Galchen's story appeared. By that time, his mother reported, Rector had left the country. He could no longer bear the American public's contempt.

Rector's experience isn't unusual. Nowadays, public shaming happens over and over. The weapons include social media, smartphone cameras, and Web sites like YouTube. The trend has grown so big that it's captured the attention of journalists. One such reporter is Jon Ronson (b. 1967). Originally from Wales, he's a veteran investigator of offbeat topics. His books include *Them: Adventures with Extremists* (2001), *The Psychopath Test: A Journey Through the Madness Industry* (2011), and *The Men Who Stare at Goats* (2004), which became a feature film. In 2015, Ronson published a book about the practice of shaming. Its title, *So You've Been Publicly Shamed*, may someday apply to all of us. Meanwhile, he researched his book by talking with people whom the title already fits.

Evidently, Ronson didn't speak with Andrew Rector, the model for Galchen's character Usl. Probably Rector's case was too recent for him to include in his book. Still, Ronson's discussion of shaming provides a context for Galchen's story. To help you connect the story with the real shamings Ronson describes, we offer the following excerpt from an article he wrote. Published in the February 12, 2015, issue of the *New York Times Magazine*, the article is a preview of Ronson's book. As its title indicates, much of this piece focuses on the case of Justine Sacco.

JON RONSON
From *"How One Stupid Tweet Blew Up Justine Sacco's Life"*

As she made the long journey from New York to South Africa, to visit family during the holidays in 2013, Justine Sacco, 30 years old and the senior director of corporate communications at IAC, began tweeting acerbic little jokes about the indignities of travel. There was one about a fellow passenger on the flight from John F. Kennedy International Airport:

"'Weird German Dude: You're in First Class. It's 2014. Get some deodorant.'—Inner monologue as I inhale BO. Thank God for pharmaceuticals."

Then, during her layover at Heathrow:

"Chilly—cucumber sandwiches—bad teeth. Back in London!"

And on Dec. 20, before the final leg of her trip to Cape Town: 5

"Going to Africa. Hope I don't get AIDS. Just kidding. I'm white!"

She chuckled to herself as she pressed send on this last one, then wandered around Heathrow's international terminal for half an hour, sporadically checking her phone. No one replied, which didn't surprise her. She had only 170 Twitter followers.

Sacco boarded the plane. It was an 11-hour flight, so she slept. When the plane landed in Cape Town and was taxiing on the runway, she turned on her phone. Right away, she got a text from someone she hadn't spoken to since high school: "I'm so sorry to see what's happening." Sacco looked at it, baffled.

Then another text: "You need to call me immediately." It was from her best friend, Hannah. Then her phone exploded with more texts and alerts. And then it rang. It was Hannah. "You're the No. 1 worldwide trend on Twitter right now," she said.

Sacco's Twitter feed had become a horror show. "In light of @JustineSacco   10
disgusting racist tweet, I'm donating to @care today" and "How did @JustineSacco get a PR job?! Her level of racist ignorance belongs on Fox News. #AIDS can affect anyone!" and "I'm an IAC employee and I don't want @JustineSacco doing any communications on our behalf ever again. Ever." And then one from her employer, IAC, the corporate owner of The Daily Beast, OKCupid and Vimeo: "This is an outrageous, offensive comment. Employee in question currently unreachable on an intl flight." The anger soon turned to excitement: "All I want for Christmas is to see @JustineSacco's face when her plane lands and she checks her inbox/voicemail" and "Oh man, @JustineSacco is going to have the most painful phone-turning-on moment ever when her plane lands" and "We are about to watch this @JustineSacco bitch get fired. In REAL time. Before she even KNOWS she's getting fired."

The furor over Sacco's tweet had become not just an ideological crusade against her perceived bigotry but also a form of idle entertainment. Her complete ignorance of her predicament for those 11 hours lent the episode both dramatic irony and a pleasing narrative arc. As Sacco's flight traversed the length of Africa, a hashtag began to trend worldwide: #HasJustineLandedYet. "Seriously. I just want to go home to go to bed, but everyone at the bar is SO into #HasJustineLandedYet. Can't look away. Can't leave" and "Right, is there no one in Cape Town going to the airport to tweet her arrival? Come on, Twitter! I'd like pictures #HasJustineLandedYet."

A Twitter user did indeed go to the airport to tweet her arrival. He took her photograph and posted it online. "Yup," he wrote, "@JustineSacco HAS in fact landed at Cape Town International. She's decided to wear sunnies as a disguise."

By the time Sacco had touched down, tens of thousands of angry tweets had been sent in response to her joke. Hannah, meanwhile, frantically deleted her friend's tweet and her account—Sacco didn't want to look—but it was far too late. "Sorry @JustineSacco," wrote one Twitter user, "your tweet lives on forever."

In the early days of Twitter, I was a keen shamer. When newspaper columnists made racist or homophobic statements, I joined the pile-on. Sometimes I led it. The journalist A.A. Gill once wrote a column about shooting a baboon on safari in Tanzania: "I'm told they can be tricky to shoot. They run up trees, hang on for grim life. They die hard, baboons. But not this one. A soft-nosed .357 blew his lungs out." Gill did the deed because he "wanted to get a sense of what it might be like to kill someone, a stranger."

I was among the first people to alert social media. (This was because Gill always gave my television documentaries bad reviews, so I tended to keep a vigilant eye on things he could be got for.) Within minutes, it was everywhere. Amid the hundreds of congratulatory messages I received, one stuck out: "Were you a bully at school?"   15

Still, in those early days, the collective fury felt righteous, powerful and effective. It felt as if hierarchies were being dismantled, as if justice were being democratized. As time passed, though, I watched these shame campaigns multiply, to the point that they targeted not just powerful institutions and public figures but really anyone perceived to have done something offensive. I also began to marvel at the disconnect between the severity of the crime and the gleeful savagery of the punishment. It almost felt as if shamings were now happening for their own sake, as if they were following a script.

Eventually I started to wonder about the recipients of our shamings, the real humans who were the virtual targets of these campaigns. So for the past two years, I've been interviewing individuals like Justine Sacco: everyday people pilloried brutally, most often for posting some poorly considered joke on social media. Whenever possible, I have met them in person, to truly grasp the emotional toll at the other end of our screens. The people I met were mostly unemployed, fired for their transgressions, and they seemed broken somehow—deeply confused and traumatized. . . .

Late one afternoon last year, I met Justine Sacco in New York, at a restaurant in Chelsea called Cookshop. Dressed in rather chic business attire, Sacco ordered a glass of white wine. Just three weeks had passed since her trip to Africa, and she was still a person of interest to the media. Websites had already ransacked her Twitter feed for more horrors. (For example, "I had a sex dream about an autistic kid last night," from 2012, was unearthed by BuzzFeed in the article "16 Tweets Justine Sacco Regrets.") A New York Post photographer had been following her to the gym.

"Only an insane person would think that white people don't get AIDS," she told me. It was about the first thing she said to me when we sat down.

Sacco had been three hours or so into her flight when retweets of her   20
joke began to overwhelm my Twitter feed. I could understand why some people found it offensive. Read literally, she said that white people don't get AIDS, but it seems doubtful many interpreted it that way. More likely it was her apparently gleeful flaunting of her privilege that angered people. But after thinking about her tweet for a few seconds more, I began to suspect that it wasn't racist but a reflexive critique of white privilege — on our tendency to naïvely imagine ourselves immune from life's horrors. Sacco, like Stone, had been yanked violently out of the context of her small social circle. Right?

"To me it was so insane of a comment for anyone to make," she said. "I thought there was no way that anyone could possibly think it was literal." (She would later write me an email to elaborate on this point. "Unfortunately, I am not a character on 'South Park' or a comedian, so I had no business commenting on the epidemic in such a politically incorrect manner on a public platform," she wrote. "To put it simply, I wasn't trying to raise awareness of AIDS or piss off the world or ruin my life. Living in America puts us in a bit of a bubble when it comes to what is going on in the third world. I was making fun of that bubble.")

I would be the only person she spoke to on the record about what happened to her, she said. It was just too harrowing — and "as a publicist," inadvisable — but she felt it was necessary, to show how "crazy" her situation was, how her punishment simply didn't fit the crime.

"I cried out my body weight in the first 24 hours," she told me. "It was incredibly traumatic. You don't sleep. You wake up in the middle of the night forgetting where you are." She released an apology statement and cut short her vacation. Workers were threatening to strike at the hotels she had booked if she showed up. She was told no one could guarantee her safety.

Her extended family in South Africa were African National Congress supporters — the party of Nelson Mandela. They were longtime activists for racial equality. When Justine arrived at the family home from the airport, one of the first things her aunt said to her was: "This is not what our family stands for. And now, by association, you've almost tarnished the family."

As she told me this, Sacco started to cry. I sat looking at her for a moment.   25
Then I tried to improve the mood. I told her that "sometimes, things need to reach a brutal nadir before people see sense."

"Wow," she said. She dried her eyes. "Of all the things I could have been in society's collective consciousness, it never struck me that I'd end up a brutal nadir."

She glanced at her watch. It was nearly 6 p.m. The reason she wanted to meet me at this restaurant, and that she was wearing her work clothes, was that it was only a few blocks away from her office. At 6, she was due in there to clean out her desk.

"All of a sudden you don't know what you're supposed to do," she said. "If I don't start making steps to reclaim my identity and remind myself of who I am on a daily basis, then I might lose myself."

The restaurant's manager approached our table. She sat down next to Sacco, fixed her with a look and said something in such a low volume I couldn't hear it, only Sacco's reply: "Oh, you think I'm going to be grateful for this?"

We agreed to meet again, but not for several months. She was determined   30 to prove that she could turn her life around. "I can't just sit at home and watch movies every day and cry and feel sorry for myself," she said. "I'm going to come back."

After she left, Sacco later told me, she got only as far as the lobby of her office building before she broke down crying. . . .

Recently, I wrote to Sacco to tell her I was putting her story in The Times, and I asked her to meet me one final time to update me on her life. Her response was speedy. "No way." She explained that she had a new job in communications, though she wouldn't say where. She said, "Anything that puts the spotlight on me is a negative."

It was a profound reversal for Sacco. When I first met her, she was desperate to tell the tens of thousands of people who tore her apart how they had wronged her and to repair what remained of her public persona. But perhaps she had now come to understand that her shaming wasn't really about her at all. Social media is so perfectly designed to manipulate our desire for approval, and that is what led to her undoing. Her tormentors were instantly congratulated as they took Sacco down, bit by bit, and so they continued to do so. Their motivation was much the same as Sacco's own — a bid for the attention of strangers — as she milled about Heathrow, hoping to amuse people she couldn't see.   [2015]

In this article and in his book, Ronson feels sorry for Justine Sacco. He thinks she was foolish to send her notorious tweet, but he doesn't believe she deserved the abuse she received. Indeed, Ronson came to sympathize with many of his interview subjects. For him, they were victims more than villains. He started to doubt the morality of shamers. Often, he sensed, their crusades are reckless and cruel.

Some cultural observers, though, defend public shaming, or at least they endorse certain types. Among these advocates is Jennifer Jacquet, a scholar and social activist. Jacquet earned a Ph.D. in natural resources management and environmental studies at the University of British Columbia. Currently she is an assistant professor of environmental studies at New York University, where she is also affiliated with the Stern School of Business. In 2015, she published a book titled *Is Shame Necessary?: New Uses for an Old Tool.* Jacquet would agree with Ronson that many kinds of shaming are awful. But in her book, she argues that other kinds have worth. On behalf of wildlife preservation, she herself has joined efforts to shame environmentally insensitive firms. In her view, there really are "new uses for an old tool." Of course, she wants to ensure that these uses are good, so she lays out principles she hopes shamers will heed. Here, in this excerpt from her book, she explains one.

JENNIFER JACQUET

From *Is Shame Necessary?*

Effective shaming should focus on a transgression for which there is no threat of a more severe or formal form of punishment. If there is a formal system of sanctioning in place—if, for example, there were a U.S. law that made voting compulsory (as there is in Australia)—there would be no need to mobilize the audience, and using shame might even be a waste of attention. The crowd itself might even find this to be a waste of its time. A Texas man filmed his neighbor vandalizing his car and not only used it against him in court, but also posted the footage online. Why publicize this crime and further shame the neighbor? The Texas man didn't need the help of the crowd for punishment— there was a system in place to punish the transgression.

When there is no legal mechanism or no enforcement of laws, then shaming moves up the list of options for social control. There were no laws regulating how AIG had to spend the government bailout money, just as there were no laws that prohibited banks from using bailout money for banker bonuses. Financial executives received almost $20 billion in bonuses in 2008, after a $245 billion government bailout. Citigroup proposed to buy a $50 million corporate jet in early 2009, shortly after receiving $45 billion in taxpayer funds. The courts could not find anything illegal in this behavior, but days later, President Obama said that Citigroup "should know better" and called the bonuses "shameful."

Occupy Wall Street was a signal that even though the legal system had not found that the banks had acted outside the law, many people felt the banks had done something wrong. Had more than one lone investment banker gone to prison after the 2008 financial crisis—as hundreds did during the last fraud-filled financial crisis, in the 1980s, which was one-seventieth the size of the one in 2008—we would have probably seen less shaming used against financial institutions and their employees. The Occupy Wall Street movement claimed some modest accomplishments—banks abandoned plans for debit-card fees, the government established a new agency to protect consumers from the financial sector, and the meme of "the one percent" was born. It also served as a reminder that when there are no formal avenues to punishment, society still has shame up its sleeve.

Law professor Toni Massaro has argued against shaming on the grounds that "shaming may convey the message that drunk drivers, child molesters, and the other offenders subjected to these penalties are less than human" and that they "deserve our contempt." In those specific cases, Massaro could be correct. But when shaming is used against bankers or nonvoters or against companies like Google, Amazon, and Starbucks for their offshore tax havens, it's not because society sees them as "less than human" (although in the case of the corporations, they might be) but because there is no alternative. For the same reason, states are left with shaming delinquent taxpayers because, unlike the federal government, states have almost no other means of recourse. (The State of California can confiscate only second homes and luxury vehicles, and only after a big legal brouhaha.)

It's not that shaming is preferable; it's just that, in some cases, sham-   5
ing is all we have. When fishermen in southern Chile are seen in areas that the community has designated as marine protected areas, other fishermen write the transgressors' names on a big sign in town that says LOS CASTIGADOS ("THE PUNISHED"). The fishermen are group-policing the area and using shame because there are no formal sanctions. International law instruments like the Universal Declaration of Human Rights have no formal avenues for punishment, so shaming is one of the main tactics of enforcement. Kenneth Roth, executive director of Human Rights Watch, wrote, "The strength of organizations like Human Rights Watch is not their rhetorical voice but their shaming methodology — their ability to investigate misconduct and expose it to public opprobrium."

Sometimes formal punishment will never be implemented, and shaming can encourage better behavior. It is not likely, for instance, that highly salty or otherwise unhealthy foods will ever be outlawed — nor that we would want them to be. Yet we also grapple with the problems associated with unhealthy diets. Research shows that shaming might help reduce consumption of unhealthy foods — not by shaming the consumers, but by shaming the foods, that is, singling out the most egregious products that they might purchase. Researchers labeled some foods at a hospital kiosk "less healthy" and sales of healthier items increased by 6 percent. Beginning in 1993, the Finnish government required a label on foods with high salt content, which led to a significant decrease in overall salt consumption.   [2015]

≡ THINKING ABOUT THE TEXT

We encourage you to link Galchen's story with the issues that Ronson and Jacquet raise. You might, through writing or discussion, tackle these specific questions.

1. Photographs of Andrew Rector sleeping at the stadium are readily available online. We could have used one of them to illustrate Galchen's story. But we chose not to. What would *your* decision have been? What would be the arguments for and against reproducing Rector's image in this book?

2. To what extent is Galchen's portrayal of Usl sympathetic? Is Ronson's portrayal of Justine Sacco equally so? Refer to specific passages in both texts.

3. Although the title character of Galchen's story has a real-life counterpart, she uses her freedom as a writer of fiction to invent certain details. How does Usl's mother play a significant role in the story? Why do you think Galchen gives Usl the particular job he has? What does she emphasize about Usl's lawsuit? What should readers make of the story's last word, "waiting"?

4. What would you say to someone who argues that the stadium jumbotron's repeated close-ups of Rector were an invasion of privacy?

5. Many of the shaming messages directed at Rector—and evidently at Usl, too—refer to his being overweight. Do you think that the shamers would be less scornful toward someone who was thinner? Why, or why not? To what extent, and in what ways, are overweight people nowadays made to feel ashamed?

6. What examples of public shaming can *you* think of? How similar are these cases to what Andrew Rector, Galchen's character Usl, and Justine Sacco experienced?

7. What would you say to someone who argues that social media companies like Twitter should exercise more control over content that insults people?

8. What do you think motivates shamers to send insulting messages about people they don't know and have never heard of before?

9. What advice would you give people who have been publicly shamed, such as Andrew Rector, Galchen's character Usl, and Justine Sacco?

10. In our excerpt from her book, Jacquet identifies one principle that shamers should follow if their act of shaming is to have value. In your own words, what is that principle? What principles would you add?

11. Jacquet says, "It's not that shaming is preferable; it's just that, in some cases, shaming is all we have." To what extent do you agree with her? Explain your reasoning.

CHAPTER 4

The Reading Process

Courses in many disciplines ask for *close reading*. But literature classes strongly emphasize it—one reason they are good preparation for other fields. Nevertheless, the steps involved in close reading are not always clear to students. Perhaps you have been told to engage in this process without knowing what it entails. Because close reading is central to literary studies, plays a big role in other courses, and yet remains murky for many students, this chapter both explains it and models it.

If you are taking a course that asks you to *write* about the literary works you study, close reading of them will help you form ideas about them worth spreading to *your* audiences. Such reading will also help you decide what details of these texts will best support your points about them. So, as we proceed to explain close reading, we treat it mainly as what some would call a method of invention. It's a way for you, as a *writer*, to discover things to say about literature.

Strategies for Close Reading

Actually, close reading consists of not one strategy but several. All of them can help you gain insights into a literary work, which you might then convey through your writing. You need not follow these strategies in the order we list them here, but try each of them.

1. Make predictions as you read.   That is, guess what will happen and how the text will turn out. If you wind up being surprised, fine. You may get a richer understanding of the text as you reflect on how it *defies* your expectations.

2. Reread the text.   Reread the text several times, focusing each time on a different element of the text and using at least one of these occasions to read aloud. Few readers of a literary work can immediately see everything important and interesting in it. You greatly increase your chances of getting ideas about a text if you read it again and again. At first, you may be preoccupied with following the plot or with figuring out the text's main theme. Only by examining the text repeatedly may you notice several of its other aspects, including features that really stir your thoughts. But don't try to study everything in the text each time you look at it. Use each reading of it to study just one characteristic. In an early stage, for example, you might trace the text's repetitions, and then you might use a later reading to pinpoint its ambiguous words. This division of labor can, in the end, generate many insights that a less focused approach would not.

Reading all of the text or portions of it out loud gives you a better sense of how the text is manipulating language. Reading aloud is especially useful in the case of poems, for you may detect rhymes or soundalike words that you would not notice when reading silently.

3. Test the text against your own experiences.   Keep in mind your experiences, beliefs, assumptions, and values as you read the text, but note ways that it challenges or complicates these things. When you first read a particular literary work, your interpretations and judgments are bound to be influenced by your personal background. This includes your beliefs, assumptions, and values, as well as things that have happened to you. Indeed, many people read a literary work hoping they can personally identify with the characters, situations, and views it presents. Moreover, this is an understandable goal. Pay attention, though, to details of the text that do *not* match your life and current thinking. After all, the author may be deliberately challenging or complicating readers' habitual attitudes. In any case, parts of the text that are hard to identify with will often provide you with great subjects when you write about the work. Bear in mind, though, that you will not interest your readers if you simply criticize characters in the work or sneer at other elements of it. In particular, try not to sum up characters with negative labels such as *immoral, weird,* or *sick.* These terms often strike readers as reflecting mere prejudice — a poor substitute for careful analysis of human complexity.

4. Look for patterns in the text and disruptions of them.   Many a literary work is organized by various patterns, which may not be evident on first reading. In fact, you might not detect a number of these patterns until you read the text several times. You may even see these better if you move back and forth in the text instead of just reading it straight through. Typically, a literary work's patterns include repetitions of words and of actions; oppositions; words similar or related in meaning; and technical methods of organization (such as rhyme schemes or frequent use of flashbacks). Just as important to note are moments in the text that are inconsistent with one or more of its patterns. Locate and think about places where the work makes a significant shift, in meaning, imagery, tone, plot, a character's behavior, narrative point of view, or even physical format (for example, a change in rhyme scheme).

5. Note ambiguities.   These are places where the text's meaning is not crystal clear and therefore calls for interpretation: for example, words that can have more than one definition, symbols that have multiple implications, and actions that suggest various things about a character.

6. Consider the author's alternatives.   That is, think about what the author *could* have done and yet did not do. The author of a literary work faces all sorts of decisions in composing it. And as you study the work, you will have more to say about it if you think about those choices. Try, then, to compare the author's handling of particular passages to other possible treatments of them. By considering, for example, why the author chose a certain word over others, you may better detect implications and effects of the author's actual language. Similarly, by reflecting on how the author *might* have portrayed a certain character more simplistically, you strengthen your ability to analyze the character's variety of traits.

7. Ask questions.   As you read, generate questions that have more than one possible answer. When we first read a literary work, most of us try to get comfortable with it. We search for passages that are clear; we groan when we encounter ones that are mysterious or confusing. Sooner or later, though, we must confront puzzles in the text if we are to analyze it in depth. Furthermore, if we plan to *write* about the text, we are more likely to come up with ideas worth communicating to our readers if we present ourselves as helping them deal with matters *not* immediately clear. After all, our audience will not need our analysis if it centers on what's obvious. Therefore, list multiple questions that the work raises for you, especially ones that have various possible answers. Then, if you focus on addressing one of these questions in your writing — providing and supporting your own particular answer to it — your readers will find value in turning to *your* text. Furthermore, when you come across literary passages that seem easy to understand, consider how they might actually involve more than one possible meaning. Even little words may prove ambiguous and, therefore, worth analyzing in your writing. Of course, you may have to consult a dictionary in order to see the different meanings that a word can have.

The questions you come up with need hardly be restricted to matters of the work's theme. After all, hardly any literary text worth studying can be reduced to a single message. Often, such texts play with multiple ideas, perhaps emphasizing tensions among them. Therefore, it may make more sense for you to refer to a work's *themes*. Actually, as we have been suggesting throughout our catalog of reading strategies, any literary text has several other features. As a writer, you may wind up with much more to say about a literary work if you consider one or more of these other elements: for example, facts obscured or absent in the text, possible definitions of key words, symbols, patterns, evaluations to be made of the characters or the overall work, the text's historical and cultural context, the text's genre, its relevance to current political debates, and cause-effect relationships. In the next chapter, we explain these elements at greater length, identifying them as *issues* you might write about.

8. Jot down possible answers.   Even while reading the text, begin developing and pulling together your thoughts by informally writing about it. See if you can generate not only good questions but also tentative answers to them. Writing need not be the final outcome of your reflections on a literary work. You can jot down ideas about the text even as you first encounter it. Such informal, preliminary writing can actually help you generate insights into the text that you would not have achieved simply by scanning it. The following are some of the specific things you might do:

- **Make notes in the text itself.**   A common method is to mark key passages, either by underlining these passages or by running a highlighter over them. Both ways of marking are popular because they help readers recall main features of the text. But use these techniques moderately if you use them at all, for marking lots of passages will leave you unable to distinguish the really important parts of the text. Also, try "talking back" to the text in its margins. Next to particular passages, you might jot down words of your own, indicating any feelings and questions you have about those parts. On any page of the text, you might circle related words and then draw lines between these words to emphasize their connection. If a word or an idea shows up on numerous pages, you might circle it each time. Furthermore, try cross-referencing by listing on at least one page the numbers of all those pages where the word or idea appears.

- **As you read the text, occasionally look away from it, and jot down anything in it you recall.**   This memory exercise lets you review your developing impressions of the text. When you turn back to its actual words, you may find that you have distorted or overlooked aspects of it that you should take into account.

- **At various moments in your reading, freewrite about the text for ten minutes or so.**   Spontaneously explore your preliminary thoughts and feelings about it, as well as any personal experiences the text leads you to recall. One logical moment to do freewriting is when you have finished reading the text. But you do not have to wait until then; as you read, you might pause occasionally to freewrite. This way, you give yourself an opportunity to develop and review your thoughts about the text early on.

- **Create a "dialectical notebook."**   So named by composition theorist Ann Berthoff, it involves using pages of your regular notebook in a particular way. On each page, draw a line down the middle to create two columns. In the left column, list various details of the text: specifically, words, images, characters, and events that strike you. In the right column, jot down for each detail one or more sentences indicating *why* you were drawn to it. Take as many pages as you need to record and reflect on your observations. You can also use the two-column format to carry out a dialogue with yourself about the text. This is an especially good way to ponder aspects of the text that you find confusing, mysterious, or complex.

- **Play with the text by revising it.**   Doing so will make you more aware of options that the author rejected and will give you a better sense of the moves that the author chose to make. Specifically, you might rearrange parts of the text, add to it, change some of its words, or shift its narrative point of view. After you revise the text, compare your alternative version with the original, considering especially differences in their effects.

A Poem for Analysis

To demonstrate what it means to read closely, we present observations that various students made about a poem. The poem is by Sharon Olds (b. 1942), who teaches at New York University and has produced many volumes of verse. "Summer Solstice, New York City" appears at the start of her 1987 book *The Gold Cell*. The poem deals with work—in this case, efforts by New York City police to prevent a suicide.

SHARON OLDS

Summer Solstice, New York City

By the end of the longest day of the year he could not stand it,
he went up the iron stairs through the roof of the building
and over the soft, tarry surface
to the edge, put one leg over the complex green tin cornice
and said if they came a step closer that was it.   5
Then the huge machinery of the earth began to work for his life,
the cops came in their suits blue-gray as the sky on a cloudy evening,
and one put on a bullet-proof vest, a
black shell around his own life,
life of his children's father, in case   10
the man was armed, and one, slung with a
rope like the sign of his bounden duty,
came up out of a hole in the top of the neighboring building
like the gold hole they say is in the top of the head,
and began to lurk toward the man who wanted to die.   15
The tallest cop approached him directly,
softly, slowly, talking to him, talking, talking,
while the man's leg hung over the lip of the next world
and the crowd gathered in the street, silent, and the
hairy net with its implacable grid was   20
unfolded near the curb and spread out and
stretched as the sheet is prepared to receive at birth.
Then they all came a little closer
where he squatted next to his death, his shirt
glowing its milky glow like something   25
growing in a dish at night in the dark in a lab and then
everything stopped
as his body jerked and he
stepped down from the parapet and went toward them
and they closed on him, I thought they were going to   30
beat him up, as a mother whose child has been
lost will scream at the child when it's found, they
took him by the arms and held him up and
leaned him against the wall of the chimney and the
tall cop lit a cigarette   35

in his own mouth, and gave it to him, and
then they all lit cigarettes, and the
red, glowing ends burned like the
tiny campfires we lit at night
back at the beginning of the world.   *[1987]*   40

Applying the Strategies

Even before you look at the students' comments, try doing what they did. We
asked each of them to read the poem several times (step 2, pp. 88–89). More
specifically, they devoted each of their readings to a specific element of the
poem:

- First, they focused on how it fulfilled or defied their predictions.
- Then they considered how the poem matched and diverged from their
  personal backgrounds.
- Then they traced the poem's patterns, as well as breaks from these.
- Then they noted places where the poem is puzzling, ambiguous, or
  unclear.
- Next, they identified at least one choice that the poem's author faced.
- They then settled on questions that have more than one possible
  answer and that therefore might be worth addressing in a formal
  essay about the poem.
- Finally, pulling their thoughts together, they came up with tentative
  answers to these questions, which they might develop in a formal
  essay.

Again, the order of these stages is not the only one possible; the important
thing is to go through them all. At each stage of their reading, the students also
did a few minutes of freewriting, using this strategy to develop thoughts about
whatever element was their focus. Below are excerpts from these informal
reflections.

MAKE PREDICTIONS

KATHERINE: I was really tense as I read this poem because I thought the man
would jump at the end and then we would get a horrible description of
him splattering on the sidewalk. I didn't predict the cops would succeed
in talking him out of it. When the poet says he "jerked," that could easily
have been the start of his jumping, but thank God he is instead stepping
back. I'm glad that they persuaded him to remain alive.

MARIA: I was like the poem's speaker expecting that they would physically
grab him and treat him roughly, and so I was surprised when they were
nice to him and even offered him a cigarette.

TREVOR: I predicted that the poem would end with the man still on the edge
of the building deciding whether or not to jump off, because I think that

in a way it would be neat to leave us guessing whether he's really going to do it. I wasn't all that surprised when he pulled back and joined the cops, because that was certainly one possible outcome. However, I was surprised when the author had them smoking cigarettes at the end like "at the beginning of the world." I didn't expect that image of prehistoric people to show up here at the end.

REFLECT ON YOUR PERSONAL BACKGROUND

JAMES: It's hard for me to sympathize with someone who commits suicide, especially because someone at my high school killed himself and all of his friends and family were terribly saddened by what he did. I think that no matter how bad things get for you, there's a way out if only you look for it. Suicide is no answer, and it hurts the people you leave behind. So I'm glad that the man in this poem winds up not committing suicide. If he had, I would have thought less of him.

CARLA: I vaguely remember seeing some movies in which a character stands on a ledge and thinks about jumping off it. In real life, I've never seen something like that. What this poem most brings to my mind are reports I heard about people jumping off the World Trade Towers to escape being killed by fire. Of course, they died anyway. As I recall, TV didn't show these people jumping, out of respect for them I guess, and I'm glad that I didn't have to see this happen. Still, I'm aware that it did. Anyway, the man thinking about suicide in this poem isn't facing the same situation. He can easily live if he wants to.

BOB: I guess the police are obligated to try rescuing the man even if they have to risk their own lives. I've never been in this position, so I'm not sure how I'd feel if I'd been assigned to save the man in this poem. Though I disapprove of suicide, maybe I wouldn't have the guts to try confronting him on the edge of the building, and I'm not sure I could talk to him calmly, because if he did jump he might take me down with him. I admire the ability of these cops to stay cool and talk him into joining them. I'm also impressed that they then treat him like a friend instead of like a potentially violent nut case that they have to get under control through force. If it were me, I think I might want to throw him to the ground and pin his arms so that he wouldn't try something like that again.

READ FOR PATTERNS AND FOR BREAKS IN PATTERNS

DOMINICK: This may be too little a thing to think about, but I notice that the word "it" is repeated in the beginning section of the poem. The first line ends with "it," and line 5 does also. I'm not sure what is meant by "it" in "he could not stand it." Obviously on one level "it" here means his life, but he seems to have something specific about his life in mind when he says this, but we don't learn what he's specifically thinking of. The second "it" seems to refer to the fact that he will kill himself if they come closer. But that reference too isn't as clear as it might be. I see that later on "it" comes up again as a word for the cigarette that the cop gives to the man (after lighting it in his own mouth, yuk!). Maybe we're supposed to connect this "it" to the "its" at the start.

BOB: After the middle of the poem we start to get a lot of birth imagery. The word "birth" is even stated, and a little later there's the image of something "growing" in a lab dish.

JARED: "World" is repeated. In the middle of the poem, there's a reference to "the next world," and the very last word of the poem is "world," meaning the world where we currently live.

COURTNEY: I found a number of references to children. There are the words "his children's father," and then toward the end the word "child" is repeated, though this time it's a mother's child. And then the last line refers to "the beginning of the world," as if the world is a child that has just been born.

FRANK: It's funny that the word "end" is one of the first words of the poem, and then the word "beginning" is one of its last words. I can more easily imagine the reverse. Anyway, "end" and "beginning" are opposites that the poet seems to want us to think about. Come to think of it, there is mention of "ends" near the conclusion, but these are the "ends" of the men's cigarettes and not the end of the world.

ALEX: The word "day" appears in the first line (it's "the longest day of the year"), but later there is the word "night" ("growing in a dish at night"), and then "night" is in the next-to-last line. Ironically, things get brighter (the man decides to live) as the poem moves from "day" to "night."

PAUL: As the poem moves along, there's a shift in pronouns. In the first half or so, we get forms of "he" and "they." Then the word "I" suddenly appears, and then the next-to-last line has the word "we."

READ FOR PUZZLES, AMBIGUITIES, AND UNCLEAR MOMENTS

KATHERINE: I just don't learn enough about this man's thinking to know why he's even planning to kill himself. This is something the poem doesn't make clear. But I guess the "I" of the poem doesn't know the man's thinking either, and meanwhile she's in the position of possibly witnessing the man falling to the pavement! Maybe the author doesn't tell us exactly why the man wants to commit suicide because we can then identify more easily with him. We can think about moments when we were incredibly unhappy, whether or not we were depressed by the same things he is.

TIM: We're told that the cop approaching the man is doing a lot of talking, but we don't find out what he specifically says, even though this may have played a big role in getting the man to step back and live.

HILLARY: The gold hole sounds like something from folklore, but I don't know the background.

RACHEL: I'm wondering how much we're supposed to focus on the speaker's reactions to what's going on, or whether we should think more about the man and the policemen.

READ FOR THE AUTHOR'S CHOICES

KATHERINE: Olds could have had the man jump and die. Even if this poem is based on a real incident where the man decided to live, she could have changed what happened. Also, if she still went with the rescue version, she could have had the policemen treat the man roughly after they rescued him.

PAUL: The word "I" could have appeared more often throughout the poem, especially because the poem is written from the point of view of someone observing this suicide attempt.

TIM: We might have been told why the man was thinking of killing himself and what the cops said to him. I realize this information would be hard for the speaker of the poem to give us, since she's just observing the whole business from the street below. Still, maybe Olds could have found a way of telling us at least a little more about what the men on the roof were saying and thinking.

BOB: The author didn't have to use birth images. She could have described this event without them. In fact, death imagery seems more appropriate when a poem is about a possible suicide.

GENERATE QUESTIONS THAT HAVE MORE THAN ONE POSSIBLE ANSWER

JENNIFER: What might the poet be trying to convey when she ends the poem with the image of "the beginning of the world"? The last line really captures my attention.

PAUL: What should we conclude when the pronouns shift from "he" and "they" to "I" and finally "we"?

VICTORIA: How should we interpret the poem's repeated references to children and to parents (both father and mother)?

BOB: How important are the cops as characters in this poem?

STATE TENTATIVE ANSWERS

JENNIFER: Maybe the poet is telling us that each time you overcome depression and decide to go on living, it's like the rebirth of the world, and you're rejoining a "we" in the sense of rejoining the rest of humanity.

PAUL: I believe that the speaker comes to identify with the man and his rescuers and then sees herself and them as all part of a common humanity, as if we all have to decide when to risk our lives and when to preserve them.

VICTORIA: In a paper, I could argue that these child and parent references are used by Olds to suggest that even as adults, we sometimes act like children and sometimes have to act like a parent, but Olds evidently prefers that we not act like a very stern parent.

BOB: The cops are very important in this poem. So much of it is about what they do and how they maybe feel. They're required to save the guy, they're part of "huge machinery," and one of them might end up sacrificing the "life of his children's father" just in order to rescue someone who wants to kill himself anyway, but then the cops turn out to be quite sympathetic toward the guy. There's even this odd religious-type moment with the sharing of a cigarette and then all the men lighting up. I think I would focus my paper on how the cops do their duty to preserve life even when they probably didn't want to, and then something spiritual happens because they didn't give up on the job they were assigned.

DAN: If I'm remembering correctly, the summer solstice is a turning point in the year, and you could say that there's a turning point in this poem when the man steps down from the ledge and chooses not to die. After the summer solstice we're heading toward winter, which is associated with death, but psychologically the poem goes in the opposite direction.

Think about your own developing understanding of Olds's poem. What aspect of it might you focus on in a formal essay? What's a claim that you might make? To us, the students' claims we have quoted seem promising topics for papers. Nevertheless, they could probably stand some polishing and further reflection. After all, they are the outcome of freewriting—an exploratory phase. In any case, what we want to stress is that you are more likely to get ideas about a literary work if you use the reading strategies that this group of students applied.

Reading Closely by Annotating

When you use such strategies, you may come up with several observations about the literary work you are reading. You may even find it helpful to record them directly on the text. Then, by reviewing the points you have annotated and connecting them to one another, you will provide yourself with a solid foundation for a paper. Here we demonstrate this process by showing how student Kara Lundquist annotated a poem by the noted writer and editor X. J. Kennedy (b. 1929) and then composed a possible opening paragraph for an essay about it.

X. J. KENNEDY

Death of a Window Washer

(He) dropped the way you'd slam an obstinate sash, — *Window washer is given no name.*

His (split) belt like a shade unrolling, flapping. — *Did his body "split" when he hit the ground? Poem avoids gruesome details to focus mostly on bystanders.*

Forgotten on his account, the mindless copying

Machine ran scores of memos no one wanted.

Heads stared from every floor, noon traffic halted   5

As though transformed to stone. Cops sealed the block — *Alliteration: What do "c" words suggest?*

With sawhorse barricades, laid canvas cover.

Nuns (crossed) themselves, flies went on being alive, — *Nuns' reaction different from insects'. But are the humans here much more sensitive?*

A broker (counted) ten shares sold as five, — *Echoes "account" in line 3. Did the dead man count (matter)?*

And by coincidence a digital clock   10

Stopped in front of a second it couldn't leap over. — *Do people prefer to "leap over" deaths like this?*

Struck wordless by his tumble from the sky

To their feet, two lovers held fast to each other

Uttering cries. But he had made no cry.

He'd made the city pause briefly to (suffer)   15 — *At first seems to mean "experience pain," then seems to mean "put up with."*

His taking ample room for once. In rather

A (tedious) while the rinsed street, left to dry, — *"Tedious" to whom? People soon get impatient for the body to go.*

Unlatched its gates that passersby might pass. — *Unusual to ask why he lived in the first place.*

Why did he live and die? His legacy — *Relates to "wordless" in line 12 and "no cry" in line 14.*

Is (mute): one final gleaming pane of glass.   20 — *"Pane of glass" (clear vision) seems opposite of "mute." Connect "pane" to "pain"?*

[2007]

Here is the paragraph that Kara composed, based on her annotations.

> X. J. Kennedy's poem "Death of a Window Washer" emphasizes not the title character's horrible accident, but rather how bystanders react to it. The poem suggests that although people may be momentarily affected by the death of an ordinary person whom they do not know, eventually they want to resume their own lives and pay him little attention. The specific situation that the poem dramatizes is the accidental plunge of a window washer from a city building. Certainly this incident shocks, at first, the passersby who witness it. Even though "flies went on being alive" (line 8), various human beings are disturbed by the man's sudden death. But as the poem proceeds, the city's inhabitants want to go back to their personal pursuits. A turning point in the poem is the word "suffer," which the speaker uses to describe the city dwellers at the end of line 15. This word might, at first, lead the reader to believe that they are tormented by the window washer's accident. But in the next line, it becomes clear that they are "suffering" in the sense that they are impatiently waiting for his corpse to be removed. Rather than permanently grieve over his having "passed" (i.e., died), they want to "pass" his body (18) and take up their daily existence once again. Therefore, although his death has been highly visible to them, they don't really bother to learn anything about him. His life is not revealed to them like the reality behind a "gleaming pane of glass" (20). The speaker's concluding use of this image is, in fact, ironic.

Further Strategies for Close Reading

IDENTIFY CHARACTERS' EMOTIONS

Your feelings about the characters in a literary work can help you write a paper about it. Especially useful to consider is *why* you view these people as you do. What specific aspects of their thinking and conduct affect your attitudes toward them? You will have more material for the paper, though, if you also examine how the characters feel. With this strategy of close reading, you patiently and carefully identify *their* emotions, not simply your own. This analysis can even wind up giving you your paper's key idea — what, in the previous chapter, we called its *main claim*.

As you pinpoint the characters' passions and moods, try not to judge these right away. Emotions that may at first seem obnoxious or odd can have interesting roots. Also, they may be stages in complex mental journeys. A character may display numerous feelings, including ones that conflict, and undergo major changes of heart. Bear in mind, too, that many people in literature repress or mask their real desires, so the reader must infer their true inner states. Identify as well any emotions that characters significantly *lack*. Noting what feelings they *might* have had helps you pinpoint those they express.

We invite you to practice this method of analysis with the following poem. "Execution" is by the veteran poet Edward Hirsch (b. 1950) and appeared in his 1989 book *The Night Parade* as well as in a 2010 retrospective on his career, *The Living Fire: New and Selected Poems*. As you read the text, try to specify the emotions of the speaker and his main subject, his former coach. We follow up the poem with specific questions about their feelings. Then, to demonstrate the potential benefit of this approach to literature, we present a few ideas that student Courtney Reeves came up with when she applied it to "Execution." The insights she gained helped her eventually construct the introduction to an essay she wrote on the poem.

EDWARD HIRSCH

Execution

The last time I saw my high school football coach
He had cancer stenciled into his face
Like pencil marks from the sun, like intricate
Drawings on the chalkboard, small *x*'s and *o*'s
That he copied down in a neat numerical hand   5
Before practice in the morning. By day's end
The board was a spiderweb of options and counters,
Blasts and sweeps, a constellation of players
Shining under his favorite word, *Execution*,
Underlined in the upper right-hand corner of things.   10
He believed in football like a new religion
And had perfect unquestioning faith in the fundamentals
Of blocking and tackling, the idea of warfare
Without suffering or death, the concept of teammates
Moving in harmony like the planets—and yet   15
Our awkward adolescent bodies were always canceling
The flawless beauty of Saturday afternoons in September,
Falling away from the particular grace of autumn,
The clear weather, the ideal game he imagined.
And so he drove us through punishing drills   20
On weekday afternoons, and doubled our practice time,
And challenged us to hammer him with forearms,
And devised elaborate, last-second plays—a flea-
Flicker, a triple reverse—to save us from defeat.
Almost always they worked. He despised losing   25
And loved winning more than his own body, maybe even
More than himself. But the last time I saw him
He looked wobbly and stunned by illness,
And I remembered the game in my senior year
When we met a downstate team who loved hitting   30
More than we did, who battered us all afternoon
With a vengeance, who destroyed us with timing

And power, with deadly, impersonal authority,
Machine-like fury, perfect execution.   *[1989]*

≣ THINKING ABOUT THE TEXT

1. To what extent does the speaker seem grief-stricken about his coach's mortal illness? Point to specific words in the text that influence your answer.

2. In line 11, the speaker says of the coach, "He believed in football like a new religion." What values would someone like the coach need to have in order to feel so passionately about this sport? Why might someone who regards "football like a new religion" not necessarily feel the same way about baseball or basketball?

3. In line 25, the speaker says that the coach "despised losing." How, if at all, did he reveal this attitude to his players? Identify specific words that help you address this question.

4. What other words in the poem indicate to you how the coach, during the speaker's youth, felt about high school football?

5. Where, if anywhere, does the speaker indicate how the players felt about the coach back then? Where, if anywhere, is the speaker evasive about what the players' attitudes toward the coach were?

6. In line 28, the speaker says that the coach now "looked wobbly and stunned by illness." What, evidently, was the coach feeling about his misfortune?

7. How does the speaker seem to feel about the football game he recalls at the end of the poem?

8. The title word, *execution*, appears twice in the poem. Do these two appearances reflect the same emotion, or different ones? Explain.

9. If the title of this poem were the name of an emotion, what emotion would you think appropriate?

After examining the characters' emotions, Courtney Reeves formed these ideas for her paper on the poem. We italicize her references to emotions.

> The speaker does not openly express *sorrow* for his former coach when he finds him both *physically and mentally suffering* from cancer. Nor is it clear that the speaker was ever extremely *fond* of the coach, although probably he *respected* him when he played for him. In general, the poem is not a blatant *sympathy* card for the coach. Instead, it seems chiefly a philosophical reflection, carried out with some *sadness*. The speaker seems mostly to *brood* about the ironies of the coach's present situation, including how these ironies apply to the speaker himself. Noticing that the coach now looks *"wobbly and stunned,"* the speaker obviously thinks that a big reason he appears this way is that cancer has physically attacked him. The speaker also seems to believe that the disease has *psychologically thrown the*

coach off balance, in at least two respects. First, although the coach is surely aware that his cancer may kill him, he cannot know for certain how long he actually has to live. The title of the poem, "Execution," refers in one sense to killing that is swift and scheduled, but the coach has now entered a period of *scary* unpredictability about his fate. Second, the coach's look of *unsteadiness and confusion* results from his lifelong belief that people can overcome their limits through skillful physical performances, another sense of the word "execution." This was a goal that the coach *strived for* when he pushed the speaker and his fellow players to achieve a perfect "execution" of plays that would enable them to defeat all opposing teams. Having cancer *shocks* the coach by showing him that he was naive in making football "a new religion" in which proper training of the body would mean success not only on the field but throughout life. He discovers that even though the game of football usually lacks real "suffering and death," these things strike all of us eventually, and that even though he "loved winning more than his own body," he depended on his body's health. The speaker, on the other hand, does not seem "wobbly and stunned" by what has happened to the coach. He suggests that during his boyhood he himself saw the reality of human limits with greater clarity and *detachment* than the coach did. Perhaps, though, the speaker is with *at least a bit of desperation* trying to ward off death by writing this well-"executed" poem about it, just as the coach *frenziedly* wrote marks on the blackboard to help the team "execute" plays.

USING TOPICS OF LITERARY STUDIES TO GET IDEAS

You can also get ideas about the text if, as you read it, you consider how it deals with **topics** that have preoccupied literary studies as a profession. Some of these topics have interested the discipline for many years. One example is work, a subject common to several selections in Chapters 1–8. Traditionally, literary studies has also been concerned with such topics as family relations, love, freedom and confinement, justice, and journeys. Moreover, the discipline has long called attention to topics that are essentially classic conflicts: for example, innocence versus experience, free will versus fate or determinism, the individual versus society, nature versus culture, and eternity versus the passing time.

Over the past few years, however, literary studies has turned to several new concerns. For instance, quite a few literary critics now consider the ways in which literary texts are often *about* reading, writing, interpretation, and evaluation. Critics increasingly refer to some of the following subjects in their analysis of literature:

- Traits that significantly shape human identity, including gender, race, ethnic background, social class, sexual orientation, cultural background, nationality, and historical context

- Representations of groups, including stereotypes held by others
- Acknowledgments — or denials — of differences among human beings
- Divisions, conflicts, and multiple forces *within* the self
- Boundaries, including the processes through which these are created, preserved, and challenged
- Politics and ideology, including the various forms that power and authority can take; acts of domination, oppression, exclusion, and appropriation; and acts of subversion, resistance, and parody
- Ways that carnivals and other festivities challenge or preserve social order
- Distinctions between what's universal and what's historically or culturally specific
- Relations between the public and the private, the social and the personal
- Relations between the apparently central and the apparently marginal
- Relations between what's supposedly normal and what's supposedly abnormal
- Relations between "high" culture and "low" (that is, mass or popular) culture
- Economic and technological developments, as well as their effects
- The role of performance in everyday life
- Values — ethical, aesthetic, religious, professional, and institutional
- Desire and pleasure
- The body
- The unconscious
- Memory, including public commemorations as well as personal memory
- Material things, including common physical objects

If you find that a literary text touches on one of these topics, try next to determine how the work specifically addresses that topic. Perhaps you will consider the topic an element of the text's themes. In any case, remember that, by itself, a topic is not the same as a theme. While a topic can usually be expressed in a word or a short phrase, a theme is a whole claim or assertion that you believe the text makes.

Actually, the topics we have identified may be most worth consulting when you have just begun analyzing a literary text and are far from establishing a theme. By using these topics, you can generate preliminary questions about the text, various issues you can then explore.

To demonstrate how these topics can stimulate inquiry, we apply some of them to the following poem, "Night Waitress." It is from the 1986 book *Ghost Memory*, by the late American poet Lynda Hull (1954–1994). Hull had been developing an impressive career in literature when she died in a car accident. This poem is also about work, the speaker being the night waitress of the title.

LYNDA HULL

Night Waitress

Reflected in the plate glass, the pies
look like clouds drifting off my shoulder.
I'm telling myself my face has character,
not beauty. It's my mother's Slavic face.
She washed the floor on hands and knees   5
below the Black Madonna, praying
to her god of sorrows and visions
who's not here tonight when I lay out the plates,
small planets, the cups and moons of saucers.
At this hour the men all look   10
as if they'd never had mothers.
They do not see me. I bring the cups.
I bring the silver. There's the man
who leans over the jukebox nightly
pressing the combinations   15
of numbers. I would not stop him
if he touched me, but it's only songs
of risky love he leans into. The cook sings
with the jukebox, a moan and sizzle
into the grill. On his forehead   20
a tattooed cross furrows,
diminished when he frowns. He sings words
dragged up from the bottom of his lungs.
I want a song that rolls
through the night like a big Cadillac   25
past factories to the refineries
squatting on the bay, round and shiny
as the coffee urn warming my palm.
Sometimes when coffee cruises my mind
visiting the most remote way stations,   30
I think of my room as a calm arrival
each book and lamp in its place. The calendar
on my wall predicts no disaster
only another white square waiting
to be filled like the desire that fills   35
jail cells, the old arrest
that makes me stare out the window or want
to try every bar down the street.
When I walk out of here in the morning
my mouth is bitter with sleeplessness.   40
Men surge to the factories and I'm too tired
to look. Fingers grip lunch box handles,
belt buckles gleam, wind riffles my uniform

and it's not romantic when the sun unlids
the end of the avenue. I'm fading   45
in the morning's insinuations
collecting in the crevices of buildings,
in wrinkles, in every fault
of this frail machinery.   *[1986]*

≡ A WRITING EXERCISE

After you read "Night Waitress," do a ten-minute freewrite in which you try
to identify how the poem relates to one or more of the topics mentioned
on pages 102–103.

We think that several of the topics now popular in literary studies are relevant to Hull's poem. Here are a few possibilities, along with questions that
these topics can generate.

Gender.   The speaker alludes to conventional roles through which men and
women relate to each other. When the speaker declares that "at this hour the
men all look / as if they'd never had mothers," she indicates that women have
often played a maternal role for men. Furthermore, she implies that often
women have been the primary caretaker of their sons. (Notice that she makes
no reference to fathers.) What is the effect of this attention to women as mothers of men? In most of the poem, the speaker refers to men as potential lovers.
Yet even as she suggests she would like a sexual relationship with a man, she
suggests as well that she has had trouble establishing worthwhile attachments.
Why has she had such difficulty, do you think? Does the problem seem due to
her personality alone, or do you sense larger forces shaping her situation?
Notice, too, that the poem refers to the factory workers as male, while the
woman who speaks is a waitress. To what extent does American society perpetuate a gendered division of labor?

Ethnic background.   Near the start of the poem, the speaker refers to her
"mother's Slavic face" and points out that her mother served "the Black
Madonna," a religious icon popular in Central European countries such as the
Czech Republic and Poland. What is the effect of these particular ethnic references? To pursue this line of inquiry, probably you will need to do research into
the Black Madonna, whether in a library or on the Internet.

Social class.   In part, considering social class means thinking about people's
ability to obtain material goods. When the speaker compares her ideal song to
"a big Cadillac," she implies that she doesn't currently possess such a luxurious
car. At the same time, she is expressing her desire for the song, not the car. Why
might the song be more important to her right now? Social class is also a matter of how various workplaces are related to one another. This poem evokes a
restaurant, factories, refineries, and bars. How are these settings connected as
parts of American society? Think, too, about how you would label the social
class of the various occupations the poem mentions. What would you say is the

social class of a waitress? To what classes would you assign people who work in factories and refineries? Who, for the most part, are the social classes that have to work at night?

Sexual orientation.   The speaker of "Night Waitress" seems heterosexual, an orientation often regarded as the only legitimate one. Because almost all societies have made heterosexuality the norm, a lot of people forget that it is a particular orientation and that not everyone identifies with it. Within literary studies, gay and lesbian critics have pointed out that a literary work may seem to deal with sexuality in general but may actually refer just to heterosexuality. Perhaps "Night Waitress" is examining heterosexuality as a specific social force. If so, how might the speaker's discontent be related to heterosexuality's influence as a particular institution? Keep in mind that you don't have to assume anything about the author's sexuality as you pursue such a question. In fact, heterosexuality may be a more important topic in Hull's poem than she intended.

Divisions, conflicts, and multiple forces within the self.   The poem's beginning indicates that the speaker experiences herself as divided. The first four lines reveal that she feels pride and disappointment in her mirror image: "I'm telling myself my face has character, / not beauty." Later, she indicates that within her mind are "remote way stations" that she visits only on occasion. Furthermore, she seems to contradict herself. Although she initially refers to her room as "a calm arrival," she goes on to describe that place negatively, as empty and confined. Early in the evening, she seems sexually attracted to the man playing the jukebox ("I would not stop him / if he touched me"), but by morning her mood is "not romantic" and she is "too tired / to look" at the male factory workers. What may be the significance of these paradoxes?

Boundaries.   In the first line, the speaker is apparently looking at a window, and later she reveals that at times she feels driven to "stare out the window" of her room. What should a reader make of these two references to such a common boundary? When the speaker observes that the men in the restaurant "do not see me," she indicates that a boundary exists between them and her. Do you think she is merely being paranoid, or do you suspect that the men are indeed ignoring her? If they *are* oblivious to her, how do you explain their behavior? Still another boundary explored in the poem is the line between night and day. What happens when the speaker crosses this line? What can night, day, and the boundary between them signify? You might also consider what the author of a literary work does with its technical boundaries. Often a poem creates boundaries in its breaks between stanzas. Yet "Night Waitress" is a continuous, unbroken text; what is the effect of Hull's making it so? At the same time, Hull doesn't always respect sentence boundaries in her lines. At several points in the poem, sentences spill over from one line to another. This poetic technique is called **enjambment**; what is its effect here?

Politics and ideology.   When, in referring to the jukebox man, the speaker declares that "I would not stop him / if he touched me," she can be taken to imply that male customers often flirt with waitresses. How might flirtation be seen as involving power, authority, and even outright domination? Do you see the poem as commenting on such things? Earlier, we raised issues of social class; these can be seen as political issues, too. How would you describe a society in which some people have "a big Cadillac" and others do not?

Carnivals and other festivities.   Although the poem does not refer to a "carnival" in any sense of that word, it does mention bars, which today are regarded by many people as places of festive retreat from work. What adjectives would you use to describe the speaker when she says that sometimes she wants "to try every bar down the street"?

Distinctions between what is universal and what is historically or culturally specific.   Try to identify anything that is historically or culturally specific about this poem's setting. Certainly the word *Slavic* and the reference to the Black Madonna indicate that the speaker has a particular background. You might also note her description of the restaurant, her use of the Cadillac as a metaphor, and her mention of the "factories" and the "refineries" that are "squatting on the bay." Although a wide range of places might fit these details, the poem's setting does not seem universal. Indeed, many readers are attracted to literature *because* it deals with specific landscapes, people, and plots. Nevertheless, these same readers usually expect to get some larger, more widely applicable meanings out of literature even as they are engaged by its specific details. Are you inclined to draw general conclusions from "Night Waitress"? If so, what general meanings do you find in it? What sorts of people do you think might learn something about themselves from reading this poem?

Relations between the public and the private, the social and the personal.   The speaker of "Night Waitress" works in a very public place, a restaurant. Yet she seems to feel isolated there, trapped in her own private world. How did she come to experience public life this way, do you think? Later, she initially seems to value her room as a private retreat, calling it "a calm arrival," but then she describes it as a place so lonely that it leads her to "stare out the window or want / to try every bar down the street." How, then, would you ultimately describe the relations between the speaker's public life and her private one? In addressing this issue, probably you need to consider whether the speaker's difficulties are merely personal or reflect a larger social disorder. When, at the end of the poem, she refers to "this frail machinery," is she referring just to herself, or is she suggesting that this phrase applies to her society in general? If she is indeed making a social observation, what do you sense are the "faults" in her society? Who else might be "fading"?

Relations between "high" culture and "low" culture.   Although the speaker does not identify the "songs / of risky love" playing on the jukebox, surely they are examples of what is called low, mass, or popular culture. Just as a lot of us are moved by such music when we hear it, so the jukebox player and the cook are engaged by it. In contrast, the poem itself can be considered an example of high culture. Often poetry is regarded as a serious art even by people who don't read it. In what ways, if any, does this poem conceivably resemble the songs it mentions? Given that author Lynda Hull is in essence playing with combinations of words, can we compare her with "the man / who leans over the jukebox nightly / pressing the combinations / of numbers"? (Actually, *numbers* has been a poetic term; centuries ago, it was commonly used as a synonym for the rhythms of poems.)

The role of performance in everyday life.   The most conspicuous performer in this poem is the cook, who "sings words / dragged up from the bottom of his lungs." But in everyday life, people often perform in the sense of taking on certain roles, even disguising their real personalities. Do you see such instances of performing in this poem? If so, where? Notice that the speaker wears a uniform; can that be considered a costume she wears while performing as a waitress?

Religious values.   The speaker clearly refers to religion when she recalls her mother's devotion to the Black Madonna, behavior that involved "praying / to her god of sorrows and visions." And although that god is "not here tonight," the speaker's description of waitressing has ritualistic overtones reminiscent of religious ceremonies. When she says, "I bring the cups. / I bring the silver," she could almost be describing preparations for Communion. In fact, she depicts the cook as wearing a religious emblem: "On his forehead / a tattooed cross furrows, / diminished when he frowns." What do you make of all this religious imagery? Might the speaker be trying to pursue certain religious values? Can she be reasonably described as looking for salvation?

Desire and pleasure.   The speaker explicitly mentions the word *desire* when she describes the emptiness she feels in her room, a feeling of desolation "that makes me stare out the window or want / to try every bar down the street." These lines may lead you to believe that her desire is basically sexual. Yet when the speaker uses the words *I want* earlier in the poem, she expresses her wish for "a song that rolls / through the night like a big Cadillac." Here, her longing does not appear sexual in nature. Is the speaker referring to at least two kinds of desire, then? Or do you see her as afflicted with basically one kind?

The body.   A notable feature of this poem is its attention to body parts. The speaker mentions her "shoulder," her "face," her mother's "face," her mother's "hands and knees," the cook's "forehead," his "lungs," her "palm," the "way stations" of her "mind," her "mouth," the factory workers' "fingers," and their "belt buckles." At the same time, the speaker never describes any particular body as a whole. What is the effect of this emphasis on mere parts? Does it connect in any way to the speaker's ultimate "fading"?

Memory.   Already we have noted the speaker's reference to her mother at the start of the poem. In what way, if any, is it significant that she engages in recollection? What circumstances in her life might have prompted the speaker to look back at the past?

Material things.   The speaker mentions cups, plates, saucers, and silverware. Evidently she's careful to "lay out" (line 8) these items in a particular order. Similarly, she reports, the room where she lives has "each book and lamp in its place" (line 32). What do you conclude from her neat ordering of these objects? Note that the only "warming" she feels in the poem comes from "the coffee urn" (line 28). Is there a possibility of her ever feeling warmth from a human being? "Box" appears multiple times: as part of the word "jukebox" (brought up twice, in lines 14 and 19) and as part of the phrase "lunch box" (line 42). With this repetition, perhaps Hull is encouraging her readers to connect "jukebox" and "lunch box" in some meaningful way. The first seems a means of entertainment, the second an object taken to work or school. But they're both part of the speaker's world; what should readers infer from that fact?

≡ A WRITING EXERCISE

We have applied several topics from our list to Lynda Hull's poem "Night Waitress." Now see you how can apply topics from the list to other literature. Next, we present two texts: the first is a famous poem, the second is a recent award-winning short story. Try to come up with several questions about one or both of these works, referring to topics on our list. Then select at least one of the questions you have formulated, and freewrite for ten minutes in response to it.

T. S. ELIOT
The Love Song of J. Alfred Prufrock

One of the most respected intellectuals of his time, Thomas Stearns Eliot (1888–1965) was a poet, playwright (Murder in the Cathedral), *and critic* (The Sacred Wood). *His poem "The Waste Land" (1922), considered a modernist masterpiece, is perhaps the last century's most influential poem. The long-running Broadway play* Cats *is based on some of Eliot's lighter poems. Born in America and educated at Harvard, Eliot lived his mature life in England. He was awarded the Nobel Prize for literature in 1948.*

> *S'io credesse che mia risposta fosse*
> *A persona che mai tornasse al mondo,*
> *Questa fiamma staria senza più scosse.*
> *Ma perciocchè giammai di questo fondo*
> *Non tornò vivo alcun, s'i'odo il vero,*
> *Senza tema d'infamia ti rispondo.°*

EPIGRAPH: **S'io . . . rispondo:** In Dante's *Inferno,* a sufferer in hell says, "If I thought I was talking to someone who might return to Earth, this flame would cease; but if what I have heard is true, no one does return; therefore, I can speak to you without fear of infamy."

Let us go then, you and I,
When the evening is spread out against the sky
Like a patient etherized upon a table;
Let us go, through certain half-deserted streets,
The muttering retreats   5
Of restless nights in one-night cheap hotels
And sawdust restaurants with oyster-shells:
Streets that follow like a tedious argument
Of insidious intent

To lead you to an overwhelming question . . .   10
Oh, do not ask, "What is it?"
Let us go and make our visit.

In the room the women come and go
Talking of Michelangelo.

The yellow fog that rubs its back upon the window panes,   15
The yellow smoke that rubs its muzzle on the window panes
Licked its tongue into the corners of the evening,
Lingered upon the pools that stand in drains,
Let fall upon its back the soot that falls from chimneys,
Slipped by the terrace, made a sudden leap,   20
And seeing that it was a soft October night,
Curled once about the house, and fell asleep.

And indeed there will be time°
For the yellow smoke that slides along the street,
Rubbing its back upon the window panes;   25
There will be time, there will be time
To prepare a face to meet the faces that you meet;
There will be time to murder and create,
And time for all the works and days° of hands
That lift and drop a question on your plate: 30
Time for you and time for me,
And time yet for a hundred indecisions,
And for a hundred visions and revisions,
Before the taking of a toast and tea.
In the room the women come and go   35
Talking of Michelangelo.
And indeed there will be time
To wonder, "Do I dare?" and, "Do I dare?" —
Time to turn back and descend the stair,

23 there will be time: An allusion to Ecclesiastes 3:1–8: "To everything there is a season,
and a time to every purpose under heaven." **29 works and days:** Hesiod's eighth-
century B.C.E. poem gave practical advice.

With a bald spot in the middle of my hair— 40
(They will say: "How his hair is growing thin!")
My morning coat, my collar mounting firmly to the chin,
My necktie rich and modest, but asserted by a simple pin—
(They will say: "But how his arms and legs are thin!")
Do I dare 45
Disturb the universe?
In a minute there is time
For decisions and revisions which a minute will reverse.

    For I have known them all already, known them all:
Have known the evenings, mornings, afternoons, 50
I have measured out my life with coffee spoons;
I know the voices dying with a dying fall
Beneath the music from a farther room.
    So how should I presume?

    And I have known the eyes already, known them all— 55
The eyes that fix you in a formulated phrase,
And when I am formulated, sprawling on a pin,
When I am pinned and wriggling on the wall,
Then how should I begin
To spit out all the butt-ends of my days and ways? 60
    And how should I presume?

    And I have known the arms already, known them all—
Arms that are braceleted and white and bare
(But in the lamplight, downed with light brown hair!)
    Is it perfume from a dress 65
    That makes me so digress?
Arms that lie along a table, or wrap about a shawl.
    And should I then presume?
    And how should I begin?

    Shall I say, I have gone at dusk through narrow streets, 70
And watched the smoke that rises from the pipes
Of lonely men in shirtsleeves, leaning out of windows? . . .
I should have been a pair of ragged claws
Scuttling across the floors of silent seas.

    And the afternoon, the evening, sleeps so peacefully! 75
Smoothed by long fingers,
Asleep . . . tired . . . or it malingers,
Stretched on the floor, here beside you and me.
Should I, after tea and cakes and ices,
Have the strength to force the moment to its crisis? 80
But though I have wept and fasted, wept and prayed,

Though I have seen my head (grown slightly bald) brought in upon a
    platter,°
I am no prophet—and here's no great matter;
I have seen the moment of my greatness flicker,
And I have seen the eternal Footman hold my coat, and snicker,   85
    And in short, I was afraid.

    And would it have been worth it, after all,
After the cups, the marmalade, the tea,
Among the porcelain, among some talk of you and me,
Would it have been worth while   90
To have bitten off the matter with a smile,
To have squeezed the universe into a ball
To roll it toward some overwhelming question,
To say: "I am Lazarus,° come from the dead,
Come back to tell you all, I shall tell you all"—   95
If one, settling a pillow by her head,
    Should say: "That is not what I meant at all;
    That is not it, at all."

    And would it have been worth it, after all,
Would it have been worth while,   100
After the sunsets and the dooryards and the sprinkled streets,
After the novels, after the teacups, after the skirts that trail along the
    floor—
And this, and so much more?—
It is impossible to say just what I mean!
But as if a magic lantern° threw the nerves in patterns on a screen: 105
Would it have been worth while
If one, settling a pillow or throwing off a shawl,
And turning toward the window, should say:
    "That is not it at all,
    That is not what I meant, at all."   110

No! I am not Prince Hamlet, nor was meant to be;
Am an attendant lord,° one that will do
To swell a progress,° start a scene or two
Advise the prince: withal, an easy tool,
Deferential, glad to be of use,   115
Politic, cautious, and meticulous;
Full of high sentence, but a bit obtuse;
At times, indeed, almost ridiculous—
Almost, at times, the Fool.

---

82 head . . . platter: Like John the Baptist (Matt. 14:1–12).   **94 "I am Lazarus":** Raised from the dead by Jesus.   **105 magic lantern:** Precursor of the slide projector. **112 attendant lord:** Like Polonius in Shakespeare's *Hamlet*.   **113 progress:** State procession.

I grow old . . . I grow old . . .   120
I shall wear the bottoms of my trowsers rolled.

    Shall I part my hair behind?° Do I dare to eat a peach?°
I shall wear white flannel trowsers, and walk upon the beach.
I have heard the mermaids singing, each to each.

I do not think that they will sing to me.   125

I have seen them riding seaward on the waves,
Combing the white hair of the waves blown back
When the wind blows the water white and black.

We have lingered in the chambers of the sea
By seagirls wreathed with seaweed red and brown,   130
Till human voices wake us, and we drown.   [1917]

121–22 trowsers rolled . . . part my hair behind: The latest fashion; **eat a peach:**
Considered a risky fruit.

ALLISON ALSUP
Old Houses

*Although she grew up in Oakland, California, Allison Alsup now lives in New Orleans.
In fact, the following story appeared in a 2012 issue of the* New Orleans Review.
Subsequently, "Old Houses" was honored by being selected for The O. Henry Prize
Stories 2014. *Besides publishing fiction, Alsup teaches in a program for high school
students called Urban League College Track. She is also coauthor of* The French
Quarter Drinking Companion *and a contributor to the New Orleans tourist site
GoNOLA.com.*

As they gather for the spring block party on the Peabodys' extra lot, the residents of Hillcrest Way think how lucky they are to live in old houses and among
the kind of people who understand old houses and their architecture—Tudor,
Colonial, Spanish Mediterranean. Every house on the street is different but in
keeping with the neighborhood, scaled and proportioned. *Houses that know
who they are,* Dennis Petersen calls them in an effort to distinguish them from
the ones down the hill. The homes on the roads below are smaller, built on
stingier lots and in some cases, built too late to have the kind of distinct identity
that old houses do. His own house is Norman, the first on the block, and built
over a century ago.

    The latecomers make their way down the sidewalks towards the Peabodys'
lot, the women holding cheese trays and pasta salads, the men bottles of wine.
They are all grateful to Richard and Katherine for having purchased the lot and
for having saved it from the builders. They have seen what developers can do.

When fire swept through the hills across town, the builders razed everything and erected rows of white boxes with no room for gardens or yards for children to play in. So after they place their offerings on the folding table buffet on the Peabodys' lawn, they all compliment Katherine on her growing collection of irises. They note, as always, with genuine delight, how the lot opens the view in just the right spot: a slice of steel blue bay and beyond, the studded grid of downtown San Francisco. The view is better they note, from *this* side.

They are fond of the phrase *original to the house*. Moldings and in-laid oak floors original to the house. Built-in cabinets, box beams, coved ceilings and stained glass original to the house. Bannisters, mullions, muntins, french doors, glass knobs, telephone niches, carved mantles, fireplace grates, chandeliers, porthole windows and *working* shutters, all original to the house. The little bedroom on the ground floor, original to the house. All the old houses on Hillcrest have one — just a few steps from the kitchen and the back stairs. They don't call it a maid's room, except in private. Of course, no one has a maid anymore, only a woman who cleans and a gardener who comes once a week to mow and round up the leaves. Live-ins are for those in the hills above, people who can't be bothered to walk their own dogs.

In some of their houses, the little room has been converted into an office, sometimes into a discreet spot for the television. Five years ago, the Welshes lined the back wall with double-glazed windows and made a music studio where he could play the violin and she the French horn. The children played too, before they went to college and moved away. Since their remodel, Judith Goldman times her evening walks to coincide with the Welshes' practice hour; sometimes Suzanne Collier joins her and they share news of their daughters who attend neighboring colleges in Massachusetts. Sometimes however, Judith prefers to walk alone. The faint sound of the Russian composers and the sight of the cool evening fog weaving through the tall pines makes her think of summers spent as a girl in upstate New York. She had her own little room remade into a library complete with a gas fireplace and matching highback chairs. When she closes the door, her husband knows not to bother her.

They stand clustered about the grass, sampling salads and refilling wine glasses. They like to think about all that their houses have witnessed. They all know the story of the Petersen's house — built for a bachelor sea captain at the turn of the last century. Of course, there had been sea captains then. They all agree that with his thick sweaters and ruddy face, Dennis Petersens' does indeed resemble a sea captain.

You never own an old house, they agree, you just safeguard it for the next generation.

By this, they mean their children, the eldest of whom have scattered. And really, given the way prices and taxes have risen, inheriting a house on Hillcrest is the next generation's only hope for an old house in a good neighborhood. Of course, they themselves will never leave. They'll have to be carried out feet first, they say, though they are careful to speak softly so that the old doctor won't hear. His house, just across the street from the Peabodys' lawn, rises above the

5

thick clump of Katherine's yellow irises. He is very old now and must decline the invitations to the block party. He sends his wishes from behind the closed curtains of his white stucco Spanish Mediterranean. They do not say so, but the other residents of Hillcrest are relieved. They have never understood why he chose to stay after what happened. They wouldn't have been able to.

Occasionally, an article appears in the paper, marking the tenth, twentieth, now thirtieth anniversary of the killings — the doctor's first wife and older daughter, home from college for a visit between semesters. The case remains unsolved; the articles end with the usual plea for information. They have written to the paper and asked that the name Hillcrest be withheld from the article; it gives the wrong impression of the neighborhood. But of course, the paper still prints the street name and inevitably one of their kids learns of the crimes and they're forced to tell the version they've agreed upon. They assure their children all this happened long before they moved in, another era really. They're more careful now. It's why Madeleine Welsh was right to phone the police about the stranger looking over the Colliers' garden gate. Below them is a different city, where hooded youths with guns roam the flat streets. There isn't a wall between them and the rest of the world. They must all watch out for one another. It's why the block parties are so important. Still, what's past is past.

They omit certain details. They don't tell the children the way the killer bound the two women with their own stockings or what he did to the girl. They don't mention that it was the younger daughter, the one still in high school, who walked home from class to find her mother and sister on the living room floor just a few feet from the piano. Nor do they say that the front door had not been forced open or that the prime suspect lived just two doors down, in what is now the Dillingers' house: a shaggy-haired, hollow-eyed teenage boy whose second story window faced the doctor's house. They do not admit what they have all imagined from the black-and-white photo of the victims reprinted in the paper each year: the scrubbed co-ed opening the door, her pressed miniskirt, her straight smile and full brunette hair. *Please, come in.* They especially do not like to think about that. As parents, they have aimed to instill good manners in their own children. The police investigated, but couldn't make a case against the boy. That hasn't changed, the adults agree. Even with all the technology now, they have no faith in the cops. Instead they tell their children, That was long time ago. They've learned to be more careful now. They watch out for one another.

Everyone claps encouragement as James and Madeleine Welsh arrive carrying their instruments in black armored cases. Each year they learn a new piece just for the party. James has never told his wife this, but he believes their music placates ghosts. Nor has Suzanne Collier ever revealed that years ago, after she saw the girl's picture in the paper, she began to hear odd noises. She said nothing of it, even to Anne Dillinger, who had confided that she once hired a woman to burn sage in every room of their house. Judith Goldman keeps most thoughts to herself. Sometimes when she closes the door to her small library, she sits in her highback chair and thinks about when the house was new. She imagines the young girls who once slept in her little room. She

10

pictures their raw fingers and plain faces, the way they rose from narrow beds early in the morning to pin back mopstraight hair and light the fireplace. She imagines the routine of their days, cooking and cleaning for a family not their own, and how the girls must have longed for the few dark hours to themselves in this tiny room. She thinks of her own daughter, now three thousand miles away in a little dorm room. When Judith calls, her daughter does not seem relieved to hear from her or interested in news from the neighborhood. Judith doesn't understand it, but she detects accusation, even disdain, in her daughter's voice.

Wine glasses are refilled, then everyone quiets as James and Madeleine settle their music stand on the grass. Anne Dillinger gently guides her husband away from the spinach dip. The first tendrils of the evening fog have crept in and some of the women slip on jackets they have knowingly brought. There is a general murmur about *San Francisco summers*. And there's a breeze; the sheet music ripples. Dennis Petersen steps forward and with thick, pink fingers, steadies the sheets. His tall frame looms to the side of the metal stand and they all smile, certain that in a past life, he held the pitted wood of a ship's wheel with the same measured calm.

Keeping their backs to the doctor's house, they tell themselves that any place as old as Hillcrest has stories. All old houses do. It's part of their character. The older neighbors stand smiling as the younger parents gather their children, pull them close and whisper, Listen. Then Madeleine's lips nestle into the brass mouthpiece of her horn, and James lowers his bow to the strings.

[2012]

CHAPTER 5

The Writing Process

In Chapter 6, we discuss how to write about each of the three literary genres featured in this book. Here, however, we suggest how to write about a literary work of any genre. To make our advice concrete, we mostly trace what one student did as she worked on a writing assignment for a course much like yours. Each student chose a single poem from the syllabus and wrote a 600-word argument paper on it for a general audience. We focus on the writing process of a student named Abby Hazelton.

Ultimately, Abby chose to write about William Wordsworth's "The Solitary Reaper." In his own day, Wordsworth (1770–1850) was poet laureate of England, and he continues to be regarded as a major British Romantic poet. He and fellow poet Samuel Taylor Coleridge collaborated on *Lyrical Ballads* (1798), a collection of verse that became a landmark of Romantic poetry. In his preface to the second edition two years later, Wordsworth famously defined *poetry* as "emotion recollected in tranquillity," contended that it should draw on "common life," and called for it to incorporate "language really used by men." Like many other Romantics, Wordsworth celebrated scenes of nature and country life while deploring the increasing spread of cities. "The Solitary Reaper" appeared in his 1807 *Poems in Two Volumes*.

Before examining Abby's writing process, read Wordsworth's poem.

WILLIAM WORDSWORTH
The Solitary Reaper

Behold her, single in the field,
    Yon solitary Highland Lass!
Reaping and singing by herself;
    Stop here, or gently pass!
Alone she cuts and binds the grain,   5
And sings a melancholy strain;
O listen! for the Vale profound
Is overflowing with the sound.

No Nightingale did ever chaunt
    More welcome notes to weary bands   10
Of travellers in some shady haunt,
    Among Arabian sands:

A voice so thrilling ne'er was heard
In spring-time from the Cuckoo-bird,
Breaking the silence of the seas   15
Among the farthest Hebrides.

Will no one tell me what she sings? —
    Perhaps the plaintive numbers flow
For old, unhappy, far-off things,
    And battles long ago: 20
Or is it some more humble lay,
Familiar matter of to-day?
Some natural sorrow, loss, or pain,
That has been, and may be again?

Whate'er the theme, the Maiden sang   25
    As if her song could have no ending;
I saw her singing at her work,
    And o'er the sickle bending; —
I listen'd, motionless and still;
And, as I mounted up the hill,   30
The music in my heart I bore,
Long after it was heard no more.   *[1807]*

Once she chose to write about Wordsworth's poem for her paper, Abby engaged in four sorts of activities: (1) exploring, (2) planning, (3) composing, and (4) revising. As we describe each, keep in mind that these activities need not be consecutive. Abby moved back and forth among them as she worked on her assignment.

Strategies for Exploring

As you read a literary work, you are bound to interpret and judge it. Yet not all reading is close reading, which can also be called **critical reading**. This process involves carefully and self-consciously analyzing various aspects of a text, including its meanings, its effects, and its treatment of typical elements of its genre. When you read a work closely and critically, you also note questions it raises for you — issues you might explore further in class discussion and writing. Indeed, close reading is a process of self-reflection. During this process, you monitor your own response to the text and try to identify why you see the text the way you do.

Exploring, the first stage of writing an essay about literature, is this particular process of reading. As we explain in Chapter 4, it specifically involves the following:

- Making predictions as you read
- Rereading the text with a different focus each time, including at least one stage in which you read aloud
- Comparing the text with your personal experience
- Tracing patterns and breaks from these patterns

- Noting ambiguities
- Considering the author's alternatives
- Generating questions
- Considering how the text deals with topics that have preoccupied literary studies
- Formulating a tentative claim
- Using informal writing to move through all these steps, including commenting in the text's margins, note-taking, freewriting, creating a "dialectical notebook," and playfully revising the text

≡ A WRITING EXERCISE

Do at least ten minutes of freewriting about Wordsworth's poem, keeping it nearby so that you can consult it if you need to. In particular, try to raise questions about the poem, and consider which of these may be worth addressing in a more formal paper.

Here is an excerpt from Abby's freewriting.

> I see that this poem consists of four stanzas, each of which is eight lines long. But these stanzas have different emphases. The first stanza is a series of commands. The speaker tells people to "Behold," "Stop here, or gently pass," and "listen." The second stanza mainly describes the reaper. The third stanza is basically a bunch of questions. The fourth is the speaker's recollection of his experience in general. So I could write a paper about how this poem changes as it moves along and why the stanzas shift in emphasis. But one problem with a paper like that is that it might get me bogged down in mechanically moving from stanza to stanza. I don't want that to happen. Another thing I could do is answer one of the speaker's own questions, which are about what kind of song the reaper is singing. Evidently this "Highland Lass" is using a Scottish dialect that he doesn't understand. But I'm just as ignorant as he is about the song. I guess I'm more likely to contribute some analysis of my own if I come up with a question myself. I'm struck by the fact that he doesn't give us much sense of the reaper's song. There's no way that a printed poem could convey the reaper's tune, but still. And the words are foreign to the speaker. But I'm surprised that he doesn't make a little effort to convey at least some of the song's lyrics even if they're foreign words that he might hear wrong or misspell. How can I as a reader join him in experiencing the beauty of her song if I don't learn any of its words? I wonder if we're supposed to see the poem as being more about the speaker than about the reaper. More specifically, maybe we're supposed to be a little disturbed that he's a British intellectual who is making a spectacle out of a foreign woman from the working class. At any rate, he seems bent on controlling this experience even as he invites us to share it. Another question for me is, Why does he shift from present tense to past tense in the

last stanza? This change is really curious to me. I don't see anything earlier on that prepares me for it. First, we're led to believe that the speaker is observing the reaper right then and there, but at the end he speaks as if this occurred in the past, though maybe the recent past. This inconsistency in the time frame makes me think that in some important way the overall poem is about time. At any rate, I'm drawn to the inconsistency because it's so blatant. If I wrote about it, I might still devote a paragraph to each stanza, but I'd be starting with the last one and referring back to the others in order to explain that stanza. What I still have to figure out, though, is what exactly the poem is saying about time when it makes the shift of tense.

Freewriting enabled Abby to raise several questions. At the same time, she realized that her paper could not deal with everything that puzzled her. When you first get an assignment like hers, you may fear that you will have nothing to say. But you will come up with a lot of material if, like Abby, you take time for exploration. As we have suggested, it's a process of examining potential subjects through writing, discussion, and just plain thinking. One of your challenges will be to choose among the various issues you have formulated. At the end of this excerpt from her freewriting, Abby is on the verge of choosing to analyze the poem's shift of tense in its final stanza. For her, this shift is an interesting change from a pattern, the poem's previous uses of present tense. Abby has not yet decided how to explain this shift; at the moment, it remains for her a mystery. But her paper would achieve little if it focused just on aspects of the poem that are easy to interpret. Though Abby has more thinking to do about the poem's shift of tense, it seems a promising subject for her precisely because it puzzles her.

Strategies for Planning

Planning for an assignment like Abby's involves five main activities:

1. Choosing the text you will analyze
2. Identifying your audience
3. Identifying the main issue, claim, and evidence you will present
4. Identifying your assumptions
5. Determining how you will organize your argument, including how you will demonstrate your process of reasoning

CHOOSE A TEXT

Abby considered several poems before choosing one for her paper. She settled on Wordsworth's for five reasons. First, it was a text that left her with plenty of questions. Second, she believed that these questions could be issues for other readers. Third, she felt increasingly able to *argue* about the poem—that is, to make and support claims about it. Fourth, she believed that she could adequately analyze the poem within the assignment's word limit. Finally, Wordsworth's poem drew her because she had heard about the Romantic movement in English literature and was curious to study an example of it.

Faced with the same assignment, you might choose a different poem than Abby did. Still, the principles that she followed are useful. Think about them whenever you are free to decide which texts you will write about. With some assignments, of course, you may need a while to decide which text is best for you. And later, after you have made your decision, you may want to make a switch. For example, you may find yourself changing your mind once you have done a complete draft. Frustrated by the text you have chosen, you may realize that another inspires you more. If so, consider making a substitution. Naturally, you will feel more able to switch if you have ample time left to write the paper, so avoid waiting to start your paper until just before it is due.

IDENTIFY YOUR AUDIENCE

To determine what your readers will see as an issue and to make your claims about it persuasive to them, you need to develop an audience profile. Perhaps your instructor will specify your audience. You may be asked, for example, to imagine yourself writing for a particular group in a particular situation. If you were Abby, how would you analyze "The Solitary Reaper" for an orchestra wanting to know what this poem implies about music? Even when not required of you, such an exercise can be fun and thought provoking for you as you plan a paper.

Most often, though, instructors ask students to write for a "general" audience, the readership that Abby was asked to address. Assume that a general audience is one that will want evidence for your claims. While this audience will include your instructor, let it also include your classmates, since in class discussions they will be an audience for you whenever you speak. Besides, your class may engage in peer review, with students giving one another feedback on their drafts.

IDENTIFY YOUR ISSUE, CLAIM, AND EVIDENCE

When you have written papers for previous classes, you may have been most concerned with coming up with a thesis. Maybe you did not encounter the term *issue* at all. But good planning for a paper does entail identifying the main issue you will address. Once you have sensed what that issue is, try phrasing it as a question. If the answer would be obvious to your readers, be cautious, for you really do not have an issue if the problem you are raising can be easily resolved.

Also, try to identify what *kind* of issue you will focus on. For help, look at our list of various types (pp. 54–61). Within "The Solitary Reaper," the speaker raises an issue of fact: he wants to know what sort of song the reaper is singing. But as someone writing about Wordsworth's poem, Abby wanted to focus on another kind of issue, which she decided is best regarded as an issue of pattern. More precisely, she thought her main question might be, What should we conclude from the inconsistency in pattern that occurs when the final stanza shifts to past tense? To be sure, Abby recognized that addressing this issue would lead to issues of theme and of cause and effect, for she would have to consider why Wordsworth shifts tenses and how the shift relates to his overall subject.

Now that she had identified her main issue, Abby had to determine her main claim. Perhaps you have grown comfortable with the term *thesis* and want to keep using it. Bear in mind, though, that your thesis is the main *claim* you will make and proceed to support. And when, as Abby did, you put your main issue as a question, then your main claim is your answer to that question. Sometimes you will come up with question and answer simultaneously. Once in a while, you may even settle on your answer first, not being certain yet how to word the question. Whatever the case, planning for your paper involves articulating both the question (the issue) and the answer (your main claim). Try actually writing both down, making sure to phrase your main issue as a question and your main claim as the answer. Again, Abby's main issue was, What should we conclude from the inconsistency in pattern that occurs when the final stanza shifts to past tense? After much thought, she expressed her main claim this way:

> One possible justification for the shift to past tense is that it reminds us of the speaker's inability to halt the passage of time. He would like to freeze his encounter with the reaper, keeping it always in the present. But as the shift in tense indicates, time goes on, making the encounter part of the speaker's past. Perhaps, therefore, the poem's real subject is the idea that time is always in flux.

Audiences usually want evidence, and as we noted earlier, most arguments you write about literature will need to cite details of the work itself. Because direct quotation is usually an effective move, Abby planned to elaborate her claim by citing several of Wordsworth's references to time. Remember, though, that you need to avoid seeming willfully selective when you quote. While Abby expected to quote from Wordsworth's last stanza, she also knew she had to relate it to earlier lines so that her readers would see her as illuminating the basic subject of the whole poem. In particular, she looked for language in the first three stanzas that might hint at the speaker's lack of control over time, thereby previewing the last stanza's emphasis.

IDENTIFY YOUR ASSUMPTIONS

Often, to think about particular challenges of your paper is to think about your assumptions. Remember that a big category of assumptions is warrants; these are what lead you to call certain things evidence for your claims. Abby knew that one of her warrants was an assumption about Wordsworth himself — that he was not being sloppy when he shifted tenses in his last stanza. Rarely will your paper need to admit all the warrants on which it relies. Most of the time, your task will be to guess which warrants your readers do want stated. Abby felt there was at least one warrant she would have to spell out — her belief that the poem's verb tenses reveal something about the speaker's state of mind.

DETERMINE YOUR ORGANIZATION

To make sure their texts seem organized and demonstrate the process of reasoning, most writers first do an **outline**, a list of their key points in the order they will appear. Outlines are indeed a good idea, but bear in mind that there are various kinds. One popular type, which you may already know, is the **sentence outline**. As the name implies, it lists the writer's key points in sentence form. Its advantages are obvious: this kind of outline forces you to develop a detailed picture of your argument's major steps, and it leaves you with sentences you can then incorporate into your paper. Unfortunately, sentence outlines tend to discourage flexibility. Because they demand much thought and energy, you may hesitate to revise them, even if you come to feel your paper would work better with a new structure.

A second, equally familiar outline is the **topic outline**, a list in which the writer uses a few words to signify the main subjects that he or she will discuss. Because it is sketchy, this kind of outline allows writers to go back and change plans if necessary. Nevertheless, a topic outline may fail to provide all the guidance a writer needs.

We find a third type useful: a **rhetorical purpose outline**. As with the first two, you list the major sections of your paper. Next, you briefly indicate two things for each section: the effect you want it to have on your audience and how you will achieve that effect. Here is the rhetorical purpose outline that Abby devised for her paper.

INTRODUCTION

The audience needs to know the text I'll discuss.	I'll identify Wordsworth's poem.
The audience must know my main issue.	I'll point out that the poem is puzzling in its shift of tenses at the end.
The audience must know my main claim.	I'll argue that the shift to past tense suggests that the poem's real subject is the inability of human beings to halt the passage of time.

ANALYSIS OF THE POEM'S FINAL STANZA

The audience needs to see in detail how the final stanza's shift to past tense signals the speaker's inability to control the passage of time.	I will point out not only the shift of tense but also other words in the last stanza that imply time moves on. I will note as well that music is an especially fleeting medium, so the reaper's song was bound to fade.

ANALYSIS OF THE PRECEDING STANZAS

To accept that the passage of time is the poem's real concern, the audience must see that the preceding stanzas hint at this subject.	I will analyze the first three stanzas in turn, showing how each implies the speaker is frustrated over his inability to control time.

CONCLUSION

The audience may need to be clearer about what I consider the ultimate *tone* of the poem.	I will say that although the poem can be thought of as a warm tribute to the singing reaper, the final emphasis on the passage of time is pessimistic in tone, and the speaker winds up as "solitary" as the reaper.

For your own rhetorical purpose outlines, you may want to use phrases rather than sentences. If you do use sentences, as Abby did, you do not have to write all that many. Note that Abby wrote relatively few as she stated the effects she would aim for and her strategies for achieving those effects. Thus, she was not tremendously invested in preserving her original outline. She felt free to change it if it failed to prove helpful.

Strategies for Composing

Composing is not always distinguishable from exploring, planning, and revising. As you prepare for your paper, you may jot down words or whole sentences. Once you begin a draft, you may alter that draft in several ways before you complete it. You may be especially prone to making changes in drafts if you use a computer, for word processing enables you to jump around in your text, revisiting and revising what you have written.

Still, most writers feel that doing a draft is an activity in its own right, and a major one at that. The next chapter presents various tips for writing about specific genres, and Chapter 7 discusses writing research-based papers. Meanwhile, here are some tips to help you with composing in general.

DECIDE ON A TITLE

You may be inclined to let your **title** be the same as that of the text you discuss. Were you to write about Wordsworth's poem, then, you would be calling your own paper "The Solitary Reaper." But often such mimicry backfires. For one thing, it may lead your readers to think that you are unoriginal and perhaps even lazy. Also, you risk confusing your audience, since your paper would actually be about Wordsworth's poem rather than being the poem itself. So take the time to come up with a title of your own. Certainly it may announce the text you will focus on, but let it do more. In particular, use your title to indicate the main claim you will be making. With just a few words, you can preview the argument to come.

MAKE CHOICES ABOUT YOUR STYLE

Perhaps you have been told to "sound like yourself" when you write. Yet that can be a difficult demand (especially if you are not sure what your "self" is really like). Above all, the **style** you choose depends on your audience and purpose. In writing an argument for a general audience, probably you would do best to avoid the extremes of pomposity and breezy informality. Try to stick with words you know well, and if you do want to use some that are only hazily familiar to you, check their dictionary definitions first.

At some point in our lives, probably all of us have been warned not to use *I* in our writing. In the course you are taking, however, you may be asked to write about your experiences. If so, you will find *I* hard to avoid. Whether to use it does become a real question when you get assignments like Abby's, which require you chiefly to make an argument about a text. Since you are supposed to focus on that text, your readers may be disconcerted if you keep referring to yourself. Even so, you need not assume that your personal life is irrelevant to the task. Your opening paragraph might refer to your personal encounters with the text as a way of establishing the issue you will discuss. A personal anecdote might serve as a forceful conclusion to your paper. Moreover, before you reach the conclusion, you might orient your readers to the structure of your paper by using certain expressions that feature the word *I*: for example, *As I suggested earlier, As I have noted, As I argue later.* In general, you may be justified in saying *I* at certain moments. When tempted to use this pronoun, though, consider whether it really is your best move.

Arguments about literature are most compelling when supported by quotations, but be careful not to quote excessively. If you constantly repeat other people's words, providing few of your own, your readers will hardly get a sense of you as an author. Moreover, a paper full of quotation marks is hard to read. Make sure to quote selectively, remembering that sometimes you can simply paraphrase. When you do quote, try to cite only the words you need. You do not have to reproduce a whole line or sentence if one word is enough to support your point.

When summarizing what happens in a literary work, be careful not to shift tenses as you go along. Your reader may be confused if you shift back and forth between past and present. We suggest that you stick primarily to the present tense, which is the tense that literary critics customarily employ. For example, instead of saying that the speaker *praised* the lass, say that he *praises* her.

DRAFT AN INTRODUCTION

As a general principle, use your introduction to identify as quickly and efficiently as possible

- the main text that you will analyze;
- the main issue about it that you will address; and
- the main claim that you will develop in response to that issue.

Don't waste time with grand philosophical statements such as "Society doesn't always appreciate the work that everyone does," or "Over the centuries, much literature has been about work," or "William Wordsworth was a great British Romantic poet."

Remember that your main issue should be a significant question with no obvious answer. Try using one or more of the following strategies to establish that issue at the start of your essay:

- **State the issue as, indeed, a question.** For example: "Why, conceivably, does Wordsworth shift to the past tense in his poem's final stanza?"

- **Apply a word like *puzzling, confusing, mysterious*, or *curious* to whatever feature your issue will be about.** For example: "Because Wordsworth uses present tense for much of the poem, it is puzzling that he turns to past tense at the very end."

- **Through personal reference, state that you were first puzzled by a particular feature of the work but are now able to interpret it.** For example: "At first, I was confused when Wordsworth shifted to the past tense, but now I have arrived at a possible explanation for this move."

- **Indicate that you aim to help other readers of the work, who may have trouble understanding the feature of it you will focus on.** For example: "Quite a few readers of Wordsworth's poem may have difficulty seeing why he shifts to the past tense at the end. There is, however, a possible explanation for this move."

- **Indicate that you will express disagreement with existing or possible interpretations.** For example: "While some readers of Wordsworth's poem may feel that his shift to the past tense shows a wonderful ability to preserve his experience with the reaper, a more plausible interpretation is that it shows his isolation after meeting her."

LIMIT PLOT SUMMARY

Short stories and plays spin tales. So do many poems and essays. But if you are writing about a literary text that is narrative in form, don't spend much of your paper just summarizing the narrative. Developing a genuine argument about the work involves more than recounting its plot. Here are strategies you can use to limit this:

- **Assume that your reader knows the basic plot and needs only a few brief reminders of its key elements.**

- **Keep in mind that your main purpose is to put forth, explain, and support a *claim* about the text—your answer to some question you raise about it.**

- **After your introduction, try to begin each new paragraph with a subclaim that helps you develop your main claim.** Use the rest of the paragraph to elaborate and provide evidence for this subclaim. *Don't* begin a paragraph simply by recording a plot incident, for doing so is liable to bog you down in sheer summary.

- **Instead of reciting plot details, write about how the work you are analyzing is *constructed*.** Make observations about specific methods that the author uses to present the story, including techniques of organization and characterization. For example, rather than saying, "The speaker in Wordsworth's poem wonders what the woman is singing," state and develop a point like "Wordsworth chooses not to translate the woman's song for us; instead, he depicts the speaker as not knowing her words, so that the poem becomes mostly about the effect of her song as sheer musical notes."

- **Instead of turning frequently to plot details, try to linger on some of the author's specific language, exploring possible definitions of particular words.** For example, rather than saying, "The speaker in Wordsworth's poem remembers the woman's music," examine possible meanings of the word *bore* in the poem's next-to-last line, "The music in my heart I bore." *Bore* can simply mean "carried," and probably that is one meaning that Wordsworth has in mind here. But it can also mean "engraved, deeply inscribed," and perhaps Wordsworth wants us to think of this definition, too.

DECIDE HOW TO REFER TO THE AUTHOR'S LIFE AND INTENTIONS

Be cautious about relating the work to the author's life. Sometimes a certain character within the work may indeed express the author's own views, but don't simply assume that a character speaks for the author. Even the *I* of a first-person poem may differ significantly from its creator. True, many literary works are at least somewhat autobiographical, based on one or more aspects of the author's life. Nevertheless, even works that are largely autobiographical may not be entirely so. Besides, knowledge of the author's life won't always help you figure out his or her text. Wordsworth may have derived "The Solitary Reaper" from a personal encounter, but we must still interpret the particular poem he proceeded to write. So,

- **Be careful in linking a work to the author's own circumstances.** Such connections can be legitimate, but the more you push them, the more you may risk distorting the work's exact design. You also risk neglecting the author's artistic achievement. Not everyone who hears a reaper sing could turn this event into a poem!

Much of what you write about a literary work will reflect your understanding of its author's intentions. Needless to say, you can't peer into the author's mind. Rather, you'll make hypotheses about the author's aims. So,

- **Sometimes, at least, admit that you are guessing at what the author thought.** Often, your reader will assume that you are speculating about the author's aims, but your argument about them can be more persuasive if, at times, you acknowledge that you're trying to come up with the best hypothesis rather than stating an absolute fact. Take care, however, to explain why your guesses are logical.

- **If you suspect that the author might object to your view of the text, feel free to acknowledge such possible disagreements.** In fact, many theorists argue that a literary work may differ from how its author sees it. They refuse, therefore, to treat the author as an absolute authority on the work. D. H. Lawrence's advice was "Trust the tale, not the teller." Even if Lawrence is right, of course, you must show how *your* interpretation of a text manages to make sense of it.

- **Feel free to concede that your analysis of the work isn't the only reasonable one.** You can develop your main claim about a literary work partly by noting and addressing ways in which other readers may disagree with you about it. Bear in mind, though, that you will annoy your own audience if you come across as dogmatic. Be as fair as you can to views different from yours. Actually, your readers will appreciate it if at times you concede that yours is not the only reasonable interpretation. You can even specify one or more alternatives. Of course, you would still try to make a case for *your* explanation, perhaps by saying why it is *more plausible* or *more helpful* than its rivals. But speak of these competitors with respect instead of just dismissing them with scorn.

RECOGNIZE AND AVOID LOGICAL FALLACIES

Although arguments presented in literary texts are often not logical, your arguments about these texts should be. Readers do not expect a poem's speaker, for example, to present cogently reasoned arguments to her lover, nor do they expect a lament for the lost passions of youth to be anything but subjective. But different kinds of writing have different conventions. What works in poetry may not be appropriate in an argument. The kinds of serious arguments you are expected to create cannot be successful using heartfelt emotion alone. When you write about literature, shaky thinking might cause your audience to dismiss your ideas. Your claims and the assumptions behind them should be clear and reasoned. If they are not, you might be committing a **fallacy**, a common term for unsound reasoning.

In the next several paragraphs, we discuss typical logical fallacies. Some of them are especially relevant to literary studies, and for all of them we provide examples related to "The Solitary Reaper." We do not want you to brood over this list, seeing it as a catalog of sins to which you might fall prey. If you constantly fear being accused of fallacies, you might be too paralyzed to make claims at all! In our discussion of fallacies, we also identify circumstances in which your audience might *not* object to a particular fallacy. In addition, we suggest how a writer might revise such claims to be more persuasive. Indeed, the main value in studying fallacies is to identify ways you might develop arguments more effectively.

One of the most common fallacies, *ad hominem* (Latin: "toward the man"), is probably the easiest to commit because it is the hardest to resist. Instead of doing the hard work of analyzing the claim and the evidence, we simply ignore them and attack the character of the person making the argument. Instead of trying to figure out what is going on in a complex work of literature, we say, "How can you take seriously a poem about love written by a manic depressive who commits suicide?" It is best to focus on the message, not the messenger.

A related fallacy, **begging the question** (a kind of circular reasoning in which the statement being argued is already assumed to have been decided) is also involved in this example since it is assumed (not proved) that unstable poets cannot have cogent insights about love.

In writing about "The Solitary Reaper," a classmate of Abby's ignored whatever argument the poem is making and focused on Wordsworth's credibility as an observer: "British intellectuals have been either romanticizing or degrading country people for centuries. Whatever Wordsworth thinks about the 'Highland Lass' is almost certainly wrong." First of all, the speaker of the poem should not be automatically equated with the poet. When they write, poets and fictional writers construct personae that may or may not reflect their own views. Second, attacking Wordsworth is a fallacy for several reasons. It first has to be demonstrated that the poet is a British intellectual, that intellectuals have consistently misrepresented rural people, and that the speaker has done so in this particular case. The classmate should revise her claim so that it deals with the words in the text, not her view of the poet's credibility.

Professional historians, mathematicians, and philosophers usually cite other professionals working in their field; that is, they **appeal to authority** to bolster their credibility. Disciplinary knowledge is created by a community of scholars who cite the ideas of its members as evidence for their claims. The warrant is that recognized authorities know what they are talking about. Quoting them is persuasive. But not completely: appeals to authority can also be fallacious. Literary critics, like other thinkers, often disagree. Just citing an expert does not conclusively prove your claim. A classmate of Abby's, for example, quoted a critic, Ian Lancashire, who says that the narrator "transcends the limitations of mortality," but the student did not give his own reasons or his own evidence for thinking this way. This appeal to critical authority without giving reasons or evidence is a fallacy because a sound argument would at least have to consider other critics. An argument is a reasoning process in which claims are supported, not simply asserted, even if they come from an expert.

A related fallacy involves using quotations from unreliable sources. Although the Internet is often a valuable tool, students sometimes use it uncritically. If you went to the search engine Google and entered Wordsworth's "The Solitary Reaper," you would quickly find Ian Lancashire's essay, and since he is a professor at the University of Toronto with many publications on this and other Romantic topics, citing him is appropriate. But some of the commentators noted by the Google search are students, perhaps English majors who have written a paper for a course on the Romantic poets. Using them as authorities would damage your judgment and credibility.

Equally harmful to the soundness of your argument is to rely too heavily on personal experience as evidence for your claim. Personal experience can sometimes be compelling and authoritative. Indeed, many critics have successfully used their own experiences with discrimination to create cogent arguments. But they rarely rely exclusively on personal experience. Instead they blend relevant experience with textual and critical specifics. Telling your readers that "The Solitary Reaper" is factually flawed because you never saw harvesters work alone when you worked on your uncle's farm would be a fallacy.

Actually, the previous example of using personal experience as authority is also unsound because the personal sample is too small to warrant a reasonable conclusion. It is hard to convince your audience if you claim too much based on limited experience. A student arguing that "The Solitary Reaper" demonstrates that field workers are melancholy would be committing a **hasty generalization** fallacy. Simply claiming less would improve the argument. In fact, this student might change the focus of her argument by doing research on other poems by Wordsworth, finding several that deal with young women in nature. Using "She Dwelt among Untrodden Ways" and "She Was a Phantom of Delight," the student might argue that Wordsworth is so enraptured by the natural world that he often blurs the boundaries between people and nature.

Another common fallacy is *post hoc, ergo propter hoc* (Latin: "After this, therefore because of this"). Few of us escape this error in cause and effect. Many superstitions probably began because of this fallacy. A man breaks a mirror and bad luck follows. Did the mirror cause the bad luck? Logic says no, but the next day he breaks a leg, and a week later his car is stolen. The coincidence is often too tempting to resist. Does smoking marijuana lead to hard drugs? Logic says no, since you could argue just as plausibly that almost anything (carrots, beer, coffee) that comes before could be said to cause what comes after. Unless a clear, logical link between the two events is demonstrated, you might be accused of the *post hoc* fallacy.

In writing about "The Solitary Reaper," you might want to argue that the "melancholy strain" the traveler heard caused him to have a deeper appreciation for the beauty and mystery of rural people. But perhaps the narrator held such an opinion for a long time, or perhaps this is just one of dozens of such encounters that the poet remembers fondly. A sounder argument would focus on the cause and effect that do seem to be in the text: the mystery of the song's content adds to the emotional response the poet has.

Most of us commit a version of the **intentional fallacy** when we defend ourselves against someone we offended by saying, "That's not what I meant. It was just a joke." The problem arises because we are not always able to carry out our intentions. Perhaps our language is not precise enough, or perhaps our intention to be sincere or honest or witty gets mixed up with other intentions we have to sound intelligent, confident, or impressive. Students are often surprised when teachers tell them that a writer's stated intentions cannot be taken as the final word on a poem's meaning. "Wordsworth knows the poem better than anyone else" is an understandable retort. But that might not be the case. Wordsworth might not be the most astute reader of his own work. And he may not be fully aware of all that he intended. A student would be committing an intentional fallacy by arguing that "The Solitary Reaper" is written in the language used by the common man because Wordsworth says so in his preface to *Lyrical Ballads*. While this student should be commended for doing extra research, another student might point out that "Vale profound," "plaintive numbers," and "humble lay" seem conventionally poetic. Like others, this fallacy is easily revised by claiming less: "Most of 'The Solitary Reaper' is written in simple diction to approximate the language used by ordinary people."

When you try to destroy someone's argument by ignoring their main point and focusing on something marginal, you are attacking a **straw man**. The student who argues that we should dismiss Wordsworth's credibility as an observer because of "his absurd declaration that 'a voice so thrilling ne'er was heard'" is committing the straw man fallacy. While it is probably true that the song he hears is not the most thrilling in the history of the world, this is hardly Wordsworth's main point. Writers gain more credibility if they deal with a writer's strongest or main claim.

A favorite tactic of traditionalists trying to hold the line against change, the **slippery slope** fallacy is used to claim that if we allow one thing to happen, then slipping into catastrophe is just around the corner. If we do not prevent students from wearing gangsta rap fashions, gangs will eventually roam the hallways; if we allow the morning-after pill, sexual anarchy will follow. A small step is seen as precipitating an avalanche.

The following claim by a student anticipates something that simply is not logically called for: "Although Wordsworth probably means well, his praise for the 'Highland Lass' is a dangerous move since she is probably illiterate and full of rural biases and superstitions. His failure to discriminate will lead to loss of judgment and standards." Again, claiming less improves the argument: Wordsworth is less interested in the content ("Whate'er the theme") than in the "music in my heart," an emotional response that we hope does not carry over into his views on medicine, engineering, and economics.

We are all guilty at times of the fallacy of **oversimplification**—of not seeing the inevitable complexity of things. At the risk of committing a hasty generalization ourselves, it is probably the case that your instructor will be impressed if you look for complexity in literary texts and in your arguments. Seeing complexity is a consequence of hard thinking. There are rarely two sides to a question. More likely, there are a dozen plausible and reasonable perspectives. The cliché that the truth often appears in shades of gray rather than in black and white gets at the idea that simple solutions are often the result of shallow thinking.

Complexity is not what the following claim reveals: "'The Solitary Reaper' is a poem about a traveler who hears a young girl 'singing by herself,' and like a catchy ad, the tune stays with him." Being exposed to other viewpoints in class discussions and in peer-group revision can help this student avoid oversimplifying the experience Wordsworth evokes, one that touches on issues of mortality, the mysteries of emotional response, the purpose of poetry, and the power of the natural world. When Henry David Thoreau, the author of *Walden* (1854), urged his contemporaries to live simply, he was talking about their lifestyles, not their thinking.

Non sequitur is a general catchall fallacy that means "it does not follow." Some principle of logic has been violated when we make a claim that the evidence cannot support. In "The Solitary Reaper," it does not follow that because the Highland Lass "sings a melancholy strain," she herself is sad. She could be happy, absentminded, or simply bored. Perhaps the song is a conventional ballad typically sung by workers to pass the time. Revising this fallacy, like many of the others, involves setting aside time in the revision process to look again at your claims and the assumptions behind them, carefully and objectively making a clear connection between your claim and the evidence you say supports it.

First Draft of a Student Paper

The following is Abby's first complete draft of her paper. Eventually, she revised this draft after a group of her classmates reviewed it and after she reflected further on it herself. For the moment, though, read this first version, and decide what you would have said to her about it.

Abby Hazelton
Professor Ramsey
English 102
4 March - - - -
The Passage of Time in
"The Solitary Reaper"

William Wordsworth, one of the most famous writers in the movement known as British Romanticism, liked to write about beautiful features of the countryside. In his poem "The Solitary Reaper," the speaker enthuses over a girl who sings as she works in the fields. Yet although he is enraptured by her "melancholy strain," (line 6), he is unsure what it is *about* because she is using a Scottish dialect that he cannot understand. By contrast, the subject of the poem seems much clearer. The very title of the poem refers to the singing girl, and the subsequent lines repeatedly praise her song as wonderfully haunting. Nevertheless, the poem has puzzling aspects. Many readers are likely to wonder if they are supposed to find the speaker guilty of cultural and class superiority when he, as a British intellectual, treats a Scottish peasant girl as a spectacle. Another issue, the one I focus on in my paper, arises when the final stanza shifts to past tense. In the first three stanzas, the speaker uses present tense, as if he is currently observing the singer whom he describes. In the concluding stanza, however, the speaker uses verbs such as "sang" (25), "saw" (27), and "listen'd" (29), as if he is *recalling* his encounter with her. How can we explain this inconsistency? One possible justification for the final shift to past tense is that it reminds us of the speaker's inability to halt the passage of time. Even though he would like to freeze the encounter, time goes on. Perhaps, therefore, the poem's real subject is the idea that time is always in flux. Indeed, even before the final stanza, the speaker betrays an awareness that he can't bend time to his will.

Simply by virtue of the shift to past tense, the last stanza indicates that time goes on despite the speaker's wishes. But other elements of this stanza convey the same notion. Recalling his experience of the girl's singing, the speaker reports that he was "motionless and still" (29), yet in the very next line he admits that he eventually moved: "I mounted up the hill" (30). When the speaker says that "the Maiden sang / As if her song could have no ending" (25–26), the words "As if" are significant, implying that the song did end for him in reality. Similarly, the poem itself has to end at some point. In fact, it concludes with the words "no more," which stress that the singer and her song now belong to the speaker's past (32). Only in his "heart" (31), apparently, can he retain them. Furthermore, the medium of print can never convey the sound of music. In fact, prior to recording technology, music was the most fleeting of media, its notes fading with each new moment. By seeking to transmit music, the speaker ensures that he will wind up being frustrated by time.

Even if the final stanza's shift of tense is jarring, the first three stanzas give hints that the speaker will end up defeated by time. Significantly, the poem's very first word is "Behold" (1). In issuing this command, the speaker evidently hopes that other people will abandon all motion and gaze at the singer, basking in her song. The speaker reinforces this call for paralysis with the command that begins line 4: "Stop here." Yet, as if acknowledging limits to his control, he adds "or gently pass!" (4). Besides referring to other human beings, these commands seem directed at time itself. The speaker hopes that time, too, will "Stop" and "Behold." Even at this point in the poem, however, he realizes that time is inclined to "pass," in which case he hopes that it will at least move on "gently" (4).

The second stanza is chiefly concerned with space. Comparing the girl's song to other sounds, the speaker ranges from "Arabian sands" (12) to "the seas / Among the farthest Hebrides" (15–16). In the third stanza, however, he focuses again on time. Trying to determine the subject of the song, he expresses uncertainty about its time frame. He wonders whether the song concerns "old, unhappy, far-off things / And battles long ago" (19–20) or instead deals with "Familiar matter of to-day" (22). Moreover, even if he suspects the song's subject is "Some natural sorrow, loss, or pain" (23), he is unsure whether this experience of despair is confined to the past ("has been") or will reoccur ("may be again") (24). Whichever of the possibilities he raises is true, the speaker is clearly limited in his ability to figure out the song's relation to time. In other words, he cannot force time into a meaningful pattern, let alone prevent its passing.

By the end of the poem, the speaker seems as "solitary" as the reaper. In addition to losing his experience with her as time moves on, he is isolated in other ways.

This situation seems to leave the speaker as "solitary" as the reaper. Throughout the poem, actually, we don't see him in the company of others. His opening "Behold" is directed at no one in particular. Furthermore, we can't be sure he is speaking to actual passersby or, rather, to the poem's hypothetical future readers. Nor, for all his praise of the singer, does he apparently talk to her. Rather, he gives the impression that he keeps at a distance. Even if he did try to converse with the reaper, he himself would still be "solitary" in the sense of failing to understand her language and failing to communicate her song to his readers. He does not even bother trying to reproduce some of the song's words. Therefore, despite the speaker's enchantment over the reaper, this poem is ultimately pessimistic. The speaker is left only with his memories of a wonderful experience. He has lost the experience itself.

Strategies for Revising

Most first drafts are far from perfect. Even experienced professional writers often have to revise their work. Besides making changes on their own, many of them solicit feedback from others. In various workplaces, writing is collaborative, with coauthors exchanging ideas as they try to improve a piece. Remain open to the possibility that your draft needs changes, perhaps several. Of course, you are more apt to revise extensively if you have given yourself enough time. Conversely, you will not feel able to change much of your paper if it is due the next day. You will also limit your ability to revise if you work only with your original manuscript, scribbling possible changes between the lines. This practice amounts to conservatism, for it encourages you to keep passages that really ought to be overhauled.

You may have trouble, however, improving a draft if you are checking many things in it at once. Therefore, read the draft repeatedly, looking at a different aspect of it each time. A good way to begin is to outline the paper you have written and then compare that outline with your original one. If the two outlines differ, your draft may or may not need adjusting; perhaps you were wise to swerve from your original plan. In any case, you should ponder your departures from that plan, considering whether they were for the best.

If, like Abby, you are writing an argument paper, our Checklist for Revising box has some topics and questions you might apply as you review your first draft. Some of these considerations overlap. Nevertheless, take them in turn rather than all at once.

≣ A CHECKLIST FOR REVISING

Logic

- Will my audience see that the issue I am focusing on is indeed an issue?

- Will the audience be able to follow the logic of my argument?

- Is the logic as persuasive as it might be? Is there more evidence I can provide? Do I need to identify more of my assumptions?

- Have I addressed all of my audience's potential concerns?

Organization

- Does my introduction identify the issue that I will focus on? Does it state my main claim?

- Will my audience be able to detect and follow the stages of my argument?

- Does the order of my paragraphs seem purposeful rather than arbitrary?

- Have I done all I can to signal connections within and between sentences? Within and between paragraphs?

- Have I avoided getting bogged down in mere summary?

- Will my conclusion satisfy readers? Does it leave any key questions dangling?

(continued on next page)

■ **A CHECKLIST FOR REVISING** (*continued*)

Clarity

- Does my title offer a good preview of my argument?

- Will each of my sentences be immediately clear?

- Am I sure how to define each word that I have used?

Emphasis

- Have I put key points in prominent places?

- Have I worded each sentence for maximum impact? In particular, is each sentence as concise as possible? Do I use active verbs whenever I can?

Style

- Are my tone and level of vocabulary appropriate?

- Will my audience think me fair-minded? Should I make any more concessions?

- Do I use any mannerisms that may distract my readers?

- Have I used any expressions that may annoy or offend?

- Is there anything else I can do to make my paper readable and interesting?

Grammar

- Is each of my sentences grammatically correct?

- Have I punctuated properly?

Physical Appearance

- Have I followed the proper format for quotations, notes, and bibliography?

- Are there any typographical errors?

We list these considerations from most to least important. When revising a draft, think first about matters of logic, organization, and clarity. There is little point in fixing the grammar of particular sentences if you are going to drop them later because they fail to advance your argument.

As we noted, a group of Abby's classmates discussed her draft. Most of these students seemed to like her overall argument, including her main issue and claim. Having been similarly confused by the poem's shift of tense, they appreciated the light that Abby shed on it. They were impressed by her willingness to examine the poem's specific words. They especially liked her closing analogy between the reaper and the speaker himself. Nevertheless, the group made several comments about Abby's paper that she took as suggestions for improvement. Ultimately, she decided that the following changes were in order.

1. She should make her introduction more concise.   The first draft is so long and dense that it may confuse readers instead of helping them sense the paper's main concerns. This problem is common to first drafts. In this preliminary phase, many writers worry that they will fail to generate *enough* words; they are hardly thinking about how to restrain themselves. Moreover, the writer of a first draft may still be unsure about the paper's whole argument, so the introduction often lacks a sharp focus. After Abby finished and reviewed her first draft, she saw ways of making her introduction tighter.

2. She should rearrange paragraphs.   After her introduction, Abby discussed the poem's last stanza in more detail. Then she moved back to stanza 1. Next, just before her paper's conclusion, she analyzed stanzas 2 and 3. Abby thought that the structure of her paper moved logically from the obvious to the hidden: the poem's last stanza emphasized the passage of time, and the earlier stanzas touched on this subject more subtly. Yet Abby's method of organization frustrated her classmates. They thought her paper would be easier to follow if, after the introduction, it moved chronologically through the poem. For them, her discussion of stanzas 2 and 3 seemed especially mislocated. Though she had positioned this discussion as her paper's climax, her classmates did not sense it to be her most significant and compelling moment of insight. Most important, they believed, were her comments on the *final* stanza, for that seemed to them the most important part of Wordsworth's poem. In other words, they thought the climax of the paper would be stronger if it focused on the climax of the poem. Abby hesitated to adopt her classmates' recommendation, but eventually she did so. When you read her final version, see if you like her rearrangement of paragraphs. Sometimes, though not always, a paper about a literary work seems more coherent if it does follow the work's chronological structure. And papers should indeed build to a climax, even if readers disagree about what its content should be.

3. She should reconsider her claim that "this poem is ultimately pessimistic."   Abby's classmates thought this claim did not fully account for the poem's last two lines: "The music in my heart I bore, / Long after it was heard no more" (31–32). While they agreed with her that the words "no more" emphasize that the singer has faded into the past, they disagreed that her song is lost as well, for it remains in the speaker's "heart." They noted that Abby had acknowledged this fact, but they felt she had done so too briefly and dismissively. In addition, one student encouraged her to think about poetry and music as ways of keeping memories alive. More specifically, he suggested that the speaker of "The Solitary Reaper" is Wordsworth himself, who is using this poem to preserve his memory of an actual encounter. After studying the poem again, Abby decided that her classmates' ideas had merit, and she incorporated them into her revision. Of course, such advice is not always worth heeding. Still, writers should accept the invitation to look more closely at whatever text they are analyzing.

Revised Draft of a Student Paper

Here is the new version of the paper that Abby wrote. Attached to it are marginal comments by us that call your attention to her strategies.

Abby Hazelton
Professor Ramsey
English 102
11 March ----

Title clearly indicates the particular work being analyzed and the aspect to be focused on.

The Passage of Time in "The Solitary Reaper"

In William Wordsworth's poem "The Solitary Reaper," the speaker enthuses over a girl who sings as she works in the fields. Throughout the poem, his rapture is evident. Yet in the last stanza, he makes a puzzling move, shifting to past tense after using present tense in the previous three stanzas. No longer does he seem to be currently observing the singer he describes; rather, now he seems to be *recalling* his encounter with her. One possible justification for this shift in tense is that it reminds us of the speaker's inability to halt the passage of time. Even though he would like to freeze the encounter, time goes on. Perhaps, therefore, the poem's real theme is that time is always in flux. Indeed, even before the final stanza, the speaker betrays an awareness that he can't bend time to his will.

Immediately refers to specific detail of text.

With "puzzling," signals issue to be addressed.

Identifies the main claim.

Connects feature of the poem to be focused on to other parts of it.

Significantly, the poem's very first word is "Behold" (line 1). In issuing this command, the speaker evidently hopes that other people will abandon all motion and gaze at the singer. The speaker reinforces this call for paralysis with the command that begins line 4: "Stop here." Yet, as if acknowledging limits to his control, he adds "or gently pass!" (4). Besides referring to other human beings, these commands seem directed at time itself. The speaker hopes that time, too, will "Stop" and "Behold." Even at this point in the poem, however, he realizes that time is inclined to "pass," in which case he hopes that it will at least move on "gently."

Analyzes an implication of the poem's particular language rather than just beginning with a plot detail.

Develops point that even the poem's early stanzas show concern about the passage of time that final stanza emphasizes.

The second stanza is chiefly concerned with space. Comparing the girl's song to other sounds, the speaker ranges from "Arabian sands" (12) to "the seas / Among the farthest

Moves chronologically through the poem, carefully pointing out how second stanza differs from the first.

Hebrides" (15–16). In the third stanza, however, he focuses again on time. Trying to determine the subject of her song, he expresses uncertainty about its time frame. He wonders whether the song concerns "old, unhappy, far-off things / And battles long ago" (19–20) or instead deals with "Familiar matter of to-day" (22). Moreover, even if he suspects the song's subject is "Some natural sorrow, loss, or pain" (23), he is unsure whether this experience of despair is confined to the past ("has been") or will reoccur ("may be again") (24). Whichever of the possibilities he raises is true, the speaker is clearly limited in his ability to figure out the song's relation to time. In other words, he cannot force time into a meaningful pattern, let alone prevent its passing.

Makes distinctions among stanzas' topics. Returns to main claim of the essay.

Refers to actual words of poem to support points.

Ends paragraph by reminding us what main claim is.

Simply by virtue of the shift to past tense, the last stanza indicates that time goes on despite the speaker's wishes. But other elements of the stanza convey this same notion. Recalling his experience of the girl's singing, the speaker reports that he was "motionless and still" (29), yet in the very next line he admits that he eventually moved: "I mounted up the hill" (30). When the speaker says that "the Maiden sang / As if her song could have no ending" (25–26), the words "As if" are significant, implying that the song did end for him in reality. Similarly, the poem itself has to end at some point. In fact, it concludes with the words "no more" (32), which stress that the singer and her song now belong to the speaker's past. Only in his "heart" (31), apparently, can he retain them.

Directs attention to part of poem with which she is most concerned.

Traces implications of poem's words, especially as these are related to main issue and claim.

This situation seems to leave the speaker as "solitary" as the reaper. Throughout the poem, actually, we don't see him in the company of others. His opening "Behold" is directed at no one in particular. Furthermore, we can't be sure he is speaking to actual passersby or, rather, to the poem's hypothetical future readers. Nor, for all his praise of the singer, does he apparently talk to her. Rather, he gives the impression that he keeps at a distance. Even if he did converse with the reaper, he himself would still be "solitary" in the sense of failing to understand her dialect and failing to communicate her words to his readers. As things stand, he is apparently unable or unwilling to reproduce any of the song's lyrics. Just as important, the medium of print can never convey the sounds of music. In fact, prior to recording technology, music was the most fleeting of media, its notes fading with each new moment. By seeking to transmit music, the speaker ensures that he will wind up being frustrated by time.

Connects last stanza to other parts of poem.

Several observations support idea that the speaker is isolated.

Concludes climactic paragraph with substantial analysis.

Yet perhaps the singer and her song are preserved in more than just the speaker's "heart." It can be argued that they are also preserved by the poem, if only to a limited extent. More generally, we can say that literature is a means by which human beings partially succeed in perpetuating things. This idea seems quite relevant to "The Solitary Reaper" if we suppose that the speaker is the poet himself and that he actually witnessed the scene he describes. If we make such assumptions, we can see Wordsworth as analogous to the speaker. After all, both engage in commemorative verbal art. Because time passes, the "strain[s]" that Wordsworth and the singer produce in their efforts to preserve time are bound to be "melancholy" (6). Still, their art matters, for through it they are imaginatively "[r]eaping" (3) experiences that would otherwise fade.

Signals that she is simply making a suggestion here, rather than asserting a definite new point.

Concluding paragraph reminds us of main issue and claim but goes beyond mere repetition to bring up some new suggestions.

To us, Abby's revision is more persuasive and compelling than her first draft. In particular, she has nicely complicated her claim about the poem's "pessimism." Nevertheless, we would hesitate to call this revision the definitive version of her paper. Maybe you have thought of things Abby could do to make it even more effective. In presenting her two drafts, we mainly want to emphasize the importance of revision. We hope, too, that you will remember our specific tips as you work on your own writing.

Strategies for Writing a Comparative Paper

Much writing about literature *compares* two or more texts. After all, you can gain many insights into a text by noting how it resembles and differs from others. We refer to the practice of critical comparison in Chapter 3, "How to Argue about Literature" (pp. 43–87), where we juxtapose stories by Daniel Orozco and Jamaica Kincaid, each of which features a point of comparison: both speakers are introducing someone to a kind of work. But in this section we offer specific advice for writing a comparative paper, a task you may be assigned in your course. We also present a sample paper that models strategies of comparative writing.

To aid our discussion, we ask that you read the following two poems. The first, "Two Trees," appears in the 2009 verse collection *Rain* by Don Paterson (b. 1963), a Scottish writer who is also a jazz musician, a professor at the University of St. Andrews, and the poetry editor for the publisher Picador Macmillan. Next comes "Regarding History," a poem from the 2005 book *Trill & Mordent* by Luisa A. Igloria (b. 1961), a Filipina American writer who is a professor of English and creative writing at Old Dominion University in Norfolk, Virginia.

DON PATERSON
Two Trees

One morning, Don Miguel got out of bed
with one idea rooted in his head:
to graft his orange to his lemon tree.
It took him the whole day to work them free,
lay open their sides, and lash them tight.   5
For twelve months, from the shame or from the fright
they put forth nothing; but one day there appeared
two lights in the dark leaves. Over the years
the limbs would get themselves so tangled up
each bough looked like it gave a double crop,   10
and not one kid in the village didn't know
the magic tree in Miguel's patio.

The man who bought the house had had no dream
so who can say what dark malicious whim
led him to take his axe and split the bole   15
along its fused seam, and then dig two holes.
And no, they did not die from solitude;
nor did their branches bear a sterile fruit;
nor did their unhealed flanks weep every spring
for those four yards that lost them everything   20
as each strained on its shackled root to face
the other's empty, intricate embrace.
They were trees, and trees don't weep or ache or shout.
And trees are all this poem is about.   *[2009]*

LUISA A. IGLORIA
Regarding History

A pair of trees on one side of the walk, leaning
now into the wind in a stance we'd call involuntary—
I can see them from the kitchen window, as I take meat
out of the oven and hold my palms above the crust, darkened
with burnt sugar. Nailed with cloves, small earth of flesh   5
still smoldering from its furnace. In truth I want to take it
into the garden and bury it in soil. There are times
I grow weary of coaxing music from silence, silence
from the circularity of logic, logic from the artifact.
Then, the possibilities of sunlight are less attractive   10
than baying at the moon. I want to take your face
in my hands, grow sweet from what it tells, tend
how it leans and turns, trellis or vine of morning-glory.

I wish for limbs pared to muscle, to climb away from
chance and all its missed appointments, its half-drunk   15
cups of coffee. Tell me what I'll find, in this
early period at the beginning of a century.
Tell me what I'll find, stumbling into a boat
and pushing off into the year's last dark hours.   *[2005]*

LIST SIMILARITIES AND DIFFERENCES

A class like yours sensed value in comparing Paterson's poem with Igloria's. So the students proceeded to brainstorm lists of specific similarities and differences—something you might do to start analyzing texts you bring together. For these two poems, the class came up with the following comparisons:

SIMILARITIES

In both poems, a prominent role is played by a real pair of trees, and their relation to each other seems important.

Both poems describe labor. In Paterson's, it's the labor of joining and then separating the trees; in Igloria's, it's the labor of cooking, burying, coaxing, climbing, and "pushing off."

The word *limbs* appears in both poems.

Both poems contain many words that have negative connotations. Paterson's poem includes such words as *shame, fright, dark malicious whim, die, sterile, unhealed, weep, strained, shackled, empty,* and *ache,* while Igloria's poem includes such words as *darkened, burnt, nailed, bury, weary, missed,* and *dark.*

More specifically, both poems contain words associated with death.

Both poems refer to the time frame of a year, with Paterson's mentioning "twelve months" and Igloria's concluding with "the year's last dark hours."

DIFFERENCES

The speaker in Igloria's poem uses first person, indicated by the pronoun *I,* while the speaker in Paterson's poem is no specific, identifiable person.

Paterson's poem does, however, name a particular character (Don Miguel) and refers to several other people (kids in the village, the man who chopped apart the trees), while the only people in Igloria's poem seem to be "I" and "you."

Paterson's poem centers on a particular image, the two trees, whereas Igloria's poem has other images besides the pair of trees.

Paterson's poem seems more like a narrative; it tells a story. Igloria's poem seems to be more the expression of the speaker's mood.

While Igloria's speaker is clearly interested in the pair of trees as metaphors for her relationship with "you," Paterson's poem leaves readers to interpret whether and how the two trees have metaphorical implications.

"Two Trees" rhymes, but "Regarding History" does not.

"Regarding History" seems in many respects a love poem, but "Two Trees" is hard to see in that way.

"Two Trees" comments on the fact that it is a poem, but "Regarding History" does not.

"Regarding History" ends with its speaker wanting to know something ("Tell me what I'll find"), but "Two Trees" may leave its *readers* wanting to know something: whether we're supposed to accept its speaker's claim that "trees are all this poem is about."

As you plan your own comparative paper, lists such as these can help you organize your thoughts. To be sure, this class did not immediately think of all the similarities and differences it ended up noting. Usually, going beyond obvious points of comparison is a gradual process, for which you should give yourself plenty of time. Similarly, once you have made lists such as the one above, take time to decide which similarities and differences truly merit your attention. At most, only a few can be part of your paper's main issue and claim.

CONSIDER "WEIGHTING" YOUR COMPARISON

Unfortunately, many students writing a comparative analysis are content to put forth main claims such as these:

There are many similarities and differences between "Two Trees" and "Regarding History."

While "Two Trees" and "Regarding History" have many similarities, in many ways they are also different.

While "Two Trees" and "Regarding History" are different in many ways, they are similar in others.

Several problems arise with these common methods of introducing a comparative paper. For one thing, they give the reader no preview of the specific ideas to come. Indeed, they could have been written by someone who never bothered to read the two poems, for any two texts are similar in certain ways and different in others. Furthermore, these sorts of claims leave no meaningful and compelling way of organizing the paper. Rather, they encourage the writer to proceed arbitrarily, noting miscellaneous similarities and differences on impulse. More precisely, claims such as these fail to identify the *issue* driving the paper. Why compare Paterson's and Igloria's poems in the first place? Comparison is a means to an end, not an end in itself. What important question is the writer using these two texts to answer? In short, what's at stake?

A more fruitful approach, we think, is to write a *weighted* comparative analysis—that is, an argument chiefly concerned with *one* text more than others. When professional literary critics compare two texts, often they mainly want to answer a question about just one of them. They bring in the second text because they believe that doing so helps them address the issue they are raising about their key text. True, a good paper can result even when you treat equally all texts you discuss. But you might write a paper that seems more purposeful and coherent if you focus basically on one work, using comparisons to resolve some issue concerning it.

A Student Comparative Paper

The following paper by student Jeremy Cooper demonstrates weighted comparative analysis. The author refers to Igloria's "Regarding History" along with Paterson's "Two Trees," but he is mostly concerned with Paterson's poem. He brings up Igloria's poem not to do comparison for its own sake but to address a question he has about Paterson's text.

Jeremy Cooper
Professor Budnoy
English 102
15 October - - - -

Title does not merely repeat title of the poem to be analyzed. Moreover, title specifies what aspect of that poem he will examine.

Don Paterson's Criticism of Nature's Owners

Until its last two lines, Don Paterson's poem "Two Trees" tells a fairly straightforward story. The title refers to an orange tree and a lemon tree that stood next to each other on an estate. The speaker in the poem recalls how these trees were treated by two different owners of the property. The first owner, Don Miguel, successfully grafted the trees together. The next owner, a man unnamed by the speaker, separated them with an axe. Given the speaker's clear description of these events, most readers would probably have no trouble understanding what happened to the trees. But the poem's concluding pair of lines is puzzling:

First sentence refers to poem he will focus on, his primary text.

They were trees, and trees don't weep or ache or shout.
And trees are all this poem is about. (lines 23–24)

On the surface, the word "all" seems equivalent to "merely." If this is the case, readers might feel that Paterson is encouraging them to take a limited view of his poem, seeing it as concerned with nothing more than trees. They would then feel

Signals issue that the paper will address.

*dis*couraged from looking for additional significance or meaning in his text. But this interpretation of Paterson's focus risks making his poem appear relatively trivial, an impression that he surely does not want to create. A likelier possibility is that the speaker is being ironic in his final declaration, stating the word "all" sarcastically. Such a tone might then move readers to question whether the poem is simply about trees. They might feel compelled to consider how its real subject is something else. Indeed, the poem's actual main topic seems to be the regrettable attitudes that human beings take toward nature when they are able to own it.

Trees play a major role in Paterson's poem, as their presence in the title suggests. In the first of the poem's two stanzas, the speaker describes Don Miguel's effort to fuse the orange tree and the lemon tree together, something that he evidently managed to accomplish so well that the trees became hard to distinguish from each other: "the limbs would get themselves so tangled up / each bough looked like it gave a double crop" (9–10). In the second stanza, the speaker turns to describing how the next owner of the trees did the opposite thing to them, splitting them apart (15–16). The poem presents no other scenic feature to compete with the two trees for the reader's attention. The speaker just briefly mentions a bed (1), a patio (12), a house (13), and an axe (15).

That the focus is very much on the trees becomes even more apparent if we compare this poem with another in which two trees figure, Luisa A. Igloria's "Regarding History." Igloria's poem begins with "A pair of trees on one side of the walk, leaning / now into the wind in a stance we'd call involuntary" (1–2). Later, the speaker seems to have these two trees still in mind when she says that she wants to hold her lover's face and feel "how it leans and turns, trellis or vine of morning-glory" (13). The close relation of the word "leans" in this line to "leaning" (1) in the earlier one implies that the trees remain a meaningful symbol for her throughout the poem. But, unlike Paterson's speaker, Igloria's turns her thoughts to a number of images other than trees. For example, besides her beloved's face, she thinks of food she has just prepared ("meat / out of the oven" [3–4], which she has evidently "Nailed with cloves" [5]), her garden (7), sunlight (10), the moon (11), muscle (14), coffee (16), and a boat (18). Basically, the two trees in this poem are just part of its many elements. By contrast, the pair of trees in Paterson's poem is much more prominent.

Introductory paragraph ends by stating the claim about the primary text that the paper will support and develop.

This is a secondary text, which he uses to reinforce the point he has just made about his primary text.

The question then becomes what we as readers should make of their central role in that poem. Some of us may be inclined to see Paterson's trees as a metaphor, their physical existence being less significant than something else they represent. The pair of trees in "Regarding History" do seem metaphorical, functioning in the speaker's mind as stand-ins for a human relationship. When she observes that the trees are "leaning / now into the wind in a stance we'd call involuntary" (1–2), she appears to be actually thinking of her relationship with her beloved. Specifically, she seems worried about pressures on their relationship that threaten their ability to keep it steady. This concern of hers comes up again later, when she expresses a desire "to take your face" (11) and "tend / how it leans and turns" (12–13). Here, too, she evidently feels that her connection to her loved one is challenged by outside forces. As in her earlier remark about the trees, she fears that she will not be able to protect her relationship from influences that will make her and her lover do "involuntary" (2) things. In comparison, though, the two trees in Paterson's poem do not appear to have a metaphorical function. In the first place, the speaker of "Two Trees" lacks a distinct personality, so that the poem does not encourage readers to interpret the trees he mentions as representing thoughts or feelings of his. Whereas Igloria's speaker dominates "Regarding History" with her clearly marked hopes and concerns, Paterson's speaker writes largely like a reporter narrating news events. Moreover, when he tells what the two property owners did to the trees, he describes these actions so precisely and concretely that he makes it hard for readers to consider the trees as symbolic rather than physical. Also, in such lines as "they did not die from solitude" (17) and "nor did their unhealed flanks weep every spring" (19) the speaker seems to be reminding the reader that they are, in fact, basically vegetation rather than images of something in the human mind. If anything, these lines discourage the reader from interpreting the trees as metaphors.

But if the two trees in Paterson's poem come across mainly as real elements of nature, the attitudes that their owners show toward them are nevertheless significant. Actually, the poem's main subject is not the trees of the title, but the intense and disturbing emotions that drove Don Miguel and the later owner to handle them roughly. The feelings that led the second owner to separate the trees seem villainous. The speaker suggests that this man "had had no dream" (13) but instead acted on some mysterious "dark

He has identified a possible interpretation but now offers a different one, which he proceeds to argue for.

He uses comparison with his secondary text to support his argument about his primary text.

He is working with the claim he put forth in his introduction.

malicious whim" that compelled him to "split" them apart
(14–15), leaving their flanks "unhealed" (19) and their roots
"shackled" (21). This language gives the impression of a
plantation owner in the pre–Civil War American South, the
type of person who cruelly divided slave families and kept
their members separated in bondage. Because the poem ends
with the physical stress inflicted upon the trees by their
second owner, some readers may be more bothered by this
man's behavior than they are by Don Miguel's. They might
even appreciate Don Miguel's interest in uniting the trees,
especially because his labor resulted in the heartening picture
of "two lights in the dark leaves" (8). But the language used
to describe his actions, too, is mostly negative. The words
"lay open" (5), "lash them tight" (5), "shame" (6), "fright"
(6), and "tangled up" (9) imply traumatic destruction, even
rape, rather than blissful harmony. In his willingness to
manipulate the trees, Don Miguel therefore seems no better
than the man who replaced him. Furthermore, Don Miguel's
behavior toward the trees did not have the excuse of being
carefully thought-out and planned. He simply awoke "with
one idea rooted in his head: / to graft his orange to his
lemon tree" (2–3). Just as the word "Don" in the first line is
an indication that he is a man of power in his community, so
the repetition of the word "his" in this line suggests that he
felt able to perform surgery on the trees merely because he
owned them. Both of the men in the poem avoided thinking
of what was best for the trees. Instead, both preferred to
exercise the authority they had as possessors of the trees, no
matter how abusive their handling of the trees might be. The
speaker in Igloria's poem calls attention to what she currently
lacks or is *unable* to do, through statements like "I want to
take your face" (11), "I wish for limbs pared to muscle" (14),
and "Tell me what I'll find" (18). Furthermore, she does not
possess the two trees that figure in "Regarding History."
Rather, she is a mere observer of them: "I can see them from
the kitchen window" (3). In Paterson's poem, on the other
hand, Don Miguel and the second man treat their trees
violently and are able to do so because the trees are legally
theirs.

Paterson does not end his poem by directly indicating
what he thinks is the proper way of treating trees like those
of his title. He does not clearly offer some sort of prescription
for their care. Many readers may, nevertheless, come away
from the poem concluding that human beings should avoid
tampering with trees and, more generally, should leave nature
alone as often as possible. In any case, Paterson's central

Again, he acknowledges the possibility of an interpretation different from his before advancing his view.

Once more, he uses comparison with his secondary text to reinforce his argument about his primary text.

He suggests that this interpretation is possible but that he is more interested in getting his readers to accept his main claim about the poem: the idea he returns to in his final sentence.

purpose seems to be to make us more aware that when humans own some of nature, they may treat it arrogantly, whether in the pursuit of unity (Don Miguel's aim when he fuses the trees) or separation (the second man's goal when he breaks them apart).

Jeremy gains much from comparing "Two Trees" with "Regarding History." In paragraph 3, the analysis of the modest role that trees play in Igloria's poem bolsters Jeremy's claim that they are the core of Paterson's poem. In paragraph 4, the discussion of how Igloria uses trees as metaphors strengthens Jeremy's point that Paterson's trees are literal. In paragraph 5, the observation that Igloria's speaker is *not* an owner of trees helps Jeremy stress that Paterson's men possess them. Obviously, though, Jeremy focuses his paper on Paterson's poem, not on both. By concentrating chiefly on "Two Trees," he enables himself to develop a tight and logical argument, whereas focusing on both poems would encourage him to roam through similarities and differences at random.

Perhaps you know the advice usually given about how to organize a comparative paper. Traditionally, writers aiming to compare two texts learn of two options: (1) discuss one text and then move to the other, comparing it with the first; (2) discuss the texts together, noting each of their similarities and differences in turn. Both of these alternatives make sense and provide a ready-made structure for your paper; either can result in a coherent essay. Still, a weighted analysis such as Jeremy's—an analysis that focuses on one text more than another—is more likely than either of the alternatives to seem the logical evolution of a pointed claim.

CHAPTER 6

■■　■■

Writing about Literary Genres

At the beginning of Chapter 3, we discussed how literary works are often understood as examples of particular **genres** (kinds or types of writing). While acknowledging that most readers think of literature as comprising the genres of fiction, poetry, and drama, we invited you to think of nonfiction (such as historical writing), creative nonfiction (such as autobiography and memoir), and essays (sometimes including argumentative prose) as literature as well. In this chapter, we present elements of literary analysis for the genres of fiction, poetry, and drama showing how various students have used these elements to generate writing about literary works. You will notice that many of these elements are useful in thinking about most genres, but different genres make different use of elements, emphasizing some more than others. We also devote a section to writing about poems and pictures; over the centuries, many poets have been prompted to create their art in response to visual images created by other kinds of artists.

Writing about Stories

Short stories can be said to resemble novels. Above all, both are works of fiction. Yet the difference in length matters. As William Trevor, a veteran writer of short stories, has observed, short fiction is "the art of the glimpse; it deals in echoes and reverberations; craftily it withholds information. Novels tell all. Short stories tell as little as they dare." Maybe Trevor overstates the situation when he claims that novels reveal everything. All sorts of texts feature what literary theorist Wolfgang Iser calls "gaps." Still, Trevor is right to emphasize that short stories usually tell much less than novels do. They demand that you understand and evaluate characters on the basis of just a few details and events. In this respect, short stories resemble poems. Both tend to rely on compression rather than expansion, seeking to affect their audience with a sharply limited number of words.

Short stories' focused use of language can make the experience of reading them wonderfully intense. Furthermore, you may end up considering important human issues as you try to interpret the "glimpses" they provide. Precisely because short stories "tell as little as they dare," they offer you much to ponder as you proceed to write about them.

In discussing the writing process, we refer often to the story that follows. Published in 1941, "A Visit of Charity" is by a pioneer of American short fiction, Eudora Welty (1909–2001). She spent her life chiefly in her hometown of Jackson, Mississippi, and most of her writing is set in the American South.

EUDORA WELTY

A Visit of Charity

It was mid-morning—a very cold, bright day. Holding a potted plant before her, a girl of fourteen jumped off the bus in front of the Old Ladies' Home, on the outskirts of town. She wore a red coat, and her straight yellow hair was hanging down loose from the pointed white cap all the little girls were wearing that year. She stopped for a moment beside one of the prickly dark shrubs with which the city had beautified the Home, and then proceeded slowly toward the building, which was of whitewashed brick and reflected the winter sunlight like a block of ice. As she walked vaguely up the steps she shifted the small pot from hand to hand; then she had to set it down and remove her mittens before she could open the heavy door.

"I'm a Campfire Girl. . . . I have to pay a visit to some old lady," she told the nurse at the desk. This was a woman in a white uniform who looked as if she were cold; she had close-cut hair which stood up on the very top of her head exactly like a sea wave. Marian, the little girl, did not tell her that this visit would give her a minimum of only three points in her score.

"Acquainted with any of our residents?" asked the nurse. She lifted one eyebrow and spoke like a man.

"With any old ladies? No—but—that is, any of them will do," Marian stammered. With her free hand she pushed her hair behind her ears, as she did when it was time to study Science.

The nurse shrugged and rose. "You have a nice *multiflora cineraria*° there," she remarked as she walked ahead down the hall of closed doors to pick out an old lady.   5

There was loose, bulging linoleum on the floor. Marian felt as if she were walking on the waves, but the nurse paid no attention to it. There was a smell in the hall like the interior of a clock. Everything was silent until, behind one of the doors, an old lady of some kind cleared her throat like a sheep bleating. This decided the nurse. Stopping in her tracks, she first extended her arm, bent her elbow, and leaned forward from the hips—all to examine the watch strapped to her wrist; then she gave a loud double-rap on the door.

"There are two in each room," the nurse remarked over her shoulder.

"Two what?" asked Marian without thinking. The sound like a sheep's bleating almost made her turn around and run back.

---

multiflora cineraria: A houseplant with brightly colored flowers and heart-shaped leaves.

One old woman was pulling the door open in short, gradual jerks, and when she saw the nurse a strange smile forced her old face dangerously awry. Marian, suddenly propelled by the strong, impatient arm of the nurse, saw next the side-face of another old woman, even older, who was lying flat in bed with a cap on and a counterpane° drawn up to her chin.

"Visitor," said the nurse, and after one more shove she was off up the hall.   10

Marian stood tongue-tied; both hands held the potted plant. The old woman, still with that terrible, square smile (which was a smile of welcome) stamped on her bony face, was waiting. . . . Perhaps she said something. The old woman in bed said nothing at all, and she did not look around.

Suddenly Marian saw a hand, quick as a bird claw, reach up in the air and pluck the white cap off her head. At the same time, another claw to match drew her all the way into the room, and the next moment the door closed behind her.

"My, my, my," said the old lady at her side.

Marian stood enclosed by a bed, a washstand, and a chair; the tiny room had altogether too much furniture. Everything smelled wet—even the bare floor. She held on to the back of the chair, which was wicker and felt soft and damp. Her heart beat more and more slowly, her hands got colder and colder, and she could not hear whether the old women were saying anything or not. She could not see them very clearly. How dark it was! The window shade was down, and the only door was shut. Marian looked at the ceiling. . . . It was like being caught in a robbers' cave, just before one was murdered.

"Did you come to be our little girl for a while?" the first robber asked.   15

Then something was snatched from Marian's hand—the little potted plant.

"Flowers!" screamed the old woman. She stood holding the pot in an undecided way. "Pretty flowers," she added.

Then the old woman in bed cleared her throat and spoke. "They are not pretty," she said, still without looking around, but very distinctly.

Marian suddenly pitched against the chair and sat down in it.

"Pretty flowers," the first old woman insisted. "Pretty—pretty . . ."   20

Marian wished she had the little pot back for just a moment—she had forgotten to look at the plant herself before giving it away. What did it look like?

"Stinkweeds," said the other old woman sharply. She had a bunchy white forehead and red eyes like a sheep. Now she turned them toward Marian. The fogginess seemed to rise in her throat again, and she bleated, "Who—are—you?"

To her surprise, Marian could not remember her name. "I'm a Campfire Girl," she said finally.

"Watch out for the germs," said the old woman like a sheep, not addressing anyone.

"One came out last month to see us," said the first old woman.   25

A sheep or a germ? wondered Marian dreamily, holding on to the chair.

"Did not!" cried the other old woman.

counterpane: Bedspread.

"Did so! Read to us out of the Bible, and we enjoyed it!" screamed the first.

"Who enjoyed it!" said the woman in bed. Her mouth was unexpectedly small and sorrowful, like a pet's.

"We enjoyed it," insisted the other. "You enjoyed it—I enjoyed it."   30

"We all enjoyed it," said Marian, without realizing that she had said a word.

The first old woman had just finished putting the potted plant high, high on the top of the wardrobe, where it could hardly be seen from below. Marian wondered how she had ever succeeded in placing it there, how she could ever have reached so high.

"You mustn't pay any attention to old Addie," she now said to the little girl. "She's ailing today."

"Will you shut your mouth?" said the woman in bed. "I am not."

"You're a story."   35

"I can't stay but a minute—really, I can't," said Marian suddenly. She looked down at the wet floor and thought that if she were sick in here they would have to let her go.

With much to-do the first old woman sat down in a rocking chair—still another piece of furniture!—and began to rock. With the fingers of one hand she touched a very dirty cameo pin on her chest. "What do you do at school?" she asked.

"I don't know . . ." said Marian. She tried to think but she could not.

"Oh, but the flowers are beautiful," the old woman whispered. She seemed to rock faster and faster; Marian did not see how anyone could rock so fast.

"Ugly," said the woman in bed.   40

"If we bring flowers—" Marian began, and then fell silent. She had almost said that if Campfire Girls brought flowers to the Old Ladies' Home, the visit would count one extra point, and if they took a Bible with them on the bus and read it to the old ladies, it counted double. But the old woman had not listened, anyway; she was rocking and watching the other one, who watched back from the bed.

"Poor Addie is ailing. She has to take medicine—see?" she said, pointing a horny finger at a row of bottles on the table, and rocking so high that her black comfort shoes lifted off the floor like a little child's.

"I am no more sick than you are," said the woman in bed.

"Oh, yes you are!"

"I just got more sense than you have, that's all," said the other old woman,   45
nodding her head.

"That's only the contrary way she talks when *you all* come," said the first old lady with sudden intimacy. She stopped the rocker with a neat pat of her feet and leaned toward Marian. Her hand reached over—it felt like a petunia leaf, clinging and just a little sticky.

"Will you hush! Will you hush!" cried the other one.

Marian leaned back rigidly in her chair.

"When I was a little girl like you, I went to school and all," said the old woman in the same intimate, menacing voice. "Not here—another town . . ."

"Hush!" said the sick woman. "You never went to school. You never   50
came and you never went. You never were anything—only here. You never

were born! You don't know anything. Your head is empty, your heart and hands and your old black purse are all empty, even that little old box that you brought with you you brought empty — you showed it to me. And yet you talk, talk, talk, talk, talk all the time until I think I'm losing my mind! Who are you? You're a stranger — a perfect stranger! Don't you know you're a stranger? Is it possible that they have actually done a thing like this to anyone — sent them in a stranger to talk, and rock, and tell away her whole long rigmarole? Do they seriously suppose that I'll be able to keep it up, day in, day out, night in, night out, living in the same room with a terrible old woman — forever?"

Marian saw the old woman's eyes grow bright and turn toward her. This old woman was looking at her with despair and calculation in her face. Her small lips suddenly dropped apart, and exposed a half circle of false teeth with tan gums.

"Come here, I want to tell you something," she whispered. "Come here!"

Marian was trembling, and her heart nearly stopped beating altogether for a moment.

"Now, now, Addie," said the first old woman. "That's not polite. Do you know what's really the matter with old Addie today?" She, too, looked at Marian; one of her eyelids dropped low.

"The matter?" the child repeated stupidly. "What's the matter with her?"   55

"Why, she's mad because it's her birthday!" said the first old woman, beginning to rock again and giving a little crow as though she had answered her own riddle.

"It is not, it is not!" screamed the old woman in bed. "It is not my birthday, no one knows when that is but myself, and will you please be quiet and say nothing more, or I'll go straight out of my mind!" She turned her eyes toward Marian again, and presently she said in the soft, foggy voice, "When the worst comes to the worst, I ring this bell, and the nurse comes." One of her hands was drawn out from under the patched counterpane — a thin little hand with enormous black freckles. With a finger which would not hold still she pointed to a little bell on the table among the bottles.

"How old are you?" Marian breathed. Now she could see the old woman in bed very closely and plainly, and very abruptly, from all sides, as in dreams. She wondered about her — she wondered for a moment as though there was nothing else in the world to wonder about. It was the first time such a thing had happened to Marian.

"I won't tell!"

The old face on the pillow, where Marian was bending over it, slowly gathered and collapsed. Soft whimpers came out of the small open mouth. It was a sheep that she sounded like — a little lamb. Marian's face drew very close, the yellow hair hung forward.   60

"She's crying!" She turned a bright, burning face up to the first old woman.

"That's Addie for you," the old woman said spitefully.

Marian jumped up and moved toward the door. For the second time, the claw almost touched her hair, but it was not quick enough. The little girl put her cap on.

"Well, it was a real visit," said the old woman, following Marian through the doorway and all the way out into the hall. Then from behind she suddenly clutched the child with her sharp little fingers. In an affected, high-pitched whine she cried, "Oh, little girl, have you a penny to spare for a poor old woman that's not got anything of her own? We don't have a thing in the world—not a penny for candy—not a thing! Little girl, just a nickel—a penny—"

Marian pulled violently against the old hands for a moment before she was   65
free. Then she ran down the hall, without looking behind her and without looking at the nurse, who was reading *Field & Stream* at her desk. The nurse, after another triple motion to consult her wrist watch, asked automatically the question put to visitors in all institutions: "Won't you stay and have dinner with *us*?"

Marian never replied. She pushed the heavy door open into the cold air and ran down the steps.

Under the prickly shrub she stooped and quickly, without being seen, retrieved a red apple she had hidden there.

Her yellow hair under the white cap, her scarlet coat, her bare knees all flashed in the sunlight as she ran to meet the big bus rocketing through the street.

"Wait for me!" she shouted. As though at an imperial command, the bus ground to a stop.

She jumped on and took a big bite out of the apple.   *[1941]*   70

A Student's Personal Response to the Story

Here is some freewriting a student did about the story you just read. By simply jotting down some observations and questions, she provided herself with the seeds of a paper.

I'm not sure which character I should be sympathizing with in
Welty's story. Right away I disliked the girl because she wasn't really
interested in seeing the old women. I don't know why the story is
called "A Visit of Charity," since she just wanted to get more points.
And yet I have to admit that when I was younger I was sort of like
her. I remember one time when my church youth group had to sing
Christmas carols at an old folks' home, and I was uneasy about having to meet all these ancient men and women I didn't know, some of
whom could barely walk or talk. It's funny, because I was always
comfortable around my grandparents, but I have to confess that
being around all those old people at once spooked me a little. I
smiled a lot at them and joined in the singing and helped hand out
candy canes afterward. But I couldn't wait to leave. Once I did, I felt
proud of myself for going there, but I guess I also felt a little guilty
because I didn't really want to be there at all. So, maybe I'm being
hypocritical when I criticize the girl in Welty's story for insensitivity.
Anyway, I expected that Welty would present in a good light any old
women that Marian encountered, just to emphasize that Marian was
being unkind and that it's really sad for people to have to live in a

retirement home (or senior citizens center or whatever they're calling such places nowadays). And yet the two old women she meets are cranky and unpleasant. Even the receptionist doesn't come off all that good. If I were Marian, I probably would have left even sooner than she did! Maybe Welty didn't want us to sympathize with anyone in the story, and maybe that's OK. I tend to want a story to make at least some of the characters sympathetic, but maybe it's unfair of me to demand that. Still, I'm wondering if I'm not appreciating Welty's characters enough. When the two old women argue, should we side with one of them, or are we supposed to be bothered by them both? Are we supposed to think any better of the girl by the time she leaves? The apple she eats immediately made me think of the Adam and Eve story, but I don't know what I'm supposed to do with that parallel.

The Elements of Short Fiction

Whether discussing them in class or writing about them, you will improve your ability to analyze stories like Welty's if you grow familiar with typical elements of short fiction. These elements include plot and structure, point of view, characters, setting, imagery, language, and theme.

PLOT AND STRUCTURE

For many readers, the most important element in any work of fiction is **plot**. As they turn the pages of a story, their main question is, What will happen next? In reading Welty's story, quite possibly you wanted to know how Marian's visit to the rest home would turn out. Indeed, plots usually center on human beings, who can be seen as engaging in actions, as being acted upon, or both. You might describe Marian as acting, noting among other things that she "jumped off the bus" (para. 1), that "she shifted the small pot from hand to hand" (para. 1), that "she pushed her hair behind her ears" (para. 4), that her "face drew very close" to Addie's (para. 60), that she "jumped up and moved toward the door" (para. 63), that she "pulled violently against the old hands" of the other elderly woman (para. 65), that "she ran to meet the big bus" (para. 68), and that she "jumped on and took a big bite out of the apple" (para. 70). But you might also describe her as being affected by other forces. For example, she is "suddenly propelled by the strong, impatient arm of the nurse" (para. 9), the "claw" of the first old woman "drew her all the way into the room" (para. 11), and she repeats the two women's language "without realizing that she had said a word" (para. 31). In any case, most short stories put characters into high-pressure situations, whether for dark or comic effect. To earn the merit points she desires, Marian has to contend with the feuding roommates.

Besides physical events, a short story may involve psychological developments. Welty's heroine goes through mental changes during her visit. One is that her interest in the two women grows; they are no longer just a dutiful task to her. This change is indicated best by a particular word: *wondered*. When the women discuss a previous visitor, Marian "wondered" about the animal imagery suddenly filling her mind (para. 26). When the first old woman perches the plant "high on the top of the wardrobe," the girl "wondered how she had ever succeeded in placing it there" (para. 32). Then, as Marian gazes upon the bedridden Addie, "She wondered about her—she wondered for a moment as though there was nothing else in the world to wonder about" (para. 58). As if to emphasize that the girl is experiencing a psychological transition, the narrator reports: "It was the first time such a thing had happened to Marian" (para. 58). Many stories do show characters undergoing complete or partial conversions. Meanwhile, a number of stories include characters who stick to their beliefs but gain a new perspective on them.

Does Marian's encounter with the two women have something to do with her ultimately biting the apple and leaping onto the bus? If so, what's the specific connection? Questions like these bring up relations of cause and effect, terms that often figure in discussions of plot. The novelist and short-story writer E. M. Forster refers to them in defining the term *plot* itself. To Forster, a plot is not simply one incident after another, such as "the king died and then the queen died." Rather, it is a situation or a whole chain of events in which there are reasons *why* characters behave as they do. Forster's example: "The king died, and then the queen died of grief."

Writers of short stories do not always make cause and effect immediately clear. Another possible plot, Forster suggests, is "The queen died, no one knew why, until it was discovered that it was through grief at the death of the king." In this scenario, all of the characters lack information about the queen's true psychology for a while, and perhaps the reader is in the dark as well. Indeed, many short stories leave the reader ignorant for a spell. For instance, only near the conclusion of her story does Welty reveal that before entering the rest home, Marian had put an apple under the shrub. Why does the author withhold this key fact from you? Perhaps Welty was silent about the apple because, had she reported it right away, its echoes of Eve might have overshadowed your interpretation of the story as you read. Worth considering are issues of effect: what the characters' behavior makes you think of them and what impact the author's strategies have on you.

When you summarize a story's plot, you may be inclined to put events in chronological order. But remember that short stories are not always linear. Alice Adams, author of many short stories, offers a more detailed outline of their typical **structure**. She has proposed the formula ABDCE: these letters stand for **action, background, development, climax**, and **ending**. More precisely, Adams has said that she sometimes begins a story with an action, follows that action with some background information, and then moves the plot forward in time through a major turning point and toward some sort of resolution. Not all writers of short stories follow this scheme. In fact, Adams does not always stick to it. Certainly a lot of short stories combine her background and development stages, moving the plot along while offering details of their characters' pasts. And sometimes a story will have several turning points rather than a single distinct climax. But by keeping Adams's formula in mind, if only as a common way to construct short stories, you will be better prepared to recognize how a story departs from chronological order.

The first paragraph of Welty's story seems to be centered on *action*. Marian arrives at the Old Ladies' Home and prepares to enter it. Even so, Welty provides some basic information in this paragraph, describing Marian and the rest home as if the reader is unfamiliar with both. Yet only in the second paragraph do you learn Marian's name and the purpose of her visit. Therefore, Welty can be said to obey Adams's formula, beginning with *action* and then moving to *background*. Note, however, that the second paragraph features *development* as well. By explaining to the receptionist who she is and why she is there, Marian takes a step closer to the central event, her meeting with the two roommates. The remainder of the story keeps moving forward in time.

What about *climax*, Adams's fourth term? Traditionally, the climax of a story has been defined as a peak moment of drama appearing near the end. Also, it is usually thought of as a point when at least one character commits a significant act, experiences a significant change, makes a significant discovery, learns a significant lesson, or perhaps does all these things. With Welty's story, you could argue that the climax is when Marian asks Addie her age, meets with refusal, sees Addie crying, and tries to bolt. Certainly this is a dramatic moment, involving intense display of emotion resulting in Marian's departure. But Welty indicates, too, that Marian here experiences inner change. When she looks on Addie "as though there was nothing else in the world to wonder about," this is "the first time such a thing had happened to Marian."

Adams's term *ending* may seem unnecessary. Why would anyone have to be reminded that stories end? Yet a story's climax may engage readers so much that they overlook whatever follows. If the climax of Welty's story is Marian's conversation with the tearful Addie, then the ending is basically in four parts: the plea that Addie's roommate makes to Marian as she is leaving; Marian's final encounter with the receptionist; Marian's retrieval of the apple; and her escape on the bus, where she bites into the apple. Keep in mind that the ending of a story may relate somehow to its beginning. The ending of Welty's "A Visit of Charity," for instance, brings the story full circle. Whereas at the start Marian gets off a bus, hides the apple, and meets the receptionist, at the conclusion she rushes by the receptionist, recovers the apple, and boards another bus. However a story ends, ask yourself if any of the characters have changed at some point between start and finish. Does the conclusion of the story indicate that at least one person has developed in some way, or does it leave you with the feeling of lives frozen since the start? As Welty's story ends, readers may have various opinions about Marian. Some may find that she has not been changed all that much by her visit to the home, while others may feel that it has helped her mature.

A common organizational device in short stories is **repetition**. It takes various forms. First, a story may repeat words, as Welty's story does with its multiple uses of the word "wondered." Second, a story may repeatedly refer to a certain image, as you see with Welty's images of the plant and the apple. Third, a story may involve repeated actions. In "A Visit of Charity," the two roommates repeatedly argue; Marian travels by bus at the beginning and at the end; and the nurse consults her wristwatch both when Marian arrives and when she leaves.

POINT OF VIEW

A short story may be told from a particular character's perspective or **point of view**. When it is written in the **first person**—narrated by someone using the pronoun *I* or, more rarely, *we*—you have to decide how much to accept the narrator's point of view, keeping in mind that the narrator may be psychologically complex. How objective does the narrator seem in depicting other people and events? In what ways, if any, do the narrator's perceptions seem influenced by his or her personal experiences, circumstances, feelings, values, and beliefs? Does the narrator seem to have changed in any way since the events recalled? How reasonable do the narrator's judgments seem? At what moments, if any, do you find yourself disagreeing with the narrator's view of things?

Not every short story is narrated by an identifiable person. Many of them are told by what has been traditionally called an **omniscient narrator**. The word *omniscient* means "all-knowing" and is often used as an adjective for God. An omniscient narrator is usually a seemingly all-knowing, objective voice. This is the kind of voice at work in Welty's story, right from the first paragraph. There, Marian is described in an authoritatively matter-of-fact tone that appears detached from her: "Holding a potted plant before her, a girl of fourteen jumped off the bus in front of the Old Ladies' Home." Keep in mind, though, that a story may rely primarily on an omniscient narrator and yet at some points seem immersed in a character's perspective. This, too, is the case with Welty's story. Consider the following passage about Marian:

> Everything smelled wet—even the bare floor. She held on to the back of the chair, which was wicker and felt soft and damp. Her heart beat more and more slowly, her hands got colder and colder, and she could not hear whether the old women were saying anything or not. She could not see them very clearly. How dark it was! The window shade was down, and the only door was shut. Marian looked at the ceiling. . . . It was like being caught in a robbers' cave, just before one was murdered.

The passage remains in the third person, referring to "she" rather than to "I." Nevertheless, the passage seems intimately in touch with Marian's physical sensations. Indeed, the sentence "How dark it was!" seems something that Marian would say to herself. Similarly, the analogy to the robbers' cave may be Marian's own personal perception, and as such, the analogy may reveal more about her own state of mind than about the room. Many literary critics use the term **free indirect style** for moments like this, when a narrator otherwise omniscient conveys a particular character's viewpoint by resorting to the character's own language.

Throughout this book, we encourage you to analyze an author's strategies by considering the options that he or she faced. You may better understand a short story's point of view if you think about the available alternatives. For example, how would you have reacted to Welty's story if it had focused on Addie's perceptions more than on Marian's?

CHARACTERS

Although we have been discussing plots, we have also referred to the people caught up in them. Any analysis you do of a short story will reflect your understanding and evaluation of its **characters**. Rarely does the author of a story provide you with extended, enormously detailed biographies. Rather, you see the story's characters at select moments of their lives. To quote William Trevor again, the short story is "the art of the glimpse."

You may want to judge characters according to how easily you can identify with them. Yet there is little reason for you to read works that merely reinforce your prejudices. Furthermore, you may overlook the potential richness of a story if you insist that its characters fit your usual standards of behavior. An author can teach you much by introducing you to the complexity of people you might automatically praise or condemn in real life. Many of us would immediately condemn someone reluctant to help old women, but Welty encourages us to analyze carefully the girl in her story rather than just denounce her. You may be tempted to dismiss the roommates in Welty's story as unpleasant, even "sick"; in any case, take the story as an opportunity to explore *why* women in a rest home may express discontent.

One thing to consider about the characters in a story is what each basically desires. At the beginning of Welty's story, for example, Marian is hardly visiting the Old Ladies' Home out of "charity," despite that word's presence in the story's title. Rather, Marian hopes to earn points as a Campfire Girl. Again, characters in a story may change, so consider whether the particular characters you are examining alter their thinking. Perhaps you feel that Marian's visit broadens her vision of life; then again, perhaps you conclude that she remains much the same.

Reading a short story involves relating its characters to one another. In part, you'll need to determine their relative importance. Even a seemingly minor character can perform some noteworthy function; the nurse in "A Visit of Charity" not only ushers Marian in and out but also marks time. Nevertheless, any reader will try to identify a story's *main* figures. When a particular character seems the focus, he or she is referred to as the story's **protagonist**. Many readers would say that Marian is the protagonist of "A Visit of Charity." When the protagonist is in notable conflict with another character, this foe is referred to as the **antagonist**. Because Marian initially finds both roommates unpleasant, you may want to call them her antagonists. But it's not a word that you *must* apply to some character in a story; the work can have a protagonist and yet *not* include an opponent. Moreover, as a story proceeds, characters may alter their relationships with one another. Marian grows more conscious of the tensions *between* the roommates, and then for a moment she sympathizes with Addie. It is possible, too, for one character to be ambivalent toward another, feeling both drawn *and* opposed to that person.

Perhaps the roommates have a love-hate relationship, needing each other's company even as they bicker. As perhaps you have found in your own experience, human relationships are often far from simple. Works of literature can prove especially interesting when they suggest as much.

What power and influence people achieve may depend on particular traits of theirs. These include their gender, social class, race, ethnic background, nationality, sexual orientation, age, and the kind of work they do. Because these attributes may greatly affect a person's life, pay attention to them as you analyze characters. For instance, in Welty's story, all the characters are female. How might their gender matter? How might the story's dynamics have differed if it had featured at least one man? Another element of the story is its gap in ages: while the roommates are old, Marian is barely a teenager. What, over their years of living, might the two women have learned that the girl doesn't know yet?

Typically, characters express views of one another, and you have to decide how accurate these are. Some characters will seem wise observers of humanity. Others will strike you as making distorted statements about the world, revealing little more than their own biases and quirks. And some characters will seem to fall in the middle, coming across as partly objective and partly subjective. On occasion, you and your classmates may find yourselves debating which category a particular character fits. One interesting case is Welty's character Addie. Look again at the speech in which she berates her roommate:

> "Hush!" said the sick woman. "You never went to school. You never came and you never went. You never were anything—only here. You never were born! You don't know anything. Your head is empty, your heart and hands and your old black purse are all empty, even that little old box that you brought with you you brought empty—you showed it to me. And yet you talk, talk, talk, talk, talk all the time until I think I'm losing my mind! Who are you? You're a stranger—a perfect stranger! Don't you know you're a stranger? Is it possible that they have actually done a thing like this to anyone—sent them in a stranger to talk, and rock, and tell away her whole long rigmarole? Do they seriously suppose that I'll be able to keep it up, day in, day out, night in, night out, living in the same room with a terrible old woman—forever?"

Some may argue that this speech is merely an unreasonable rant, indicating Addie's dour mood rather than her roommate's true nature. (For one thing, contrary to Addie's declaration, the roommate must have been born!) Yet it can also be argued that Addie shrewdly diagnoses her situation. Perhaps statements like "you never were born," "your head is empty," and "you're a stranger" are true in a metaphorical sense.

SETTING

Usually a short story enables readers to examine how people behave in concrete circumstances. The characters are located in a particular place or **setting**. Moreover, they are shown at particular moments in their personal histories.

Sometimes the story goes further, referring to them as living at a certain point in world history.

As the word *sometimes* implies, short stories vary in the precision with which they identify their settings. They differ as well in the importance of their setting. Sometimes location serves as a mere backdrop for the plot. At other times, the setting can be a looming presence. When Welty's character Marian visits the Old Ladies' Home, we get her vivid impressions of it. Even when a story's setting seems ordinary, it may become filled with drama and meaning as the plot develops. One way of analyzing characters is to consider how they accommodate themselves — or fail to accommodate themselves — to their surroundings. The two roommates in Welty's story are evidently frustrated with living in the Old Ladies' Home, and they take out their frustration on each other.

IMAGERY

Just like poems, short stories often use **imagery** to convey meaning. Sometimes a character in the story may interpret a particular image just the way you do. Some stories, though, include images that you and the characters may analyze quite differently. One example is the apple in Welty's story. Whereas Marian probably views the apple as just something to eat, many readers would make other associations with it, thinking in particular of the apple that Adam and Eve ate from the tree of knowledge in the Garden of Eden. By the end of Welty's story, perhaps Marian has indeed become like Adam and Eve, in that she has lost her innocence and grown more aware that human beings age. At any rate, many readers would call Marian's apple a **symbol**. Traditionally, that is the term for an image seen as representing some concept or concepts. Again, Marian herself probably does not view her apple as symbolic; indeed, characters within stories rarely use the word *symbol* at all.

Images may appear in the form of metaphors or other figures of speech. For example, when Marian enters the Old Ladies' Home, she experiences "a smell in the hall like the interior of a clock." Welty soon builds on the clock image as she describes the receptionist checking her wristwatch, an action that this character repeats near the end. Welty's whole story can be said to deal with time and its effects, both on the old and on the young.

Images in short stories usually appeal to the reader's visual sense. Most often, they are things you can picture in your mind. Yet stories are not limited to rendering visual impressions. They may refer to other senses, too, as when Welty's young heroine notices the odor in the hall.

LANGUAGE

Everything about short stories we have discussed so far concerns **language**. After all, works of literature are constructed entirely out of words. Here, however, we call your attention to three specific uses of language in stories: title, predominant style, and dialogue.

A story's **title** may be just as important as any words in the text. Not always will the relevance of the title be immediately clear to you. Usually you have to read a story all the way through before you can sense fully how its title applies. In any case, play with the title in your mind, considering its various possible meanings and implications. In analyzing the title of Welty's "A Visit of Charity," you may find it helpful to think about this famous passage from the King James translation of the New Testament: "And now abideth faith, hope, charity, these three; but the greatest of these is charity" (1 Corinthians 13:13). You may also want to look up the word *charity* in a dictionary.

Not all short stories have a uniform **style**. Some feature various tones, dialects, vocabularies, and levels of formality. Welty's story incorporates different types of speech almost from its start. When, using rather formal language, the nurse asks Marian, "Acquainted with any of our residents?" (para. 3), the girl puts this question more plainly: "With any old ladies?" (para. 4). Stories that do have a predominant style are often told in the first person, thus giving the impression of a presiding "voice." Charlotte Perkins Gilman's "The Yellow Wallpaper" (p. 244) teems with the anguished expressions of its beleaguered narrator.

Dialogue may serve more than one purpose in a short story. By reporting various things, characters may provide you with necessary background for the plot. In Welty's story, it's only from the roommates' fragmentary remarks that Marian — and the reader — can learn anything about their lives up until now. Actually, dialogue can also be thought of as an action in itself, moving the plot along. Try to identify the particular kinds of acts that characters perform when they speak. When the first roommate asks the departing Marian for a coin, she seems to be begging, but perhaps she is also doing whatever she can to hold the girl there; her having "clutched the child" (para. 64) suggests as much. Indeed, dialogue may function to reveal shifts in characters' relations with one another.

THEME

We have already discussed the term **theme** on pages 55–57. There, we identified issues of theme as one kind of issue that comes up in literary studies. At the same time, we suggested that the term *theme* applies to various literary genres, not just short stories. Later in this chapter, we examine theme in connection with poems, plays, and essays. Here, though, we consider theme as an element of short fiction. In doing so, we review some points from our earlier discussion, applying them now to Welty's story.

Recall that we defined the theme of a work as the main claim it seems to make. Furthermore, we identified it as an assertion, a proposition, or a statement rather than as a single word. "Charity" is obviously a *topic* of Welty's story, but because it is just one word, it is not an adequate expression of the story's *theme*. The following exercise invites you to consider just what that theme may be.

1. Try to state a text's theme as a midlevel generalization.   If you were to put it in very broad terms, your audience would see it as fitting a great many works besides the one you have read. If you went to the opposite extreme, tying the theme completely to specific details of the text, your audience might think the theme irrelevant to their own lives.

The phrase "the moral of the story" suggests that a story can usually be reduced to a single message, often a principle of ethics or religion. Plenty of examples can be cited to support this suggestion. In the New Testament, for instance, Jesus tells stories—they are called *parables*—to convey some of his key ideas. In any number of cultures today, stories are used to teach children elements of good conduct. Moreover, people often determine the significance of a real-life event by building a story from it and by drawing a moral from it at the same time. These two processes conspicuously dovetailed when England's Princess Diana was killed in a car crash. Given that she died fleeing photographers, many people saw her entire life story as that of a woman hounded by the media. The moral was simultaneous and clear: thou shalt honor the right to privacy.

It is possible to lose sight of a story's theme by placing too much emphasis on minor details of the text. The more common temptation, however, is to turn a story's theme into an all-too-general cliché. Actually, a story is often most interesting when it *complicates* some widely held idea that it seemed ready to endorse. Therefore, a useful exercise is to start with a general thematic statement about the story and then make it increasingly specific. With "A Visit of Charity," for example, you might begin by supposing that a theme is "everyone must give up their dreams of innocence and paradise, just as Adam and Eve did." Your next step would be to identify the specific spin that Welty's story gives this idea. How does her story differ from others on this theme? Note, for instance, that Marian comes literally face to face with the mortality of women much older than she is and that the experience fills her momentarily with "wonder." Try to rephrase our version of Welty's theme so that it seems more in touch with these specific details of the text.

2. A theme of a text may be related to its title. It may also be expressed by some statement made within the text. But often various parts of the text merit consideration as you try to determine its theme.

In our discussion of a short story's language, we called attention to the potential significance of its title. The title may serve as a guide to the story's theme. What clues, if any, do you find in the title "A Visit of Charity"? Of course, determining a story's theme entails going beyond the title. You have to read, and usually reread, the entire text. In doing so, you may come across a statement that seems a candidate for the theme because it is a philosophical generalization. Nevertheless, take the time to consider whether the story's essence is indeed captured by this statement alone.

3. You can state a text's theme either as an observation or as a recommendation. Each way of putting it evokes a certain image of the text's author. When you state the theme as an **observation**, you depict the author as a psychologist, a philosopher, or some other kind of analyst. When you state the theme as a **recommendation**—which often involves your using the word *should*—you depict the author as a teacher, preacher, manager, or coach. That is, the author comes across as telling readers what to do.

As we have noted, stories are often used to teach lessons. Moreover, often the lessons are recommendations for action, capable of being phrased as "Do X" or "Do not do X." The alternative is to make a generalization about some state of affairs. When you try to express a particular story's theme, which of these two options should you follow? There are several things to consider in making your decision. First is your personal comfort: do you feel at ease with both ways of stating the theme, or is one of these ways more to your taste? Also worth pondering is the impression you want to give of the author: do you want to portray this person as a maker of recommendations, or do you want to assign the author a more modest role?

4. Consider stating a text's theme as a problem.   That way, you are more apt to convey the complexity and drama of the text.

We have suggested that short stories often pivot around conflicts between people and conflicts within people. Perhaps the most interesting stories are ones that pose conflicts not easily resolved. Probably you will be more faithful to such a text if you phrase its theme as a problem. In the case of Welty's story, for example, you might state the theme as follows: "Young people may sense an older person's infirmity, but, especially if that person is a stranger, they may as yet lack sufficient maturity and confidence to stay and help."

5. Rather than refer to *the* theme of a text, you might refer to *a* theme of the text, implying that the text has more than one.   You would still be suggesting that you have identified a central idea of the text. Subsequently, you might have to defend your claim.

Unlike the average novel, the typical short story pivots around only a few ideas. Yet you need not insist that the story you are analyzing has a single theme. The shortest piece of short fiction may have more than one, and your audience may well appreciate your admitting this. One theme of Welty's story may be that none of us can escape the passage of time. The old roommates aside, teenaged Marian seems on the brink of adulthood, and her concluding bus ride suggests that she is moving further into it. But additional themes are possible. A second idea, dramatized by the roommates' feud, may be that old age can test a person's spirit even as it hurts the person's body. Of course, to call either of these ideas a theme of the story is still to make a claim that requires support.

Perhaps the biggest challenge you will face in writing about short stories is to avoid long stretches of plot summary. Selected details of the plot will often serve as key evidence for you. You will need to describe such moments from the story you are discussing, even if your audience has already read it. But your readers are apt to be frustrated if you just repeat plot at length. They will feel that they may as well turn back to the story itself rather than linger with your rehash. Your paper is worth your readers' time only if you provide insights of your own, *analyzing* the story rather than just *summarizing* it.

To understand what analysis of a short story involves, let's turn to student Tanya Vincent. Assigned to write an argument paper about a short story, Tanya decided to focus on Welty's. She realized that for her paper to be effective, she had to come up with an issue worth addressing, a claim about that issue, and evidence for that claim. Moreover, she had to be prepared to identify her process of reasoning and her assumptions.

For most writing assignments, settling on an issue will be your most important preliminary step. Without a driving question, you will have difficulty producing fresh, organized, and sustained analysis. For her paper on "A Visit of Charity," Tanya chose to address this issue: What does the story suggest charity can mean? In part, she was drawn to this question because the word *charity* appears in the story's title and because it comes up in the famous passage from 1 Corinthians that we quoted earlier. But the question also enticed her because Welty's protagonist doesn't appear truly compassionate. A conventional definition of *charity* is that it is an expression of a sincere desire to help people. Given that Marian appears to lack this desire, is Welty's title ironic? Or does charity in some *other* sense of the word operate in the story? Tanya realized that she would be tackling an issue of definition. She would need to examine various possible meanings of *charity* and determine which are relevant to specific details of Welty's text.

A paper about a short story doesn't have to mention explicitly all the elements of short fiction we've identified. Nevertheless, thinking of these elements can help you plan such a paper, providing you with some preliminary terms for your analysis. Tanya perceived that her paper would be very much about characters and plot; it might also dwell upon imagery and language. She knew, too, that she would be more apt to persuade her readers if she included quotations from the story. Yet, as with plot summary, quoting should be limited, so that the paper seems an original argument—not a recycling of the literary work's own words. Tanya sensed that practically every sentence of Welty's story could be quoted and then interpreted. At the same time, she realized that she should quote only *some* words, not all.

Final Draft of a Student Paper

Here is Tanya's final draft of her paper about "A Visit of Charity." As you read it, keep in mind that it emerged only after she had done several preliminary drafts, in consultation with some of her classmates as well as her instructor. Although Tanya's paper is a good example of how to write about a short story, most drafts can stand to be revised further. What do you think Tanya has done well in her paper? If she planned to do yet another revision, what suggestions would you make?

Tanya Vincent
Professor Stein
English 1A
3 November - - - -

The Real Meaning of "Charity"
in "A Visit of Charity"

Many people would define the word "charity" as an act in which an individual or institution sincerely offers material or *An assumption, but seems a reasonable one.* spiritual comfort to someone less fortunate. In this respect,

charity is a form of love. Such is the meaning implied in the
King James translation of the most famous statement about
charity, 1 Corinthians 13:13: "And now abideth faith, hope,
charity, these three; but the greatest of these is charity." In
fact, some other translations of this biblical passage use
"love" instead of "charity," thereby suggesting that the two
terms are more or less equivalent. But Marian, the protagonist
of Eudora Welty's short story "A Visit of Charity," does not
appear to demonstrate this concept of charity when she
visits the Old Ladies' Home. She gives no indication that
she sincerely cares about any of its residents. Rather, she
approaches the visit as a mechanical task that she must
perform to raise her standing as a Campfire Girl. Nor does she
seem to become much more empathetic after spending time
at the Home. Several readers of the story, therefore, might
think its title ironic.

    This view may, however, be too limited. Welty may be
encouraging us to move past our familiar concept of
"charity" and give the word a meaning that *can* apply to her
text in a nonironic way. It is true that Marian does not act
lovingly or even compassionately on her trip to the Home.
Yet maybe her brief moments with the two elderly roommates
provide charity to Marian herself, making her a beneficiary of
it rather than a donor of it. After all, her encounter with the
two women helps to make her at least a bit more aware of
the stresses that old age can bring. Charity in *this* sense
would mean the providing of a necessary lesson about what
life can be like as an adult. Even though the two roommates
do not intend to be benevolent teachers of the girl, her
meeting with them has some value, for it gives her a preview
of realities she will have to deal with more extensively as she
grows up.

    When we first meet her in the story, Marian seems
anything but passionately devoted to improving life for the
Home's inhabitants. Probably "Old Ladies' Home" is not the
building's real name to begin with, but instead Marian's own
insensitive designation. Clearly she looks upon her visit as a
chore. To her, it is just something she must do to earn points.
Later, we readers learn that she has even computed the specific amounts available to her: "She had almost said that if
Campfire Girls brought flowers to the Old Ladies' Home, the
visit would count one extra point, and if they took a Bible
with them on the bus and read it to the old ladies, it counted
double" (line 124). When, back at the story's start, she introduces herself to the nurse, she does not even pretend to be a
true Angel of Mercy pursuing a higher spiritual purpose: "I'm

*Starts to introduce her issue
and claim by referring to
readers who are possibly
superficial.*

*A qualification. Tanya holds
back from claiming certainty
about Welty's intentions.*

*Introduction ends with main
issue (a definitional kind) and
main claim.*

*Concession to readers who
have trouble finding "charity"
in the story.*

a Campfire Girl. . . . I have to pay a visit to some old lady"
(122). So indifferent is she to the Home's aged occupants
that she candidly announces "any of them will do" (line 122).
When she does meet with the two roommates, she chooses
not to stay long with them. Nor does she offer charity in a
traditional sense when one of the roommates begs. While the
woman asks, "have you a penny to spare for a poor old woman
that's not got anything of her own?" (126), Marian is anxious
to flee. Nor, when she does leave the pair, is her exit gradual,
patient, and kind: she "jumped up and moved toward the door";
"pulled violently against the old hands"; "ran down the hall,
without looking behind her and without looking at the nurse";
"quickly . . . retrieved a red apple"; "ran to meet the big bus";
"shouted" at the bus; and "jumped on" (126). These frenzied
motions indicate that Marian is ultimately *repelled* by the two
women, not drawn to them as clients for her kindness.

Nevertheless, perhaps Marian's experience with them con-
fers a sort of charity upon *her* by alerting her to facts she will
eventually have to face. When she first meets the roommate
who is supposedly healthier, she is struck by the "terrible,
square smile (which was a smile of welcome) stamped on her
bony face" (123). This seems more an image of death than of
life, suggesting that Marian is beginning to grow conscious of
mortality. This implication gets even stronger when Marian
comes to the bed of the sicker woman, Addie: "She wondered
about her — she wondered for a moment as though there was
nothing else in the world to wonder about. It was the first
time such a thing had happened to Marian" (125). More precisely, Marian seems to discover that people soon to die may
become a mixture of helplessness and fierce self-assertion. To
the girl, Addie repeatedly comes across as a sheep or lamb, a
species of animal traditionally associated with innocence.
Even before she enters the room, Marian twice experiences
Addie's voice as that of a sheep "bleating" (122), and at
Addie's bedside she mentally compares the tearful, suffering
woman to "a little lamb" (125). Yet Addie is also someone
capable not only of refusing to tell her age, but also of berat-
ing her roommate: "And yet you talk, talk, talk, talk, talk all
the time until I think I'm losing my mind!" (125). In turn,
the object of this scorn displays to Marian a similar blend of
powerlessness and ferocity. "In an affected, high-pitched
whine," this roommate refers to herself as "a poor old
woman," but at the same time "she suddenly clutched the
child with her sharp little fingers" (125–26). Indeed, if Addie
comes across to Marian as a sheep or lamb, the girl senses
right from the start of the meeting that the other woman is

Here and elsewhere in the paper, Tanya quotes from Welty's text.

Transition to development of main claim.

As earlier, with "wondered," Tanya shows attention to repetition.

an aggressive bird: "Suddenly Marian saw a hand, quick as a bird claw, reach up in the air and pluck the white cap off her head" (123). In general, neither of the roommates fits the sentimental stereotype of the sweet old lady. But their difference from this image is precisely what can be educational for Marian. Their nearness to death, and the complex behavior they show in response to their fate, are matters that the girl will have to contend with a lot once she herself becomes a full-fledged adult.

While admitting that the sentence about "the first time" appears significant, some readers may doubt that Marian learns anything from this experience. Their skepticism would be understandable, given that she does not philosophize at length about the visit and ends it rather speedily. Welty does, however, suggest the stirrings of mental change in Marian by drawing our attention to the bodily disorientation she goes through in the old women's room. Immediately upon meeting them, she "stood tongue-tied" (123). Soon, "her heart beat more and more slowly, her hands got colder and colder, and she could not hear whether the old women were saying anything or not" (123). Moreover, "she could not see them very clearly" (123). A moment later, she winds up "pitched against the chair" (123) and forgets her own name. Eventually "her heart nearly stopped beating altogether" (125). These disabilities, though temporary, indicate that at *some* level of consciousness, Marian is having perceptions that she did not have before. Specifically, she seems to have glimmers of how death increasingly enters people's lives as they age.

Concession to readers with a different view.

The story's very last sentence further suggests that Marian either learns this lesson or vaguely intuits it. By taking "a big bite out of the apple" (126), she resembles Adam and Eve, whose own eating of an apple resulted in their becoming mortal. But in writing her story, Welty may also have had in mind a second biblical passage. Occurring just two lines before the famous statement about charity I have quoted, it is a well-known review of life's journey: "When I was a child, I spake as a child, I understood as a child, I thought as a child: but when I became a man, I put away childish things" (1 Corinthians 13:11). Although Marian is female, the line can still apply to her. Before her visit to the Home, she has been "a child," and she acts that way for much of her time there. But the visit may make her more inclined to "put away childish things," in which case she herself would receive a form of charity from it.

Again, acknowledges that she can't be certain about Welty's thinking.

Writing about Poems

Some students are put off by poetry, perhaps because their early experiences with it were discouraging. They imagine that poems have deep hidden meanings they can't uncover. Maybe their high-school English teacher always had the right interpretation, and they rarely did. This need not be the case. Poetry can be accessible to all readers.

The problem is often a confusion about the nature of poetry, since poetry is more compressed than prose. Poetry focuses more on connotative, emotional, or associative meanings and conveys meaning more through suggestion, indirection, and the use of metaphor, symbol, and imagery than prose does. It seldom hands us a specific meaning. Poetic texts suggest certain possibilities, but the reader completes the transaction. Part of the meaning comes from the writer, part from the text itself, and part from the reader. Even students who are the same age, race, religion, and ethnicity are not duplicates of one another. Each has unique experiences, family histories, and emotional lives. If thirty people read a poem about conformity or responsibility, all thirty will have varying views about these concepts, even though they will probably have some commonalities. (Most societies are so saturated with shared cultural experiences that it is nearly impossible to avoid some overlap in responses.)

In a good class discussion, then, we should be aware that even though we might be members of the same culture, each of us reads from a unique perspective, a perspective that might also shift from time to time. If a woman reads a poem about childbirth, her identity as a female will seem more relevant than if she were reading a poem about death, a more universal experience. In other words, how we read a poem and how significant and meaningful the poem is for us depends both on the content of the poem and on our specific circumstances. Suppose you are fourteen when you first read a poem about dating; you would likely have very different responses rereading it at nineteen, twenty-five, and fifty. We read poems through our experiences. As we gain new experiences, our readings change.

One reason to respond in writing to your first reading is to be able to separate your first thoughts from those of your classmates. They too will bring their own experiences, values, and ideas to the discussion. In the give-and-take of open discussion, it may be difficult to remember what you first said. Of course, the point of a classroom discussion is not simply to defend your initial response, for then you would be denying yourself the benefit of other people's ideas. A good discussion should open up the poem, allow you to see it from multiple viewpoints, and enable you to expand your perspective, to see how others make sense of the world.

This rich mixture of the poet's text, the reader's response, and discussion among several readers can create new possibilities of meaning. Even more than fiction or drama, poetry encourages creative readings that can be simultaneously true to the text and to the reader. A lively class discussion can uncover a dozen or more plausible interpretations of a poem, each backed up with valid evidence from both the poem and the reader's experience. You may try to persuade others that your views about the poem are correct; others may do the same to you. This negotiation is at the heart of a liberal, democratic education. In fact, maybe the most respected and repeated notion about being well educated is the ability to empathize with another's point of view, to see as another sees. Reading, discussing, and writing about poetry can help you become a person who can both create meaning and understand and appreciate how others do. This is one important way literature matters.

The following three poems are about work—about the joys and sorrows, the satisfactions and frustrations of physical labor. Some people might think of poets as intellectuals who are far removed from the experiences of the working class, but this is not the case. Indeed, many poets were themselves brought up in working-class homes and know firsthand the dignity and value of such work. Even among poets who do not toil with their hands, few lack the imaginative empathy that would allow them to write perceptively about firefighters and factory workers, cleaning women and mill workers. These three poems are especially relevant today when physical work is becoming less and less a reality among middle-class Americans. Poems that matter are poems about real life— about love and death, about pain and loss, about beauty and hope. These three poems about work are about all of these and more.

The first poem, Mary Oliver's (b. 1935) "Singapore," appeared in *House of Light* (1992). She has won a Pulitzer Prize for her poetry. "Blackberries" is by Yusef Komunyakaa (b. 1947), who has become known for exploring various aspects of African-American experience; the poem is from *Magic City* (1992). Edwin Arlington Robinson's "The Mill" is the oldest poem in the cluster. Robinson (1869–1935) is considered the first major poet of twentieth-century America.

MARY OLIVER
Singapore

In Singapore, in the airport,
a darkness was ripped from my eyes.
In the women's restroom, one compartment stood open.
A woman knelt there, washing something
        in the white bowl.   5

Disgust argued in my stomach
and I felt, in my pocket, for my ticket.

A poem should always have birds in it.
Kingfishers, say, with their bold eyes and gaudy wings.
Rivers are pleasant, and of course trees.   10
A waterfall, or if that's not possible, a fountain
        rising and falling.
A person wants to stand in a happy place, in a poem.

When the woman turned I could not answer her face.
Her beauty and her embarrassment struggled together, and   15
    neither could win.
She smiled and I smiled. What kind of nonsense is this?
Everybody needs a job.
Yes, a person wants to stand in a happy place, in a poem.
But first we must watch her as she stares down at her labor,   20
    which is dull enough.
She is washing the tops of the airport ashtrays, as big as
    hubcaps, with a blue rag.
Her small hands turn the metal, scrubbing and rinsing.
She does not work slowly, nor quickly, but like a river.   25
Her dark hair is like the wing of a bird.

I don't doubt for a moment that she loves her life.
And I want her to rise up from the crust and the slop
    and fly down to the river.
This probably won't happen.   30
But maybe it will.
If the world were only pain and logic, who would want it?

Of course, it isn't.
Neither do I mean anything miraculous, but only
the light that can shine out of a life. I mean   35
the way she unfolded and refolded the blue cloth,
the way her smile was only for my sake; I mean
the way this poem is filled with trees, and birds.   *[1992]*

YUSEF KOMUNYAKAA

Blackberries

They left my hands like a printer's
Or thief's before a police blotter
& pulled me into early morning's
Terrestrial sweetness, so thick
The damp ground was consecrated   5
Where they fell among a garland of thorns.

Although I could smell old lime-covered
History, at ten I'd still hold out my hands
& berries fell into them. Eating from one
& filling a half gallon with the other,   10
I ate the mythology & dreamt
Of pies & cobbler, almost

Needful as forgiveness. My bird dog Spot
Eyed blue jays & thrashers. The mud frogs
In rich blackness, hid from daylight.   15

An hour later, beside City Limits Road
I balanced a gleaming can in each hand,
Limboed between worlds, repeating *one dollar.*
The big blue car made me sweat.
Wintertime crawled out of the windows.   20
When I leaned closer I saw the boy
& girl my age, in the wide back seat
Smirking, & it was then I remembered my fingers
Burning with thorns among berries too ripe to touch.   *[1992]*

EDWIN ARLINGTON ROBINSON
The Mill

The miller's wife had waited long,
    The tea was cold, the fire was dead;
And there might yet be nothing wrong
    In how he went and what he said:
"There are no millers any more,"   5
    Was all that she had heard him say;
And he had lingered at the door
    So long that it seemed yesterday.

Sick with fear that had no form
    She knew that she was there at last;   10
And in the mill there was a warm
    And mealy fragrance of the past.
What else there was would only seem
    To say again what he had meant;
And what was hanging from a beam   15
    Would not have heeded where she went.

And if she thought it followed her,
    She may have reasoned in the dark
That one way of the few there were
    Would hide her and would leave no mark: 20
Black water, smooth above the weir
    Like starry velvet in the night,
Though ruffled once, would soon appear
    The same as ever to the sight.   *[1920]*

A Student's Personal Responses to the Poems

The following are selections from the response journal of student Michaela
Fiorucci, who chose to focus on boundaries—on the various divisions we set
up between ourselves and other people, such as income, race, gender, sexual
preference, and religion. It seemed to her an interesting way to talk about work

since Michaela had observed barriers of all kinds between workers at her job at the university.

Using an explorative strategy, Michaela did some freewriting on the three poems, hoping to discover an argument about boundaries that might fit. The following are selections from her response journal.

> In "Singapore," there is a clear boundary between the middle-class American tourist and the cleaning lady, so much so that at first the narrator says, "Disgust argued in my stomach." The cleaning woman also seems to believe in a barrier and continues to work in a steady way. The narrator finally sees beauty in her dedication to her work. When the narrator does see beauty in her work habits, it helps close the barrier between them. There are also the issues of boundaries between fantasy and reality and between a world of pain and logic and one with birds and rivers. But at the end these boundaries also seem to be closing.
>
> In "Blackberries," the young boy seems to be living in a rural paradise, beyond the city boundaries, outside the usual urban and suburban environment. He lives in a land of bird dogs, jays, thrashers, and mud frogs. He makes comparisons between blackness and light that seem to anticipate the economic boundary that appears in the last stanza, the one between the poor boy and the rich kids in the car. It is this division between the children in air-conditioned comfort and the narrator on the outside looking in that seems to be the main point of this poem. Some boundaries cause us pain.
>
> "The Mill" tells the sad story of a miller who could not see a boundary between himself and his job. When he tells his wife "there are no millers any more," he is really saying that his life is over; he has no reason to live. And so he crosses the boundary between life and death. Tragically, his wife also has difficulty seeing herself outside her role as wife and housekeeper, and so she also crosses that ultimate boundary. She does so, however, in a completely different way: she drowns herself, so no one will know. She passes through life's boundary without leaving a trace.

After reading these brief freewrites to her response group, Michaela still didn't have a focus, but she liked the idea that boundaries, like walls, sometimes serve a purpose and sometimes they don't. She remembered a discussion of Robert Frost's "Mending Wall" from another course that focused on negotiating the walls we build between us. Her professor liked this idea since it helped her considerably narrow the concept of boundaries.

After reviewing her freewriting, Michaela wrote the following first draft and read it to her response group. She then discussed with her instructor her plans for a revision. Her instructor made a number of specific and general comments. After reading her first draft, what feedback would you give Michaela? Her revision appears later in this chapter on pp. 182–84.

First Draft of a Student Paper

Michaela Fiorucci
Mr. Hardy
English 102
15 April ----

Boundaries in Robinson, Komunyakaa, and Oliver

Although most sophomores I know at school value their privacy, they also want to create intimate relationships. It is often hard to reconcile these two impulses. Most middle-class students are lucky enough to have their own rooms, private enclaves against annoying sisters and brothers, intrusive mothers and fathers. But a room is also more than a physical boundary; it is also a symbolic assertion of identity. It says, "I'm separate from others, even within the closeness of the family." Such a commitment to physical privacy might be innocent enough, but it does contain dangerous seeds, especially when extended beyond the home to neighborhoods. When different ethnic groups want boundaries between them, it is no longer innocent. When the upper classes need to be separated from workers because they see each other as radically different, a dangerous boundary has been erected.

It would be reductive, however, to say all boundaries need to be erased. Edwin Arlington Robinson's "The Mill" is a good example of the dangerous consequences of a missing boundary. The poem narrates the sad story of a farm couple who commit suicide — the husband because he feels useless, the wife because she can't imagine life without her husband. During my first few readings, I was struck by the lack of communication between the couple. He must have been depressed for a long time, but it seems they never discussed his feelings. Keeping an emotional distance from others was probably a typical part of the way men and women dealt with each other a hundred years ago. It was a boundary not to be crossed. Apparently he could not say, "I feel terrible that I am going to lose my job." And his wife accepts his reticence, even though he might have been having second thoughts as he "lingered at the door". Clearly this is a boundary that should have been breached. But after several readings I began to realize that the boundary that should have been established wasn't — the idea that a person's value or worth is synonymous with his or her identity is dehumanizing. And it probably isn't something that just happened in the past. Nor is the equally dehumanizing idea that a wife is nothing without her husband. When the miller's wife decides to "leave no mark" by jumping into the pond, she is admitting she is not a worthwhile person by herself. Both identify totally with a role that in my view should be only one aspect of a complex human life. The final barrier she crosses, from life to death, is symbolically represented in the poem as a feminine domestic gesture: she doesn't want to leave a mess. The boundaries of person and occupation should be made clear; the arbitrary boundaries between genders should not.

When the narrator in Yusef Komunyakaa's "Blackberries" claims that he is "Limboed between worlds" (18), he means the rural paradise of "Terrestrial sweetness" (4) and "rich blackness" (15) he temporarily lives in versus the commercial, urban work that "made me sweat" (19). He has constructed a boundary between the ancient picking of berries and the technology of automobiles, between a natural closeness with nature and the artificial "Wintertime crawled out of the windows" (20). Even though the narrator is only ten, he senses the sensual joys of being one with nature. He seems to reject "old lime-covered / History" (7–8) in favor of "mythology" (11), which seems to suggest a conscious rejection or maybe repression of the contemporary world. But this boundary cannot stand. He needs the outside world to survive, and when the car approaches, it is the modern world and all its pluses and minuses that draw near. When he looks in, he sees "Smirking" (23) children; he sees class prejudice, hierarchy, and economic reality. The smirkers of the world are in charge. This realization dissolves the protective boundary around his Garden of Eden, and he feels physical pain. But really he feels the pain of initiation, the pain of having to cross a boundary he wanted to delay as long as possible. Although we can sympathize with the young narrator, he would probably have fared better by not making his boundary so extreme.

The narrator in Mary Oliver's "Singapore" at first sees a significant boundary between herself as a middle-class traveler and a cleaning woman washing a toilet. It is a separation we might all make, given our socialization to see this kind of physical labor as degrading. College-educated people in America have a tendency to see themselves as distinct from workers. For most, a woman washing something in a compartment is beyond the pale, a clear indication that the woman is other. But Oliver does have some conflicting ideas since she says a "Disgust argued in my stomach" (6). Since we are also socialized to be tolerant and open-minded, she knows she shouldn't think this way. And since she is also a writer with ideas about how a poem should "always have birds in it" (8), she looks harder at the cleaning woman, finally seeing in her face, in her hair, and in the way she works slowly, "like a river" (25), the positive aspects she probably wants to find. Oliver does not simply accept the boundaries that her culture constructs but negotiates with herself, eventually seeing that "light . . . can shine out of a life" (35) even where we do not expect it. In the woman's careful folding and unfolding of her blue work cloth and in her smile, Oliver eclipses the social boundary and ends up with a life-affirming vision "filled with trees, and birds" (38).

The Elements of Poetry

SPEAKER AND TONE

The voice we hear in a poem could be the poet's, but it is better to think of the speaker as an artistic construction—perhaps a **persona** (mask) for the poet or perhaps a character who does not resemble the poet at all. For example, the speaker in Lynda Hull's "Night Waitress" (p. 104) is not the poet herself but a struggling worker. In large part, to describe any poem's speaker is to pinpoint the person's tone or attitude. Sometimes this is hard to discern. The tone could be ironic or sentimental, joyful or morose, or a combination of emotions. To get a precise sense of it, read the poem aloud, actually performing the speaker's role. Bear in mind that his or her tone may change over the course of the poem. For instance, as the speaker in Yusef Komunyakaa's "Blackberries" recalls a day in his childhood when he picked fruit and then tried to sell it on a highway, he shifts from nostalgia (remembering "Terrestrial sweetness") to bitter recognition of class bias (the "Smirking" of the children who passed him in their car).

The narrator of "The Mill" immediately creates a somber, foreboding tone of anxiety and dread with the tea is "cold" and the fire is "dead," which also foreshadows the death of the miller. Likewise, his brief statement that "there are no millers any more" reinforces and intensifies the sense of impending doom that permeates the plot and theme of the poem. And, of course, such a grim tone is warranted by the dual suicides. Interestingly, the ominous tone of the poem noticeably shifts in the last four lines to one of quiet, smooth repose as the once ruffled pond appears "like starry velvet in the night." Perhaps the miller and his wife are finally at peace.

DICTION AND SYNTAX

Although we would all agree that poets rely on the meaning of words to express their feelings and their ideas, what words mean is no simple matter. Perplexed over what a poet might have intended, we often consult a dictionary. And that certainly might help demystify a puzzling passage. But poetry is often more about complicating than clarifying. Most poets are more interested in opening up words than pinning them down. Unlike journalists or science writers, poets often intend to be ambiguous. They like a word's possibilities, its rich emotional overtones. That's one reason readers see in poems different things; one reader may think of the line "Wintertime crawled out of the window" as meaning air conditioning and another as meaning the chilly arrogance and distaste of the privileged for laborers. Only Komunyakaa knows exactly what he meant by "wintertime."

Looking up *wintertime* in the dictionary would give us the denotative meaning, which wouldn't be much help here. But the emotional overtones or associations for individual readers give us the complex multiplicity that poets hope will enrich the poem's meaning. When in "Singapore," for example, the narrator says "a darkness was ripped from my eyes," the objective denotative meaning is probably not what she is after. More likely Oliver is counting on the more subjective, emotional associations of "darkness." Perhaps lack of understanding or ignorance is suggested. Perhaps intolerance or fear of otherness comes to mind. And in the background lie all the negative associations of the unknown, the uncertainty and the danger of things unseen. These are the word's connotations, and they are crucial to the evocative suggestiveness of poems. Oliver wants readers to allow connotation to do its work in expanding and personalizing the meaning of words. In this sense, the word *darkness* contains within it infinite subjective and cultural possibilities.

The same is true for "light" in line 38 of the last stanza. It is the connotative possibilities that infuse "light" with significance, especially when contrasted with the darkness of the first stanza. Seen in the context of the poem, "light" might suggest beauty or integrity or perhaps dedication, commitment, or the ability to find in work something valuable and beautiful. For religious readers, "light" might suggest the beauty and worthiness of each human soul, while for the political thinkers, the dedication and skill of laborers might come to mind. What other connotations can you suggest for these two words?

The last line of the poem offers a clear distinction between denotation and connotation when Oliver says, "this poem is filled with trees, and birds." Literally, of course, trees and birds do not fill the page (except for the actual words), but if we think of trees and birds connoting or suggesting delicate beauty or the majesty of nature or perhaps simply positive and pleasant thoughts, then through her diction, Oliver's meaning is both clarified and expanded.

FIGURES OF SPEECH

When we use figures of speech, we mean something other than the words' literal meaning. In the first sentence of "Singapore," Mary Oliver writes that "a darkness was ripped from my eyes." This direct comparison is a **metaphor**. Had she been more indirect, she might have written "it was like a darkness . . . ," a common literary device called a **simile**. Poets use metaphors and similes to help us see in a fresh perspective. Comparing love to a rose encourages us to think differently about love, helping us see its delicate beauty. Of course, today that comparison is no longer novel and can even be a cliché, suggesting that a writer is not trying to be original and is settling instead for an easy comparison. When Robert Burns wrote "my love is like a red, red rose" more than two hundred years ago, it was a fresh comparison that excited new ways of looking at love. Indeed, some theorists, like the contemporary American philosopher Richard Rorty, think that metaphors can change our ways of looking at the world. Our thinking about time, for example, might be different if we didn't think with linear metaphors about the past being behind us and the future up ahead. What if, as some American Indian languages do, ours used a circular metaphor, having just one day that constantly repeated itself? Would our perceptions of time change?

What if Mary Oliver had begun her poem by saying that "a misunderstanding was corrected," instead of "a darkness was ripped from my eyes"? Her metaphor is not only more dramatic and memorable but also more suggestive. Darkness deepens the idea of lack of knowledge, suggesting not only intellectual blindness but also a host of negative connotations that readers might associate with the dark. Fresh metaphors can be expansive and illuminating. They help us understand the world differently.

Oliver creatively uses metaphors and similes throughout "Singapore." "Disgust argued" is an interesting metaphor or perhaps a personification, in which the speaker's stomach is given the ability to argue. She interrupts her observation of the cleaning woman in the third stanza to make a comment on the function of poetry itself, claiming that poems should have birds, rivers, and trees in them. Is she suggesting metaphorically that poems should be pleasant? Is that the only thing birds, rivers, and trees suggest to you?

She returns to the woman, and they exchange glances. Apparently, the speaker is struggling with her own socialization that sees this kind of physical labor as demeaning. She directly describes the woman's "scrubbing and rinsing" but then returns to similes, describing her work as being "like a river" and her hair "like the wing of a bird." These comparisons seem for a moment to clarify the event for the speaker, helping her see this seemingly oppressive job positively. Amazingly, she wants the woman actually to become a bird and "rise up from the crust and the slop and fly."

But in the final stanza, she reminds us that she isn't really expecting that kind of physical miracle; instead, she wants to remind us that how we describe the woman working controls how we feel about her. If we see the folding and unfolding of her washcloth metaphorically, then we might see her differently; we might see her natural dignity, her beauty, and how her "light" was able to illuminate the speaker's "darkness."

Sometimes the poet chooses words like *darkness* and *light* that are so rich in texture that they can be examined as both metaphor and connotation. Such words might also be thought of as examples of synecdoche or metonymy. **Synecdoche** substitutes part of something for the whole, as in "I love my new wheels," referring to a car. **Metonymy** substitutes something associated with a thing, as in "Hollywood is resisting censorship" referring to the entire film industry. Oliver's "eyes" might be a synecdoche for her mind, and "darkness" and "light" can be metonymies for ignorance and beauty. Locate examples in our three poems of metaphor, connotation, synecdoche, and metonymy, if you can.

Although students often seem perplexed when professors find hidden **symbols** in poems, writers rarely plant such puzzling images deep in the recesses of their texts. The best symbols grow naturally out of the meaning-making process that readers go through. In the context of a particular poem, symbols are usually objects that can stand for general ideas. And like metaphors and similes, they suggest different things to different readers. The whale in *Moby-Dick*, for example, can be read as a symbol for implacable evil or perhaps the mysteries of the universe. In "Singapore," the specific event of the speaker watching a woman washing ashtrays in a toilet could be symbolic of anything we find unpleasant or strange or alien. And the whole event, including her eventual understanding, could easily be an **allegory** or extended symbol for the necessity for all of us to transcend our cultural socialization to understand other cultures and other attitudes toward working.

SOUND

The English poet Alexander Pope hoped that poetry's **sound** could become "an echo to [its] sense," that what the ear hears would reinforce what the mind understands. To many people, **rhyme** is the most recognizable aspect of poetry. The matching of final vowel and consonant sounds can make a poem trite or interesting. The now-familiar rhyming of "moon" and "June" with "swoon" suggests a poet who will settle for a cliché rather than do the hard work of being fresh. Rhyme, of course, is pleasing to the ear and makes the poem easier to remember, but it also gives the poem psychological force. Most contemporary poets choose not to rhyme, preferring the flexibility and freedom of free verse. But sound is still a high priority.

One of the most famous and effective examples of how sound can "echo" its sense is found in Robert Frost's "Stopping by Woods on a Snowy Evening," especially in the last two stanzas:

> He gives his harness bells a shake
> To ask if there is some mistake.
> The only other sound's the sweep
> Of easy wind and downy flake.
>
> The woods are lovely, dark and deep,
> But I have promises to keep,
> And miles to go before I sleep,
> And miles to go before I sleep.

Skilled poets like Frost use **alliteration** to connect words near each other by repeating the initial consonant sound. A variation, **assonance**, repeats vowel sounds. Frost obviously and subtly employs these sound techniques to echo both theme and mood. The alliterative -s's in "shake," "some," "sound's," and "sweep" also connect the meaning of these words, which are also reinforced by the -s's in "gives," "his," "harness," "bells," "asks," "is," "mistake," "sound's," and "easy." And when alliteration is combined with the assonance of "sweep" and "easy," as well as "downy" and "sound's," visual, tactile, and aural images are joined to create a soothing, restful, and idyllic scene of beauty and peace. All of these choices prepare the reader for the -e's of "keep" and "deep" and the -s's of the repeated "woods," "promises," "miles," and "sleep." In this way, the serenity and retreat of the woods are verbally and thematically contrasted with the demands of life's duties, culminating in the deadly temptation to escape responsibility by entering the winter woods.

Notice how Mary Oliver uses alliteration in her first stanza to link "women's," "woman," "washing," and "white." Komunyakaa's first stanza too links "printers," "police," and "pulled" as well as "they," "thief's," "Terrestrial," "thick," and "thorns." What effect do these and other elements of sound have on the impact and meaning of the poems?

☰ A WRITING EXERCISE

Note the use of alliteration and assonance in all three poems. How might these devices enhance meaning?

RHYTHM AND METER

Many poets in the early twentieth century chose to have their poems rhyme. Edwin Arlington Robinson's "The Mill" employs a typical **rhyme scheme** in which in each stanza the last words in lines 1 and 3 sound the same and the last words in lines 2 and 4 sound the same. We indicate such a pattern with letters—*abab*. The second half of the first stanza would then be *cdcd* and so forth.

Rhythm in poetry refers to the beat, a series of stresses, pauses, and accents. We are powerfully attuned to rhythm, whether it is our own heartbeat or the throb of the bass guitar in a rock band. When we pronounce a word, we give more **stress** (breath, emphasis) to some syllables than to others. When these stresses occur at a regular interval over, say, a line of poetry, we refer to it as **meter**. When we scan a line of poetry, we try to mark its stresses and pauses. We use ´ to indicate a stressed syllable and ˘ for an unstressed one. The basic measuring unit for these stressed and unstressed syllables in English is the **foot**. There are four usual feet: *iambic, trochaic, anapestic,* and *dactylic.* An **iamb** is an unstressed syllable followed by a stressed one, as in "the woóds." Reversed we have a **trochee**, as in "tigĕr." An **anapest** contains three syllables that are unstressed, then unstressed, then stressed, as in "Whĕn thĕ blúe / wăve rŏlls níghtlў / ŏn deép Gălĭleé." The reverse, the **dactyl,** can be heard in the Mother Goose rhyme, "Pússў cát, / pússў cát / whére hăvĕ yŏu / beén?" If you look at the first four lines of "The Mill" again, you can hear a regular beat of iambs:

> Thĕ mill / ĕr's wife / hăd waít / ĕd lóng,
>
> Thĕ téa / wăs cóld, / thĕ fire / wăs deád;
>
> Ănd thére / mĭght yét / bĕ nóth / ĭng wróng
>
> Ĭn hów / hĕ wént / ănd whát / hĕ saíd:

Depending on the number of feet, we give lines various names. If a line contains one foot, it is a **monometer**; two, a **dimeter**; three, a **trimeter**; four, a **tetrameter**; five, a **pentameter**; six, a **hexameter**; seven, a **heptameter**; and eight, an **octometer**. So Robinson's lines are iambic tetrameter. Most lines in Shakespeare's sonnets are iambic pentameter, or five iambs.

Note the punctuation in Robinson's poem. When a line ends with a comma, we are meant to pause very briefly; when a line ends with a period (end stop), we pause a bit longer. But when there is no punctuation (line 7), we are meant to continue on until the end of the next line. This is known as *enjambment.* These poetic techniques improve the sound and flow of the poem and enhance the thoughts and feelings that give poetry its memorable depth and meaningfulness.

THEME

Some readers are fond of extracting ideas from poems, claiming, for example, that the theme of "Blackberries" is the loss of innocence or that the theme of "The Mill" is the loss of identity. In a sense, these thematic observations are plausible enough, but they are limiting and misleading. "Blackberries" certainly seems to have something to do with the interruption of a certain view about physical labor, but the significance for each reader might be much more specific, having to do with the noble savage; the Garden of Eden; hierarchy in society; the arrogance of the rich; or sensitivity, cruelty, and dignity. "The Mill" could also be about gender relations, economic cruelty, or the responsibility of communities. Reducing a complex, ambiguous poem to a bald statement robs the poem of its evocative power, its mystery, and its art.

Some critics stress the response of readers; others care only for what the text itself says; still others are concerned with the social and cultural implications of the poem's meaning. Psychoanalytic readers may see poems as reflections of the psychological health or illness of the poet; source-hunting or intertextual readers want to find references and hints of other literary works hidden deep within the poem. Feminist readers may find sexism, Marxists may find economic injustice, and gay and lesbian readers may find heterosexual bias. Readers can and will find in texts a whole range of issues. Perhaps we find what we are looking for, or we find what matters most to us.

This does not mean that we should think of committed readers as biased or as distorting the text to fulfill their own agenda, although biased or distorted readings are not rare. In a literature course, readers are entitled to read poems according to their own interpretations as long as they follow the general convention of academic discourse. That is, it is possible to make a reasonable case that "Blackberries" is really about rejecting contemporary technology in favor of rural life. The reason that some themes sound more plausible than others is that these critics marshal their evidence from the text and their own experience. Usually the evidence that fits best wins: if you can persuade others that you have significant textual support for your theme and if you present a balanced and judicious persona, you can usually carry the day. Poems almost always have several reasonable themes. The critic's job is to argue for a theme that seems to make the most sense in relation to the support. Often the same evidence can be used to bolster different themes because themes are really just higher-level generalizations than the particulars found in the text. Critics use the concrete elements of a poem to make more general abstract statements. In "Blackberries," for example, the same textual support could be used to uphold a theme about the cruelty of children, the more general notion of an initiation in a class-conscious culture, or the even more general idea of the inevitable loss of innocence.

Revised Draft of a Student Paper

Michaela Fiorucci
Mr. Hardy
English 102
25 April - - - -

Negotiating Boundaries

Although most college students value their privacy, they
also want to create intimate relationships; it is often hard to
reconcile these two impulses. Most middle-class students are
lucky enough to have their own bedrooms, private enclaves
against annoying sisters and brothers, intrusive mothers and
fathers. But such boundaries are more than physical barriers;
they are also a symbolic assertion of identity. They say, "I'm
separate from you even within the closeness of our family."
Such a commitment to physical privacy might be innocent
enough, but it does contain dangerous seeds, especially when
extended beyond the home to neighborhoods. When different
ethnic groups want boundaries between them, it is no longer
innocent. When the upper classes want to be separated from
workers because they see each other as radically different, a
dangerously undemocratic boundary has been erected.
Boundaries clearly serve a protective function, but unneeded ones
can also prevent us from helping and understanding each other.
Writers like Edwin Arlington Robinson, Yusef Komunyakaa, and
Mary Oliver understand that we must negotiate boundaries,
building them when they increase privacy and self-worth and
bridging them when human solidarity can be enhanced.

> *Creates context about boundaries, moving from the personal to neighborhoods and beyond.*

> *Announces her focus on need to negotiate.*

It would be reductive to say that boundaries are either
good or bad, since their value depends so much on context.
Robinson's "The Mill" is a good example of the dangerous consequences of a failure to cross a boundary that should not exist
and then a failure to establish a boundary where one should
exist. The poem narrates the sad story of a farm couple who
commit suicide — the husband because he feels useless, the
wife because she can't imagine life without her husband.
A contemporary reader is struck by the lack of communication
between the couple. He must have been depressed for a long
time, but it seems they never discussed his feelings. Keeping
such an emotional boundary between husband and wife was
probably typical of the way men and women dealt with each
other one hundred years ago. Apparently, it was a constructed
barrier that few could cross. He simply could not bare his heart
by saying, "I feel terrible that I am going to lose my job." And
his wife accepts his reticence, even though he might have been

> *Begins first concrete supporting example.*

> *Example of harmful tradition boundary.*

having second thoughts as he "lingered at the door". Clearly, this is a boundary that should have been breached. The time for their solidarity was before he kills himself, not after.

After several readings, it is clear that the boundary that should have been established wasn't. The miller is the victim of the demeaning idea that a person's worth is synonymous with his or her occupation. When his job disappears, so must he. Although Robinson's tone is flat, we sense his frustration with the inevitability of this grim tragedy, one that is compounded by the equally dehumanizing idea that a wife cannot exist without her husband. When the miller's wife decides to "leave no mark" by jumping into the pond, she is admitting that she is useless outside her matrimonial role. Both identify with a role that should be only one aspect of a complex human life. The final barrier she crosses, from life to death, is symbolically represented in the poem as a feminine domestic gesture: she doesn't want to leave a mess. She continues as a housewife even in death. The boundaries between a person and occupation should be clear, but the arbitrary boundaries between husbands and wives should continue to be eradicated.

Concrete reference to poems strengthens argument.

Concludes paragraph with example of a boundary needing negotiating.

When the ten-year-old narrator in "Blackberries" claims that he is "Limboed between worlds" (18), he means the rural paradise of "Terrestrial sweetness" (4) and "rich blackness" (15) he temporarily lives in versus the commercial urban world that seems to make him anxious. He has constructed a boundary between the ancient task of picking berries and the modern technology of automobiles, between a closeness with nature and the artificial air-conditioning of the car. Although the narrator enjoys being one with nature, he seems to be cutting himself off from the realities of the world. He seems to reject "old lime-covered / History" (7–8) in favor of "mythology" (11), which seems to suggest a conscious rejection of the present. But this is a boundary that cannot stand. He needs the outside world to survive financially, and so when the car approaches, it is the modern world and all its complexity that draws near. When he looks into the car, he sees "Smirking" (23) children; he sees class prejudice, hierarchy, and economic reality. The smirkers of the world are in charge. It is this realization that dissolves the protective boundary around his Garden of Eden; consequently, he feels physical pain, but it is really the pain of initiation into reality that he feels. He must now cross a boundary he tried to delay. Although we can sympathize with the young narrator, like the couple in "The Mill," he would have been better off not making his boundary so extreme.

Second concrete example of problematic boundary.

Notes consequences of not negotiating.

Connection to previous poem increases essay's unity.

The narrator in Mary Oliver's "Singapore" also imagines that she sees a significant boundary, here between herself as a middle-class traveler and a cleaning woman laboring over a toilet. It is a separation we might all make, given our socialization in America to consider this kind of physical labor as degrading. College-educated people have a tendency to see themselves as distinct from the working class. For many, a woman washing an ashtray in a toilet bowl is beyond the pale, a clear indication that the woman is Other. But Oliver does not simply give into her cultural conditioning; she contests the boundary, asserting that a "Disgust argued in my stomach"(6). Since part of our democratic socialization is also to be tolerant and open-minded, Oliver knows that she shouldn't stereotype workers. And since she is also a writer with ideas about how a poem should "always have birds in it" (8), she looks hard at the cleaning woman, finally seeing in her face, in her hair, and in the way she works, slowly "like a river" (25), the positive aspects of the woman that most of us would probably miss.

Third concrete example of boundaries.

Explicit example of negotiating a boundary.

Oliver does not simply accept the boundaries that her culture constructs. Instead, she negotiates internally, eventually seeing that a "light . . . can shine out of a life" (35) even where we would not expect it. In the woman's careful folding and unfolding of her blue work cloth and in her smile, Oliver sees a beauty that helps her eclipse a social boundary, ending with a life-affirming vision "filled with trees, and birds" (38). Such an insight does not come easily to us because we usually accept our given cultural boundaries. The miller and his wife are tragically unequipped to bridge the divide between them. Likewise, the boy in "Blackberries" is unable to sustain his fantasy boundaries. Oliver's traveler, however, struggles to negotiate boundaries and is thereby able to increase human solidarity even across class structures and cultures.

Notes benefits of breaching a boundary.

Concludes by uniting all three poems in support of claim.

Comparing Poems and Pictures

Although literature and visual art may seem quite different media, they have often been closely connected. For one thing, any page of literature is a visual image, whether or not readers are always conscious of this fact. Also, most publishers of literature carefully design the covers of their books, aiming to lure readers in. Specific genres and authors, however, have forged even stronger relations between literature and art. Beginning in classical times and continuing today, many poems have precisely described existing paintings and sculptures; this tradition of verse is called **ekphrasis**. In the late eighteenth century, William Blake made highly ornamental engravings of his poems, so that they were striking works of art and not just written texts. In the nineteenth century, many novels included illustrations, a tradition evident today in children's picture books. At present, perhaps you are a fan of **graphic novels**: comic books that combine words and images to tell stories aimed at adults.

Aside from this history of connections, comparing a literary text with an image is a good mental exercise. The process can help you acquire more insights into each work. Given this possibility, we present a pairing on pages 186–87 of an Edward Hopper painting and a Rolando Perez poem, both titled *Office at Night*. In this case, the poem was written in response to the image. In other cases you may wish to connect a poem and an image for the first time, to trace their similarities and differences. With any such pairing, comparison can help you generate ideas for writing, a principle we stress throughout this book.

ANALYZING VISUAL ART

You can better understand a work of visual art—and develop ideas for an essay about it—if you raise certain questions about it and try to answer them. These questions apply to various types of pictures. Bear in mind that even photographs are not mere reproductions of reality. People who create them are, consciously or not, choosing their subject and figuring out how best to represent it. Especially in the age of digital technologies such as Photoshop, images caught by the camera can be tweaked in all sorts of ways. Moreover, the scene depicted might be a staged fantasy in the first place.

Here are the questions to ask yourself as you examine a picture with an eye to analyzing it:

1. What details do you see in the picture? Besides recognizable objects and figures (human beings or animals), consider shapes, colors, lighting, and shading. Do not list just the picture's most prominent elements, for those that at first seem trivial may turn out to be important for you.

2. What are aspects of the picture's *style*—the artist's particular way of handling the subject? Among other things, consider what the artist does and does not allow the viewer to see, how realistic or abstract the work seems, and whether anyone in the picture looks directly at the viewer.

3. How has the artist organized the picture? Note especially patterns of resemblance and contrast. Think, too, about whether the picture's design directs the viewer's attention to a particular part of it.

4. What mood does the picture evoke? Consider emotions that you experience as a viewer, as well as those that seem to be felt by any living figures in the scene.

5. What is at least one detail of the picture that strikes you as puzzling (and therefore especially in need of interpretation)?

6. Does the picture seem to tell a story or appear to be part of a story that has already begun and will continue?

7. How does the picture relate to its title and (where applicable) to its caption?

8. What are some options that the artist could have explored but did not pursue?

WRITING AN ESSAY THAT COMPARES LITERATURE AND ART

Before you write an essay comparing a work of literature with a work of art, collect as many details as you can about each. The questions above can help you do this with the artwork. For aid in gathering observations about the literary text, see Chapter 4, "The Reading Process," especially the section on Strategies for Close Reading. Then, as you proceed to write, keep the following principles especially in mind:

- You do not have to give equal space to each work. Rather, you may prefer to come up with an issue and a main claim by focusing on interpreting *one* of the works: either the literary text *or* the visual image. Your secondary work will still play some role in the essay, but your primary one will receive greater attention. The result will be what in Chapter 5 we call a *weighted* comparison. (See that chapter for more tips.)
- Assume that your reader is at least somewhat familiar with both the literary work and the image but needs to be reminded of their basic details. In particular, help your audience *visualize* the art you discuss.
- Refer at least sometimes to the author of the literary work and to the artist who created the image. Doing so will help you analyze how their productions involve particular strategies of representation — attempts to affect audiences in particular ways.

ROLANDO PEREZ

Office at Night

It is past nine o'clock, and she has stayed late to help him. How many times did he dream of this very same scenario: her standing there in her tight blue dress, with her black pumps and flesh-colored stockings. And now it has finally happened. Without him having to ask — not that he would have dared — she volunteered all on her own.   5

He had to "open the window."

"This office at night is a bit stuffy."

A sheet of paper that once lay on top of other papers on his desk, now lies on the green carpet — to his right — gently carried there by the wind. Standing at a black filing cabinet, searching for some old bills, she has noticed the paper   10
lying on the floor. The desk lamp throws a shadow on the desk, and illuminates his hands. And a patch of light, reflected on the wall, touches them both . . . lightly, very lightly . . . as with finger tips.

Will she bend over to pick it up?

If only the phone beside him would ring, then he would do something, he   15
would act, produce the correct combination of words that would elicit the correct series of reactions from her. He might even suggest that they lock up and go for a drink somewhere. But having heard too many truths in the past, now history holds him back. In his suit, with his shirt buttoned to the top, and his tie still on, he hasn't moved, and she hasn't moved; and the wind-swept   20

Edward Hopper, *Office at Night*. 1940. Oil on canvas. 30-5/16 × 33-15/16 × 2-3/4″ framed. Collection Walker Art Center, Minneapolis. Gift of the T. B. Walker Foundation, Gilbert M. Walker Fund, 1948.

paper will stay on the floor, halfway between his desk and her cabinet, timidly undisturbed, in this wounded and frozen infinity.   *[2002]*

A Sample Paper Comparing a Poem and a Picture

To give you a better idea of what an essay comparing literature and art looks like, we present a paper by student Karl Magnusson. He connects Edward Hopper's painting *Office at Night* to the prose poem of the same title by Rolando Perez. As you will see, Karl's essay is a weighted comparison; it focuses mostly on Perez's poem.

Karl Magnusson
Professor Kemper
English W350
16 May - - - -

Lack of Motion and Speech in
Rolando Perez's "Office at Night"

Edward Hopper's painting *Office at Night* depicts a man and a woman working in the kind of setting indicated by the title. The man is apparently the boss of the woman, who seems to be his secretary. He sits at a desk by an

Immediately refers to the painting and then proceeds to summarize its key details.

open window, studying a document that he holds in front of him. She is positioned to the left and slightly to the rear of him. More precisely, she stands at a filing cabinet with her right hand resting on an open drawer. Their respective postures suggest that she is waiting to hear what he will say next. Perhaps she has just asked him a question and he is thinking about how to answer, or perhaps she is simply expecting him, as her superior, to issue her a new order. In any case, viewers of the painting are free to interpret their interaction, and different spectators might come up with different ideas about what these people really mean to each other. Indeed, not everyone would conceive their relationship to be what Rolando Perez imagines it as being in his poem about Hopper's artwork. Also entitled "Office at Night," Perez's poem speculates that the man and woman have a romantic interest in each other that neither he nor she can express. Furthermore, the poem conveys their reticence in terms that have often been used to describe the medium of painting in general.

Now turns to the poem, which will be the primary work in this weighted comparison.

This is the essay's main claim, which is about the poem.

The poem draws attention more to the self-repression of the boss. The secretary, too, evidently does not feel able to speak frankly about their emotions, perhaps because she is after all his employee. But the text tends to focus on *his* reluctance to reveal that he is enamored of her. This mixture of lust and hesitation is evident right near the start of the poem. There, just before describing the secretary's alluring clothes, the poem's speaker wonders, "How many times did he [the boss] dream of this very same scenario" (lines 1–2). The implication is that the boss has entertained sensual visions of his employee in his mind while doing nothing to bring them about. He merely fantasizes a romance with her, not actually helping it come to life. Soon after, the reader learns that *she* had to prompt *him* to "open the window" (5) and let fresh air in. Evidently she wishes to stimulate their senses and admit their real feelings, but this is behavior that he apparently would never "have dared" (4) to engage in on his own. Later, he resists actually inviting her to take their office working relationship in a romantic direction. Although he apparently considers the possibility that "he would do something, he would act, produce the correct combination of words" (14–15) to initiate a courtship, he remains silent and still. The implication is that he is restrained by the memory of his previous disappointments in love — "too many truths in the past" (17). Whatever specific episodes

Proceeds to support the main argument with specific lines from the poem.

in his past he is thinking of, the result is that "now history holds him back" (17). Rather than "suggest[ing] that they lock up and go for a drink somewhere" (16), he stays emotionally locked up, not letting his true attachment to her emerge.

In describing physical details of the office, the poem's speaker sums up the couple's inability to be emotionally open with each other. In part, the speaker does this by sometimes using images of motion that underscore by contrast how the man and woman fail to act on their feelings. The "patch of light" that "touches them both . . . lightly, very lightly . . . as with fingertips" (10–12) is a reminder that these two people do not physically touch each other at all. The phrase "gently carried there by the wind" (8) — used in reference to a piece of paper on the floor — indirectly emphasizes that the couple will not let themselves be carried away by passion. When, however, near the end of the poem, the speaker describes the paper as "timidly undisturbed" (20), the symbolism is more direct: the word "timidly" seems to fit the couple as well, for they have been too scared to confess their emotional bond. Moreover, the speaker's observation that "he hasn't moved, and she hasn't moved" (18–19) directly reinforces their *psychological* paralysis. The poem's final phrase, "wounded and frozen infinity" (20), is not just an overview of this late-night office environment. The speaker is also indicating the basic state of the couple's relationship. They are "wounded" in the sense that they suffer unfulfilled desires for each other. They are "frozen" in the sense that they cannot reveal these desires. The word "infinity" implies that, given their inertia, their situation is unlikely to change.

Not every poem about Hopper's *Office at Night* painting would necessarily focus on its two human figures. Nor would every poem about the painting necessarily depict their relationship in the way that Perez's does. Indeed, a distinctive feature of his poem is that his portrait of the couple attributes to them characteristics often associated with the medium of painting itself. Aware, like most people, that figures in a painting do not move, Perez takes this fact and makes it an element of the couple's behavior. The static nature of painting in general is echoed in their paralytic inhibition. Furthermore, just as people in paintings do not speak aloud, so the couple in Perez's poem resist articulating what they really feel. Also, just as viewers of a painting have to guess the thoughts of anyone shown in it, so Perez's man and woman force themselves to guess what is on each other's mind.

Perez could be seen as tolerating and even encouraging affairs between bosses and their secretaries. In this respect, his text seems more in keeping with the world of 1940, the year Hopper painted *Office at Night*. Back then, expressions of love between a manager and a subordinate might have been smiled upon, perceived as what the poem's speaker calls "the correct combination of words" and "the correct series of reactions" (15–16). The same expressions now, however, might be condemned as politically and even legally *in*correct. Certainly, government and company policies on sexual harassment warn executives not to seduce the employees who serve them. Nevertheless, it would be unfair simply to dismiss Perez's poem or Hopper's painting as outdated, especially because the audiences for these works do not have to take them as being just about romance in the office. Both the poem and the painting allow for interpretations that see the couple as universal — as people who might exist anywhere. In this case, their reticence toward each other would be a widespread human problem: the difficulty of communicating the stirrings of one's heart.

The concluding paragraph does not simply repeat what has already been said. It touches on a new subject: changes in policies on office affairs.

Writing about Plays

Most plays incorporate elements also found in short fiction, such as plot, characterization, dialogue, setting, and theme. But, in contrast to short fiction and other literary genres, plays are typically enacted live, in front of an audience. Theater professionals distinguish between the written *script* of a play and its actual *performances*. When you write about a play, you may wind up saying little or nothing about performances of it. When you first read and analyze a play, however, try to imagine ways of staging it. You might even research past productions of the play, noting how scenery, costumes, and lighting — as well as particular actors — were used.

Because a play is usually meant to be staged, its readers are rarely its only interpreters. Audiences at productions of the play also ponder its meanings. So, too, do members of the casts; no doubt you have heard of actors "interpreting" their parts. When a play is put on, even members of the backstage team are involved in interpreting it. The technical designers' choices of sets, costumes, and lighting reflect their ideas about the play, while the director works with cast and crew to implement a particular vision of it. No matter what the author of the script intended, theater is a collaborative art: all of the key figures involved in a play's production are *active* interpreters of the play, in that they influence the audience's understanding and experience of it. Therefore, you can develop good ideas when you read a play if you imagine yourself directing a production of it. More specifically, think what you would say to the actors as you guide them through their parts. As you engage in this thought experiment, you will see that you have options, for even directors keen on staying faithful to the script know it can be staged in any number of ways. Perhaps your course will give you and other students the chance to perform a scene together; if so, you will be deciding what interpretation of the scene to set forth.

To help you understand how to write about plays, we will refer often to the one-act play that follows. *The Stronger* was first performed in 1889. Its Swedish author, August Strindberg (1849–1912), is widely acknowledged as a founder of modern drama. Throughout his career, Strindberg experimented with a variety of theatrical styles. With this particular play, an encounter between two actresses, he dared to have one of the women speak and the other remain silent.

AUGUST STRINDBERG
The Stronger
Translated by Edith and Warner Oland

CHARACTERS

MRS. X, *an actress, married*
MISS Y, *an actress, unmarried*
A WAITRESS

SCENE: *The corner of a ladies' café. Two little iron tables, a red velvet sofa, several chairs. Enter Mrs. X, dressed in winter clothes, carrying a Japanese basket on her arm.*

Miss Y sits with a half empty beer bottle before her, reading an illustrated paper, which she changes later for another.

MRS. X: Good afternoon, Amelie. You're sitting here alone on Christmas eve like a poor bachelor!

Miss Y looks up, nods, and resumes her reading.

MRS. X: Do you know it really hurts me to see you like this, alone, in a café, and on Christmas eve, too. It makes me feel as I did one time when I saw a bridal party in a Paris restaurant, and the bride sat reading a comic paper, while the groom played billiards with the witnesses. Huh, thought I, with such a beginning, what will follow, and what will be the end? He played billiards on his wedding eve! (*Miss Y starts to speak.*) And she read a comic paper, you mean? Well, they are not altogether the same thing.

A waitress enters, places a cup of chocolate before Mrs. X, and goes out.

MRS. X: You know what, Amelie! I believe you would have done better to have kept him! Do you remember, I was the first to say "Forgive him?" Do you remember that? You would be married now and have a home. Remember that Christmas when you went out to visit your fiancé's parents in the country? How you gloried in the happiness of home life and really longed to quit the theater forever? Yes, Amelie dear, home is the best of all, the theater next and children—well, you don't understand that.

Miss Y looks up scornfully.

   Mrs. X sips a few spoonfuls out of the cup, then opens her basket and shows Christmas presents.

MRS. X: Now you shall see what I bought for my piggywigs. *(Takes up a doll.)* Look at this! This is for Lisa, ha! Do you see how she can roll her eyes and turn her head, eh? And here is Maja's popgun. *(Loads it and shoots at Miss Y.)*

Miss Y makes a startled gesture.

MRS. X: Did I frighten you? Do you think I would like to shoot you, eh? On my soul, if I don't think you did! If you wanted to shoot *me* it wouldn't be so surprising, because I stood in your way—and I know you can never forget that—although I was absolutely innocent. You still believe I intrigued and got you out of the Stora theater, but I didn't. I didn't do that, although you think so. Well, it doesn't make any difference what I say to you. You still believe I did it. *(Takes up a pair of embroidered slippers.)* And these are for my better half. I embroidered them myself—I can't bear tulips, but he wants tulips on everything.

Miss Y looks up ironically and curiously.

MRS. X *(putting a hand in each slipper):*   What little feet Bob has! What? And you should see what a splendid stride he has! You've never seen him in slippers! *(Miss Y laughs aloud.)* Look! *(She makes the slippers walk on the table. Miss Y laughs loudly.)* And when he is grumpy he stamps like this with his foot. "What! damn those servants who can never learn to make coffee. Oh, now those creatures haven't trimmed the lamp wick properly!" And then there are draughts on the floor and his feet are cold. "Ugh, how cold it is; the stupid idiots can never keep the fire going." *(She rubs the slippers together, one sole over the other.)*

Miss Y shrieks with laughter.

MRS. X: And then he comes home and has to hunt for his slippers which Marie has stuck under the chiffonier—oh, but it's sinful to sit here and make fun of one's husband this way when he is kind and a good little man. You ought to have had such a husband, Amelie. What are you laughing at? What? What? And you see he's true to me. Yes, I'm sure of that, because he told me himself—what are you laughing at?—that when I was touring in Norway that that brazen Frédérique came and wanted to seduce him! Can you fancy anything so infamous? *(Pause.)* I'd have torn her eyes out if she had come to see him when I was at home. *(Pause.)* It was lucky that Bob told me about it himself and that it didn't reach me through gossip. *(Pause.)*

But would you believe it, Frédérique wasn't the only one! I don't know why, but the women are crazy about my husband. They must think he has influence about getting them theatrical engagements, because he is connected with the government. Perhaps you were after him yourself. I didn't use to trust you any too much. But now I know he never bothered his head about you, and you always seemed to have a grudge against him someway.

Pause. They look at each other in a puzzled way.

Come and see us this evening, Amelie, and show us that you're not put out with us,—not put out with me at any rate. I don't know, but I think it would be uncomfortable to have you for an enemy. Perhaps it's because I stood in your way or—I really—don't know why—in particular.

Pause. Miss Y stares at Mrs. X curiously.

MRS. X *(thoughtfully)*:   Our acquaintance has been so queer. When I saw you for the first time I was afraid of you, so afraid that I didn't dare let you out of my sight; no matter when or where, I always found myself near you—I didn't dare have you for an enemy, so I became your friend. But there was always discord when you came to our house, because I saw that my husband couldn't endure you, and the whole thing seemed as awry to me as an ill-fitting gown—and I did all I could to make him friendly toward you, but with no success until you became engaged. Then came a violent friendship between you, so that it looked all at once as though you both dared show your real feelings only when you were secure—and then—how was it later? I didn't get jealous—strange to say! And I remember at the christening, when you acted as godmother, I made him kiss you—he did so, and you became so confused—as it were; I didn't notice it then—didn't think about it later, either—have never thought about it until—now! *(Rises suddenly.)* Why are you silent? You haven't said a word this whole time, but you have let me go on talking! You have sat there, and your eyes have reeled out of me all these thoughts which lay like raw silk in its cocoon—thoughts—suspicious thoughts, perhaps. Let me see—why did you break your engagement? Why do you never come to our house any more? Why won't you come to see us tonight?

Miss Y appears as if about to speak.

MRS. X: Hush, you needn't speak—I understand it all! It was because—and because—and because! Yes, yes! Now all the accounts balance. That's it. Fie, I won't sit at the same table with you. *(Moves her things to another table.)* That's the reason I had to embroider tulips—which I hate—on his slippers, because you are fond of tulips; that's why *(Throws slippers on the floor.)* we go to Lake Mälarn in the summer, because you don't like salt water; that's why my boy is named Eskil—because it's your father's name; that's why I wear your colors, read your authors, eat your favorite dishes, drink your drinks—chocolate, for instance; that's why—oh—my God—it's terrible, when I think about it; it's terrible. Everything, everything came from you to me, even your passions. Your soul crept into mine, like a worm into an apple, ate and ate, bored and bored, until nothing was left but the rind and a little black dust within. I wanted to get away from you, but I couldn't; you lay like a snake and charmed me with your black eyes; I felt that when I lifted my wings they only dragged me down; I lay in the water with bound feet, and the stronger I strove to keep up the deeper I worked myself down, down, until I sank to the bottom, where you lay like a giant crab to clutch me in your claws—and there I am lying now.

I hate you, hate you, hate you! And you only sit there silent—silent and indifferent; indifferent whether it's new moon or waning moon, Christmas or New Year's, whether others are happy or unhappy; without power to hate or to love; as quiet as a stork by a rat hole—you couldn't scent your prey and capture it, but you could lie in wait for it! You sit here in your corner of the café—did you know it's called "The Rat Trap" for you?— and read the papers to see if misfortune hasn't befallen someone, to see if someone hasn't been given notice at the theater, perhaps; you sit here and calculate about your next victim and reckon on your chances of recompense like a pilot in a shipwreck. Poor Amelie, I pity you, nevertheless, because I know you are unhappy, unhappy like one who has been wounded, and angry because you are wounded. I can't be angry with you, no matter how much I want to be—because you come out the weaker one. Yes, all that with Bob doesn't trouble me. What is that to me, after all? And what difference does it make whether I learned to drink chocolate from you or someone else. *(Sips a spoonful from her cup.)*

Besides, chocolate is very healthful. And if you taught me how to dress— *tant mieux!*—[*so much the better!*] that has only made me more attractive to my husband; so you lost and I won there. Well, judging by certain signs, I believe you have already lost him; and you certainly intended that I should leave him—do as you did with your fiancé and regret as you now regret; but, you see, I don't do that—we mustn't be too exacting. And why should I take only what no one else wants?

Perhaps, take it all in all, I am at this moment the stronger one. You received nothing from me, but you gave me much. And now I seem like a thief since you have awakened and find I possess what is your loss. How could it be otherwise when everything is worthless and sterile in your hands? You can never keep a man's love with your tulips and your passions—but I can keep it. You can't learn how to live from your authors, as I have learned. You have no little Eskil to cherish, even if your father's name was Eskil. And why are you always silent, silent, silent? I thought that was strength, but perhaps it is because you have nothing to say! Because you never think about anything! *(Rises and picks up slippers.)*

Now I'm going home—and take the tulips with me—*your* tulips! You are unable to learn from another; you can't bend—therefore, you broke like a dry stalk. But I won't break! Thank you, Amelie, for all your good lessons. Thanks for teaching my husband how to love. Now I'm going home to love him. *(Goes.)*   [1889]

A Student's Personal Response to the Play

Trish Carlisle was enrolled in a class that read and discussed Strindberg's *The Stronger*. Below is some freewriting that Trish did about the play.

> Near the end of Strindberg's play, Mrs. X says that "I am at this moment the stronger one." But is she? I guess that depends on what Strindberg meant by "the stronger" when he gave his play that title. As I was reading, I started to think that the stronger woman is actually the silent one, Miss Y, because she seems to have more self-control than Mrs. X does. I mean, Miss Y doesn't apparently feel that she has to make long, loud speeches in defense of her way of life. I can even believe that with her silence she is manipulating Mrs. X into getting fairly hysterical. Also, I guess we're to think that Amelie has managed to lure away Mrs. X's husband, at least for a while. Furthermore, we don't have to believe Mrs. X when at the end she claims that she has triumphed over Miss Y. Maybe people who have really succeeded in life don't need to proclaim that they have, as Mrs. X does.
>
> Nevertheless, I can see why some students in this class feel that Mrs. X is in fact the stronger. If she has her husband back and wants her husband back, and if Miss Y is really without companionship at the end and has even lost her job at the theater, then probably Mrs. X is entitled to crow. Was Strindberg being deliberately unclear? Did he want his audience to make up their own minds about who is stronger? Maybe neither of these women is strong, because each of them seems dependent on a man, and Mrs. X's husband may not even be such a great person in the first place. If I were Mrs. X, maybe I wouldn't even take him back. I guess someone could say that it's Mrs. X's husband who is the stronger, since he has managed to make the two women fight over him while he enjoys his creature comforts. Anyway, Strindberg makes us guess what he is really like. Because he's offstage, he's just as silent as Miss Y is, although his wife imitates his voice at one point.
>
> In a way, I feel that this play is too short. I want it to go on longer so that I can be sure how to analyze the two women and the man. But I realize that one of the reasons the play is dramatic is that it's brief. I might not be interested in it if it didn't leave me hanging. And it's also theatrical because Miss Y is silent even as Mrs. X lashes out at her. I wonder what the play would be like if we could hear Miss Y's thoughts in a sort of voice-over, like we find in some movies. It's interesting to me that the play is *about*

actresses. I wonder if these characters are still "performing" with each other even if they're not acting in a theater at the moment.

Trish's freewriting would eventually help her develop ideas for a paper in which she had to analyze Strindberg's play. Compare your responses to the play with hers. Did the same issues come up for you? How do you feel about the women characters? What, if anything, do you wish the playwright had made clearer? What would you advise Trish to think about as she moved from freewriting to drafting a paper?

The Elements of Drama

You strengthen your ability to write about plays if you grow familiar with typical elements of drama. These elements include plot and structure, characterization, stage directions and setting, imagery, language, and theme.

PLOT AND STRUCTURE

Most plays, like most short stories, have a **plot**. When you read them, you find yourself following a narrative, a sequence of interrelated events. Even plays as short as *The Stronger* feature a plot, though the onstage action occurs in just one place and takes just a little while. As with short fiction, the reader of a play is often anxious to know how the events will turn out. The reader may especially feel this way when the play contains a mystery that characters are trying to solve. In Strindberg's play, for example, Mrs. X is apparently bent on discovering what relation her husband has had with her friend.

In summarizing the play, you might choose to depict the plot as a detective story. Then again, you might prefer to emphasize the characters' emotional conflicts as you describe how the play proceeds. In fact, there are various ways you can describe Strindberg's plot; just bear in mind that your account should be grounded in actual details of the text. However you summarize a play will reflect your sense of which characters are central to it. Is the offstage husband Bob in *The Stronger* as important as the two women onstage? More important than they are? Less important? Your summary will also reflect your sense of which characters have power. Do you think the two women in Strindberg's drama equally influence that play's events? In addition, your summary ought to acknowledge the human motives that drive the play's action. Why do you think Mrs. X feels compelled to confront Miss Y?

Summarizing the plot of a play can mean arranging its events chronologically. Yet bear in mind that some of the play's important events may have occurred in the characters' pasts. In many plays, actually, characters learn things about the past that they did not know and must now try to accept. For example, important events mentioned in *The Stronger* take place before the play begins. By the time the curtain rises, Miss Y's close relationship with Bob is well in the past. A typical summary would begin with the events on stage, but you could also summarize Strindberg's play as a chronicle of the relationship that precedes the scene in the café.

In discussing the structure of short stories, we noted that many of them follow Alice Adams's formula *ABDCE* (Action, Background, Development, Climax, and Ending). This scheme, however, does not fit many plays. In a sense, the average play is entirely Action, for its performers are constantly engaged in physical movement of various sorts. Furthermore, as we have been suggesting, information about Background can surface quite often as the play's characters talk. Yet the terms *Development*, *Climax*, and *Ending* do seem appropriate for many plays. Certainly the plot of *The Stronger* develops, as Mrs. X becomes increasingly hostile to Miss Y. Certainly, the play can be said to reach a Climax, a moment of great significance and intensity, when Mrs. X moves to another table and declares her hatred for Miss Y. The term *Ending* can also apply to this play, although readers may disagree about exactly when its Climax turns into its Ending. Certainly, Mrs. X is in a different state of mind at the play's last moment; at that point, she stops haranguing Miss Y and leaves, declaring that she will save her own marriage.

Like short stories, plays often use repetition as an organizational device. The characters in a play may repeat certain words; Mrs. X's variations on "silence" multiply as Miss Y retreats from interacting with her. Also, a play may show repeated actions, such as Mrs. X's interruptions of Miss Y. In addition, a play may suggest that the onstage situation echoes previous events, as when Mrs. X alludes to confrontations between her husband and Miss Y in the past.

The Stronger is a short, one-act play. But many other plays are longer and divided conspicuously into subsections. The ancient Greek drama *Antigone* alternates choral sections with scenes involving only the title character and her uncle Creon. All of Shakespeare's plays, and most modern ones, are divided into acts, which are often further divided into scenes. Even within a one-act play, however, you can detect various stages in the action. This task is easier when the one-act play is fairly lengthy, but even a very short play like *The Stronger* can be broken down into stages, although you will have to decide exactly what those stages are.

CHARACTERS

Many short stories have a narrator who reveals the characters' inner thoughts. Most plays, however, have no narrator at all. To figure out what the characters think, you must study what they *say* and how they *move*, if the author has indeed provided stage directions. To be sure, some characters say a great deal, leaving you with several clues to their psyche. If you are familiar with Shakespeare's lengthy play *Hamlet*, you may recall that it contains thousands of lines. Moreover, when the title character is alone on stage making long speeches to the audience, he seems to be baring his very soul. Yet despite such moments, Hamlet's mental state remains far from clear; scholars continue to debate his sanity. Thus, as a reader of *Hamlet* and other plays, you have much room for interpretation. Often you will have to decide whether to accept the judgments that characters express about one another. For example, how fair and accurate does Strindberg's Mrs. X seem to you as she berates Miss Y?

As with short stories, a good step toward analyzing a play's characters is to consider what each desires. The drama or comedy of many plays arises when the desires of one character conflict with those of another. Strindberg's Mrs. X feels that Miss Y has been a threat to her marriage, and while we cannot be sure of Miss Y's thoughts, evidently she is determined not to answer Mrs. X's charges. At the end of the play, the women's conflict seems to endure, even though Mrs. X proclaims victory. Many other plays end with characters managing to resolve conflict because one or more of them experiences a change of heart. Whatever the play you are studying, consider whether any of its characters change. Is any character's thinking transformed? If so, whose?

The main character of a play is often referred to as its **protagonist**, and a character who notably opposes this person is often referred to as the **antagonist**. As you might guess without even reading Shakespeare's play, Prince Hamlet is the protagonist of *Hamlet*; his uncle Claudius, who succeeded Hamlet's father to the throne of Denmark, serves as his antagonist. To be sure, applying these terms may be tricky or impossible in some instances. The two women in *The Stronger* oppose each other, but each can be called the protagonist and each can be called the antagonist. Can you think of other plays you have read in which the protagonist and antagonist are not readily identifiable?

In discussing the elements of short fiction, we referred to point of view, the perspective from which a story is told. Since very few plays are narrated, the term *point of view* fits this genre less well. While it is possible to claim that much of Shakespeare's *Hamlet* reflects the title character's point of view, he is offstage for stretches, and the audience may focus on other characters even when he appears. Also, do not overlook the possible significance of characters who are not physically present. A character may be important even when he or she never appears onstage. In *The Stronger*, the two women's conflict is partly about Mrs. X's unseen husband.

In most plays, characters' lives are influenced by their social standing, which in turn is influenced by particular traits of theirs. These may include their gender, their social class, their race, their ethnic background, their nationality, their sexual orientation, and the kind of work they do. Obviously *The Stronger* deals with gender relationships. Mrs. X defines herself in gendered terms: wife, mother, and insecure lover in competition with a rival for her husband's affections. But there are elements of social class too—of the circumstances of upper-middle-class Swedish women in Stockholm in the late nineteenth century—that may require research.

STAGE DIRECTIONS AND SETTING

When analyzing a script, pay attention to the staging directions it gives, and try to imagine additional ways that the actors might move around. Through a slight physical movement, performers can indicate important developments in their characters' thoughts. When Mrs. X fires a popgun at Miss Y, audience members may flinch in surprised sympathy with Miss Y's "startled gesture." But they may be just as startled by Miss Y's mirthful response, culminating in a "shriek of laughter," when Mrs. X uses her husband's slippers to mime and mock him. Is Miss Y's laughter hysterical, or knowing, or something else? How does it set up the "puzzled," curious looks Mrs. X and Miss Y exchange moments later?

You can get a better sense of how a play might be staged if you research its actual production history. Granted, finding out about its previous stagings may be difficult. But at the very least, you can discover some of the theatrical conventions that must have shaped presentations of the play, even one that is centuries old. Consider Sophocles' classical tragedy *Antigone* and Shakespeare's *Hamlet*, canonical plays that you may have read or seen performed in films or theater. While classical scholars would like to learn more about early performances of *Antigone*, they already know that it and other ancient Greek plays were staged in open-air arenas. They know, too, that *Antigone*'s Chorus turned in unison at particular moments, and that the whole cast wore large masks. Although the premiere of *Hamlet* was not videotaped, Shakespeare scholars are sure that, like other productions in Renaissance England, it made spare use of scenery and featured an all-male cast. By contrast, *The Stronger* is anchored in the nineteenth-century realist tradition that values in literary works an accurate and plausible presentation of everyday life and events.

Some plays can be staged in any number of styles and still work well. Shakespeare wrote *Hamlet* back in Renaissance England, but quite a few successful productions of it have been set in later times, such as late-nineteenth-century England. Even modern plays that seem to call for realist productions can be staged in a variety of ways. Note Strindberg's description of the setting for *The Stronger*: "The corner of a ladies' café. Two little iron tables, a red velvet sofa, several chairs." Many productions of this play have remained within the conventions of realism, striving to make the audience believe that it is seeing a late-nineteenth-century Stockholm café. But a production of *The Stronger* may present the audience with only a few pieces of furniture that barely evoke the café. Furthermore, the production might have Mrs. X's husband physically hover in the background, as if he were a ghost haunting both women's minds. You may feel that such a production would horribly distort Strindberg's drama; a boldly experimental staging of a play can indeed become a virtual rewriting of it. Nevertheless, remember that productions of a play may be more diverse in style than the script would indicate.

Remember, too, that a particular theater's architecture may affect a production team's decisions. Realism's illusion of the "fourth wall" works best on a proscenium stage, which is the kind probably most familiar to you. In brief, a proscenium is a boxlike space where the actors perform in front of the entire audience. In a proscenium production of *The Stronger*, the ladies' café can be depicted in great detail. The performing spaces at some theaters, however, are "in the round": that is, the audience completely encircles the stage. What would have to be done with the café then? List some items in the café that an "in the round" staging could accommodate.

In referring to possible ways of staging a play, we have inevitably been referring as well to its setting. A play may not be all that precise in describing its setting; Strindberg provides set designers with few guidelines for creating his Stockholm café. More significant, perhaps, than the place of the action is its *timing*: Mrs. X finds Miss Y sitting alone on Christmas eve. Yet a play may stress to its audience that its characters are located in particular places, at particular moments in their personal histories, and/or at a particular moment in *world* history. For example, *The Stronger* calls attention to the fact that it is set in a ladies' café, a female space. Are there gendered public arenas today where Mrs. X might play out her conflict with Miss Y? Could the play be set in a women's locker room? What would happen if the setting were not for women only?

You can learn much about a play's characters by studying how they accommodate themselves—or fail to accommodate themselves—to their settings. When Strindberg's Mrs. X can no longer bear sitting next to Miss Y, her shift to another table dramatically signifies her feelings. Of course, much of the drama in Strindberg's play occurs because there is a *single* setting, in which at least one character feels confined. Other plays employ a wider variety of settings to dramatize their characters' lives.

IMAGERY

When plays use images to convey meaning, sometimes they do so through dialogue. At the beginning of *The Stronger*, for instance, Mrs. X recalls "a bridal party in a Paris restaurant," where "the bride sat reading a comic paper, while the groom played billiards with the witnesses." The play proceeds to become very much about divisions between husband and wife; moreover, the two women engage in a tense "game" that seems analogous to billiards. But just as often, a play's meaningful images are physically presented in the staging: through gestures, costumes, lighting, and props. For instance, consider the slippers embroidered with tulips that Mrs. X flourishes early in the play. The slippers and the tulips gain meaning as the play progresses. The audience may be ever more inclined to see them as *symbolic*. As we note on page 161, *symbol* is the term traditionally used for an image that represents some concept or concepts.

Keep in mind that *you* may interpret an image differently than the characters within the play do. When Strindberg's Mrs. X refers to billiards, she may not think at all that she will be playing an analogous game with Miss Y. You, however, may make this connection, especially as the play proceeds.

LANGUAGE

As we have been suggesting, a play's meaning and impact may be apparent only when the play is physically staged. Nevertheless, you can learn much from studying the language in its script. For example, the play's very title may be important. At the climax of Strindberg's play, Mrs. X even refers to herself as "the stronger." Obviously, the playwright is encouraging audiences to think about the title's implications. Yet not always will the meaning of a play's title be immediately clear. In her freewriting, Trish wonders how to define "stronger" and which of Strindberg's characters fit the term. Even if you think the title of a play is easily explainable, pause to see whether that title can actually lead to an issue of definition. In other words, don't take the title for granted.

In most plays, language is a matter of dialogue. The audience tries to figure out the play by focusing on how the characters address one another. But remember that the pauses or silences within a play may be just as important as its dialogue. In fact, a director may *add* moments of silence that the script does not explicitly demand. In many plays, however, the author does specify moments when one or more characters significantly fail to speak. *The Stronger* is a prominent example: Miss Y is notably silent throughout the play, and as a reader you probably find yourself wondering why she is. Ironically, the play's *absence* of true dialogue serves to remind us that plays usually *depend* on dialogue.

Consider this moment in *The Stronger* when Miss Y fails to speak:

MRS. X: . . . Why are you silent? You haven't said a word this whole time, but you have let me go on talking! You have sat there, and your eyes have reeled out of me all these thoughts which lay like raw silk in its cocoon—thoughts—suspicious thoughts, perhaps. Let me see— why did you break your engagement? Why do you never come to our house any more? Why won't you come to see us tonight?

Miss Y appears as if about to speak.

MRS. X: Hush, you needn't speak—I understand it all! . . .

An interesting discussion might result from imagining what Miss Y might have said had she not been cut off. It's also worth reflecting on what Strindberg conceivably gains by *not* having Miss Y speak at that moment.

THEME

We have already discussed *theme* in short fiction (pp. 162–164), and here we will build on some points from our earlier discussion. Again, a *theme* is the main claim—an assertion, a proposition, or a statement—that a work seems to make. As with other literary genres, try to state a play's theme as a *midlevel generalization* (pp. 162–163). If expressed in very broad terms, it will seem to fit many other works besides the one you have read; if narrowly tied to the play's characters and their particular situation, it will seem irrelevant to most other people's lives. With *The Stronger*, an example of a very broad theme would be "Women should not fight over a man." At the opposite extreme, a too-narrow theme would be "Women should behave well toward each other on Christmas eve, even if one of them has slept with the other's husband." If you are formulating Strindberg's theme, you might *start* with the broad generalization we have cited and then try to narrow it to a midlevel one. You might even think of ways that Strindberg's play *complicates* that broad generalization. What might, in fact, be a good midlevel generalization in Strindberg's case?

As we have noted, the very title of *The Stronger* seems significant. Indeed, a play's theme may be related to its title or to some other parts of the text. Nevertheless, be wary of couching the theme in terms drawn solely from the title or from some passage within the text. The play's theme may not be reducible to these words alone. Remember that the title of Strindberg's play can give rise to issues of definition in the first place.

You can state a play's theme as an observation or as a recommendation. With Strindberg's play, an observation-type theme would be "Marriage and career may disrupt relations between women." A recommendation-type theme would be either the broad or narrow generalization that we cited above. Neither way of stating the theme is automatically preferable, but remain aware of the different tones and effects they may carry. Consider, too, the possibility of stating the theme as a problem, as in this example: "We may be inclined to defend our marriages when they seem threatened, but in our defense we may cling to illusions that can easily shatter." Furthermore, consider the possibility of referring to *a* theme of the play rather than *the* theme, thereby acknowledging the possibility that the play is making several important claims.

When you write about a play, certainly you will refer to the text of it, its **script**. But probably the play was meant to be staged, and most likely it has been. Thus, you might refer to actual productions of it and to ways it can be performed. Remember, though, that different productions of the play may stress different meanings and create different effects. In your paper, you might discuss how much room for interpretation the script allows those who would stage it. For any paper you write about the play, look beyond the characters' dialogue and study whatever stage directions the script gives.

Undoubtedly your paper will have to offer some plot summary, even if your audience has already read the play. After all, certain details of the plot will be important support for your points. But, as with papers about short fiction, keep the amount of plot summary small, mentioning only events in the play that are crucial to your overall argument. Your reader should feel that you are analyzing the play rather than just recounting it.

To understand more what analysis of a play involves, let's return to Trish Carlisle, the student whose freewriting you read earlier. Trish was assigned to write a 600-word paper about Strindberg's *The Stronger*. She was asked to imagine herself writing to a particular audience: performers rehearsing a production of the play she chose. More specifically, she was to identify and address some question that these performers might have, an issue that might be bothering them as they prepared to put on the play. Trish knew that, besides presenting an issue, her paper would have to make a main claim and support it with evidence. Moreover, the paper might have to spell out some of the warrants or assumptions behind her evidence.

Because finding an issue was such an important part of the assignment, Trish decided to review her freewriting about Strindberg's play, noting questions she had raised there about it. Trish saw that the chief issue posed for her by *The Stronger* was "Which character is the stronger?" Nevertheless, Trish recognized that the issue "Which character is the stronger?" still left her with various decisions to make. For one thing, she had to decide what kind of an issue she would call it. Trish saw that it could be considered an issue of fact, an issue of evaluation, or an issue of definition. Although it could fit into all of these categories, Trish knew that the category she chose would influence the direction of her paper. Eventually she decided to treat "Which character is the stronger?" as primarily an issue of definition, because she figured that, no matter what, she would be devoting much of her paper to defining *stronger* as a term.

Of course, there are many different senses in which someone may be "stronger" than someone else. Your best friend may be a stronger tennis player than you, in the sense that he or she always beats you at that game. But you may be a stronger student than your friend, in the sense that you get better grades in school. In the case of Strindberg's play, Trish came to see that a paper focused on which character is *morally* stronger would differ from one focused on who is *emotionally* stronger, and these papers would differ in turn from one focused on which character is *politically* stronger, more able to impose his or her will. These reflections led Trish to revise her issue somewhat. She decided to address the question "Which particular sense of the word 'stronger' is most relevant to Strindberg's play?" In part, Trish came up with this reformulation of her issue because she realized that the two women feuding in the play are actresses, and that they behave as actresses even when they are not professionally performing. Trish's answer to her revised question was that the play encourages the audience to consider which woman is the stronger *actress*— which woman is more able, that is, to convey her preferred version of reality.

When you write about a play, you may have to be selective, for your paper may not be able to accommodate all the ideas and issues that occur to you. Trish was not sure which woman in Strindberg's play is the stronger actress. She felt that a case can be made for Mrs. X or Miss Y; indeed, she suspected that Strindberg was letting his audience decide. But she decided that her paper was not obligated to resolve this matter; she could simply mention the various possible positions in her final paragraph. In the body of her paper, Trish felt she would contribute much if she focused on addressing her main issue with her main claim. Again, her main issue was "Which particular sense of the word 'stronger' is most relevant to Strindberg's play?" Her main claim was that "The play is chiefly concerned with which woman is the stronger actress, 'stronger' here meaning 'more able to convey one's version of reality.'"

Although a paper about a play need not explicitly mention the elements of plays we have identified, thinking about these elements can provide you with a good springboard for analysis. Trish saw that her paper would be very much concerned with the title of Strindberg's play, especially as that title applied to the characters. Also, she would have to refer to stage directions and imagery, because Miss Y's silence leaves the reader having to look at her physical movements and the play's props for clues to her thinking. The play does not really include dialogue, a term that implies people talking with each other. Nevertheless, Trish saw that there are utterances in the script that she could refer to, especially as she made points about the play's lone speaker, Mrs. X.

Indeed, a persuasive paper about a play is one that quotes from characters' lines and perhaps from the stage directions, too. Yet the paper needs to quote selectively, for a paper chock full of quotations may obscure instead of enhance the writer's argument.

Final Draft of a Student Paper

Here is Trish's final draft of her paper about *The Stronger*. It emerged out of several drafts, and after Trish had consulted classmates and her instructor. As you read this version of her paper, note its strengths, but also think of any suggestions that might help Trish make the paper even better.

Trish Carlisle
Professor Zelinsky
English 102
28 April ----

Which Is the Stronger Actress
in August Strindberg's Play?

You have asked me to help you solve difficulties you may be experiencing with August Strindberg's script for *The Stronger* as you prepare to play the roles of Mrs. X and Miss Y. These female characters seem harder to judge than the three women who are the focus of Susan Glaspell's play *Trifles*, the play you are performing next month. Obviously, Glaspell is pushing us to think well of Mrs. Hale, Mrs. Peters, and Minnie Wright. The two women in Strindberg's play are another matter; in particular, you have probably been wondering which of these two women Strindberg thinks of as "the stronger." If you knew which character he had in mind with that term, you might play the roles accordingly. As things stand, however, Strindberg's use of the term in his title is pretty ambiguous. It is not even clear, at least not immediately, which particular sense of the word *stronger* is most relevant to the play. I suggest that the play is chiefly concerned with which character is the stronger actress. In making this claim, I am defining *stronger* as "more able to convey one's version of reality."

You may feel that Strindberg is clarifying his use of the word *stronger* when he has Mrs. X bring up the word in the long speech that ends the play. In that final speech, she declares to Miss Y that "I am . . . the stronger one" (line 166) and that Miss Y's silence is not the "strength" that Mrs. X previously thought it was. At this point in the play, Mrs. X is evidently defining *stronger* as "more able to keep things, especially a man." She feels that she is the stronger because she is going home to her husband, while Miss Y is forced to be alone on Christmas Eve. Yet there is little reason to believe that Mrs. X is using the word *stronger* in the sense that the playwright has chiefly in mind. Furthermore, there is little reason to believe that Mrs. X is an accurate judge of the two women's situations. Perhaps she is telling herself that she is stronger because she simply needs to believe that she is. Similarly, perhaps she is telling herself that she now has control over her husband when in actuality he may still be emotionally attached to Miss Y. In addition, because Miss Y does not speak and because Mrs. X sweeps out without giving her any further opportunity to do so, we don't know if Miss Y agrees with Mrs. X's last speech.

Since Mrs. X's final use of the word *stronger* is so questionable, we are justified in thinking of other ways that the term might be applied. In thinking about this play, I have entertained the idea that the stronger character is actually Mrs. X's husband Bob, for he has two women fighting over him and also apparently has the creature comforts that servants provide. But now I tend to think that the term applies to one or both of the two women. Unfortunately, we are not given many facts about them, for it is a brief one-act play and one of the major characters does not even speak. But as we try to figure out how Strindberg is defining the term *stronger*, we should notice one fact that we are indeed given: Each of these women is an actress. Both of them have worked at Stockholm's Grand Theater, although apparently Mrs. X got Miss Y fired from the company. Furthermore, Mrs. X engages in a bit of theatrical illusion when she scares Miss Y by firing the toy pistol at her. Soon after, Mrs. X plays the role of her own husband when she puts her hands in the slippers she has bought for him and imitates not only his walk but also the way he scolds his servants. Miss Y even laughs at this "performance," as if she is being an appreciative audience for it. In addition, if Mrs. X is right about there being an adulterous affair between her husband and Miss Y, then those two people have basically been performing an act for Mrs. X. It is possible, too, that Mrs. X has not been quite so naïve; perhaps she has deliberately come to the café in order to confront Miss Y about the affair and to proclaim ultimate victory over her. In that case, Mrs. X is performing as someone more innocent than she really is. On the other hand, Miss Y might be using her silence as an actress would, manipulating her audience's feelings by behaving in a theatrical way.

Because we do know that these women are professional actresses, and because Strindberg gives us several hints that they are performing right there in the café, we should feel encouraged to think that he is raising the question of which is the stronger *actress*. Of course, we would still have to decide how he is defining the term *stronger*. But if he does have in mind the women's careers and behavior as actresses, then he seems to be defining *stronger* as "more able to convey one's version of reality." Obviously, Mrs. X is putting forth her own version of reality in her final speech, although we do not know how close her version comes to the actual truth. Again, we cannot be sure of Miss Y's thoughts because she does not express them in words; nevertheless, she can be said to work at influencing Mrs. X's version of reality by making strategic use of silence.

I realize that the claim I am making does not solve every problem you might have with the play as you prepare to perform it. Frankly, I am not sure who *is* the stronger actress. I suspect that Strindberg is being deliberately ambiguous; he wants the performers to act in a way that will let each member of the audience arrive at his or her own opinion. Still, if you accept my claim, each of you will think of yourself as playing the part of an actress who is trying to shape the other woman's sense of reality.

CHAPTER 7

Writing Researched Arguments

Maybe the word *research* makes you anxious. It gives many people qualms. It brings to mind for them big and complex assignments in high school. Back then, they experienced "the research paper" as a major challenge. It loomed for them as a hurdle, one they struggled to leap. Often they couldn't figure out its rationale. Why do all this labor? Why hunt for materials, base a long essay on them, then end with a formatted bibliography? Such toil can prove overwhelming. A student might lose sight of its point.

Take heart. Research needn't be a daunting and valueless exercise. Indeed, it's become a common and rewarding pursuit. Millions now own devices that make the process easy. Just by tapping on keyboards or smartphones, they mine the Web's vast data. We bet you cruise cyberspace for answers to lots of questions. You might not call these voyages *research*, but that is what they are. Of course, frequently you're looking for a less-than-momentous fact: where to buy hoverboards, when the next *Star Wars* premieres, who's performing at local clubs, what folks think of your town's new restaurant, how your school's football team ranks. But probably you also turn to the Internet for more crucial knowledge. You may seek details about a disease that afflicts a family member. You may wish to compare online mortgage rates. A job you hold may require you to monitor several websites, gleaning data that will help your firm serve its clientele. Maybe you assist a nonprofit cause that's quite Internet-oriented; many of them search online for possible donors and allies. In general, the digital era is an age of research. It's a tool people use to manage their day.

Nevertheless, we can imagine you saying something like this: "OK, I realize now that I do research every day. But I'm still not confident I can do academic research—the kind of research that college teachers want. And I'm by no means sure I can turn it into essays—the kind of writing they expect." We understand the concern you may feel about these tasks. In the rest of this chapter, we explain and demonstrate ways to handle them.

Here at the start, we stress this fact: most college instructors don't assign something called "the research paper." They consider this label too vague. Yes, they'll require essays based on personal research. But they'll be more precise about the goal. Most often, they'll want you to compose researched *arguments*. You'll write essays addressed to an audience. You'll raise issues and put forth claims. You'll offer evidence and reasons. And you'll do research to prepare for this kind of writing. You'll seek materials that will help you build a persuasive case.

If you'll mainly write about a particular work, that's your **primary source**. Your other findings are your **secondary sources**. Some may prove not as useful as you predicted. Leave them out of your essay; don't sweat to jam them in. The rest of your sources should each play a clear role in your text. You'll have to decide their functions. Overall, use your essay to **synthesize** your sources. Put them in conversation. Make plain how they relate to one another; show how they connect to *your* chief issue and claim.

Begin Your Research by Giving It Direction

As you start your research, you may know already what your essay will argue. Certainty can be an advantage, productively steering your hunt. But it risks narrowing your scope. You may settle for sources that just reinforce your existing ideas. Research should expand your thinking. Let it be a means of inquiry. Even if you're sure of the claim you'll make, stay open to changing your mind. Consider the claim a hypothesis that your research will test. Don't stick with findings that preserve views you currently hold. Look for materials that may send you down exciting new paths.

Of course, your opening mood might be different. Perhaps you'll be hazy about your topic. You may not know what research to do. Still, you can give it direction. If you've chosen a particular literary work to write about, read it several times. If it's in this book, review what we tell you about its author. Take a look at our questions and comments about it. Then ask questions of your own about the work. Strive to come up with a question whose answer isn't obvious — an issue that demands you conduct research.

Another strategy is to list keywords: terms that occur to you as you study the work. These can become your search terms. The list below is an example. It concerns Charlotte Perkins Gilman's "The Yellow Wallpaper," an 1892 story based partly on the writer's life. Heading the list are the story's title and the author's name. They're followed by terms that often arise when the story is discussed in class. For research on Gilman's tale, these items could serve as guides:

- "The Yellow Wallpaper"
- Charlotte Perkins Gilman
- Nineteenth-century theories about women's health, psychology, and work
- Nineteenth-century American feminism
- Nineteenth-century fiction by American women
- The rest cure
- Postpartum depression
- Psychological abuse
- S. Weir Mitchell (Gilman's doctor in real life)
- Woman-centered horror stories as a genre
- The *New England Magazine*
- Nineteenth-century American periodicals

No item on the list is a *claim* about Gilman's story. Finding and developing a claim would be a goal of your research. But any of the terms could be a point of departure for you. They are words you would put in a search box to launch your probe.

Search for Sources in the Library and Online

Once you have your topic in mind and perhaps sketched a tentative claim, begin looking for research sources. Many different types of sources for literary research are available, and the types you will need will depend largely on the type of claim you choose to defend. If your issue is primarily one of interpretation—about the theme, patterns, or symbolism of the text, for instance—you will most likely need to consult literary criticism to see what has been said in the past about the literature you are discussing. If your issue concerns historical or cultural context, including issues of social policy, you may need to consult newspapers, magazines, and similar sorts of cultural documents. Some topics might require several different types of sources.

Not many years ago, for most people the word *research* was synonymous with hours spent in the library hunting for books and articles. For many students today, *research* has become synonymous with the Internet, which they turn to in the belief that everything is available online. But this is simply not true. Many of the best and most reliable sources are still available only in print. In particular, lots of potentially useful books haven't been digitized yet. They remain in your school library, so you'll have to go there if you hope to read them. The library may also house relevant documents and scholarly journals that aren't online. The library's computerized **catalog** will alert you to its holdings, helping you locate useful texts. Typically, the catalog entry for a book lists various subject headings for it. By clicking on a heading, you'll find other books on that topic. When you go to the library's shelves for a book, browse through neighboring volumes, for perhaps they also address your subject of study.

Of course, a wealth of information is available on the Internet. As with the library, your goal is to find useful information efficiently, evaluate it carefully, and employ it effectively in your paper. Unfortunately, and unlike a library's sources, information on the Internet is not indexed and organized to make it easily accessible to researchers. Many students go right away to Wikipedia, hoping to find most of their needed data there. Indeed, a Wikipedia entry may contain some useful facts. Nevertheless, you shouldn't accept on faith everything that the entry says. It's the product of anonymous people, many of whom may not really be experts on the subject they claim to know. Wikipedia can be a decent *starting* point for online searches, especially because it provides links to Web sites that may be more authoritative. But many teachers will object if you depend on Wikipedia itself as a source. Consider it a launch pad, not a destination.

You will need to do a certain amount of "surfing" if you are to find appropriate online materials for your project. A number of **search engines** (programs for finding information) are designed to help you track down materials on the Web. If you are an old hand on the Internet, probably you can depend on search engines that have served you well in the past. Bear in mind, however, that relying on just one search engine may not lead you to all the sources that would benefit you. Many students pursuing a research topic go immediately to Google. They type their subject into the box, click a mouse, and expect to see terrific sources pop right up on-screen. Yet often this search method proves exasperating. For one thing, it may succeed all *too* well in generating items. Our three sample researched arguments discuss "The Yellow Wallpaper"; a Google search using this title elicits around 628,000 results. The first paper also deals with postpartum depression; if you Google this term, you'll come up with roughly 3,820,000 results. Even if you combine "The Yellow Wallpaper" with "postpartum depression," you'll get roughly 6,110 results. It can take forever to sift through these avalanches for whatever gems they contain. Faced with such landslides, some writers just pounce on the first few results they obtain. But "first" doesn't necessarily mean "best." An ideal article may surface late in a Google list.

You can narrow your results by adding words to your search, making it more exact. Or you might turn to Google Scholar, which sticks with academic texts. There, combining "The Yellow Wallpaper" with "postpartum depression" produces about 125 results. This is certainly a more manageable number. Still, Google addiction will limit you as a researcher. See what other Web sites can do for you. If your college or university makes available to you sites such as JSTOR, Academic Search Premier, and Project Muse, these will give you access to hundreds of scholarly journals and books. The Internet service LexisNexis offers current articles from newspapers and magazines, as well as transcripts of radio and TV broadcasts.

When you take a course, find out what search engines serve its field. For literary research, a great one is the *MLA International Bibliography*, sponsored by the Modern Language Association (MLA) and carried by many schools. It lists books and articles on a wide range of topics in literary studies. Later in this chapter are sample researched arguments by students who used MLA's service. They looked for sources related to "The Yellow Wallpaper." For instance, Sarah Michaels was curious how the story might add to current debates about postpartum depression. Therefore, one of her search terms was this disorder's name. Typing it into the MLA search box, she found a useful article on how TV reports the problem. Katie Johnson was focused on literary criticism about Gilman's story. Using its title to search with, she found analyses of the tale.

Like most search engines, MLA's enables you to filter. Say you're looking for studies of "The Yellow Wallpaper." Once you insert this title into MLA's search box, you can restrict the results to articles published in journals. You can also have the results appear in reverse chronological order, so that the most recent articles come first. They'll mention older articles and books that have proven important, and you could turn to those next.

In several journals, each article is prefaced by a summary called an **abstract**. This overview, usually a paragraph, immediately tells you the article's main claim. Whenever you discover an article or book relevant to your project, examine its bibliography as well. Often, this will have the heading **Works Cited**. Likely to be listed there are other texts you'll find useful. In general, scholars refer to previous works on their subject. They extend, challenge, or refine their predecessors' claims. Notice how they treat these prior views. You'll get a sense of the conversation your topic has already stirred. You may also see how to join this dialogue with ideas of your own.

Evaluate the Sources

Whatever method you use to locate your research materials, remember that not all sources are created equal. Take care to **evaluate** those you come across. When tempted to use a writer's work, ask yourself the following: What do I want my audience to think about this person? Often, you'll hope your readers will accept him or her as some sort of authority. In a way, you have to think about **ethos**, a term we discussed in our first two chapters. There, you may recall, we defined *ethos* as the image that an author projects. Many writers try to be persuasive by constructing an admirable ethos — a version of themselves that will impress their readers. Similarly, when you incorporate sources into a researched argument, you will often want your audience to respect them. These sources may not agree with one another — heck, *you* may not agree with them all — but they'll need to have recognizable expertise. Otherwise, why should your readers pay attention to them?

Suppose you plan to write a research paper on "The Yellow Wallpaper." An online search leads you to an analysis of the story. You might refer to this study in your essay. But you need to determine whether the author is someone your readers would take seriously. You have to look for credentials. Perhaps the writer is a professor publishing in a scholarly journal. Maybe, like Paul Goldberger in Chapter 1, this person is an award-winning authority in a certain field (in this case, architecture). Another writer in the same chapter, David Barno, is a veteran military officer affiliated with a distinguished think tank. Sometimes you can learn writers' professional status by visiting the Web sites of institutions they work for. At any rate, be skeptical when a Web post's author is shrouded in mystery. The views expressed may be interesting, but if their advocate is a phantom, you can't expect your readers to care about them. Useful to bear in mind is the famous *New Yorker* magazine cartoon about the digital age. One canine, perched at a computer, tells another that "on the Internet, nobody knows you're a dog." In short, the Web can fool you. Although someone posting on it is probably human, hunt for details of the person's background. Your audience will expect you to have this information about a source, even if you don't include every bit of it in your paper.

A teacher may require a number of your sources to be articles from "peer-reviewed" academic journals. Such journals publish a manuscript only after it has been evaluated by experts in its subject. Usually, a journal's Web site will indicate whether it falls into this category. Some search engines have a feature that, when you activate it, confines your results to peer-reviewed works.

For example, both Academic Search Premier and the MLA International Bibliography enable you to restrict your search this way. Most books published by academic and university presses have also been peer reviewed. Of course, even when it doesn't come with this label, a book or an article may still be worth consulting. In many popular newspapers (such as the *New York Times* and the *Washington Post*) and magazines (such as *The New Yorker* and the *Atlantic*), you'll find thoughtful, well-grounded reports and opinion pieces.

In general, you should ask the following basic questions of your sources: (1) Is the information recent, and if not, is the validity of the information likely to have changed significantly over time? (2) How credible is the author? Is he or she a recognized expert on the subject? (3) Is the source published by an established, respectable press, or does it appear in a well-respected journal or periodical (the *Los Angeles Times* has more credibility than the *National Enquirer*, for example) or Web site (one supported by a university or library, for instance)? (4) Based on what you've learned about responsible argument, do the arguments in your source seem sound, fair, and thoughtful? Is the evidence convincing? Is the development of the argument logical?

You increase your own credibility with your audience by using the most reliable research materials available to you, so do not just stick with whatever comes to hand if you have the opportunity to find a stronger source.

Record Your Sources' Key Details

As your research proceeds, record your discoveries. In a computer file or handwritten notes, jot down key details of each source. Don't expect that you'll simply recall this information. Memory is imperfect; data can fade from your mind.

Above all, specify each source by using bibliographical form. You'll then have an entry ready to put in your essay's Works Cited section. In a literature course, the format you'll usually follow is that of the MLA. Later in this chapter, we explain MLA's guidelines at length. At the moment, here are sample MLA-formatted entries by the two students we've mentioned. Sarah, who found the article about postpartum depression, logged it in her notes this way:

> Dubriwny, Tasha N. "Televison News Coverage of Postpartum Disorders and the Politics of Medicalization." *Feminist Media Studies*, vol. 10, no. 3, Sept. 2010, pp. 285–303.

Katie, who investigated literary criticism, recorded one of her articles as follows:

> Johnson, Greg. "Gilman's Gothic Allegory: Rage and Redemption in `The Yellow Wallpaper.'" *Studies in Short Fiction*, vol. 26, no. 4, Fall 1989, pp. 521–30.

What else about a source might you write down? You have several options.

A *summary* of the source — one or two sentences indicating in your own words the author's main claim. Such summaries guarantee that you understand the gist of an author's argument and (since they are in your own words) can readily be incorporated in your paper. You might think of a summary as a restatement of the author's principal claim, perhaps with a brief indication of the types of supporting evidence he or she marshals. You can also write summaries of supporting points — subsections of an author's argument — if they seem applicable to your paper. A summary should not, however, include quotations, exhaustive detail about subpoints, or a list of all the evidence in a given source. A summary is meant to provide a succinct overview — to demonstrate that you have grasped a point and convey it to your readers.

A possible summary of Durbriwny's article:

> In the period of 2000–2007, television reports on postpartum disorders used expert and personal testimonies to depict these disorders as the medical problems of individuals. It is more appropriate, however, to put these conditions in a social context, for the women suffering from them are actually challenging the destructive cultural stereotype of the "good" mother.

A possible summary of Johnson's article:

> The heroine of "The Yellow Wallpaper" emerges not as a pathetic madwoman, but as someone who asserts her freedom and creativity by imagining a Gothic fantasy for herself and writing about it in her diary.

***Quotations* (with page numbers) that you might incorporate into your essay.** A quotation may be a word, a phrase, a sentence, or an entire passage.

A striking sentence in Dubriwny's article:

> Women's varied emotions and behaviors during the postpartum period — their feelings of anger, distress, sadness, and guilt as well as happiness — point to a substantial gap between the lived reality of mothering and the discourse of essential/good motherhood. (287)

A memorable sentence from Johnson:

> Thus as the story progresses, the heroine follows both her childlike promptings and her artistic faith in creating a Gothic alternative to the stifling daylight world of her husband and the society at large. (524)

***Paraphrasing* (with page numbers) that you might incorporate in your essay.** A paraphrase puts a statement in new words. Think of it as a translation that attempts to convey the basic idea of the original passage. It has two advantages over a quotation. First, an accurate paraphrase proves that you understand the material you've read. Second, a paraphrase is easier to integrate into your essay than a quotation, since it is already written in your own words and style. When you paraphrase, you need to identify the original page number, just as you do with quotations.

A statement by Dubriwny:

> Unfortunately, the struggle over the definition of postpartum disorders is, in television news, not much of a struggle at all, as only a few voices exist to challenge the complete medicalization of postpartum disorders. (299)

A possible paraphrase of Dubriwny's statement:

> Sadly, televised reports tend to depict postpartum depression and similar maladies as medical problems, rarely giving air time to activists who propose other ways of understanding such conditions (299).

A statement by Johnson, about Gilman's heroine:

> Her experience should finally be viewed not as a final catastrophe but as a terrifying, necessary stage in her progress toward self-identity and personal achievement. (523)

A possible paraphrase of Johnson's statement:

> At the end of the story, the heroine may seem doomed but actually is not, for she has to engage in such frightening behavior if she is eventually to become a fulfilled, accomplished individual (523).

Texts and other materials with which the source is in conversation. When you note these, you put the source in context. You become more aware of the issues that the source addresses.

> Dubriwny analyzes how postpartum disorders were represented in television reports from 2000 to 2007. She focuses on a selection of tapes available in the Vanderbilt Television News Archives. They're her primary source. Motivating her research was recent public attention to certain events, including Andrea Yates's murder of her children and Tom Cruise's disapproval of Brooke Shields's reliance on antidepressants. Dubriwny is influenced, too, by advocacy groups and sociologists who critique the role that dominant models of mother-hood play in diagnoses of postpartum conditions. Also driving her to write is the relative lack of scholarship on the biases that shape media representations of these disorders.
>
> Johnson takes Gilman's story as his primary source. He argues that its heroine's behavior at the end is a creative, self-affirming protest against the patriarchal society that her husband represents. Johnson opposes interpretations of the story that see the heroine as simply mad. But when he cites specific studies of the story, he tends to choose those that support his view. He also develops his claim by referring to Gilman's nonfiction autobiographical writings; to other women writers (Emily Dickinson, Charlotte Bronte, Sylvia Plath); and to scholarship on the Gothic literary tradition.

Strategies for Integrating Sources

Throughout your research, you'll aim to evolve an argument of your own. It's something *you'll* contribute to discussions taking place. The student essays at the conclusion of this chapter are examples. Each recruits sources to advance a claim that the student herself has produced.

Once you've finished your research, take time to reflect. If you've come up with an issue and claim, think about them again. In light of all your findings, is your argument still good? Does it need fine-tuning? Should you even change topics? Maybe, though, you remain unsure what to argue. To gain focus, review the issues your sources raise. What debates do they participate in? What sides in these debates do *you* favor? What issues do these debates ignore or slight? For help in getting ideas, you might also review the categories of issues we present on pages 54–61 of Chapter 3.

As you draft your essay, show that you're using your sources. Don't let them overshadow *your* contribution. They should clearly serve your argument, not crowd it out. Whenever you summarize, paraphrase, or quote, identify your source's function. Indicate the role it plays in a conversation you run. If you've taken many notes in your research, your essay may not have room for all. Cast aside those that fail to help.

Use direct quotations sparingly. Hordes of them make for choppy reading and may obscure your ideas. When you're tempted to quote, consider paraphrasing instead. If you still feel that quoting is necessary, try to limit the number of words. Perhaps you needn't quote an entire sentence or passage. A bit of phrasing may suffice. Here are examples of selective quotation.

Original (from Dubriwny's article):

> The medical experts interviewed in the news coverage engage in a process of decontextualizing postpartum distress. What I mean is that the experts take the distress out of the social context of mothering and focus almost solely on biological causes of postpartum disorders. (290)

Limited quoting:

> Dubriwny is concerned that TV reports on postpartum conditions use medical authorities to emphasize "biological causes" rather than "the social context of mothering" (290).

Original (from Johnson's article):

> Two of the story's major structural devices are its contrasting of the husband's daylight world and his wife's nocturnal fantasy, and the religious imagery by which she highlights the liberating and redemptive qualities of her experience. (523)

Limited quoting:

> Johnson contends that although the heroine seems tormented, she actually finds her interaction with the wallpaper "liberating and redemptive" (523).

When quoting up to four lines of prose or three lines of poetry, integrate the quotation directly into your paragraph, enclosing the quoted material in double quotation marks and checking to make sure that the quotation accurately reflects the original. Longer quotations are set off from the text by starting a new line and indenting one inch on the left margin only; these are called **block quotations**. For these, quotation marks are omitted since the indention is enough to indicate that the material is a quotation. Examples of the correct format for both long and short quotations appear in Katie Johnson's paper (pp. 234–38).

When a short quotation is from a poem, line breaks in the poem are indicated by slash marks, with single spaces on either side. The following example demonstrates the format for a short quotation, in this case from Yusef Komunyakaa's poem "Blackberries" (featured in Chapter 6). The numbers in parentheses specify which lines in the poem are being quoted:

> The poem's speaker recalls the scene as sinister, noting: "The big blue car made me sweat. / Wintertime crawled out of the windows" (19–20).

While it is essential to quote accurately, sometimes you may need to alter a quotation slightly, either by deleting text for brevity or by adding or changing text to incorporate it grammatically. If you delete words from a quotation, indicate the deletion by inserting an ellipsis (three periods with spaces between them), as demonstrated by the following quotation from Robert Frost's poem "Mending Wall" (Chapter 3):

> The speaker makes his neighbor sound warlike, describing him as "Bringing a stone . . . / In each hand, like an old-stone savage armed" (39–40).

If you need to change or add words for clarity or grammatical correctness, indicate the changes with square brackets. If, for instance, you wanted to clarify the meaning of "They" in Komunyakaa's opening line "They left my hands like a printer's," you could do so like this:

> The speaker recalls that "[The blackberries] left my hands like a printer's" (1).

No quotation is self-sufficient. Nor is its meaning always self-evident. When you put a quotation in your essay, help your audience see why it's there. Introduce it clearly. Follow it with any additional explanation it needs. The longer the quotation, the more analysis readers want.

Avoid Plagiarism

Plagiarism is a serious violation of academic standards. Most colleges have policies that explain how they define and treat it. You should learn your institution's guidelines. But there are general rules of thumb to follow when you quote, summarize, or paraphrase. The major one is this: indicate clearly which ideas are yours and which are other people's. You commit **plagiarism** if you claim credit for another person's thoughts. Even if you put them in your own words, they came from someone else. If you don't attribute these ideas to their source, you mislead your readers. You betray your audience's trust.

To see better what we mean, look at the sentence below, which is on page 527 of Greg Johnson's article about Gilman's "The Yellow Wallpaper." Johnson refers to the story's heroine, who records her distress in her diary:

> An experienced writer, she understands the healing power which inheres in the act of writing and recognizes intuitively that her physician husband's rest cure can lead only to her psychic degeneration.

You would be committing plagiarism if you presented Johnson's sentence — or parts of it — as your own prose:

> We should remember that the heroine is an experienced writer. She understands intuitively the healing power that writing has. Indeed, writing in her diary is a means by which she tries to head off the degeneration of her mind that her physician husband's rest cure will cause.

You would also be plagiarizing if you paraphrased Johnson's sentence without noting that it's his:

> A veteran crafter of prose, the heroine perceives that her journal-keeping is important for her mental health. At some level of consciousness, she also realizes that the treatment her doctor spouse is putting her through will result in the decay of her mind.

Here is a way you could quote from Johnson's sentence, give him credit for it, identify its page number, and make clear what you're doing with him as a source:

> Many analysts of the story overlook the fact that its narrator writes. Specifically, she maintains a diary of her ordeal. As Greg Johnson points out, her journal-keeping has for her a "healing power," whereas the treatment her husband is putting her through "can lead only to her psychic degeneration" (527). Johnson may be overestimating how perceptive the narrator is when he claims that "she understands" (527) the diary's therapeutic function. Perhaps she isn't as aware of its value as he thinks. Still, writing is a resource for her as she tries to cope with the medical treatment her husband inflicts.

Sometimes authors unintentionally plagiarize. They forget that certain ideas they recorded during their research are actually quotations or paraphrases. Nevertheless, most readers will see "accidental" plagiarism as still plagiarism. So be precise in your research notes. Put within quotation marks anything you copy. The moment your notes quote or restate someone else's words, jot down information about the source. Of course, you should record the page number, but do even more. Include all the details you'll need for a Works Cited entry, because your essay may end up referring to the source. In general, equip yourself to give credit.

What *does not* need to be referenced is **common knowledge**: factual information that the average reader can be expected to know or that is readily available in many easily accessible sources. For example, it is common knowledge that Charlotte Perkins Gilman was an American writer. It is also common knowledge that she was born in 1860 and died in 1935, even though most people would have to look that information up in an encyclopedia or a biographical dictionary to verify it.

Strategies for Documenting Sources (MLA Format)

Documentation is the means by which you give credit to the authors of all primary and secondary sources cited within a researched argument. It serves two principal purposes: (1) it allows your readers to find out more about the origin of the ideas you present, and (2) it protects you from charges of plagiarism. Every academic discipline follows slightly different conventions for documentation, but the method most commonly used for writing about literature is the format devised by the MLA. This documentation method encompasses **in-text citations**, which briefly identify within the body of your paper the source of a particular quotation, summary, or paraphrase, and a bibliography, called **Works Cited**, which gives more complete publication information.

While mastering the precise requirements of MLA punctuation and format can be time consuming and even frustrating, getting them right adds immeasurably to the professionalism of a finished paper. More detailed information, including special circumstances and documentation styles for types of sources not covered here, will be found in the *MLA Handbook for Writers of Research Papers*, Eighth Edition (New York: Modern Language Association, 2016). Of course, if your instructor requests that you follow a different documentation method, you should follow his or her instructions instead.

MLA IN-TEXT CITATION

Each time you include information from any outside source—whether in the form of a summary, a paraphrase, or a quotation—you must provide your reader with a brief reference indicating the author and page number of the original. This reference directs the reader to the Works Cited list, where more complete information is available.

There are two basic methods for in-text citation. The first, and usually preferable, method is to include the author's name in the text of your essay and note the page number in parentheses at the end of the citation. The following paraphrase and quotation from "The Yellow Wallpaper" show the format to be followed for this method. Note that the page number (without

the abbreviation "p." or additional punctuation) is enclosed within parentheses and that the final punctuation for the sentence occurs after
the parenthetical reference, effectively making the reference part of the
preceding sentence. For a direct quotation, the closing quotation marks
come before the page reference, but the final period is still saved until after
the reference.

> Gilman's narrator believes her husband trivializes her disorder (230).

> Gilman's narrator sadly reports that her husband considers her
> disorder to be just "a slight hysterical tendency" (230).

The method is similar for long quotations (those set off from the main text of
your essay). The only differences are that the final punctuation mark comes
before the parenthetical page reference, and that the quotation is not enclosed
within quotation marks.

In those cases where citing the author's name in your text would be awkward or difficult, you may include both the author's last name and the page
reference in the parenthetical citation. The following example draws a quotation from Greg Johnson's article about Gilman's story.

> According to one interpreter of the story, the heroine's final behavior
> is a "necessary stage in her progress toward self-identity and
> personal achievement" (Johnson 523).

If you cite more than one work by the same author, you must specify from
which of these works each citation comes. Many Internet sources don't number their pages; the parenthetical reference needs to include only the author's
last name (or, if the work is anonymous, an identifying title.) In the case of
poems, use line numbers (rather than page numbers) if they're provided, and
precede your first use of a line number with the word "line." If the poem lacks
line numbers, cite it by giving the page number. But if the poem is just one page
long, you don't need to cite any numbers within your text. The page number
must appear, though, in your Works Cited.

MLA WORKS CITED

The second feature of the MLA format is the Works Cited list, or bibliography. This list should begin on a new page of your paper and should be double-
spaced throughout and use hanging indention, which means that all lines
except the first are indented one-half inch. The list is alphabetized by
author's last name (or by the title in the case of anonymous works) and
includes every primary and secondary source referred to in your paper. The
format for the most common types of entries is given below. If any of the
information called for is unavailable for a particular source, simply skip that
element and keep the rest of the entry as close as possible to the given format. An anonymous work, for instance, skips the author's name and is
alphabetized under the title.

▤ DIRECTORY TO MLA WORKS-CITED ENTRIES

Books

A book by a single author or editor (221)

A book with multiple authors or editors (221)

A book with a corporate author (221)

A recent edition of a book originally published much earlier (221)

Short Works from Collections and Anthologies

A single work from a collection or anthology (222)

Multiple works from the same collection or anthology (222)

Multiple Works by the Same Author (222)

Works in Periodicals

A work in a scholarly journal (223)

An article in a magazine (223)

An article in a newspaper (223)

A book review in a scholarly journal (224)

A book review in a magazine (224)

A book review in a newspaper (224)

Online Sources

An article in an online journal (224)

An article in a print journal that you access through an online database (224)

A book review that appears online (225)

A comment posted at a Web site (225)

A contribution to a listserv or similar online forum (225)

An e-mail message (225)

An online video, such as those available at YouTube (225)

Citation Formats for Other Kinds of Sources

An interview you conducted (226)

An episode of a television series (226)

A film (226)

Books

Here are typical elements of a book citation, in the order they should appear:

1. The author, last name first. If the book has an editor rather than an author, put the last name first but then add a comma and the word "editor." An author might be corporate; in that case, put the name of the organization.

2. The full title, in italics. If the book has a subtitle, put a colon between title and subtitle.

3. If the book has both an author and an editor, now put the words "edited by" and then the editor's name.
4. If the book has a translator, now put the words "translated by" and the translator's name.
5. If the book is in an edition other than the first, put the edition number.
6. Put the name of the publisher. If the publisher is a university, abbreviate "University" as "U" and Press as "P": for example, U of Chicago P or Indiana UP.
7. Put the year of publication.

Rules of punctuation: Follow the author's name with a period. Do the same for the book's full title. Usually, in the rest of the entry, your chief form of punctuation will be a comma. If you use a period again, it will be for abbreviations and for the entry's final punctuation mark. There are a few exceptions to this rule, which we will point out later.

A book by a single author or editor.

> Cima, Gay Gibson. *Performing Women: Female Characters, Male Playwrights, and the Modern Stage.* Cornell UP, 1993.
> Booth, Wayne C. *The Rhetoric of Fiction.* 2nd ed., U of Chicago P, 1983.
> Tucker, Robert C., editor. *The Marx-Engels Reader.* Norton, 1972.
> O'Connor, Flannery. *The Habit of Being: Letters of Flannery O'Connor.* Edited by Sally Fitzgerald, Farrar, Straus, and Giroux, 1979.

A book with multiple authors or editors.   If there are two, identify the additional person by first and last name. If there are three or more, just give the first person's name followed by "et al."

> Leeming, David, and Jake Page. *God: Myths of the Male Divine.* Oxford UP, 1996.
> Arrow, Kenneth Joseph, et al., editors. *Education in a Research University.* Stanford UP, 1996.

A book with a corporate author.

> National Conference on Undergraduate Research. *Proceedings of the National Conference on Undergraduate Research.* U of North Carolina, 1995.

A recent edition of a book originally published much earlier.   If you want your reader to know the first publication date, give it a sentence of its own after the book's title.

> Bronte, Emily. *Wuthering Heights.* 1847. Penguin Classics, 2002.

Short Works from Collections and Anthologies

Many scholarly books are collections of articles on a single topic by several different authors. When you cite an article from such a collection, include the information given below. The format is the same for works of literature that appear in an anthology, such as this one.

1. The name of the author(s) of the article or literary work.
2. The title of the short work, enclosed in quotation marks.
3. The title of the anthology, italicized.
4. The name(s) of the editor(s) of the collection or anthology.
5. All relevant publication information, in the same order and format as it would appear in a book citation.
6. The inclusive page numbers for the shorter work.
7. The medium of publication.

A single work from a collection or an anthology. Begin with the author of the single work, and then the work's title. Follow this with the book's title, its editor, and other information you would normally provide for a book. Conclude the entry with the page numbers of the single work.

> Kirk, Russell. "Eliot's Christian Imagination." *The Placing of T. S. Eliot*, edited by Jewel Spears Brooker, U of Missouri P, 1991, pp. 136–44.
>
> Silko, Leslie Marmon. "Yellow Woman." *The Story and Its Writer: An Introduction to Short Fiction*, edited by Ann Charters, 9th ed., Bedford, 2015, pp. 1209–15.

Multiple works from the same collection or anthology. Write a single general entry that provides full publication information for the collection or anthology as a whole. The entry for each shorter work then contains only its author and title, the names of the book's editors, and the page numbers of the shorter work, with all of these facts separated by commas.

> Charters, Ann, editor. *The Story and Its Writer: An Introduction to Short Fiction*. 9th ed., Bedford, 2015.
>
> Faulkner, William. "A Rose for Emily." Charters, pp. 409–15.

Multiple Works by the Same Author

If you cite more than one work by a single author, alphabetize the individual works by title. Give the author's full name only for the first citation in the Works Cited. Any subsequent entry for that author begins not with the name but with three hyphens followed by a period.

> Faulkner, William. "A Rose for Emily." *The Story and Its Writer: An Introduction to Short Fiction*, edited by Ann Charters, 9th ed., Bedford, 2015, pp. 454–60.
>
> - - -. *The Sound and the Fury*. Modern Library, 1956.

Works in Periodicals

When you cite articles and other short works from journals, magazines, or newspapers, include the following information, in the given order and format:

1. The name(s) of the author(s) of the short work, as for a book publication.
2. The title of the short work, in quotation marks.
3. The title of the periodical, italicized.
4. The volume number, issue number, and date of the issue. See the model citations below for examples of how to abbreviate volume, number, and date in the citations.
5. The page numbers of the short work.

Rules of punctuation: Follow the author's name with a period. Do the same for the short work's title. Usually, in the rest of the entry, your chief form of punctuation will be a comma. If you use a period again, it will be for abbreviations and for the entry's final punctuation mark. There are a few exceptions to this rule, which we will point out later.

A work in a scholarly journal.   Publication information for works from scholarly and professional journals should include the volume number, the issue number, the month or season of the issue, and the year.

> Charles, Casey. "Gender Trouble in *Twelfth Night.*" *Theatre Journal*,
>   vol. 49, no. 2, May 1997, pp. 121–41.

An article in a magazine.   Publication information for articles in general-circulation magazines includes the month(s) of publication for a monthly (or bimonthly), or the date (day, abbreviated month, then year) for a weekly or biweekly.

> Cowley, Malcolm. "It Took a Village." *Utne Reader*, Nov.-Dec. 1997,
>   pp. 48–49.
> Kolbert, Elizabeth. "Unnatural Selection." *New Yorker*, 18 April 2016,
>   pp. 22–28.

An article in a newspaper.   When citing an article from a newspaper, include the date (day, abbreviated month, year), followed by the edition, the section number, or the section letter (if applicable).

> Bray, Hiawatha. "New FCC Rules Draw Criticism." *Boston Globe*,
>   17 May 2016, p. C2.

A book review in a scholarly journal.

> Hawkins, Ty. Review of *Vietnam and Beyond: Tim O'Brien and the Power of Storytelling*, by Stefania Ciocia. *Studies in the Novel*, Vol. 45, No. 4, Winter 2013, pp. 705–07.

A book review in a magazine.

> Plumly, Stanley. Review of *Those Who Write for Immortality: Romantic Reputations and the Dream of Lasting Fame*, by H. J. Jackson. *The American Scholar*, vol. 84, no. 2, Spring 2015, pp. 152–53.

A book review in a newspaper.

> Yardley, Jonathan. Review of *One Matchless Time: A Life of William Faulkner*, by Jay Parini. *The Washington Post*, 24 Oct. 2004, p. T2.

Online Sources

Documentation for online sources should include as much of the following information as possible, in the order and format specified:

1. The name(s) of the author(s), as for a book publication.
2. The title of the work accessed, in quotation marks. For e-mails and postings, the title is the subject line.
3. The title of the periodical, italicized.
4. The volume number, issue number, and date of the issue. See the model citations below for examples of how to abbreviate volume, number, and date in the citations.
5. The URL or, better yet, the DOI. The letters "DOI" stand for "digital object identifier." A DOI is a permanent tag, enabling an online source to be located even when the URL changes. Not every Internet document has a DOI, but if you can find one for your source, list that rather than the URL.
6. If there is no date of issue, you may indicate the date you accessed the site, e.g., "Accessed 2 May 2016".

Rules of punctuation: Follow the author's name with a period. Do the same for the work's title. Usually, in the rest of the entry, your chief form of punctuation will be a comma. If you use a period again, it will be for abbreviations and for the entry's final punctuation mark. There are a few exceptions to this rule, which we will point out later.

An article in an online journal.

> Abowitz, Richard. "The Hughes Blues." *The Smart Set*, 2 Mar. 2016, http://thesmartset.com/the-langston-hughes-blues/.

An article in a print journal that you access through an online database.   Provide all the information you would give if you were citing the print version of the article. End this section with a period. Then put the name of the database (in italics), a comma, the URL or the DOI, and a final period.

> De Baerdemaeker, Ruben. "Performative Patterns in Hemingway's 'Soldier's Home.'" *The Hemingway Review*, vol. 27, no. 1, Fall 2007, pp. 55–73. *Project Muse*, doi: 10.1353/hem.2007.0017.

A book review that appears online.

> Livingston, James. Review of *The Age of the Crisis of Man*, by Mark Greif. *Bookforum*, 9 Mar. 2015, http://www.bookforum.com /review/14328.

A comment posted at a Web site.   Begin the entry with whatever name the commenter has used. Then write "Comment on," followed by the title (in quotation marks) of the text that the comment responds to. Next, using commas, give the title of the journal or Web site where the comment appears, followed by the date that the comment was posted, the time it was posted (if available), and the URL.

> Stefan. Comment on "How Should We Live in a Diverse Society?" *Pandaemonium*, 4 May 2016, 10:25 p.m., https://kenanmalik .wordpress.com/2016/05/02/how-should-we-live-in-a-diverse -society/.

A contribution to a listserv or similar online forum. In this case, the title is the subject line.

> Bean, Joyce. "Re: Is fiction w/ community as subject still viable?" *Writing Program Administration*, 10 May 2016, 12:08 p.m., https://lists.asu.edu/cgi-bin/wa?A2=ind1605&L=WPA -L&D=0&P=149100.

An e-mail message.   Again, the title is the subject line. Then you should identify who received the message, along with the date it arrived.

> Hardy, Rachel. "Re: Flannery O'Connor's stories." Received by Jacob Ravitz, 5 Apr. 2016.

An online video, such as those available at YouTube.   For an entry like this, you have options. Your choices should reflect what you want to stress. Note the following options for citing a certain YouTube video. The first example starts with the video's title, which would surely help your readers track down the video. But if you wish to stress the title *and* acknowledge who posted the video, you could include that person's name, as our second example does. Maybe, though, you'll want to emphasize the video's director; our third example begins with his name and production role.

> "A Conversation with Tobias Wolff Directed by Lawrence Bridges." *YouTube*, 30 Nov. 2013, https://www.youtube.com/watch?v =0MZ3oKPFf90.

> "A Conversation with Tobias Wolff Directed by Lawrence Bridges."
>   *YouTube*, posted by Lawrence Bridges, 30 Nov. 2013, https://
>   www.youtube.com/watch?v=0MZ3oKPFf90.
> Bridges, Lawrence, director. "A Conversation with Tobias Wolff
>   Directed by Lawrence Bridges." *YouTube*, 30 Nov. 2013, https://
>   www.youtube.com/watch?v=0MZ3oKPFf90.

Citation Formats for Other Kinds of Sources

An interview you conducted.   In the author slot, identify the person you interviewed. Follow this information with "Personal interview," a comma, and the interview's date.

> McCorkle, Patrick. Personal interview, 12 Mar. 2004.

An episode of a television series.   Begin with the episode's title. Using commas, follow this with the series title, the season and episode numbers, the network or production company, and the date of first airing. Our first example refers to the notorious "red wedding" episode of the TV series *Game of Thrones*. If you want to call attention to particular contributors, you can do so by adding information about them as our second example does.

> "The Rains of Castamere." *Game of Thrones*, season 3, episode 9,
>   HBO, 2 June 2013.
> "The Rains of Castamere." *Game of Thrones*, created by David Benioff
>   and D. B. Weiss, performances by Richard Madden, Michelle
>   Fairley, and Oona Chaplin, season 3, episode 9, HBO, 2
>   June 2013.

A film.   Many film citations indicate title and director. Depending on which you want to emphasize, you can begin with either. Our first and second examples show these options. If you want to call attention to other contributors, you can do so by adding information about them as our third example does. In any case, end your entry by identifying the main production company and the year of first release.

> *The Dark Knight*. Directed by Christopher Nolan, Warner Bros., 2008.
> Nolan, Christopher, director. *The Dark Knight*, Warner Bros., 2008.
> *The Dark Knight*. Directed by Christopher Nolan, performances by
>   Christian Bale and Heath Ledger, Warner Bros, 2008.

A Note on Endnotes

Occasionally, you may have an idea or find a piece of information that seems important to your paper but that you just cannot work in smoothly without interrupting the flow of ideas. Such information can be included in the form of **endnotes**. A small superscript number in your text signals a note, and the notes themselves appear on a separate page at the end of your paper, before the Works Cited. Often, endnotes point readers to sources that they can then investigate if they wish. Any source mentioned in an endnote must be listed in the Works Cited.

Three Annotated Student Researched Arguments

We end this chapter with three researched arguments written by students. All of the essays refer to Charlotte Perkins Gilman's short story "The Yellow Wallpaper." But they model different ways to write about it. In order, the essays are:

- An argument that uses a literary work to examine a social issue
- An argument that deals with existing interpretations of a literary work
- An argument that places a literary work in historical and cultural context

Each argument demonstrates strategies we've discussed. Each also shows how to cite sources using MLA format. We annotate these essays in their margins, with comments that point out specific moves they make. After each essay, we review how it uses its sources. You'll see that the authors draw on research to create a conversation. They synthesize their findings as they build a case of their own.

AN ARGUMENT THAT USES A LITERARY WORK TO EXAMINE SOCIAL ISSUES

Some research papers mention a literary work but then focus on examining a social issue related to that work. An example of such a paper is the following essay by student Sarah Michaels. To prepare for writing her paper, Sarah consulted numerous sources, and she turns to them during the course of her essay. The chief danger in a project like this is that it will become a mere "data dump"—that is, a paper in which the writer uncritically cites one source after another without really making an original argument. In writing an essay like Sarah's, be sure to identify your main issue and claim clearly. Present yourself as someone who is genuinely *testing* your sources, determining the specific ways in which they are relevant to your argument. Keep in mind that even if you are representing a source as useful, you can indicate how its ideas need to be further complicated. With at least some of your sources, analyze specific terms they employ, lingering over their language. Moreover, try to relate your sources to one another. We think Sarah accomplishes all these objectives. Even if you disagree, aim to practice her strategies yourself.

Sarah Michaels
Professor Swain
English L202
21 May - - - -

"The Yellow Wallpaper" as a Guide
to Social Factors in Postpartum Depression

In 2005, actor Brooke Shields's memoir *Down Came the Rain: My Journey through Postpartum Depression* drew much public attention to the psychological problem mentioned in its subtitle.[1] But during the last couple of decades, postpartum depression has been the subject of reports by many medical institutions and media outlets. By now, lots of people other than health professionals are aware of this problem and can at least roughly define it. If asked, most of them would probably say that although it can exhibit varying degrees of severity, postpartum depression is basically a state of despair suffered by a significant number of women who have just given birth. This is, in fact, the main image of it presented in a recent document about it, an October 2010 report by Marian Earls and a committee of the American Academy of Pediatrics. Besides explaining what postpartum depression is, the report urges pediatricians and other primary care providers to screen new mothers for it. Given that many members of the public already know that the problem is widespread, the report has not sparked much disagreement. Responding to it in the online magazine *Slate*, however, Emily Anthes does challenge its almost total emphasis on mothers. She argues that the Academy's committee makes a questionable assumption in writing as if only females are traumatized by birth. In her article entitled "Dads Get Blue, Too," she criticizes the report's authors for not acknowledging at greater length that new fathers can experience postpartum depression as well.[2] More generally, her article suggests that discussions of this disorder can be skewed by ideological views that need to be recognized. But, more than a century ago, Charlotte Perkins Gilman's story "The Yellow Wallpaper" made pretty much the same point by showing how a woman diagnosed with a label like postpartum depression is a victim of her domestic circumstances and her society's ideas about gender, not just a person who has become ill on her own. When juxtaposed with the Academy's report, Gilman's 1892 tale is a reminder that today's doctors should look beyond an individual woman's symptoms of post-birth distress, because the social arrangements in which she lives may significantly affect her health.

Calls attention to an endnote.

Quickly identifies social issue that the paper will focus on.

Introduces the literary work that the paper will relate to the social issue.

The term *postpartum depression* has for a long time appeared in analyses of "The Yellow Wallpaper" and of the personal experience that Gilman based the story on. Veronica Makowsky points out that this clinical phrase has even "become a critical commonplace" (329) in studies of the relationship between the story and Gilman's life. Gilman does not, however, actually use the term *postpartum depression* in the tale. Instead, the heroine's husband, John, declares that she suffers from "temporary nervous depression — a slight hysterical tendency" (230), and the character herself refers to her "nervous troubles" (232). Nor does Gilman bring up the term in her accounts of the real-life despair she went through when she gave birth to her daughter. In her essay "Why I Wrote 'The Yellow Wallpaper,'" she recalls being tormented much of her life by "a severe and continuous nervous break-down tending to melancholia" (792). In her book-length autobiography *The Living of Charlotte Perkins Gilman*, she describes herself as suffering from "nervous prostration" (90). Indeed, the *Oxford English Dictionary*'s entry for *postpartum depression* indicates that the term was not recorded until 1929, when it showed up in an issue of the *American Journal of Psychiatry*.

Concedes that the term is used by scholars rather than by the author herself.

Nevertheless, the phrase does seem to fit the condition of Gilman's narrator. According to the American Academy of Pediatrics report, the symptoms of postpartum depression can range from "crying, worrying, sadness, anxiety, and mood swings" to more disturbing signs like "paranoia, mood shifts, hallucinations, [and] delusions" (1033). Gilman's character can be said to display most of these things once her child is born. At the estate that is the story's setting, she has trouble sleeping, she comes to doubt her husband's love, and, most dramatically, she rips off the wallpaper in her bedroom to free a woman whom she imagines wanting to creep away.

Directly connects language of the report to the story.

But simply labeling the heroine's distress as postpartum depression risks ignoring the conditions surrounding her that contribute to her suffering. Commenting on "The Yellow Wallpaper," literary critic Paula A. Treichler points out that a medical diagnosis can block understanding of "social, cultural, and economic practices" (69), even though these may support the doctor's claim to expertise, play a role in the patient's anguish, and become more important to confront than the patient's individual pain.[3] In Gilman's story, John uses his social authority as physician and husband to control his wife. Specifically, he isolates her on the estate and makes her give up real activity, just as Gilman's real-life doctor, S. Weir

Uses another interpreter of the story to advance this paper's argument.

Mitchell, demanded that she rest. As a result, the heroine feels obligated to surrender to the stereotypical passive female role, even though she would welcome more interaction with others and suspects that "congenial work, with excitement and change, would do me good" (780). When she proceeds to hallucinate the woman in the wallpaper, this is something that she is *driven* to do by John's assertion of masculine power, just as Weir Mitchell's prescription for inertia drove Gilman "near the border line of utter mental ruin" ("Why" 792).

Key quote from the story.

With "The Yellow Wallpaper" in mind, readers of the American Academy of Pediatrics report might examine how it downplays what Treichler calls "social, cultural, and economic practices" in its focus on diagnosing postpartum depression in women. Although the report does note that "Paternal depression is estimated at 6%" (1032), it does not linger on this fairly significant figure. In addition, the committee mentions only in passing that while "as many as 12% of all pregnant or postpartum women experience depression in a given year," the percentage is twice as much "for low-income women" (1032). Similarly brief is the recognition that "Eighteen percent of fathers of children in Early Head Start had symptoms of depression" (1033), a distinctly high figure that again suggests one's social class can affect one's health. Nor does the report develop its brief notice that possible causes of postpartum depression include "domestic violence" (1034), which would be a serious problem in the patient's environment rather than a malfunction within the patient herself. Instead of insisting that "Treatment must address the mother-child dyad relationship" (1036), the committee might also have called for addressing the chance that the mother suffers from a lack of money or the presence of an abusive partner.

Uses the story to examine the issue raised by the report.

Paper works with specific examples and language from the report.

Juxtaposing Gilman's story with the Academy's report does not mean that readers of this recent document about postpartum depression have to declare its authors evil. The attitudes and recommendations of the committee are not as morally disturbing as those of Gilman's character John. But her story should encourage the report's readers to notice where, in its call for screening women for postpartum depression, it risks screening *out* social influences on people diagnosed with this clinical problem.

Heads off possible misunderstanding.

Endnotes

[1] Shields also discussed her postpartum depression in a *New York Times* op-ed column, in which she defended herself against actor Tom Cruise's charge that she should have relied on vitamins and exercise rather than on the prescription drug Paxil.

[2] For an article that supports Anthes's attention to fathers even though she does not mention it, see Kim and Swain.

[3] For an article that expresses a position like Treichler's, see Dubriwny's critique of how modern-day TV news broadcasts represent postpartum disorders.

The endnotes provide additional information not easily incorporated into the paper's main text.

Works Cited

Anthes, Emily. "Dads Get Blue, Too." *Slate*, 4 Nov. 2010,
    http://slate.com/articles/double_x/doubleex/2010/11
    /dads_gett_blue_too.html.

Dubriwny, Tasha N. "Televison News Coverage of Postpartum
    Disorders and the Politics of Medicalization." *Feminist
    Media Studies*, vol. 10, no. 3, Sept. 2010, pp. 285–303.

Earls, Marian F., and the Committee on Psychosocial Aspects
    of Child and Family Health. "Clinical Report: Incorporat-
    ing Recognition and Management of Perinatal and
    Postpartum Depression into Pediatric Practice. *Pediatrics*,
    vol. 26, no. 5, Nov. 2010, pp. 1032–38, doi:
    10.1542/peds.2010-2348.

Gilman, Charlotte Perkins. *The Living of Charlotte Perkins
    Gilman: An Autobiography*. 1935. Arno Press, 1972.

- - -. "Why I Wrote 'The Yellow Wallpaper.'" 1913. Schilb and
    Clifford, pp. 258–59.

- - -. "The Yellow Wallpaper." 1892. Schilb and Clifford,
    pp. 244–57.

Kim, Pilyoung, and James E. Swain. "Sad Dads: Paternal
    Postpartum Depression." *Psychiatry*, Feb. 2007,
    pp. 36–47.

Makowsky, Veronica. "Fear of Feeling and the Turn-of-the-
    Century Woman of Letters." *American Literary History*,
    vol. 5, no. 2, Summer 1993, pp. 326–34.

Schilb, John, and John Clifford, editors. *Arguing about
    Literature*. 2nd ed., Bedford, 2017.

Shields, Brooke. *Down Came the Rain: My Journey through
    Postpartum Depression*. Hyperion, 2005.

- - -. "War of Words." *New York Times*, 1 July 2005, late ed.,
    p. A17.

Treichler, Paula A. "Escaping the Sentence: Diagnosis and
    Discourse in 'The Yellow Wallpaper.'" *Tulsa Studies in
    Women's Literature*, vol. 3, nos. 1–2, Spring-Autumn
    1984, pp. 61–77.

Citation for an online article.

Citation for a book.

*Note style for multiple works
by same author. Note, too,
that when you cite more than
one work from the same book,
you give each book its own
entry and cite each work from
it in the shorthand form you
see here.*

Citation for a print article.

▤ HOW SARAH USES HER SOURCES

Sarah's primary source. The October 2010 report on postpartum
depression by the Earls Committee of the American Academy of
Pediatrics; Sarah's argument is mainly a critique of this report

Gilman, "The Yellow Wallpaper." To point out social contexts that
the Earls Committee ignored

Shields. To indicate that postpartum depression has become a big public issue (so that the topic deserves the attention Sarah will give it)

Anthes. To indicate that the Committee's report has received *some* criticism (which Sarah will add to)

Makowsky. To confirm that it's not unusual for literary critics to associate Gilman and her story with postpartum depression

Gilman, autobiographical nonfiction. To acknowledge that Gilman herself didn't use the term *postpartum depression*, though it now seems applicable to her and her story

Treichler. To support Sarah's focus on the social contexts of postpartum depression

Kim and Swain. To reinforce the argument made by Anthes (whom Sarah uses to suggest that criticism of the Earls Committee report is appropriate)

Dubriwny. To support Sarah's focus on the social contexts of postpartum depression

AN ARGUMENT THAT DEALS WITH EXISTING INTERPRETATIONS OF A LITERARY WORK

A researched writing assignment may require you to develop a claim about a literary work by relating your analysis to previous interpretations of the text. In the following essay, student Katie Johnson makes an argument about Charlotte Perkins Gilman's story "The Yellow Wallpaper" by incorporating statements made by people who have already written about it. To prepare for writing her essay, she especially consulted the *MLA International Bibliography*, through which she located several published articles about Gilman's tale. The bibliographies of these articles led her to still more interpretations of the story. The biggest challenge in writing an essay like this is to stay focused on developing an idea of your own rather than just inserting and echoing opinions held by others. Katie ended up examining an element of Gilman's story that she felt had not been adequately noted, let alone properly interpreted, by literary critics. As her essay proceeds, therefore, she does not simply agree with all the interpreters she cites. She treats with respect, however, those she finds fault with, civilly pointing out how her own thoughts differ. In addition, she clearly takes seriously the specific language of the critics she mentions, pondering their actual words rather than superficially summarizing their views.

Katie Johnson
Professor Van Wyck
English L141
5 May - - - -

The Meaning of the Husband's Fainting
in "The Yellow Wallpaper"

At the end of Charlotte Perkins Gilman's short story "The Yellow Wallpaper," the narrator is in a state that many people observing her would consider madness. She has torn off the wallpaper in her room and now seems proud of being able to "creep smoothly on the floor" (791). Her outwardly bizarre behavior at this point, along with her telling of the whole story beforehand, has led most literary critics to focus on analyzing her final conduct, as if it was the only really noteworthy feature of this concluding scene. Just as striking, however, is the final behavior of the narrator's husband, John. Up until the ending, he has acted as an authority on his wife's medical condition, and he has tried to assert power by always telling her what to do. At the conclusion, though, his mastery plainly vanishes. After finding the key to his wife's room, letting himself in, and beholding her crawling, he faints. Both the narrator and her husband end up on the floor. The narrator herself is highly aware of John's collapse, as she shows when she complains that "I had to creep over him every time!" (791). Because John's fainting is a dramatic reversal of his previous behavior and resembles the narrator's final physical position, it is surprising that only some literary critics have bothered to comment on John's breakdown, and even then the comments are relatively few. This neglect is a shame because, through John's fainting, Gilman seems to imply that he is left without any clear gender role to support him when his wife defies his manly effort to keep her what his society would consider sane.

Concisely summarizes the story's conclusion in first paragraph, which ends by stating main claim the essay will develop.

Until the last scene, John has repeatedly attempted to control his wife in the way that his society would expect of a man. This effort of his is reinforced by the professional standing he has achieved as a doctor. His masculine authority is interconnected with his medical authority. As we readers are made aware, he does not succeed in thoroughly bending his wife's will to his. Much of her narration is about her secret rebellion against him, which takes the form of imagining women trapped in the wallpaper of her room. Despite her hidden thoughts, however, he is often issuing commands to her, and she finds it hard to resist his domination. She admits to us that "I take pains to control myself — before him, at least, and that makes me very tired" (781). His attempts at enforcing his power over her include shutting her up in an odd country house in the first place. When she expresses suspicion of the estate, he simply "laughs" and "scoffs" (780), as he seems to do whenever she reveals independent thinking. She also says that he "hardly lets me stir without special direction" and gives her "a schedule prescription for each hour in the day" (781). Furthermore, he discourages her from writing, does not want to let her have visitors, and refuses to leave the estate when she informs him that she is not getting any better. Actually, he treats her more like his child than his wife, which is revealed when he asks "What is it, little girl?" (786) one night when she wakes up bothered by the wallpaper. All in all, he fits the nineteenth-century image of the ideal man as someone who gives his wife orders and expects her to follow them, though John tries to disguise his bossiness by declaring that he loves her and is looking out for her best interests.

The literary critics who do write about John's fainting at the end of the story tend to see it as a moment of irony, because in their view this masculine authority figure winds up physically collapsing in a way that is stereotypically associated with women. For example, Carol Margaret Davison states that when John faints, he is "assuming the traditional role of frail female" (66). Greg Johnson describes John's fall as "Gilman's witty inversion of a conventional heroine's confrontation with Gothic terror" (529), and similarly, Beverly A. Hume says that what happens is that John is "altering his conventional role as a soothing, masculine figure to that of a stereotypically weak nineteenth-century female" (478). These comments are not unreasonable, because during the nineteenth century, fainting was indeed something that women were believed to do more often than men. But a pair of literary critics has made another observation that, even though it sounds like the ones I have just quoted, points in a different direction that seems worth pursuing. Sandra M. Gilbert and Susan Gubar refer to John's fainting as an "unmasculine swoon of surprise" (91). They sound as if they are saying that he now seems feminine, but actually the word "unmasculine" simply indicates that he is no longer acting like a stereotypical male, so that readers of the story have to wonder whether he has any kind of identity left to him now. In fact, John's fainting seems like a total falling apart, as if he has become incapable of performing any further role at all, whether it is stereotypically feminine or masculine. Though

Synthesizes comments from critics, combining them to indicate the pattern she finds in interpretations of the story.

Does not flatly declare critics wrong but will develop an idea they have not mentioned.

Carefully analyzes a particular word that this pair of critics uses. Rest of paragraph develops main claim.

his wife is creeping, at least she is still able to move, whereas
he lies paralyzed. Overall, he appears to suffer a complete loss
of identity rather than take on a female identity. Because his
wife has fallen into what he sees as madness despite his
efforts to control her, he experiences a shattering of his male
ego, the result being not that he is left with a "womanly" self
but that he now lacks any sense of self at all. Just as he has
only leased the estate instead of owning it, so too has his
personhood proven impermanent because his ability to treat
his wife as his property has apparently gone. At the very end
of the story, the narrator even refers to her husband merely as
"that man" (791), suggesting that he is no longer recognizable as an individual human being.

More than one literary critic has argued that John has
suffered a loss of power only momentarily and that he will
soon dominate his wife just as much as he did before. Judith
Fetterley contends that "when John recovers from his faint,
he will put her in a prison from which there will be no
escape" (164), and Paula Treichler claims that

> As the ending of her narrative, her madness will no
> doubt commit her to more intense medical treatment,
> perhaps to the dreaded Weir Mitchell of whom her
> husband has spoken. The surrender of patriarchy is
> only temporary; her husband has merely fainted,
> after all, not died, and will no doubt move swiftly
> and severely to deal with her. Her individual escape
> is temporary and compromised. (67)

Because quotation from Treichler is somewhat lengthy, Katie puts it in block form.

Unfortunately, Gilman did not write a sequel called "The
Yellow Wallpaper: The Next Day" to let us know exactly what
happens to the couple after the husband wakes up. Fetterley
and Treichler might have been right if the events of this story
had taken place in real life and involved a real married
couple. Though it was based on Gilman's actual situation,[1]
the story should be treated as a work of fiction, and Gilman
has chosen to conclude it by showing John as physically
overcome. If she had wanted to suggest that he will
quickly regain power, presumably she would have done
so. As the text stands, the final scene emphasizes his new
weakness, not signs of a strength that will soon be restored
to him.

Synthesizes two critics' observations, putting them together as examples of a view that she questions.

Directs readers to endnote.

Disagrees with two critics but carefully explains why and avoids using hostile tone.

Although both the husband and the wife are in a bad
physical state at the end, we as readers do not have to
sympathize with them equally. Especially by having the wife
narrate the story, Gilman has designed it so that we are
encouraged to care far more about her than about John. A

Uses final paragraph not only to restate main claim but also to add the point that readers of story do not have to feel as sorry for John as they do for his wife.

lot of readers might even feel joy at his collapse, regarding it as the bringing down of a tyrant. In any case, his fainting is worth paying attention to as a sign that he has experienced a loss of masculine power that leaves him unable to function as any kind of self.

Endnote

[1] Gilman recalls the personal experience that motivated her to write her story in her essay "Why I Wrote 'The Yellow Wallpaper.'"

Endnote provides information that could not be easily integrated into main text of essay.

Works Cited

Davison, Carol Margaret. "Haunted House/Haunted Heroine: Female Gothic Closets in 'The Yellow Wallpaper.'" *Women's Studies*, vol. 33, no. 1, Jan.–Feb. 2004, pp. 47–75.

Fetterley, Judith. "Reading about Reading: 'A Jury of Her Peers,' 'The Murders in the Rue Morgue,' and 'The Yellow Wallpaper.'" *Gender and Reading: Essays on Readers, Texts, and Contexts*, edited by Elizabeth A. Flynn and Patrocinio P. Schweickart, Johns Hopkins UP, 1986, pp. 147–64.

Gilbert, Sandra M., and Susan Gubar. *The Madwoman in the Attic: The Woman Writer and the Nineteenth-Century Literary Imagination*. Yale UP, 1979.

Gilman, Charlotte Perkins. "Why I Wrote 'The Yellow Wallpaper.'" 1913. Schilb and Clifford, pp. 258–59.

- - -. "The Yellow Wallpaper." 1892. Schilb and Clifford, pp. 244–57.

Hume, Beverly A. "Gilman's 'Interminable Grotesque': The Narrator of 'The Yellow Wallpaper.'" *Studies in Short Fiction*, vol. 28, no. 4, Fall 1991, pp. 477–84.

Johnson, Greg. "Gilman's Gothic Allegory: Rage and Redemption in 'The Yellow Wallpaper.'" *Studies in Short Fiction*, vol. 26, no. 4, Fall 1989, pp. 521–30.

Schilb, John, and John Clifford, editors. *Arguing about Literature*. 2nd ed., Bedford, 2017.

Treichler, Paula A. "Escaping the Sentence: Diagnosis and Discourse in 'The Yellow Wallpaper.'" *Tulsa Studies in Women's Literature*, vol. 3, nos. 1–2, Spring–Autumn 1984, pp. 61–77.

Citation for article in scholarly journal.

Citation for work in anthology.

Citation for book.

Note style for multiple works by the same author. Note, too, that when you cite more than one work from the same book, you give the book its own entry and then cite each work from it in the shorthand form you see here.

Citation for anthology.

≡ HOW KATIE USES HER SOURCES

Katie's primary source. Gilman's "The Yellow Wallpaper"; Katie's argument is mainly an interpretation of the story's ending, specifically the husband's fainting

Davison, Johnson, Hume. To indicate a perspective that Katie doesn't quite accept and will go beyond

Gilbert and Gubar. To indicate a perspective that seems close to Katie's own but isn't really the same as hers

Fetterley, Treichler. To indicate an interpretation of the story's ending that Katie disagrees with

Gilman, article on her writing of the story. To acknowledge that the story has roots in real life

AN ARGUMENT THAT PLACES A LITERARY WORK IN HISTORICAL AND CULTURAL CONTEXT

When scholars do research on a literary work, often they aim to place it in its original situation. They investigate the background from which it emerged. How can they relate the work to its historical and cultural context? This is the basic issue they pursue. Perhaps you'll write a researched argument that addresses this question by applying it to a literary text you've read. If so, you'll probably make use of various sources. But you'll need to develop a claim of your own. The following essay demonstrates how. Brittany Thomas connects Gilman's "The Yellow Wallpaper" to its original era. In order to do this, she examined autobiographical nonfiction by Gilman. She studied as well a lecture by S. Weir Mitchell, Gilman's doctor. She also consulted scholarship on nineteenth-century medical treatments of women. Gradually, she came to focus on the "rest cure" Gilman suffered. After all, it was the ordeal that led Gilman to write her tale. Brittany realized the story leaves out a feature of this therapy: the massages that it usually involved. She suspected that this omission was deliberate. Her essay states and elaborates a claim about it. She argues that Gilman probably wanted to stress the narrator's isolation from human touch.

Brittany Thomas
Professor Schneebaum
English L202
25 April ----

The Relative Absence of the Human Touch
in "The Yellow Wallpaper"

In her essay "Why I Wrote 'The Yellow Wallpaper,'" Charlotte Perkins Gilman reveals that her famous story was inspired by a personal depression that got worse when she underwent a "rest cure" prescribed to her by "a noted specialist in nervous diseases, the best known in the country" (792). Though she does not name this doctor in the essay, we are aware today that he was S. Weir Mitchell, a name that she actually brings up briefly in "The Yellow Wallpaper." The rest cure that the story's narrator goes through, however, does not seem to have all the features that Weir Mitchell's did. Interestingly, neither by reading the essay nor by reading Gilman's story would you realize that Weir Mitchell's treatment involved massage. The question for an interpreter of the story thus becomes, Why did Gilman leave massage out of "The Yellow Wallpaper"? Because we can only guess at her intentions, perhaps a better way of putting the question is this: What is the effect of omitting massage from the story? One important consequence is that there is less of a literal human touch in the story than there might have been, and so the heroine's alienation from others and her withdrawal into fantasy seem stronger than they might have been.

Immediately mentions one of her sources, but only to set up main claim about Gilman's story, which she states at end of paragraph.

Using question form helps signal cause/effect issue that the essay will address.

This is the essay's main claim.

Weir Mitchell himself seems to have regarded massage as a very big component of his rest cure. He gives it a lot of attention in his 1904 lecture "The Evolution of the Rest Treatment." There he describes at length two cases, one of a man and one of a woman, where he found out that rubbing the body helped the person overcome depression. He recalls arriving at the conclusion "that massage was a tonic of extraordinary value" (796), and he continues his lecture by giving a brief account of the larger world history of what he terms "this invaluable therapeutic measure" (797). Evidently Weir Mitchell did not perform massage himself; in his lecture, he describes having others do it for him. Perhaps he thought that if he personally rubbed a patient's body, he would run the risk of being accused of a sexual advance. Despite his use of stand-ins for him, he clearly considered massage a necessary feature of his rest cure. One reason was that he thought the depressed person's body needed some form of physical stimulation, which the person would not otherwise be getting by lying around so much of the time. He states in his lecture that massage was something that "enabled me to use rest in bed without causing the injurious effects of unassisted rest" (796). Probably this method also reflected a more general belief of his, which Jane F. Thrailkill describes as the assumption "that the efficacy of his cure lay in its treatment of a patient's material body, not in what we might now term the psychological effects of isolation or of his own charismatic presence" (532). Thrailkill goes on to point out that Weir Mitchell was not alone in this belief: "[T]he medical wisdom of the day . . . conceived of a patient as a conceptually inert bundle of physiological processes" (552).[1] Massage was a means of helpfully manipulating the physique, which for Weir Mitchell and other doctors of his era was the main source of difficulties that today might be seen as chiefly mental.

Given that massage was so important to Weir Mitchell, it is significant that Gilman's references to it are not consistent. She does recall being massaged when she discusses how Weir Mitchell treated her medically in her autobiography *The Living of Charlotte Perkins Gilman*. In that book, she says that besides being "put to bed and kept there," she was "fed, bathed, [and] rubbed" (96). She does not refer to massage, however, in "Why I Wrote 'The Yellow Wallpaper.'" More important for interpretations of the story, she does not make massage part of "The Yellow Wallpaper" itself. It plays no role at all in the plot. The elements of the rest cure that come up in the story are, instead, physical seclusion and forced abandonment of work.

Briefly summarizes Weir Mitchell's lecture, focusing on his remarks about massage rather than spending additional time on other topics of his speech.

Analyzes at length one particular source, Weir Mitchell's lecture.

Square brackets indicate alteration of text being quoted. Ellipses indicate words deleted from original text.

Synthesis of three texts, comparing what they do with the topic of massage. More specifically, compares Gilman's autobiography, Gilman's essay on writing the story, and the story itself.

If massage were a major element of the rest cure that the narrator goes through in "The Yellow Wallpaper," the story would probably feature a lot more human touching than it presently does. The way the story is written, the heroine experiences relatively little physical contact with other people, or at least she does not tell us that she is having much of this. What is especially interesting is that we do not find many instances of her being physically touched by her husband, John. There are, in fact, a few places in the text where he does touch her. She says that when she informs him that she is disturbed by the wallpaper, "he took me in his arms and called me a blessed little goose" (782). When she weeps because he will not leave the house to visit relatives, "dear John gathered me up in his arms, and just carried me upstairs and laid me on the bed, and sat by me and read to me till it tired my head" (785). When she complains that he is wrong to think she is getting better, he gives her "a big hug" and says "'Bless her little heart! . . . she shall be as sick as she pleases!'" (786). Yet his moments of touching her not only are very few but also reflect his insensitivity toward her. His folding her in his arms seems an effort to control her and trivialize her protests, not an expression of genuine love. Moreover, she takes no real comfort from his touch. If this amounts to rubbing her, then from her point of view, he is rubbing her the wrong way. Again, however, massage is significantly absent from this story, and because what touches there are seem so few and inhumane, readers are led to feel that the narrator is pretty much alone in her concerns. She has only the imaginary woman in the wallpaper to bond with, and she seems drawn to that woman in large part because her human companions have no true understanding of the distress that caused her to need some sort of cure in the first place.

In effect, admits it would be misleading to claim there are no instances of touching in the story. Proceeds to bring together (to synthesize) various examples of such contact.

Accounts for details of story that might seem to conflict with main claim.

In calling attention to the role of massage in S. Weir Mitchell's rest cure, I do not mean to minimize the importance of his treatment's other components. The physical rest he demanded of his patients was certainly a big element of the cure, so that we can easily see why Gilman made it central to her story. In his lecture, Weir Mitchell also points out that he applied electrical charges to the patient's body. Historians of women's health Barbara Ehrenreich and Deirdre English argue that Weir Mitchell relied heavily as well on "the technique of healing by *command*" (119, emphasis in original), constantly and firmly giving orders to his patients so that they felt obligated to obey his wishes and to get better on the precise schedule he had in mind. Massage certainly figured, however, in Weir Mitchell's mode of treatment,

Heads off possible misunderstanding of argument; dealing with it enables her to write a concluding paragraph that does more than just repeat main claim.

including his handling of Gilman's own case, so that her omission of it from "The Yellow Wallpaper" seems a deliberate strategy for giving other things emphasis. Above all, the quite limited role of human touching in the story serves to make readers highly aware that the narrator is without the loving, intimate company she really needs to recover from her depression.

Endnote

[1] Thrailkill spends much of her article tracing how an emphasis on treating depression through physical means (the approach taken by Weir Mitchell) gave way late in the nineteenth century to a more psychological and verbal form of therapy (such as Sigmund Freud practiced).

Endnote provides information that could not be easily integrated into main text of the essay.

Works Cited

Ehrenreich, Barbara, and Deirdre English. *For Her Own Good: 150 Years of the Experts' Advice to Women*. Doubleday-Anchor, 1978.

Gilman, Charlotte Perkins. *The Living of Charlotte Perkins Gilman: An Autobiography*. 1935. Arno Press, 1972.

- - - . "Why I Wrote 'The Yellow Wallpaper.'" 1913. Schilb and Clifford, pp. 258–59.

- - - . "The Yellow Wallpaper." 1892. Schilb and Clifford, pp. 244–57.

Schilb, John, and John Clifford, editors. *Arguing about Literature*. 2nd ed., Bedford, 2017.

Thrailkill, Jane F. "Doctoring 'The Yellow Wallpaper.'" *ELH*, vol. 69, no. 2, Summer 2002, pp. 525–66.

Weir Mitchell, S. Excerpt from "The Evolution of the Rest Treatment." 1904. Schilb and Clifford, pp. 259–63.

Citation for book.

Note style for multiple works by same author.

When you cite more than one work from the same book, you give the book its own entry and cite each work from it in the shorthand form you see here.

Citation for anthology.

Citation for scholarly article.

≡ HOW BRITTANY USES HER SOURCES

Brittany's primary source. Gilman's "The Yellow Wallpaper"; Brittany's argument is mainly a consideration of why Gilman left massage out of the story

Mitchell. To indicate that Gilman's own doctor valued massage as a therapeutic measure, even if he used other methods as well

Gilman, autobiography. To prove that Mitchell used massage in treating Gilman

Gilman, article on her writing of the story. (1) To emphasize that Gilman based her story on Mitchell's treatment of her; (2) to acknowledge that Gilman didn't always mention that massage was one of Mitchell's tools

Thrailkill. To emphasize that massage was an important tool for Mitchell and reflected a basic medical belief of his era

Ehrenreich and English. To acknowledge that massage wasn't Mitchell's only method

CHARLOTTE PERKINS GILMAN, "The Yellow Wallpaper"

CULTURAL CONTEXTS:
CHARLOTTE PERKINS GILMAN, "Why I Wrote 'The Yellow Wallpaper' "

S. WEIR MITCHELL, From *"The Evolution of the Rest Treatment"*

JOHN HARVEY KELLOGG, From *The Ladies' Guide in Health and Disease*

When doctors make a medical or psychiatric diagnosis, they pinpoint their patient's condition but also often accept or reject their society's definition of *health.* The social context of diagnoses seems especially worth considering when a particular condition afflicts one gender much more than the other. Today, many more women than men appear to suffer from depression, anorexia, bulimia, and dissociative identity disorder. Why? Perhaps traditional female roles encourage these illnesses; perhaps gender bias affects how doctors label and treat them. Charlotte Perkins Gilman raised both these possibilities in her 1892 short story "The Yellow Wallpaper." In her own life, the consequences from her egregious treatment were not as serious as she depicts in her story. But Gilman was the exception. Many women suffered terribly from doctors who ignored the cultural causes of depression. Besides Gilman's story, we include her account of why she wrote it, an excerpt from a lecture by Silas Weir Mitchell about his cure, and some advice about motherhood from John Kellogg, another influential doctor of the time.

■ **BEFORE YOU READ**

How is mental illness depicted in movies and television shows you have seen? Which representations of mental illness have you appreciated the most? Which have you especially disliked? State your criteria for these judgments.

CHARLOTTE PERKINS GILMAN
The Yellow Wallpaper

Charlotte Perkins Gilman (1860–1935) was a major activist and theorist in America's first wave of feminism. During her lifetime, she was chiefly known for her 1898 book Women and Economics. *In it she argued that women should not be confined to the household and made economically dependent on men. Gilman also advanced such ideas through her many public-speaking appearances and her magazine* The Forerunner, *which she edited from 1909 to 1916. Gilman wrote many articles and works of fiction for* The Forerunner, *including a tale called* Herland *(1915) in which she envisioned an all-female utopia. Today, however, Gilman is best*

*known for her short story "The Yellow Wallpaper," which she published first in an
1892 issue of the* New England Magazine. *The story is based on Gilman's struggle
with depression after the birth of her daughter Katharine in 1885. Seeking help for
emotional turmoil, Gilman consulted the eminent neurologist Silas Weir Mitchell,
who prescribed his famous "rest cure." This treatment, which forbade Gilman to
work, actually worsened her distress. She improved only after she moved to California,
divorced her husband, let him raise Katharine with his new wife, married someone
else, and plunged fully into a literary and political career. As Gilman noted in her
posthumously published autobiography,* The Living of Charlotte Perkins Gilman
*(1935), she never fully recovered from the debilitation that had led her to Dr. Mitchell,
but she ultimately managed to be enormously productive. Although "The Yellow
Wallpaper" is a work of fiction rather than a factual account of her experience with
Mitchell, Gilman used the story to criticize the doctor's patriarchal approach as well
as society's efforts to keep women passive.*

It is very seldom that mere ordinary people like John and myself secure ances-
tral halls for the summer.

A colonial mansion, a hereditary estate, I would say a haunted house and reach the height of romantic felicity—but that would be asking too much of fate!

Still I will proudly declare that there is something queer about it.

Else, why should it be let so cheaply? And why have stood so long untenanted?

John laughs at me, of course, but one expects that in marriage.   5

John is practical in the extreme. He has no patience with faith, an intense horror of superstition, and he scoffs openly at any talk of things not to be felt and seen and put down in figures.

John is a physician, and *perhaps*—(I would not say it to a living soul, of course, but this is dead paper and a great relief to my mind)—*perhaps* that is one reason I do not get well faster.

You see, he does not believe I am sick!

And what can one do?

If a physician of high standing, and one's own husband, assures friends   10
and relatives that there is really nothing the matter with one but temporary nervous depression—a slight hysterical tendency° —what is one to do?

My brother is also a physician, and also of high standing, and he says the same thing.

So I take phosphates or phosphites—whichever it is, and tonics, and journeys, and air, and exercise, and am absolutely forbidden to "work" until I am well again.

Personally, I disagree with their ideas.

Personally, I believe that congenial work, with excitement and change, would do me good.

But what is one to do?   15

I did write for a while in spite of them; but it *does* exhaust me a good deal— having to be so sly about it, or else meet with heavy opposition.

I sometimes fancy that in my condition if I had less opposition and more society and stimulus—but John says the very worst thing I can do is to think about my condition, and I confess it always makes me feel bad.

So I will let it alone and talk about the house.

The most beautiful place! It is quite alone, standing well back from the road, quite three miles from the village. It makes me think of English places that you read about, for there are hedges and walls and gates that lock, and lots of separate little houses for the gardeners and people.

There is a *delicious* garden! I never saw such a garden—large and shady,   20
full of box-bordered paths, and lined with long grape-covered arbors with seats under them.

There were greenhouses, too, but they are all broken now.

There was some legal trouble, I believe, something about the heirs and coheirs; anyhow, the place has been empty for years.

hysterical tendency: It was common among Victorian doctors to believe women had an innate tendency to be overly emotional; now a discredited assumption.

That spoils my ghostliness, I am afraid, but I don't care—there is something strange about the house—I can feel it.

I even said so to John one moonlight evening, but he said what I felt was a *draught*, and shut the window.

I get unreasonably angry with John sometimes. I'm sure I never used to be   25
so sensitive. I think it is due to this nervous condition.

But John says if I feel so, I shall neglect proper self-control; so I take pains to control myself — before him, at least, and that makes me very tired.

I don't like our room a bit. I wanted one downstairs that opened on the piazza and had roses all over the window, and such pretty old-fashioned chintz hangings! but John would not hear of it.

He said there was only one window and not room for two beds, and no near room for him if he took another.

He is very careful and loving, and hardly lets me stir without special direction.

I have a schedule prescription for each hour in the day; he takes all care   30
from me, and so I feel basely ungrateful not to value it more.

He said we came here solely on my account, that I was to have perfect rest and all the air I could get. "Your exercise depends on your strength, my dear," said he, "and your food somewhat on your appetite; but air you can absorb all the time." So we took the nursery at the top of the house.

It is a big, airy room, the whole floor nearly, with windows that look all ways, and air and sunshine galore. It was nursery first and then playroom and gymnasium, I should judge; for the windows are barred for little children, and there are rings and things in the walls.

The paint and paper look as if a boys' school had used it. It is stripped off — the paper—in great patches all around the head of my bed, about as far as I can reach, and in a great place on the other side of the room low down. I never saw a worse paper in my life.

One of those sprawling flamboyant patterns committing every artistic sin.

It is dull enough to confuse the eye in following, pronounced enough to   35
constantly irritate and provoke study, and when you follow the lame uncertain curves for a little distance they suddenly commit suicide—plunge off at outrageous angles, destroy themselves in unheard of contradictions.

The color is repellant, almost revolting; a smouldering unclean yellow, strangely faded by the slow-turning sunlight.

It is a dull yet lurid orange in some places, a sickly sulphur tint in others.

No wonder the children hated it! I should hate it myself if I had to live in this room long.

There comes John, and I must put this away,—he hates to have me write a word.

We have been here two weeks, and I haven't felt like writing before, since that   40
first day.

I am sitting by the window now, up in this atrocious nursery, and there is nothing to hinder my writing as much as I please, save lack of strength.

John is away all day, and even some nights when his cases are serious.

I am glad my case is not serious!

But these nervous troubles are dreadfully depressing.

John does not know how much I really suffer. He knows there is no *reason*   45
to suffer, and that satisfies him.

Of course it is only nervousness. It does weigh on me so not to do my duty
in any way!

I meant to be such a help to John, such a real rest and comfort, and here I
am a comparative burden already!

Nobody would believe what an effort it is to do what little I am able, — to
dress and entertain, and order things.

It is fortunate Mary is so good with the baby. Such a dear baby!

And yet I *cannot* be with him, it makes me so nervous.   50

I suppose John never was nervous in his life. He laughs at me so about this
wallpaper!

At first he meant to repaper the room, but afterward he said that I was letting it get the better of me, and that nothing was worse for a nervous patient
than to give way to such fancies.

He said that after the wallpaper was changed it would be the heavy bedstead, and then the barred windows, and then that gate at the head of the
stairs, and so on.

"You know the place is doing you good," he said, "and really, dear, I don't
care to renovate the house just for a three months' rental."

"Then do let us go downstairs," I said, "there are such pretty rooms there."   55

Then he took me in his arms and called me a blessed little goose, and said he
would go down cellar, if I wished, and have it whitewashed into the bargain.

But he is right enough about the beds and windows and things.

It is an airy and comfortable room as anyone need wish, and, of course, I
would not be so silly as to make him uncomfortable just for a whim.

I'm really getting quite fond of the big room, all but that horrid paper.

Out of one window I can see the garden, those mysterious deep-shaded   60
arbors, the riotous old-fashioned flowers, and bushes and gnarly trees.

Out of another I get a lovely view of the bay and a little private wharf
belonging to the estate. There is a beautiful shaded lane that runs down there
from the house. I always fancy I see people walking in these numerous paths
and arbors, but John has cautioned me not to give way to fancy in the least. He
says that with my imaginative power and habit of story-making, a nervous
weakness like mine is sure to lead to all manner of excited fancies, and that I
ought to use my will and good sense to check the tendency. So I try.

I think sometimes that if I were only well enough to write a little it would
relieve the press of ideas and rest me.

But I find I get pretty tired when I try.

It is so discouraging not to have any advice and companionship about my
work. When I get really well, John says we will ask Cousin Henry and Julia
down for a long visit; but he says he would as soon put fireworks in my pillow-
case as to let me have those stimulating people about now.

I wish I could get well faster.   65

But I must not think about that. This paper looks to me as if it *knew* what a vicious influence it had!

There is a recurrent spot where the pattern lolls like a broken neck and two bulbous eyes stare at you upside down.

I get positively angry with the impertinence of it and the everlastingness. Up and down and sideways they crawl, and those absurd, unblinking eyes are everywhere. There is one place where two breadths didn't match, and the eyes go all up and down the line, one a little higher than the other.

I never saw so much expression in an inanimate thing before, and we all know how much expression they have! I used to lie awake as a child and get more entertainment and terror out of blank walls and plain furniture than most children could find in a toy-store.

I remember what a kindly wink the knobs of our big, old bureau used to   70
have, and there was one chair that always seemed like a strong friend.

I used to feel that if any of the other things looked too fierce I could always hop into that chair and be safe.

The furniture in this room is no worse than inharmonious, however, for we had to bring it all from downstairs. I suppose when this was used as a play-room they had to take the nursery things out, and no wonder! I never saw such ravages as the children have made here.

The wallpaper, as I said before, is torn off in spots, and it sticketh closer than a brother—they must have had perseverance as well as hatred.

Then the floor is scratched and gouged and splintered, the plaster itself is dug out here and there, and this great heavy bed, which is all we found in the room, looks as if it had been through the wars.

But I don't mind it a bit—only the paper.   75

There comes John's sister. Such a dear girl as she is, and so careful of me! I must not let her find me writing.

She is a perfect and enthusiastic housekeeper, and hopes for no better profession. I verily believe she thinks it is the writing which made me sick!

But I can write when she is out, and see her a long way off from these windows.

There is one that commands the road, a lovely shaded winding road, and one that just looks off over the country. A lovely country, too, full of great elms and velvet meadows.

This wallpaper has a kind of sub-pattern in a different shade, a particularly   80
irritating one, for you can only see it in certain lights, and not clearly then.

But in the places where it isn't faded and where the sun is just so—I can see a strange, provoking, formless sort of figure, that seems to skulk about behind that silly and conspicuous front design.

There's sister on the stairs!

Well, the Fourth of July is over! The people are all gone and I am tired out. John thought it might do me good to see a little company, so we just had mother and Nellie and the children down for a week.

Of course I didn't do a thing. Jennie sees to everything now.

But it tired me all the same.   85

John says if I don't pick up faster he shall send me to Weir Mitchell° in the fall.

But I don't want to go there at all. I had a friend who was in his hands once, and she says he is just like John and my brother, only more so!

Besides, it is such an undertaking to go so far.

I don't feel as if it was worthwhile to turn my hand over for anything, and I'm getting dreadfully fretful and querulous.

I cry at nothing, and cry most of the time.   90

Of course I don't when John is here, or anybody else, but when I am alone.

And I am alone a good deal just now. John is kept in town very often by serious cases, and Jennie is good and lets me alone when I want her to.

So I walk a little in the garden or down that lovely lane, sit on the porch under the roses, and lie down up here a good deal.

I'm getting really fond of the room in spite of the wallpaper. Perhaps *because* of the wallpaper.

It dwells in my mind so!   95

I lie here on this great immovable bed—it is nailed down, I believe—and follow that pattern about by the hour. It is as good as gymnastics, I assure you. I start, we'll say, at the bottom, down in the corner over there where it has not been touched, and I determine for the thousandth time that I *will* follow that pointless pattern to some sort of a conclusion.

I know a little of the principle of design, and I know this thing was not arranged on any laws of radiation, or alternation, or repetition, or symmetry, or anything else that I ever heard of.

It is repeated, of course, by the breadths, but not otherwise.

Looked at in one way each breadth stands alone, the bloated curves and flourishes—a kind of "debased Romanesque" with *delirium tremens*—go waddling up and down in isolated columns of fatuity.

But, on the other hand, they connect diagonally, and the sprawling out-   100
lines run off in great slanting waves of optic horror, like a lot of wallowing seaweeds in full chase.

The whole thing goes horizontally, too, at least it seems so, and I exhaust myself in trying to distinguish the order of its going in that direction.

They have used a horizontal breadth for a frieze, and that adds wonderfully to the confusion.

There is one end of the room where it is almost intact, and there, when the crosslights fade and the low sun shines directly upon it, I can almost fancy radiation after all,—the interminable grotesques seem to form around a common center and rush off in headlong plunges of equal distraction.

It makes me tired to follow it. I will take a nap I guess.

Weir Mitchell: Dr. S. Weir Mitchell (1829–1914) was an eminent Philadelphia neurologist who advocated "rest cures" for nervous disorders. He was the author of *Diseases of the Nervous System, Especially of Women* (1881).

* * *

I don't know why I should write this.   105

I don't want to.

I don't feel able.

And I know John would think it absurd. But I *must* say what I feel and think in some way—it is such a relief!

But the effort is getting to be greater than the relief.

Half the time now I am awfully lazy, and lie down ever so much.   110

John says I mustn't lose my strength, and has me take cod liver oil and lots of tonics and things, to say nothing of ale and wine and rare meat.

Dear John! He loves me very dearly, and hates to have me sick. I tried to have a real earnest reasonable talk with him the other day, and tell him how I wish he would let me go and make a visit to Cousin Henry and Julia.

But he said I wasn't able to go, nor able to stand it after I got there; and I did not make out a very good case for myself, for I was crying before I had finished.

It is getting to be a great effort for me to think straight. Just this nervous weakness I suppose.

And dear John gathered me up in his arms, and just carried me upstairs   115
and laid me on the bed, and sat by me and read to me till it tired my head.

He said I was his darling and his comfort and all he had, and that I must take care of myself for his sake, and keep well.

He says no one but myself can help me out of it, that I must use my will and self-control and not let any silly fancies run away with me.

There's one comfort, the baby is well and happy, and does not have to occupy this nursery with the horrid wallpaper.

If we had not used it, that blessed child would have! What a fortunate escape! Why, I wouldn't have a child of mine, an impressionable little thing, live in such a room for worlds.

I never thought of it before, but it is lucky that John kept me here after all, 120
I can stand it so much easier than a baby, you see.

Of course I never mention it to them any more—I am too wise, but I keep watch of it all the same.

There are things in the wallpaper that nobody knows but me, or ever will.

Behind that outside pattern the dim shapes get clearer every day.

It is always the same shape, only very numerous.

And it is like a woman stooping down and creeping about behind that pat-   125
tern. I don't like it a bit. I wonder—I begin to think—I wish John would take me away from here!

It is so hard to talk with John about my case, because he is so wise, and because he loves me so.

But I tried it last night.

It was moonlight. The moon shines in all around just as the sun does.

I hate to see it sometimes, it creeps so slowly, and always comes in by one window or another.

John was asleep and I hated to waken him, so I kept still and watched the   130
moonlight on that undulating wallpaper till I felt creepy.

The faint figure behind seemed to shake the pattern, just as if she wanted
to get out.

I got up softly and went to feel and see if the paper *did* move, and when I
came back John was awake.

"What is it, little girl?" he said. "Don't go walking about like that—you'll
get cold."

I thought it was a good time to talk, so I told him that I really was not gaining here, and that I wished he would take me away.

"Why, darling!" said he, "our lease will be up in three weeks, and I can't see   135
how to leave before.

"The repairs are not done at home, and I cannot possibly leave town just
now. Of course if you were in any danger, I could and would, but you really are
better, dear, whether you can see it or not. I am a doctor, dear, and I know. You
are gaining flesh and color, your appetite is better, I feel really much easier
about you."

"I don't weigh a bit more," said I, "nor as much; and my appetite may be
better in the evening when you are here but it is worse in the morning when
you are away!"

"Bless her little heart!" said he with a big hug, "she shall be as sick as she
pleases! But now let's improve the shining hours by going to sleep, and talk
about it in the morning!"

"And you won't go away?" I asked gloomily.

"Why, how can I, dear? It is only three weeks more and then we will take a   140
nice little trip of a few days while Jennie is getting the house ready. Really dear
you are better!"

"Better in body perhaps—" I began, and stopped short, for he sat up
straight and looked at me with such a stern, reproachful look that I could not
say another word.

"My darling," said he, "I beg you, for my sake and for our child's sake, as well
as for your own, that you will never for one instant let that idea enter your mind!
There is nothing so dangerous, so fascinating, to a temperament like yours. It is
a false and foolish fancy. Can you trust me as a physician when I tell you so?"

So of course I said no more on that score, and we went to sleep before long.
He thought I was asleep first, but I wasn't, and lay there for hours trying to
decide whether that front pattern and the back pattern really did move together
or separately.

On a pattern like this, by daylight, there is a lack of sequence, a defiance of law,
that is a constant irritant to a normal mind.

The color is hideous enough, and unreliable enough, and infuriating   145
enough, but the pattern is torturing.

You think you have mastered it, but just as you get well underway in following, it turns a back-somersault and there you are. It slaps you in the face,
knocks you down, and tramples upon you. It is like a bad dream.

The outside pattern is a florid arabesque, reminding one of a fungus. If you can imagine a toadstool in joints, an interminable string of toadstools, budding and sprouting in endless convolutions—why, that is something like it.

That is, sometimes!

There is one marked peculiarity about this paper, a thing nobody seems to notice but myself, and that is that it changes as the light changes.

When the sun shoots in through the east window—I always watch for 150 that first long, straight ray—it changes so quickly that I never can quite believe it.

That is why I watch it always.

By moonlight—the moon shines in all night when there is a moon—I wouldn't know it was the same paper.

At night in any kind of light, in twilight, candlelight, lamplight, and worst of all by moonlight, it becomes bars! The outside pattern I mean, and the woman behind it is as plain as can be.

I didn't realize for a long time what the thing was that showed behind, that dim sub-pattern, but now I am quite sure it is a woman.

By daylight she is subdued, quiet. I fancy it is the pattern that keeps her so 155 still. It is so puzzling. It keeps me quiet by the hour.

I lie down ever so much now. John says it is good for me, and to sleep all I can.

Indeed he started the habit by making me lie down for an hour after each meal.

It is a very bad habit I am convinced, for you see I don't sleep.

And that cultivates deceit, for I don't tell them I'm awake—O, no!

The fact is I am getting a little afraid of John. 160

He seems very queer sometimes, and even Jennie has an inexplicable look.

It strikes me occasionally, just as a scientific hypothesis,—that perhaps it is the paper!

I have watched John when he did not know I was looking, and come into the room suddenly on the most innocent excuses, and I've caught him several times *looking at the paper*! And Jennie too. I caught Jennie with her hand on it once.

She didn't know I was in the room, and when I asked her in a quiet, a very quiet voice, with the most restrained manner possible, what she was doing with the paper—she turned around as if she had been caught stealing, and looked quite angry—asked me why I should frighten her so!

Then she said that the paper stained everything it touched, that she had 165 found yellow smooches on all my clothes and John's, and she wished we would be more careful!

Did not that sound innocent? But I know she was studying that pattern, and I am determined that nobody shall find it out but myself!

Life is very much more exciting now than it used to be. You see I have something more to expect, to look forward to, to watch. I really do eat better, and am more quiet than I was.

John is so pleased to see me improve! He laughed a little the other day, and said I seemed to be flourishing in spite of my wallpaper.

I turned it off with a laugh. I had no intention of telling him it was *because* of the wallpaper — he would make fun of me. He might even want to take me away.

I don't want to leave now until I have found it out. There is a week more,   170
and I think that will be enough.

I'm feeling ever so much better! I don't sleep much at night, for it is so interesting to watch developments; but I sleep a good deal in the daytime.

In the daytime it is tiresome and perplexing.

There are always new shoots on the fungus, and new shades of yellow all over it. I cannot keep count of them, though I have tried conscientiously.

It is the strangest yellow, that wallpaper! It makes me think of all the yellow things I ever saw — not beautiful ones like buttercups, but old foul, bad yellow things.

But there is something else about that paper — the smell! I noticed it the   175
moment we came into the room, but with so much air and sun it was not bad. Now we have had a week of fog and rain, and whether the windows are open or not, the smell is here.

It creeps all over the house.

I find it hovering in the dining-room, skulking in the parlor, hiding in the hall, lying in wait for me on the stairs.

It gets into my hair.

Even when I go to ride, if I turn my head suddenly and surprise it — there is that smell!

Such a peculiar odor, too! I have spent hours in trying to analyze it, to find   180
what it smelled like.

It is not bad — at first, and very gentle, but quite the subtlest, most enduring odor I ever met.

In this damp weather it is awful, I wake up in the night and find it hanging over me.

It used to disturb me at first. I thought seriously of burning the house — to reach the smell.

But now I am used to it. The only thing I can think of that it is like is the *color* of the paper! A yellow smell.

There is a very funny mark on this wall, low down, near the mopboard. A   185
streak that runs round the room. It goes behind every piece of furniture, except the bed, a long, straight, even *smooch*, as if it had been rubbed over and over.

I wonder how it was done and who did it, and what they did it for. Round and round and round — round and round and round — it makes me dizzy!

I really have discovered something at last.

Through watching so much at night, when it changes so, I have finally found out.

The front pattern *does* move — and no wonder! The woman behind shakes it!

Sometimes I think there are a great many women behind, and some-   190
times only one, and she crawls around fast, and her crawling shakes it all
over.

Then in the very bright spots she keeps still, and in the very shady spots she
just takes hold of the bars and shakes them hard.

And she is all the time trying to climb through. But nobody could climb
through that pattern — it strangles so; I think that is why it has so many
heads.

They get through, and then the pattern strangles them off and turns them
upside down, and makes their eyes white!

If those heads were covered or taken off it would not be half so bad.

I think that woman gets out in the daytime!   195

And I'll tell you why — privately — I've seen her!

I can see her out of every one of my windows!

It is the same woman, I know, for she is always creeping, and most women
do not creep by daylight.

I see her in that long shaded lane, creeping up and down. I see her in those
dark grape arbors, creeping all around the garden.

I see her on that long road under the trees, creeping along, and when a   200
carriage comes she hides under the blackberry vines.

I don't blame her a bit. It must be very humiliating to be caught creeping
by daylight!

I always lock the door when I creep by daylight. I can't do it at night, for I
know John would suspect something at once.

And John is so queer now, that I don't want to irritate him. I wish he would
take another room! Besides, I don't want anybody to get that woman out at
night but myself.

I often wonder if I could see her out of all the windows at once.

But, turn as fast as I can, I can only see out of one at one time.   205

And though I always see her, she *may* be able to creep faster than I can turn!

I have watched her sometimes away off in the open country, creeping as
fast as a cloud shadow in a high wind.

If only that top pattern could be gotten off from the under one! I mean to try it,
little by little.

I have found out another funny thing, but I shan't tell it this time! It does
not do to trust people too much.

There are only two more days to get this paper off, and I believe John is   210
beginning to notice. I don't like the look in his eyes.

And I heard him ask Jennie a lot of professional questions, about me. She
had a very good report to give.

She said I slept a good deal in the daytime.

John knows I don't sleep very well at night, for all I'm so quiet!

He asked me all sorts of questions too, and pretended to be very loving
and kind.

As if I couldn't see through him!   215

Still, I don't wonder he acts so, sleeping under this paper for three months.

It only interests me, but I feel sure John and Jennie are secretly affected by it.

Hurrah! This is the last day, but it is enough. John is to stay in town over night, and won't be out until this evening.

Jennie wanted to sleep with me — the sly thing! But I told her I should undoubtedly rest better for a night all alone.

That was clever, for really I wasn't alone a bit! As soon as it was moonlight and   220
that poor thing began to crawl and shake the pattern, I got up and ran to help her.

I pulled and she shook, I shook and she pulled, and before morning we had peeled off yards of that paper.

A strip about as high as my head and half around the room.

And then when the sun came and that awful pattern began to laugh at me, I declared I would finish it to-day!

We go away to-morrow, and they are moving all my furniture down again to leave things as they were before.

Jennie looked at the wall in amazement, but I told her merrily that I did it   225
out of pure spite at the vicious thing.

She laughed and said she wouldn't mind doing it herself, but I must not get tired.

How she betrayed herself that time!

But I am here, and no person touches this paper but me, — not *alive*!

She tried to get me out of the room — it was too patent! But I said it was so quiet and empty and clean now that I believed I would lie down again and sleep all I could, and not to wake me even for dinner — I would call when I woke.

So now she is gone, and the servants are gone, and the things are gone,   230
and there is nothing left but that great bedstead nailed down, with the canvas mattress we found on it.

We shall sleep downstairs to-night, and take the boat home to-morrow.

I quite enjoy the room, now it is bare again.

How those children did tear about here!

This bedstead is fairly gnawed!

But I must get to work.   235

I have locked the door and thrown the key down into the front path.

I don't want to go out, and I don't want to have anybody come in, till John comes.

I want to astonish him.

I've got a rope up here that even Jennie did not find. If that woman does get out, and tries to get away, I can tie her!

But I forgot I could not reach far without anything to stand on!   240

This bed will *not* move!

I tried to lift and push it until I was lame, and then I got so angry I bit off a little piece at one corner — but it hurt my teeth.

Then I peeled off all the paper I could reach standing on the floor. It sticks horribly and the pattern just enjoys it! All those strangled heads and bulbous eyes and waddling fungus growths just shriek with derision!

I am getting angry enough to do something desperate. To jump out of the window would be admirable exercise, but the bars are too strong even to try.

Besides I wouldn't do it. Of course not. I know well enough that a step like that is improper and might be misconstrued.   245

I don't like to *look* out of the windows even — there are so many of those creeping women, and they creep so fast.

I wonder if they all come out of that wallpaper as I did?

But I am securely fastened now by my well-hidden rope — you don't get *me* out in the road there!

I suppose I shall have to get back behind the pattern when it comes night, and that is hard!

It is so pleasant to be out in this great room and creep around as I please!   250

I don't want to go outside. I won't, even if Jennie asks me to.

For outside you have to creep on the ground, and everything is green instead of yellow.

But here I can creep smoothly on the floor, and my shoulder just fits in that long smooch around the wall, so I cannot lose my way.

Why, there's John at the door!

It is no use, young man, you can't open it!   255

How he does call and pound!

Now he's crying for an axe.

It would be a shame to break down that beautiful door!

"John dear!" said I in the gentlest voice, "the key is down by the front steps, under a plantain leaf!"

That silenced him for a few moments.   260

Then he said — very quietly indeed, "Open the door, my darling!"

"I can't," said I. "The key is down by the front door under a plantain leaf!"

And then I said it again, several times, very gently and slowly, and said it so often that he had to go and see, and he got it of course, and came in. He stopped short by the door.

"What is the matter?" he cried. "For God's sake, what are you doing!"

I kept on creeping just the same, but I looked at him over my shoulder.   265

"I've got out at last," said I, "in spite of you and Jane. And I've pulled off most of the paper, so you can't put me back!"

Now why should that man have fainted? But he did, and right across my path by the wall, so that I had to creep over him every time!   *[1892]*

≡ THINKING ABOUT THE TEXT

1. What psychological stages does the narrator go through as the story progresses?

2. How does the wallpaper function as a symbol in this story? What do you conclude about the narrator when she becomes increasingly interested in the woman she finds there?

3. Explain your ultimate view of the narrator by using specific details of the story and by identifying some of the warrants or assumptions behind your opinion. Do you admire her? Sympathize with her? Recoil from her? What would you say to someone who simply dismisses her as crazy?

4. The story is narrated in the present tense. Would its effect be different if it were narrated in the past tense? Why, or why not?

5. In real life, Gilman's husband and her doctor were two separate people. In the story, the narrator's husband is her doctor as well. Why do you think Gilman made this change? What is the effect of her combining husband and doctor?

CHARLOTTE PERKINS GILMAN
Why I Wrote "The Yellow Wallpaper"

Gilman published the following piece in the October 1913 issue of her magazine, The Forerunner.

Many and many a reader has asked that. When the story first came out, in the *New England Magazine* about 1891, a Boston physician made protest in *The Transcript.* Such a story ought not to be written, he said; it was enough to drive anyone mad to read it.

Another physician, in Kansas I think, wrote to say that it was the best description of incipient insanity he had ever seen, and — begging my pardon — had I been there?

Now the story of the story is this:

For many years I suffered from a severe and continuous nervous breakdown tending to melancholia — and beyond. During about the third year of this trouble I went, in devout faith and some faint stir of hope, to a noted specialist in nervous diseases, the best known in the country. This wise man put me to bed and applied the rest cure, to which a still good physique responded so promptly that, he concluded there was nothing much the matter with me, and sent me home with solemn advice to "live as domestic a life as far as possible," to "have but two hours' intellectual life a day," and "never to touch pen, brush, or pencil again as long as I lived." This was in 1887.

I went home and obeyed those directions for some three months, and came   5
so near the border line of utter mental ruin that I could see over.

Then, using the remnants of intelligence that remained, and helped by a wise friend, I cast the noted specialist's advice to the winds and went to work again — work, the normal life of every human being; work, in which is joy and growth and service, without which one is a pauper and a parasite; ultimately recovering some measure of power.

Being naturally moved to rejoicing by this narrow escape, I wrote *The Yellow Wallpaper,* with its embellishments and additions to carry out the ideal

(I never had hallucinations or objections to my mural decorations) and sent a copy to the physician who so nearly drove me mad. He never acknowledged it.

The little book is valued by alienists° and as a good specimen of one kind of literature. It has to my knowledge saved one woman from a similar fate — so terrifying her family that they let her out into normal activity and she recovered.

But the best result is this. Many years later I was told that the great specialist had admitted to friends of his that he had altered his treatment of neurasthenia since reading *The Yellow Wallpaper.*

It was not intended to drive people crazy, but to save people from being driven crazy, and it worked.   [1913]

10

alienists: Nineteenth-century term for psychiatrists.

≡ THINKING ABOUT THE TEXT

1. S. Weir Mitchell was the "noted specialist in nervous diseases" (para. 4) whom Gilman mentions. Yet she does not identify him by name. Why not, do you think? Some historians argue that, contrary to Gilman's claim here, Mitchell continued to believe his "rest cure" valid. Does this issue of fact matter to your judgment of her piece? Why, or why not?

2. Look again at Gilman's last sentence. Do you believe that her story could indeed "save people from being driven crazy"? Why, or why not?

3. Does this piece as a whole affect your interpretation and opinion of Gilman's story? Why, or why not? In general, how much do you think readers of a story should know about its author's life?

S. WEIR MITCHELL
From *"The Evolution of the Rest Treatment"*

Charlotte Perkins Gilman sought help from Silas Weir Mitchell (1829–1914) because he was a well-known and highly respected physician who had treated many women's mental problems. Mitchell developed his "rest cure" while serving as an army surgeon during the Civil War. Ironically, like Gilman, he was also a writer. Besides producing numerous monographs on medical subjects, he published many short stories and novels. The following is an excerpt from a lecture that Mitchell gave to the Philadelphia Neurological Society in 1904, twelve years after "The Yellow Wallpaper" appeared. As you will see, Mitchell was still enthusiastic about his "rest cure," although he had changed it in certain respects since devising it.

I have been asked to come here to-night to speak to you on some subject connected with nervous disease. I had hoped to have had ready a fitting paper for so notable an occasion, but have been prevented by public engagements and private business so as to make it quite impossible. I have, therefore, been driven to ask whether it would be agreeable if I should speak in regard to the mode in which the treatment of disease by rest was evolved. This being favorably received, I am here this evening to say a few words on that subject.

You all know full well that the art of cure rests upon a number of sciences, and that what we do in medicine, we cannot always explain, and that our methods are far from having the accuracy involved in the term *scientific*. Very often, however, it is found that what comes to us through some accident or popular use and proves of value, is defensible in the end by scientific explanatory research. This was the case as regards the treatment I shall briefly consider for you to-night.

The first indication I ever had of the great value of mere rest in disease, was during the Civil War, when there fell into the hands of Doctors Morehouse, Keen, and myself, a great many cases of what we called acute exhaustion. These were men, who, being tired by much marching, gave out suddenly at the end of some unusual exertion, and remained for weeks, perhaps months, in a pitiable state of what we should call today, Neurasthenia. In these war cases, it came on with strange abruptness. It was more extreme and also more certainly curable than are most of the graver male cases which now we are called on to treat.

I have seen nothing exactly like it in civil experience, but the combination of malaria, excessive exertion, and exposure provided cases such as no one sees today. Complete rest and plentiful diet usually brought these men up again and in many instances enabled them to return to the front.

In 1872 I had charge of a man who had locomotor ataxia° with extreme   5
pain in the extremities, and while making some unusual exertion, he broke his right thigh. This confined him to his bed for three months, and the day he got up, he broke his left thigh. This involved another three months of rest. At the end of that time he confessed with satisfaction that his ataxia was better, and that he was, as he remained thereafter, free from pain. I learned from this, and two other cases, that in ataxia the bones are brittle, and I learned also that rest in bed is valuable in a proportion of such cases. You may perceive that my attention was thus twice drawn towards the fact that mere rest had certain therapeutic values.

In 1874 Mrs. G., of B——, Maine, came to see me in the month of January. I have described her case elsewhere, so that it is needless to go into detail here, except to say that she was a lady of ample means, with no special troubles or annoyances, but completely exhausted by having had children in rapid succession and from having undertaken to do charitable and other work to an extent far beyond her strength. When first I saw this tall woman, large, gaunt, weighing under a hundred pounds, her complexion pale and acneous, and heard her story, I was for a time in a state of such therapeutic despair as usually fell upon physicians of that day when called upon to treat such cases. She had been to

ataxia: An inability to control muscular movements that is symptomatic of some nervous diseases.

Spas, to physicians of the utmost eminence, passed through the hands of gyne-cologists, worn spinal supporters, and taken every tonic known to the books. When I saw her she was unable to walk up stairs. Her exercise was limited to moving feebly up and down her room, a dozen times a day. She slept little and, being very intelligent, felt deeply her inability to read or write. Any such use of the eyes caused headache and nausea. Conversation tired her, and she had by degrees accepted a life of isolation. She was able partially to digest and retain her meals if she lay down in a noiseless and darkened room. Any disturbance or the least excitement, in short, any effort, caused nausea and immediate rejection of her meal. With care she could retain enough food to preserve her life and hardly to do more. Anemia, which we had then no accurate means of measuring, had been met by half a dozen forms of iron, all of which were said to produce headache, and generally to disagree with her. Naturally enough, her case had been pronounced to be hysteria, but calling names may relieve a doctor and comfort him in failure, but does not always assist the patient, and to my mind there was more of a general condition of nervous excitability due to the extreme of weakness than I should have been satisfied to label with the apologetic label hysteria.

I sat beside this woman day after day, hearing her pitiful story, and dis-tressed that a woman, young, once handsome, and with every means of enjoy-ment in life should be condemned to what she had been told was a state of hopeless invalidism. After my third or fourth visit, with a deep sense that every-thing had been done for her that able men could with reason suggest, and many things which reason never could have suggested, she said to me that I appeared to have nothing to offer which had not been tried over and over again. I asked her for another day before she gave up the hope which had brought her to me. The night brought counsel. The following morning I said to her, if you are at rest you appear to digest your meals better. "Yes," she said. "I have been told that on that account I ought to lie in bed. It has been tried, but when I remain in bed for a few days, I lose all appetite, have intense constipation, and get up feeling weaker than when I went to bed. Please do not ask me to go to bed." Nevertheless, I did, and a week in bed justified her statements. She threw up her meals undigested, and was manifestly worse for my experiment. Sometimes the emesis° was mere regurgitation, sometimes there was nausea and violent straining, with consequent extreme exhaustion. She declared that unless she had the small exercise of walking up and down her room, she was infallibly worse. I was here between two difficulties. That she needed rest I saw, that she required some form of exercise I also saw. How could I unite the two?

As I sat beside her, with a keen sense of defeat, it suddenly occurred to me that some time before, I had seen a man, known as a layer on of hands, use very rough rubbing for a gentleman who was in a state of general paresis.° Mr. S. had asked me if I objected to this man rubbing him. I said no, and that I should like to see him do so, as he had relieved, to my knowledge, cases of rheu-matic stiffness. I was present at two sittings and saw this man rub my patient.

emesis: Vomiting. **paresis:** Brain syphilis.

He kept him sitting in a chair at the time and was very rough and violent like the quacks now known as osteopaths. I told him he had injured my patient by his extreme roughness, and that if he rubbed him at all he must be more gentle. He took the hint and as a result there was every time a notable but temporary gain. Struck with this, I tried to have rubbing used on spinal cases, but those who tried to do the work were inefficient, and I made no constant use of it. It remained, however, on my mind, and recurred to me as I sat beside this wreck of a useful and once vigorous woman. The thought was fertile. I asked myself why rubbing might not prove competent to do for the muscles and tardy circulation what voluntary exercise does. I said to myself, this may be exercise without exertion, and wondered why I had not long before had this pregnant view of the matter.

Suffice it to say that I brought a young woman to Mrs. G.'s bedside and told her how I thought she ought to be rubbed. The girl was clever, and developed talent in that direction, and afterwards became the first of that great number of people who have since made a livelihood by massage. I watched the rubbing two or three times, giving instructions, in fact developing out of the clumsy massage I had seen, the manual of a therapeutic means, at that time entirely new to me. A few days later I fell upon the idea of giving electric passive exercise and cautiously added this second agency. Meanwhile, as she had always done best when secluded, I insisted on entire rest and shut out friends, relatives, books, and letters. I had some faith that I should succeed. In ten days I was sure the woman had found a new tonic, hope, and blossomed like a rose. Her symptoms passed away one by one. I was soon able to add to her diet, to feed her between meals, to give her malt daily, and, after a time, to conceal in it full doses of pyro-phosphates of iron. First, then, I had found two means which enabled me to use rest in bed without causing the injurious effects of unassisted rest; secondly, I had discovered that massage was a tonic of extraordinary value; thirdly, I had learned that with this combination of seclusion, massage, and electricity, I could overfeed the patient until I had brought her into a state of entire health. I learned later the care which had to be exercised in getting these patients out of bed. But this does not concern us now. In two months she gained forty pounds and was a cheerful, blooming woman, fit to do as she pleased. She has remained, save for time's ravage, what I made her.

It may strike you as interesting that for a while I was not fully aware of the   10
enormous value of a therapeutic discovery which employed no new agents, but owed its usefulness to a combination of means more or less well known.

Simple rest as a treatment had been suggested, but not in this class of cases. Massage has a long history. Used, I think, as a luxury by the Orientals for ages, it was employed by Ling in 1813. It never attained perfection in the hands of the Swedes, nor do they to-day understand the proper use of this agent. It was over and over recognized in Germany, but never generally accepted. In France, at a later period, Dreyfus, in 1841, wrote upon it and advised its use, as did Recamier and Lainé in 1868. Two at least of these authors thought it useful as a general agent, but no one seems to have accepted their views, nor was its value as a tonic spoken of in the books on therapeutics or recommended on any text-book as a powerful toning agent. It was used here in the Rest Treatment, and this, I think, gave it vogue and caused the familiar use of this invaluable therapeutic measure.

A word before I close. My first case left me in May, 1874, and shortly afterwards I began to employ the same method in other cases, being careful to choose only those which seemed best suited to it. My first mention in print of the treatment was in 1875, in the Sequin Lectures, Vol. 1, No. 4, "Rest in the Treatment of Disease." In that paper I first described Mrs. G.'s case. My second paper was in 1877, an address before the Medico-Chirurgical faculty of Maryland, and the same year I printed my book on "Rest Treatment." The one mistake in the book was the title. I was, however, so impressed at the time by the extraordinary gain in flesh and blood under this treatment that I made it too prominent in the title of the book. Let me say that for a long time the new treatment was received with the utmost incredulity. When I spoke in my papers of the people who had gained half a pound a day or more, my results were questioned and ridiculed in this city as approaching charlatanism. At a later date in England some physicians were equally wanting in foresight and courtesy. It seems incredible that any man who was a member of the British Medical Association could have said that he would rather see his patients not get well than have them cured by such a method as that. It was several years before it was taken up by Professor Goodell, and it was a longer time in making its way in Europe when by mere accident it came to be first used by Professor William Playfair.

I suffered keenly at that time from this unfair criticism, as any sensitive man must have done, for some who were eminent in the profession said of it and of me things which were most inconsiderate. Over and over in consultation I was rejected with ill-concealed scorn. I made no reply to my critics. I knew that time would justify me: I have added a long since accepted means of helping those whom before my day few helped. This is a sufficient reward for silence, patience, and self-faith. I fancy that there are in this room many who have profited for themselves and their patients by the thought which evolved the Rest Treatment as I sat by the bedside of my first rest case in 1874. Playfair said of it at the British Association that he had nothing to add to it and nothing to omit, and to this day no one has differed as to his verdict.

How fully the use of massage has been justified by the later scientific studies of Lauder Brunton, myself, and others you all know. It is one of the most scientific of remedial methods.   *[1904]*

≡ **THINKING ABOUT THE TEXT**

1. How would you describe Mitchell's tone in this lecture? What self-image does he seem to cultivate? Support your answers by referring to specific words in the text.

2. Why does Mitchell consider Mrs. G.'s case significant? In what ways does she resemble Gilman and the narrator of Gilman's story?

3. Mitchell indicates that his patients have included male as well as female hysterics. Are we therefore justified in concluding that gender did not matter much in his application of the "rest cure"? Why, or why not?

JOHN HARVEY KELLOGG
From *The Ladies' Guide in Health and Disease*

John Harvey Kellogg (1852–1943) was an American physician who wrote much advice about how to discipline one's sexual desires and, in the case of women, how to be a good mother. As founder and superintendent of the Battle Creek Sanitarium in Michigan, Dr. Kellogg urged that his patients eat cereals as part of their treatment, and eventually, his brother established the cereal company that bears their family name. Dr. Kellogg's keen interest in cereals and health foods is satirized in T. Coraghessan Boyle's 1993 novel, The Road to Wellville, *and the film based on that book. The following piece is an excerpt from Kellogg's 1882* Ladies' Guide in Health and Disease: Girlhood, Maidenhood, Wifehood, Motherhood. *In this selection, he virtually equates womanhood with motherhood and discusses what a woman must do to produce outstanding children. Kellogg's advice reflects the view that much of his society held about women—or at least about middle- and upper-class white women. His discussion of "puerperal mania" is especially relevant to Gilman's story.*

The special influence of the mother begins with the moment of conception. In fact it is possible that the mental condition at the time of the generative act has much to do with determining the character of the child, though it is generally conceded that at this time the influence of the father is greater than that of the mother. Any number of instances have occurred in which a drunken father has impressed upon his child the condition of his nervous system to such a degree as to render permanent in the child the staggering gait and maudlin manner which in his own case was a transient condition induced by the poisonous influence of alcohol. A child born as the result of a union in which both parents were in a state of beastly intoxication was idiotic.

Another fact might be added to impress the importance that the new being should be supplied from the very beginning of its existence with the very best conditions possible. Indeed, it is desirable to go back still further, and secure a proper preparation for the important function of maternity. The qualities which go to make up individuality of character are the result of the summing up of a long line of influences, too subtle and too varied to admit of full control, but still, to some degree at least, subject to management. The dominance of law is nowhere more evident than in the relation of ante-natal influences to character.

The hap-hazard way in which human beings are generated leaves no room for surprise that the race should deteriorate. No stock-breeder would expect anything but ruin should he allow his animals to propagate with no attention to their physical conditions or previous preparation.

Finding herself in a pregnant condition, the mother should not yield to the depressing influences which often crowd upon her. The anxieties and fears which women sometimes yield themselves to, grow with encouragement, until they become so absorbed as to be capable of producing a profoundly evil impression on the child. The true mother who is prepared for the functions of maternity, will welcome the evidence of pregnancy, and joyfully enter upon the Heaven-given task of molding a human character, of bringing into the world a new being whose life-history may involve the destinies of nations, or change the current of human thought for generations to come.

The pregnant mother should cultivate cheerfulness of mind and calmness   5
of temper, but should avoid excitements of all kinds, such as theatrical performances, public contests of various descriptions, etc. Anger, envy, irritability of temper, and, in fact, all the passions and propensities should be held in check. The fickleness of desire and the constantly varying whims which characterize the pregnant state in some women should not be regarded as uncontrollable, and to be yielded to as the only means of appeasing them. The mother should be gently encouraged to resist such tendencies when they become at all marked, and to assist her in the effort, her husband should endeavor to engage her mind by interesting conversation, reading, and various harmless and pleasant diversions.

If it is desired that the child should possess a special aptitude for any particular art or pursuit, during the period of pregnancy the mother's mind should be constantly directed in this channel. If artistic taste or skill is the trait desired, the mother should be surrounded by works of art of a high order of merit. She should read art, think art, talk, and write about art, and if possible, herself engage in the close practical study of some one or more branches of art, as painting, drawing, etching, or modeling. If ability for authorship is desired, then the mother should devote herself assiduously to literature. It is not claimed that by following these suggestions any mother can make of her children great artists or authors at will; but it is certain that by this means the greatest possibilities in individual cases can be attained; and it is certain that decided results have been secured by close attention to the principles laid down. It should be understood, however, that not merely a formal and desultory effort on the part of the mother is what is required. The theme selected must completely absorb her mind. It must be the one idea of her waking thoughts and the model on which is formed the dreams of her sleeping hours.

The question of diet during pregnancy as before stated is a vitally important one as regards the interests of the child. A diet into which enters largely such unwholesome articles as mustard, pepper, hot sauces, spices, and other stimulating condiments, engenders a love for stimulants in the disposition of the infant. Tea and coffee, especially if used to excess, undoubtedly tend in the same direction. We firmly believe that we have, in the facts first stated, the key to the constant increase in the consumption of ardent spirits. The children of the present generation inherit from their condiment-consuming, tea-, coffee-, and liquor-drinking, and tobacco-using parents, not simply a readiness for the acquirement of the habits mentioned, but a propensity for the use of stimulants which in persons of weak will-power and those whose circumstances are not the most favorable, becomes irresistible.

The present generation is also suffering in consequence of the impoverished diet of its parents. The modern custom of bolting the flour from the different grains has deprived millions of infants and children of the necessary supply of bone-making material, thus giving rise to a greatly increased frequency of the various diseases which arise from imperfect bony structure, as rickets, caries, premature decay of the teeth, etc. The proper remedy is the disuse of fine-flour bread and all other bolted grain preparations. Graham-flour bread, oatmeal, cracked wheat, and similar preparations, should be relied upon as the leading articles of diet. Supplemented by milk, the whole-grain preparations constitute a complete form of nourishment, and render a large amount of animal food not only unnecessary but really harmful on account of its stimulating character. It is by no means so necessary as is generally supposed that meat, fish, fowl, and flesh in various forms should constitute a large element of the dietary of the pregnant or nursing mother in order to furnish adequate nourishment for the developing child. We have seen the happiest results follow the employment of a strictly vegetarian dietary, and do not hesitate to advise moderation in the use of flesh food, though we do not recommend the entire discontinuance of its use by the pregnant mother who has been accustomed to use it freely.

A nursing mother should at once suspend nursing if she discovers that pregnancy has again occurred. The continuance of nursing under such circumstances is to the disadvantage of three individuals, the mother, the infant at the breast, and the developing child.

Sexual indulgence during pregnancy may be suspended with decided benefit to both mother and child. The most ancient medical writers call attention to the fact that by the practice of continence° during gestation, the pains of childbirth are greatly mitigated. The injurious influences upon the child of the gratification of the passions during the period when its character is being formed, is undoubtedly much greater than is usually supposed. We have no doubt that this is a common cause of the transmission of libidinous tendencies to the child; and that the tendency to abortion is induced by sexual indulgence has long been a well-established fact. The females of most animals resolutely resist the advances of the males during this period, being guided in harmony with natural law by their natural instincts which have been less perverted in them than in human beings. The practice of continence during pregnancy is also enforced in the harems of the East, which fact leads to the practice of abortion among women of this class who are desirous of remaining the special favorites of the common husband.

10

continence: Chastity, abstinence, or restraint.

The general health of the mother must be kept up in every way. It is especially important that the regularity of the bowels should be maintained. Proper diet and as much physical exercise as can be taken are the best means for accomplishing this. When constipation is allowed to exist, the infant as well as the mother suffers. The effete products which should be promptly removed from the body, being long retained, are certain to find their way back into the system again, poisoning not only the blood of the mother but that of the developing fetus. . . .

Puerperal Mania. —This form of mental disease is most apt to show itself about two weeks after delivery. Although, fortunately, of not very frequent occurrence, it is a most serious disorder when it does occur, and hence we may with propriety introduce the following somewhat lengthy, but most graphic description of the disease from the pen of Dr. Ramsbotham, an eminent English physician: —

"In mania there is almost always, at the very commencement, a troubled, agitated, and hurried manner, a restless eye, an unnaturally anxious, suspicious, and unpleasing expression of face; —sometimes it is pallid, at others more flushed than usual; —an unaccustomed irritability of temper, and impatience of control or contradiction; a vacillation of purpose, or loss of memory; sometimes a rapid succession of contradictory orders are issued, or a paroxysm of excessive anger is excited about the merest trifle. Occasionally, one of the first indications will be a sullen obstinacy, or listlessness and stubborn silence. The patient lies on her back, and can by no means be persuaded to reply to the questions of her attendants, or she will repeat them, as an echo, until, all at once, without any apparent cause, she will break out into a torrent of language more or less incoherent, and her words will follow each other with surprising rapidity. These symptoms will sometimes show themselves rather suddenly, on the patient's awakening from a disturbed and unrefreshing sleep, or they may supervene more slowly when she has been harassed with wakefulness for three or four previous nights in succession, or perhaps ever since her delivery. She will very likely then become impressed with the idea that some evil has befallen her husband, or, what is still more usual, her child; that it is dead or stolen; and if it be brought to her, nothing can persuade her it is her own; she supposes it to belong to somebody else; or she will fancy that her husband is unfaithful to her, or that he and those about her have conspired to poison her. Those persons who are naturally the objects of her deepest and most devout affection, are regarded by her with jealousy, suspicion, and hatred. This is particularly remarkable with regard to her newly born infant; and I have known many instances where attempts have been made to destroy it when it has been incautiously left within her power. Sometimes, though rarely, may be observed a great anxiety regarding the termination of her own case, or a firm conviction that she is speedily about to die. I have observed upon occasions a constant movement of the lips, while the mouth was shut; or the patient is incessantly rubbing the inside of her lips with her fingers, or thrusting them far back into her mouth; and if questions are asked, particularly if she be desired to put out her tongue, she will often compress the lips forcibly together, as if with an obstinate determination of resistance. One peculiarity attending some cases of puerperal mania is the immorality and obscenity of the expressions uttered; they are often such, indeed, as to excite our astonishment that women in a respectable station of society could ever have become acquainted with such language."

The insanity of childbirth differs from that of pregnancy in that in the latter cases the patient is almost always melancholy,° while in the former there is active mania. Derangement of the digestive organs is a constant accompaniment of the disease.

If the patient has no previous or hereditary tendency to insanity, the prospect of a quite speedy recovery is good. The result is seldom immediately fatal, but the patient not infrequently remains in a condition of mental unsoundness for months or even years, and sometimes permanently.   15

Treatment: When there is reason to suspect a liability to puerperal mania from previous mental disease or from hereditary influence, much can be done to ward off an attack. Special attention must be paid to the digestive organs, which should be regulated by proper food and simple means to aid digestion. The tendency to sleeplessness must be combatted by careful nursing, light massage at night, rubbing of the spine, alternate hot and cold applications to the spine, cooling the head by cloths wrung out of cold water, and the use of the warm bath at bed time. These measures are often successful in securing sleep when all other measures fail.

The patient must be kept very quiet. Visitors, even if near relatives, must not be allowed when the patient is at all nervous or disturbed, and it is best to exclude nearly every one from the sick-room with the exception of the nurse, who should be a competent and experienced person.

When the attack has really begun, the patient must have the most vigilant watchcare, not being left alone for a moment. It is much better to care for the patient at home, when possible to do so efficiently, than to take her to an asylum.

When evidences of returning rationality appear, the greatest care must be exercised to prevent too great excitement. Sometimes a change of air, if the patient is sufficiently strong, physically, will at this period prove eminently beneficial. A visit from a dear friend will sometimes afford a needed stimulus to the dormant faculties. Such cases as these of course require intelligent medical supervision.   *[1882]*

melancholy: Mental state characterized by severe depression, somatic problems, and hallucinations or delusions.

≡ THINKING ABOUT THE TEXT

1. What specific responsibilities does Kellogg assign to women? What are some key assumptions he makes about them?

2. Quite possibly Kellogg would have said that the narrator of Gilman's story suffers from puerperal mania. What details of the story would

support this diagnosis? What significant details of the narrator's life, if any, would Kellogg be ignoring if he saw her as *merely* a case of puerperal mania?

3. If Kellogg's advice were published today, what parts of it do you think readers would accept? What parts do you think many readers would reject?

≡ WRITING ABOUT ISSUES

1. After reading the three essays given here, research women's psychological disorders of the nineteenth century and write an essay that argues that those "disorders" were the result of male attitudes toward women.

2. Research the term *female hysteria* and write a report that includes the ideas of S. Weir Mitchell and other prominent nineteenth-century doctors. Include in your report your evaluation of their credibility.

3. Research how mental illness was diagnosed and treated within a particular period of American history. Then, write an essay that argues for seeing the culture of that period as an influence on how mental illness was conceived then.

4. Research such contemporary psychological problems as depression, bulimia, anorexia, and dissociative identity disorders. Write an essay that tries to explain why these diseases seem to affect mostly women.

CHAPTER 8

Writing with Critical Approaches to Literature

Exploring the topics of literary criticism can help readers understand the various ways literature can matter. One popular way to investigate critical approaches to literature is to group critics into schools. Critics who are concerned primarily with equality for women, for example, are often classified as feminist critics, and those concerned with the responses of readers are classified as reader-response critics. Likewise, critics who focus on the unconscious are said to belong to the psychoanalytic school, and those who analyze class conflicts belong to the Marxist school.

Classifying critics in this way is probably more convenient than precise. Few critics like to be pigeonholed or thought predictable, and many professional readers tend to be eclectic — that is, they use ideas from various schools to help them illuminate the text. Nevertheless, knowing something about contemporary schools of criticism can make you a more informed reader and help literature matter to you even more.

There is a commonsense belief that words mean just what they say — that to understand a certain passage in a text, a reader simply needs to know what the words mean. But meaning is rarely straightforward. Scholars have been arguing over the meaning of passages in the Bible, in the Constitution, and in Shakespeare's plays for centuries without reaching agreement. Pinning down the exact meaning of words like *sin, justice,* and *love* is almost impossible, but even more daunting is the unacknowledged theory of reading that each person brings to any text, including literature. Some people who read the Bible or the Constitution, for example, believe in the literal meaning of the words, and some think the real meaning lies in the original intention of the writer, while others believe that the only meaning we can be sure of is our own perspective. For these latter readers, there is no objective meaning, and no absolutely true meaning is possible.

Indeed, a good deal of what a text means depends on the perspective that readers bring with them. Passages can be read effectively from numerous points of view. A generation ago, most English professors taught their students to pay attention to the internal aspects of a poem and not to the poem's larger social and political contexts. So oppositions, irony, paradox, and coherence — not gender equality or social justice — were topics of discussion. Proponents of this approach were said to belong to the New Critical school. In the past twenty-five years or so, however, professors have put much more emphasis on the external aspects of interpretation, stressing social, political, cultural, sexual, and gender-based perspectives. Each one of these perspectives can give us a valuable window on a text, helping us see the rich possibilities of literature. Even though each approach can provide insights into a text, it can also be blind to other textual elements. When we read in too focused a way, we can sometimes miss the opportunity to see what others see.

In this chapter, however, we want to present our interpretation in a clear, logical, and reflective manner as we take a position and try to persuade others of its reasonableness. Since there are many possible lenses to see a text through, you can be sure your classmates will see things differently. Part of the excitement and challenge of making arguments that matter is your ability to analyze and clarify your ideas, gather and organize your evidence, and present your claim in carefully revised and edited prose.

Contemporary Schools of Criticism

The following nine approaches are just a few of the many different literary schools or perspectives a reader can use in engaging a text. Think of them as intellectual tools or informed lenses that you can employ to enhance your interpretation of a particular literary text:

- New Criticism
- Feminist criticism
- Psychoanalytic criticism
- Marxist criticism
- Deconstruction
- Reader-response criticism
- Postcolonial criticism
- New Historicism
- Queer theory

NEW CRITICISM

New Criticism was developed about seventy years ago as a way to focus on "the text itself." Although it is no longer as popular as it once was, some of its principles are still widely accepted, especially the use of specific examples from the text as evidence for a particular interpretation. Sometimes called *close reading*, this approach does not see either the writer's intention or the reader's personal response as relevant. It is also uninterested in the text's social context, the spirit of the age, or its relevance to issues of gender, social justice, or oppression. These critics are interested, for example, in a poem's internal structure, images, symbols, metaphors, point of view, plot, and characterizations. Emphasis is placed on literary language — on the ways connotation, ambiguity, irony, and paradox all reinforce the meaning. In fact, *how* a poem means is inseparable from *what* it means. The primary method for judging the worth of a piece of literature is its organic unity or the complex way all the elements of a text contribute to the poem's meaning.

Critics often argue that their interpretations are the most consistent with textual evidence. A popular approach is to note the oppositions in the text and to focus on tensions, ironies, and paradoxes. Typically, a paradox early in the text is shown at the end not to be that contradictory after all. The critic then argues that all the elements of the text can be seen as contributing to this resolution.

FEMINIST CRITICISM

Feminist criticism developed during the 1970s as an outgrowth of a resurgent women's movement. The goals of the feminist critic and the feminist political activist are similar — to contest the patriarchal point of view as the standard for all moral, aesthetic, political, and intellectual judgments and to assert that gender roles are primarily learned, not universal. They hope to uncover and challenge essentialist attitudes that hold it is normal for women to be kept in domestic, secondary, and subservient roles, and they affirm the value of a woman's experiences and perspectives in understanding the world. Recently, both female and male critics have become interested in gender studies, a branch of theory concerned with the ways cultural practices socialize us to act in certain ways because of our gender. Focused primarily on issues of identity, gender criticism looks at the ways characters in literary texts are represented or how they are constructed in a particular culture as feminine or masculine. Like the broader area of feminism, many gender specialists hope that studying the arbitrary ways we are expected to dress, walk, talk, and behave can help us widen the conventional notions of gender.

PSYCHOANALYTIC CRITICISM

Psychoanalytic criticism began with Sigmund Freud's theories of the unconscious, especially the numerous repressed wounds, fears, unresolved conflicts, and guilty desires from childhood that can significantly affect behavior and mental health in our adult lives. Freud developed the tripart division of the mind into the ego (the conscious self), the superego (the site of what our culture has taught us about good and bad), and the id (the primitive unconscious and source of our sexual drive). Psychoanalytic critics often see literature as a kind of dream, filled with symbolic elements that often mask their real meaning. Freud also theorized that young males were threatened by their fathers in the competition for the affection of their mothers. Critics are alert to the complex ways this Oedipal drama unfolds in literature.

MARXIST CRITICISM

Marxist criticism is based on the political and economic theories of Karl Marx. Marxists think that a society is propelled by its economy, which is manipulated by a class system. Most people, especially blue-collar workers (the proletariat), do not understand the complex ways their lives are subject to economic forces beyond their control. This false consciousness about history and material well-being prevents workers from seeing that their values have been socially constructed to keep them in their place. What most interests contemporary Marxists is the way ideology shapes our consciousness. And since literature both represents and projects ideology, Marxist critics see it as a way to unmask our limited view of society's structures.

DECONSTRUCTION

Deconstruction is really more a philosophical movement than a school of literary criticism, but many of its techniques have been used by Marxist and feminist literary critics to uncover important concepts they believe are hidden in texts. Made famous by the French philosopher Jacques Derrida, deconstruction's main tenet is that Western thought has divided the world into binary opposites. To gain a semblance of control over the complexity of human experience, we have constructed a worldview in which good is clearly at one end of a continuum and bad at the other. Additional examples of binary opposites include masculine and feminine, freedom and slavery, objective and subjective, mind and body, and presence and absence. According to Derrida, however, this arbitrary and illusory construct simply reflects the specific ideology of one culture. Far from being opposed to each other, masculinity and femininity, for example, are intimately interconnected, and traces of the feminine are to be found within the masculine. The concepts need each other for meaning to occur, an idea referred to as *différance*. Derrida also notes that language, far from being a neutral medium of communication, is infused with our biases, assumptions, and values — which leads some of us to refer to sexually active women as "sluts" and to sexually active men as "studs." One term ("sluts") is marginalized, and the other ("studs") is privileged because our culture grants men more power than women in shaping the language that benefits them.

Thus, language filters, distorts, and alters our perception of the world. For deconstructors or deconstructive critics, language is not stable or reliable, and when closely scrutinized, it becomes slippery and ambiguous, constantly overflowing with implications, associations, and contradictions. For Derrida, this endless free play of meaning suggests that language is always changing, always in flux — especially so when we understand that words can be viewed from almost endless points of view or contexts. That is why deconstructionists claim that texts (or individuals or systems of thought) have no fixed definition, no center, no absolute meaning. And so one way to deconstruct or lay bare the arbitrary construction of a text is to show that the oppositions in the text are not really absolutely opposed, that outsiders can be seen to be insiders, and that words that seem to mean one thing can mean many things.

READER-RESPONSE CRITICISM

Reader-response criticism is often misunderstood to be simply giving one's opinion about a text: "I liked it," "I hate happy endings," "I think the characters were unrealistic." But reader-response criticism is actually more interested in why readers have certain responses. The central assumption is that texts do not come alive and do not mean anything until active readers engage them with specific assumptions about what reading is. New Critics think a reader's response is irrelevant because a text's meaning is timeless. But response critics, including feminists and Marxists, maintain that what a text means cannot be separated from the reading process used by readers as they draw on personal and literary experiences to make meaning. In other words, the text is not an object but an event that occurs in readers over time.

Response criticism includes critics who think that the reader's contribution to the making of meaning is quite small as well as critics who think that readers play a primary role in the process. Louise Rosenblatt is a moderate response critic since she thinks the contributions are about equal. Her transactive theory claims that the text guides our response, like a printed musical score that we adjust as we move through the text. She allows for a range of acceptable meanings as long as she can find reasonable textual support in the writing.

Response critics like Stanley Fish downplay individual responses, focusing instead on how communities influence our responses to texts. We probably all belong to a number of these interpretive communities (such as churches, universities, neighborhoods, political parties, and social class) and have internalized their interpretive strategies, their discourse, or their way of reading texts of all kinds. Fish's point is that we all come to texts already predisposed to read them in a certain way: we do not interpret stories, but we create them by using the reading tools and cultural assumptions we bring with us. Our reading then reveals what is in us more than what is in the text. We find what we expect to see.

POSTCOLONIAL CRITICISM

Postcolonial criticism, like feminist criticism, has developed because of the dramatic shrinking of the world and the increasing multicultural cast of our own country. It is mainly interested in the ways nineteenth-century European political domination affects the lives of people living in former colonies, especially the way the dominant culture becomes the norm and those without power are portrayed as inferior. Postcolonial critics often look for stereotypes in texts as well as in characters whose self-image has been damaged by being forced to see themselves as Other, as less than. As oppressed people try to negotiate life in both the dominant and the oppressed cultures, they can develop a double consciousness that leads to feelings of alienation and deep conflicts.

Literary critics often argue that being caught between the demands of two cultures—one dominant and privileged, the other marginalized and scorned—causes a character to be "unhomed," a psychological refugee who is uncomfortable everywhere.

NEW HISTORICISM

New historicism was developed because critics were dissatisfied with the old historicism, a long-standing traditional approach that viewed history simply as a background for understanding the literary text. History was thought to be an accurate record of what happened because the professional historian used objective and proven methods. But most literary critics no longer hold to this view of history. Instead, history is now thought to be just one perspective among many possibilities, inevitably subjective and biased. Influenced by the theorist Michel Foucault, history is seen as one of many discourses that can shed light on the past. But the dominant view is that all of us, including historians, writers, and critics, live in a particular culture and cannot escape its influences. And since these social, cultural, literary, economic, and political influences are all interrelated, all texts can tell us something important. Stories, histories, diaries, laws, speeches, newspapers, and magazines are all relevant. Culture permeates all texts, influencing everyone to see society's view of reality, of what's right and wrong and which values, assumptions, and truths are acceptable. Critics and historians try to interpret a vast web of interconnected discourses and forces in order to understand an era. Naturally, since many of these forces are competing for power, critics are always looking for power struggles among discourses. Think of the present struggle over the amount of influence religion should have in politics or who has the right to marry. Literature is one of the texts in a culture that shapes our views and which critics investigate to unearth these competing ideas.

QUEER THEORY

Influenced by the social, cultural, and academic advances of feminist theory in the 1980s, gay and lesbian critics in the 1990s began to join the critical conversation taking place in universities. Besides uncovering the possible homosexuality or bisexuality of canonical authors (such as Christopher Marlowe, Willa Cather, Emily Dickinson, and Henry James), these critics sought to reveal and discredit long-held stereotypes of gay and lesbian fictional characters. By challenging the homophobic prejudice they found in literature and society, lesbian and gay critics hoped to raise awareness of the complex ways society privileges heterosexual behavior and marginalizes any deviation from its norms. Adrienne Rich, an influential lesbian theorist, popularized the term "compulsive heterosexuality" to suggest the subtle and explicit ways the dominant straight culture unthinkingly socializes us to see heterosexuality as a given, the taken-for-granted default sexual identity for all. As a result, same-sex relationships suffer the disempowering injustices allotted to those judged abnormal. Therefore, another concern of gay and lesbian critics has been to suggest that sexual identity is not a stable or an absolute given. Again, Adrienne Rich is helpful with her idea of a "lesbian continuum" where sexual identity is not absolute but is best seen as contextual and fluid, ranging from young girls holding hands (homosocial) to same-sex flirting and kissing (homoerotic) to genital sex (homosexual).

The idea of sexual identity as fluid and contingent can be seen as a bridge to queer theory, an umbrella term that became popular in the 1990s in the Lesbian-Gay-Bisexual-Transgender-Questioning-Intersex-Asexual (LGBTQIA) community. Although *queer* had been a term of homophobic abuse, it was rehabilitated to refer to whatever is at odds with the norm, the accepted, and the dominant. Practitioners of queer theory want to challenge the many institutions in which heteronormativity is so deeply embedded. Like deconstructionists, queer theorists do not believe in stable identities; consequently, they always debunk and question conventional gender identity and roles. Performance is more important than what you are; action counts, not biology.

Working with the Critical Approaches

Keep these brief descriptions of the critical approaches in mind as you read the following story by James Joyce, one of the most important writers of the twentieth century. Joyce (1882–1941) was born in Ireland, although he spent most of his life in self-imposed exile on the European continent. "Counterparts" is from *Dubliners* (1914), a collection of stories set in the Irish city of his childhood years.

JAMES JOYCE
Counterparts

The bell rang furiously and, when Miss Parker went to the tube, a furious voice called out in a piercing North of Ireland accent:

—Send Farrington here!

Miss Parker returned to her machine, saying to a man who was writing at a desk:

—Mr Alleyne wants you upstairs.

The man muttered *Blast him!* under his breath and pushed back his chair   5
to stand up. When he stood up he was tall and of great bulk. He had a hanging face, dark wine-coloured, with fair eyebrows and moustache: his eyes bulged forward slightly and the whites of them were dirty. He lifted up the counter and, passing by the clients, went out of the office with a heavy step.

He went heavily upstairs until he came to the second landing, where a door bore a brass plate with the inscription *Mr Alleyne*. Here he halted, puffing with labor and vexation, and knocked. The shrill voice cried:

—Come in!

The man entered Mr Alleyne's room. Simultaneously Mr Alleyne, a little man wearing gold-rimmed glasses on a cleanshaven face, shot his head up over a pile of documents. The head itself was so pink and hairless that it seemed like a large egg reposing on the papers. Mr Alleyne did not lose a moment:

—Farrington? What is the meaning of this? Why have I always to complain of you? May I ask you why you haven't made a copy of that contract between Bodley and Kirwan? I told you it must be ready by four o'clock.

—But Mr Shelley said, sir—   10

—*Mr Shelley said, sir.* . . . Kindly attend to what I say and not to what *Mr Shelley says, sir.* You have always some excuse or another for shirking work.

Let me tell you that if the contract is not copied before this evening I'll lay the matter before Mr Crosbie. . . . Do you hear me now?

—Yes, sir.

—Do you hear me now? . . . Ay and another little matter! I might as well be talking to the wall as talking to you. Understand once for all that you get a half an hour for your lunch and not an hour and a half. How many courses do you want, I'd like to know. . . . Do you mind me, now?

—Yes, sir.

Mr Alleyne bent his head again upon his pile of papers. The man stared   15
fixedly at the polished skull which directed the affairs of Crosbie & Alleyne, gauging its fragility. A spasm of rage gripped his throat for a few moments and then passed, leaving after it a sharp sensation of thirst. The man recognized the sensation and felt that he must have a good night's drinking. The middle of the month was passed and, if he could get the copy done in time, Mr Alleyne might give him an order on the cashier. He stood still, gazing fixedly at the head upon the pile of papers. Suddenly Mr Alleyne began to upset all the papers, searching for something. Then, as if he had been unaware of the man's presence till that moment, he shot up his head again, saying:

—Eh? Are you going to stand there all day? Upon my word, Farrington, you take things easy!

—I was waiting to see . . .

—Very good, you needn't wait to see. Go downstairs and do your work.

The man walked heavily towards the door and, as he went out of the room, he heard Mr Alleyne cry after him that if the contract was not copied by evening Mr Crosbie would hear of the matter.

He returned to his desk in the lower office and counted the sheets which   20
remained to be copied. He took up his pen and dipped it in the ink but he continued to stare stupidly at the last words he had written: *In no case shall the said Bernard Bodley be*. . . . The evening was falling and in a few minutes they would be lighting the gas: then he could write. He felt that he must slake the thirst in his throat. He stood up from his desk and, lifting the counter as before, passed out of the office. As he was passing out the chief clerk looked at him inquiringly.

—It's all right, Mr Shelley, said the man, pointing with his finger to indicate the objective of his journey.

The chief clerk glanced at the hat-rack but, seeing the row complete, offered no remark. As soon as he was on the landing the man pulled a shepherd's plaid cap out of his pocket, put it on his head and ran quickly down the rickety stairs. From the street door he walked on furtively on the inner side of the path towards the corner and all at once dived into a doorway. He was now safe in the dark snug of O'Neill's shop, and, filling up the little window that looked into the bar with his inflamed face, the color of dark wine or dark meat, he called out:

—Here, Pat, give us a g.p., like a good fellow.

The curate brought him a glass of plain porter. The man drank it at a gulp and asked for a caraway seed. He put his penny on the counter and, leaving the curate to grope for it in the gloom, retreated out of the snug as furtively as he had entered it.

Darkness, accompanied by a thick fog, was gaining upon the dusk of   25
February and the lamps in Eustace Street had been lit. The man went up by the
houses until he reached the door of the office, wondering whether he could
finish his copy in time. On the stairs a moist pungent odor of perfumes saluted
his nose: evidently Miss Delacour had come while he was out in O'Neill's. He
crammed his cap back again into his pocket and re-entered the office assuming
an air of absent-mindedness.

—Mr Alleyne has been calling for you, said the chief clerk severely. Where
were you?

The man glanced at the two clients who were standing at the counter as if
to intimate that their presence prevented him from answering. As the clients
were both male the chief clerk allowed himself a laugh.

—I know that game, he said. Five times in one day is a little bit. . . . Well,
you better look sharp and get a copy of our correspondence in the Delacour
case for Mr Alleyne.

This address in the presence of the public, his run upstairs, and the porter
he had gulped down so hastily confused the man and, as he sat down at his
desk to get what was required, he realized how hopeless was the task of finishing his copy of the contract before half past five. The dark damp night was
coming and he longed to spend it in the bars, drinking with his friends amid the
glare of gas and the clatter of glasses. He got out the Delacour correspondence
and passed out of the office. He hoped Mr Alleyne would not discover that the
last two letters were missing.

The moist pungent perfume lay all the way up to Mr Alleyne's room. Miss   30
Delacour was a middle-aged woman of Jewish appearance. Mr Alleyne was
said to be sweet on her or on her money. She came to the office often and stayed
a long time when she came. She was sitting beside his desk now in an aroma
of perfumes, smoothing the handle of her umbrella, and nodding the great
black feather in her hat. Mr Alleyne had swivelled his chair round to face her
and thrown his right foot jauntily upon his left knee. The man put the correspondence on the desk and bowed respectfully but neither Mr Alleyne nor
Miss Delacour took any notice of his bow. Mr Alleyne tapped a finger on the
correspondence and then flicked it towards him as if to say: *That's all right: you
can go.*

The man returned to the lower office and sat down again at his desk. He
stared intently at the incomplete phrase: *In no case shall the said Bernard Bodley
be* . . . and thought how strange it was that the last three words began with the
same letter. The chief clerk began to hurry Miss Parker, saying she would never
have the letters typed in time for post. The man listened to the clicking of the
machine for a few minutes and then set to work to finish his copy. But his head
was not clear and his mind wandered away to the glare and rattle of the public-
house. It was a night for hot punches. He struggled on with his copy, but when
the clock struck five he had still fourteen pages to write. Blast it! He couldn't
finish it in time. He longed to execrate aloud, to bring his fist down on something violently. He was so enraged that he wrote *Bernard Bernard* instead of
Bernard Bodley and had to begin again on a clean sheet.

He felt strong enough to clear out the whole office singlehanded. His body ached to do something, to rush out and revel in violence. All the indignities of his life enraged him. . . . Could he ask the cashier privately for an advance? No, the cashier was no good, no damn good: he wouldn't give an advance. . . . He knew where he would meet the boys: Leonard and O'Halloran and Nosey Flynn. The barometer of his emotional nature was set for a spell of riot.

His imagination had so abstracted him that his name was called twice before he answered. Mr Alleyne and Miss Delacour were standing outside the counter and all the clerks had turned round in anticipation of something. The man got up from his desk. Mr Alleyne began a tirade of abuse, saying that two letters were missing. The man answered that he knew nothing about them, that he had made a faithful copy. The tirade continued: it was so bitter and violent that the man could hardly restrain his fist from descending upon the head of the manikin before him.

—I know nothing about any other two letters, he said stupidly.

—*You—know—nothing.* Of course you know nothing, said Mr Alleyne.   35
Tell me, he added, glancing first for approval to the lady beside him, do you take me for a fool? Do you think me an utter fool?

The man glanced from the lady's face to the little egg-shaped head and back again; and, almost before he was aware of it, his tongue had found a felicitous moment:

—I don't think, sir, he said, that that's a fair question to put to me.

There was a pause in the very breathing of the clerks. Everyone was astounded (the author of the witticism no less than his neighbors) and Miss Delacour, who was a stout amiable person, began to smile broadly. Mr Alleyne flushed to the hue of a wild rose and his mouth twitched with a dwarf's passion. He shook his fist in the man's face till it seemed to vibrate like the knob of some electric machine:

—You impertinent ruffian! You impertinent ruffian! I'll make short work of you! Wait till you see! You'll apologize to me for your impertinence or you'll quit the office instanter! You'll quit this, I'm telling you, or you'll apologize to me!

He stood in a doorway opposite the office watching to see if the cashier would   40
come out alone. All the clerks passed out and finally the cashier came out with the chief clerk. It was no use trying to say a word to him when he was with the chief clerk. The man felt that his position was bad enough. He had been obliged to offer an abject apology to Mr Alleyne for his impertinence but he knew what a hornet's nest the office would be for him. He could remember the way in which Mr Alleyne had hounded little Peake out of the office in order to make room for his own nephew. He felt savage and thirsty and revengeful, annoyed with himself and with everyone else. Mr Alleyne would never give him an hour's rest; his life would be a hell to him. He had made a proper fool of himself this time. Could he not keep his tongue in his cheek? But they had never pulled together from the first, he and Mr Alleyne, ever since the day Mr Alleyne had overheard him mimicking his North of Ireland accent to amuse Higgins and

Miss Parker: that had been the beginning of it. He might have tried Higgins for the money, but sure Higgins never had anything for himself. A man with two establishments to keep up, of course he couldn't. . . .

He felt his great body again aching for the comfort of the public-house. The fog had begun to chill him and he wondered could he touch Pat in O'Neill's. He could not touch him for more than a bob—and a bob was no use. Yet he must get money somewhere or other: he had spent his last penny for the g.p. and soon it would be too late for getting money anywhere. Suddenly, as he was fingering his watch-chain, he thought of Terry Kelly's pawn-office in Fleet Street. That was the dart! Why didn't he think of it sooner?

He went through the narrow alley of Temple Bar quickly, muttering to himself that they could all go to hell because he was going to have a good night of it. The clerk in Terry Kelly's said *A crown!* but the consignor held out for six shillings; and in the end the six shillings was allowed him literally. He came out of the pawn-office joyfully, making a little cylinder of the coins between his thumb and fingers. In Westmoreland Street the footpaths were crowded with young men and women returning from business and ragged urchins ran here and there yelling out the names of the evening editions. The man passed through the crowd, looking on the spectacle generally with proud satisfaction and staring masterfully at the office-girls. His head was full of the noises of tram-gongs and swishing trolleys and his nose already sniffed the curling fumes of punch. As he walked on he preconsidered the terms in which he would narrate the incident to the boys:

—So, I just looked at him—coolly, you know, and looked at her. Then I looked back at him again—taking my time, you know. *I don't think that that's a fair question to put to me*, says I.

Nosey Flynn was sitting up in his usual corner of Davy Byrne's and, when he heard the story, he stood Farrington a half-one, saying it was as smart a thing as ever he heard. Farrington stood a drink in his turn. After a while O'Halloran and Paddy Leonard came in and the story was repeated to them. O'Halloran stood tailors of malt, hot, all round and told the story of the retort he had made to the chief clerk when he was in Callan's of Fownes's Street; but, as the retort was after the manner of the liberal shepherds in the eclogues, he had to admit that it was not so clever as Farrington's retort. At this Farrington told the boys to polish off that and have another.

Just as they were naming their poisons who should come in but Higgins!   45 Of course he had to join in with the others. The men asked him to give his version of it, and he did so with great vivacity for the sight of five small hot whiskies was very exhilarating. Everyone roared laughing when he showed the way in which Mr Alleyne shook his fist in Farrington's face. Then he imitated Farrington, saying, *And here was my nabs, as cool as you please,* while Farrington looked at the company out of his heavy dirty eyes, smiling and at times drawing forth stray drops of liquor from his moustache with the aid of his lower lip.

When that round was over there was a pause. O'Halloran had money but neither of the other two seemed to have any; so the whole party left the shop somewhat regretfully. At the corner of Duke Street Higgins and Nosey Flynn bevelled off to the left while the other three turned back towards the city. Rain was drizzling down on the cold streets and, when they reached the Ballast Office, Farrington suggested the Scotch House. The bar was full of men and loud with the noise of tongues and glasses. The three men pushed past the whining match-sellers at the door and formed a little party at the corner of the counter. They began to exchange stories. Leonard introduced them to a young fellow named Weathers who was performing at the Tivoli as an acrobat and knock-about *artiste*. Farrington stood a drink all round. Weathers said he would take a small Irish and Apollinaris. Farrington, who had definite notions of what was what, asked the boys would they have an Apollinaris too; but the boys told Tim to make theirs hot. The talk became theatrical. O'Halloran stood a round and then Farrington stood another round, Weathers protesting that the hospitality was too Irish. He promised to get them in behind the scenes and introduce them to some nice girls. O'Halloran said that he and Leonard would go but that Farrington wouldn't go because he was a married man; and Farrington's heavy dirty eyes leered at the company in token that he understood he was being chaffed. Weathers made them all have just one little tincture at his expense and promised to meet them later on at Mulligan's in Poolbeg Street.

When the Scotch House closed they went round to Mulligan's. They went into the parlor at the back and O'Halloran ordered small hot specials all round. They were all beginning to feel mellow. Farrington was just standing another round when Weathers came back. Much to Farrington's relief he drank a glass of bitter this time. Funds were running low but they had enough to keep them going. Presently two young women with big hats and a young man in a check suit came in and sat at a table close by. Weathers saluted them and told the company that they were out of the Tivoli. Farrington's eyes wandered at every moment in the direction of one of the young women. There was something striking in her appearance. An immense scarf of peacock-blue muslin was wound round her hat and knotted in a great bow under her chin; and she wore bright yellow gloves, reaching to the elbow. Farrington gazed admiringly at the plump arm which she moved very often and with much grace; and when, after a little time, she answered his gaze he admired still more her large dark brown eyes. The oblique staring expression in them fascinated him. She glanced at him once or twice and, when the party was leaving the room, she brushed against his chair and said *O, pardon!* in a London accent. He watched her leave the room in the hope that she would look back at him, but he was disappointed. He cursed his want of money and cursed all the rounds he had stood, particularly all the whiskies and Apollinaris which he had stood to Weathers. If there was one thing that he hated it was a sponge. He was so angry that he lost count of the conversation of his friends.

When Paddy Leonard called him he found that they were talking about feats of strength. Weathers was showing his biceps muscle to the company and boasting so much that the other two had called on Farrington to uphold the national honor. Farrington pulled up his sleeve accordingly and showed his biceps muscle to the company. The two arms were examined and compared and finally it was agreed to have a trial of strength. The table was cleared and the two men rested their elbows on it, clasping hands. When Paddy Leonard said *Go!* each was to try to bring down the other's hand on to the table. Farrington looked very serious and determined.

The trial began. After about thirty seconds Weathers brought his opponent's hand slowly down on to the table. Farrington's dark wine-coloured face flushed darker still with anger and humiliation at having been defeated by such a stripling.

—You're not to put the weight of your body behind it. Play fair, he said.   50

—Who's not playing fair? said the other.

—Come on again. The two best out of three.

The trial began again. The veins stood out on Farrington's forehead, and the pallor of Weathers' complexion changed to peony. Their hands and arms trembled under the stress. After a long struggle Weathers again brought his opponent's hand slowly on to the table. There was a murmur of applause from the spectators. The curate, who was standing beside the table, nodded his red head towards the victor and said with loutish familiarity:

—Ah! that's the knack!

—What the hell do you know about it? said Farrington fiercely, turning on   55
the man. What do you put in your gab for?

—Sh, sh! said O'Halloran, observing the violent expression of Farrington's face. Pony up, boys. We'll have just one little smahan more and then we'll be off.

A very sullen-faced man stood at the corner of O'Connell Bridge waiting for the little Sandymount tram to take him home. He was full of smouldering anger and revengefulness. He felt humiliated and discontented; he did not even feel drunk; and he had only twopence in his pocket. He cursed everything. He had done for himself in the office, pawned his watch, spent all his money; and he had not even got drunk. He began to feel thirsty again and he longed to be back again in the hot reeking public-house. He had lost his reputation as a strong man, having been defeated twice by a mere boy. His heart swelled with fury and, when he thought of the woman in the big hat who had brushed against him and said *Pardon!* his fury nearly choked him.

His tram let him down at Shelbourne Road and he steered his great body along in the shadow of the wall of the barracks. He loathed returning to his home. When he went in by the side-door he found the kitchen empty and the kitchen fire nearly out. He bawled upstairs:

—Ada! Ada!

His wife was a little sharp-faced woman who bullied her husband when he   60
was sober and was bullied by him when he was drunk. They had five children. A little boy came running down the stairs.

—Who is that? said the man, peering through the darkness.

—Me, pa.

—Who are you? Charlie?

—No, pa. Tom.

—Where's your mother?   65

—She's out at the chapel.

—That's right. . . . Did she think of leaving any dinner for me?

—Yes, pa. I—

—Light the lamp. What do you mean by having the place in darkness? Are the other children in bed?

The man sat down heavily on one of the chairs while the little boy lit the 70 lamp. He began to mimic his son's flat accent, saying half to himself: *At the chapel. At the chapel, if you please!* When the lamp was lit he banged his fist on the table and shouted:

—What's for my dinner?

—I'm going . . . to cook it, pa, said the little boy.

The man jumped up furiously and pointed to the fire.

—On that fire! You let the fire out! By God, I'll teach you to do that again!

He took a step to the door and seized the walking-stick which was standing 75 behind it.

—I'll teach you to let the fire out! he said, rolling up his sleeve in order to give his arm free play.

The little boy cried *O, pa!* and ran whimpering round the table, but the man followed him and caught him by the coat. The little boy looked about him wildly but, seeing no way of escape fell upon his knees.

—Now, you'll let the fire out the next time! said the man, striking at him viciously with the stick. Take that, you little whelp!

The boy uttered a squeal of pain as the stick cut his thigh. He clasped his hands together in the air and his voice shook with fright.

—O, pa! he cried. Don't beat me, pa! And I'll . . . I'll say a *Hail Mary* for 80 you. . . . I'll say a *Hail Mary* for you, pa, if you don't beat me. . . . I'll say a *Hail Mary.* . . .   *[1914]*

A thorough critical analysis of "Counterparts" using any one of these approaches would take dozens of pages. The following are brief suggestions for how such a reading might proceed.

NEW CRITICISM

A New Critic might want to demonstrate the multiple ways the title holds the narrative together, giving it unity and coherence—for example, Farrington and his son Tom are counterparts since Tom is the victim of his father's bullying just as Farrington is bullied by Mr. Alleyne at work. You can also probably spot other counterparts: Farrington and his wife, for example, trade off bullying each other, and their means of escaping from the drudgery of their lives, the bar and the church, are also parallel. And naturally when Weathers, the acrobat, defeats the much larger Farrington in arm wrestling, we are reminded of the verbal beating Farrington must endure from his equally diminutive boss, Mr. Alleyne. New Critics are fond of finding the ways all the elements of a text reinforce one another.

A New Critic might argue that these counterparts or oppositions introduce tensions into the story from the first few lines when the "bell rang furiously" for Farrington to report to Mr. Alleyne for a dressing down. The irony is that Farrington is big and Alleyne is small, that Farrington is powerful and Alleyne is fragile as an egg. But it is Mr. Alleyne who breaks Farrington; it is Farrington who is weak. Throughout the story, tensions, oppositions, and ironies continue, for example, when Farrington is defeated by the smaller Weathers. In the last scene, the tension is finally resolved when the larger Farrington beats his small son, making him a counterpart to both Alleyne and Weathers in oppressing the weak. The final evidence that Farrington is ethically powerless is cruelly obvious as the son promises to pray for his abusing father.

FEMINIST CRITICISM

Feminist critics and their first cousins, gender critics, would naturally be struck by the violent masculinity of Farrington, his fantasies of riot and abuse, his savage feelings of revenge, and his "smouldering anger" (para. 57). Farrington is depicted not only as crude and brutish but also as a kind of perverse stereotype of male vanity, self-centeredness, and irresponsibility. His obsession with obtaining money for drinking completely disregards his role as the provider for a large family, and, of course, the beatings of his son are a cruel parody of his role as paternal protector. And if he had not wasted his money on drink, Farrington would also be a womanizer ("Farrington's eyes wandered at every moment in the direction of one of the young women," para. 47). Gender critics would be interested in the social and cultural mechanisms that could construct such primitive masculinity.

A reasonable argument might focus on the representation of women in the story. Miss Parker, Miss Delacour, Farrington's wife, and the performer Farrington sees in the bar are marginal characters. One student made the following claim: "The women in Farrington's world, and Irish society in general, have no agency: they are prevented from taking an active part in determining their lives and futures." Another student argued differently, saying, "While women in general are oppressed by the raw and brutal masculinity represented by Farrington, the women in this story do hold a degree of power over men." Based on their own analysis and interpretations, these students demonstrated that there was reasonable textual evidence to support their claims.

PSYCHOANALYTIC CRITICISM

A psychoanalytic critic would first notice the extreme pattern of behavior Farrington exhibits, as he repeatedly withdraws from his adult work responsibilities and as he fantasizes about being physically violent against his supervisors. Critics would argue that such behavior is typical of Farrington's repressed wounds and his unresolved conflicts with his own father. Farrington seems to be playing out painful childhood experiences. Given the violent displacement (taking it out on someone else) visited on Tom, we can imagine that Farrington is beating not only his boss, Mr. Alleyne, but also perhaps his own abusive father. The fantasies at work in Farrington also suggest the psychological defense of projection, since Farrington is blaming his problems on Mr. Alleyne and his job. Although his tasks do seem to be tedious, they certainly cannot account for his "spasm of rage" (para. 15) or his desire "to clear out the whole office singlehanded" (para. 32). When Farrington feels "humiliated and discontented" (para. 57), it is only in part because of his immediate context. It is the return of the repressed that plagues Farrington, a resurfacing of a buried pain. These ideas should also be tied to Farrington's death wish, especially his stunningly self-destructive behavior at work. Freudian critics would also argue that these specific actions are related to other core issues that would include intense loss of self-esteem, fear of intimacy, and betrayal.

MARXIST CRITICISM

A Marxist critic would be interested in focusing on the specific historical moment of "Counterparts" and not on Farrington's individual psyche, which can only distract us from the real force that affects human experience — the economic system in which Farrington is trapped. Economic power — not the Oedipal drama or gender — is the crucial human motivator. Farrington's material circumstances and not timeless values are the key to understanding his behavior. The real battle lines are drawn between Crosbie and Alleyne (the "haves") and Farrington (a "have-not") — that is, between the bourgeoisie and the proletariat, between those who control economic resources and those who perform the labor that fills the coffers of the rich. In a Marxist analysis, critics would argue that Farrington is a victim of class warfare. His desperation, his humiliation, his rage, his cruel violence are all traceable to classism — an ideology that determines people's worth according to their economic class. Although Farrington does appear shiftless and irresponsible, it is not because of his class; it is because of the meaninglessness of his work and the demeaning hierarchy that keeps him at the bottom. In his alienation, he reverts to a primitive physical masculinity, a false consciousness that only further diminishes his sense of his worth.

Marxists are often interested in what lies beneath the text in its political unconscious. To get at the unconscious, Marxists, like psychoanalytic critics, look for symptoms on the surface that suggest problems beneath. Typically, such symptomatic readings reveal class conflicts that authors are sometimes unaware of themselves. Marxist critics might debate whether Joyce himself understood that the root cause of Farrington's aberrant behavior was economic and not psychological. This makes sense since for Marxists both reader and writer are under the sway of the same ideological system that they see as natural.

One student made the following claim: "Farrington's role as proletarian results in his feelings of inferiority, resentment over lack of entitlement, and an expectation of disappointment." This same student, like many Marxist critics who see the function of literature through a pragmatic lens, concluded her essay with an appeal toward change, arguing that "The remedy does not lie in changing Farrington's consciousness, but rather in changing the economic and political discourse of power that has constituted him."

DECONSTRUCTION

One of many possible deconstructions of "Counterparts" would involve focusing on a troubling or puzzling point called an *aporia*. Some deconstructive critics have looked at the incomplete phrase that Farrington copies, "*In no case shall the said Bernard Bodley be . . .*" as an aporia, an ambiguous and not completely understandable textual puzzle but one that might be a way into the story's meaning. The oppositions that are being deconstructed or laid bare here are *presence* and *absence, word* and *reality*. Working off the implications of the title "Counterparts," Bernard Bodley can be seen as a double or counterpart for Farrington, a character like Bodley whose existence is in doubt. Although Farrington's size suggests that he is very much physically present, his behavior might suggest otherwise. He spends his time copying other people's words and has a compelling need to repeat the narrative of his encounter with Mr. Alleyne, as if he must demonstrate his own existence through repetition. He does not have a viable inner life, an authentic identity. Farrington's essence is not present but absent. His identity is insubstantial. He tries to fill the emptiness at the center of his being with camaraderie and potency, but his efforts produce the opposite — escape, loneliness, and weakness. In other words, the said Farrington does not really exist and cannot be. In this way, we can deconstruct "Counterparts" as a story in which presence is absence, strength is weakness, Farrington's actions lead only to paralysis and repetition, and Farrington's frustration with his impotence makes his oppressors more powerful.

One student working with similar interpretations of "Counterparts" noted other oppositions, especially between male and female, escape and confinement. She argued that Farrington spends most of his time trying to avoid being thought of as stereotypically feminine. However, the more exaggerated his masculine aggression, drinking, violence, and irresponsibility become, the weaker, the more stereotypically feminine he becomes. Similarly, the more Farrington tries to escape, the more ensnared he is. In this way, the student argued, our conventional understandings of these opposing terms are deconstructed, so that we are no longer confident about the meaning of escape, masculinity, or strength.

READER-RESPONSE CRITICISM

Willa Ervinman, a student, was asked to respond to the story by using Stanley Fish's ideas and noting the conflicts between the interpretive or discourse communities Willa belonged to and those depicted in the story. The following are excerpts from her response journal:

> I was upset by Farrington's lack of responsibility at work. He is
> completely unreliable and demonstrates very little self-esteem. He
> must know that the people he works with consider him a slacker and
> a fake. I was raised in a middle-class home where both my parents
> worked hard in a bank from 9 to 5. Just the idea that they would
> sneak out of work to drink in dark bars is absurd. My belief in the

> discourse of middle-class responsibility or perhaps the Protestant work ethic makes it almost impossible for me to see Farrington with sympathy even though I can see that his work is probably completely mechanical and unfulfilling. . . .
>
> Farrington's domestic violence against his son is such a violation of the discourse of domesticity that it is hard to understand any other response. Someone in my response group thought that Farrington was a victim of his working-class discourse of masculinity. I can see how he was humiliated by the smaller men, Mr. Alleyne and Weathers, but beating his innocent son as a kind of revenge cannot be forgiven. My grandmother tells me that it was common for children to be physically punished in her day, but in the interpretive community I was raised in, there is no excuse for domestic violence. It is more than a character flaw; it is criminal behavior, and I judge Farrington to be a social menace, beyond compassion.

Willa went on to argue that Farrington's violent behavior is inexcusable, interpreting our current understandings of domestic violence and responsible masculinity as evidence. She blended this personal view with textual support. Her warrant for her claim was that historical circumstances and norms should not be used to excuse reprehensible behavior.

POSTCOLONIAL CRITICISM

"Counterparts" was written in the early twentieth century at a time when the Ireland Joyce writes about was still a colony of the British Empire. Farrington is, then, a colonial subject and subject to political domination. At the story's opening, Farrington, a Catholic from the south of Ireland, is summoned by a "furious voice" from Northern Ireland, a stronghold of British sympathy and Protestant domination. The tension is announced early because it is crucial to Farrington's behavior and his internalized and colonized mindset. Many colonials have a negative self-image because they are alienated from their own indigenous culture. Indeed, Farrington seems completely ill suited to the office copying task he is relegated to. He seems more suited to some physical endeavor, but given the difficult economics of Dublin, he probably has few career options.

Farrington is the Other in the discourse of colonialism, and he is made to seem inferior at every turn, from the verbal lashing of Mr. Alleyne to the physical defeat by Weathers, who is probably British. Symbolically, Farrington tries to resist his subjugation by the British establishment but fails. He is what postcolonial theorists refer to as *unhomed* or *displaced*. He is uncomfortable at work, in the bars where he seeks solace, and finally in his ultimate refuge, a place unprepared even to feed him. Indeed, in an act likely to perpetuate abuse upon future generations, Farrington turns on his own family, becoming, through his enraged attack on his child Tom, a metaphor for the conflicted, tormented, and defeated Ireland. When a colonial is not "at home" even in his own home, he is truly in psychological agony and exile. Joyce represents the trauma of British domination through one subject's self-destructive and self-hating journey, a journey made even more cruelly ironic by Farrington's attack—in a mimicry of British aggression and injustice—on his own subjected son.

NEW HISTORICISM

A critic influenced by Foucault and New Historicism might argue that Farrington is a victim of an inflexible discourse of masculinity, that he has been socialized by working-class norms of how a man should behave to such an extent that he cannot change. Growing up in a working-class culture, Farrington would have received high marks among his peers for his size and strength, just as Mr. Alleyne would be diminished in status for his. And in another context, say, on a construction site, Farrington's sense of masculinity might be a plus. But in an office, his aggressive masculinity is a liability. In all cultures, people are subject to multiple discourses that pull them one way then another. Farrington's sarcasm, his drinking, his longing for camaraderie, and his resorting to violence to solve problems are the results of being too enmeshed in a discourse of masculinity from working-class Dublin and not enough in the middle-class business assumptions about discipline, responsibility, and concentration. Farrington is defeated at work, in the pubs, and at home because he is unable to move from one discourse to another. He is stuck in a subject position that only reinforces his powerlessness. His self-esteem is so damaged by the end of the story that he even violates his own code of masculinity by beating a defenseless child.

QUEER THEORY

Because queer theorists are as concerned with gender identities as they are with sexuality, they would be interested in the asymmetrical power relationship between Farrington's "great bulk" (para. 5) and Mr. Alleyne's "little man" with a "pink and hairless head" (para. 8). Farrington is surely performing as a queer character when he betrays his traditional masculine role by being thoroughly emasculated at work; he is incompetent at simple tasks, and his status in the hierarchy is diminishing. And the reader knows that Farrington's occupation as a copier will soon be obsolete, replaced by legions of female typists. He is a queer figure in a queer job. However, his sexuality is less of an issue than the idea that heterosexuality as a pervasive and rigid institution causes Farrington intense humiliation and anguish as he fails at every traditional (albeit arbitrary) masculine standard.

Farrington seeks solace and escape from his newfound queerness in the male homosocial pubs of Dublin. Here, he does seem to perform masterfully with the retelling of his witty put-down of his boss. But the reader is well aware that Farrington has queered the real narrative of his confrontation with Mr. Alleyne. In actuality, he was forced to apologize abjectly for his remarks and will pay dearly for not knowing his place. It is also here in his beloved pub space that he receives the greatest blow to what remains of his masculinity. He is humiliated in a contest of strength by an "artiste," "a mere boy" (para. 56).

When as an alienated outcast he returns home in rage and anger, and "viciously" (para. 78) beats his own son in a traditionally female space, the kitchen, his impotence is complete. In a good example of fluid gender roles, his wife, Ada, "who bullied [Farrington] when he was sober and was bullied by him when he was drunk" (para. 60), temporarily abandons her traditional role of caring for him. Their relationship is indeed queer. Farrington's performative queerness is never clearer than in his final violent undoing of the conventional role of the protective father, making a mockery of masculine decency, compassion, and fairness.

Alert to the inconsistencies, contradictions, and ambiguities of conventional gender behaviors, protocols, and values, queer theorists offer provocative and enriching readings that remind readers how easy it is to oversimplify the bewildering complexities of being men and women.

Sample Student Essay

The following essay was written by a first-year student using a postcolonial perspective.

Molly Frye
Prof. Christine Hardee
English 102
10 May - - - -

A Refugee at Home

It is difficult to argue that Farrington, the main character in James Joyce's "Counterparts," should be seen in a sympathetic light. After all, he seems an extreme stereotype of an aggressive, irresponsible drinker. Although his character traits certainly do not conform to our modern standards of mature masculinity, I want to argue that although we do not want to condone Farrington's brutal behavior, we can find it understandable. As an Irish subject in the British Empire, Farrington is more sinned against than sinner, more victim than victimizer. Farrington is not simply an obnoxious male since his actions can be understood as stemming from his colonial consciousness in struggling vainly against his powerlessness. His frustrations are especially clear in the three spaces Farrington inhabits: his office, the bars, and his home.

After setting up a context, states her claim supported by three examples.

Farrington's first appearance is telling. Because of his poor job performance, his boss demands to see him: "Send Farrington here!" Farrington, who most often is referred to as

"the man," mutters his first words, "Blast him!" This typical
antagonistic relationship in a colonial context foreshadows
the rest of the story. Farrington is the working-class subject
caught in a menial and unsatisfying job he can never complete under a boss who has social and cultural power. This
counterpart relationship is similar to the positions of Ireland
and England where the colony is disparaged and oppressed by
the empire. In his office run by Protestants loyal to the
British, Farrington is ironically "tall and of great bulk," while
his boss, Mr. Alleyne, is "a little man" whose head, "pink and
hairless," resembles a "large egg." Farrington's only asset, his
size and strength, is irrelevant because he is so economically
and socially weak. This disparity only increases Farrington's
frustration and precipitates fantasies of violence against his
oppressor. When Mr. Alleyne rebukes him, "Do you mind me
now," Farrington is sent into a "spasm of rage." He cannot,
of course, act on his aggressive urges, so he represses these
feelings by rationalizing that he must have a "good night's
drinking." Thus begins a pattern of self-destructive behavior
that only increases Farrington's marginal position in society.

First concrete example of Farrington as frustrated colonial subject.

Transition to explanation of Farrington's failures at work.

Farrington is so uncomfortable at work, a postcolonial
condition known as being unhomed, that he cannot concentrate on anything but drinking. He seems quite unsuited for
the tedious task of copying legal documents, staring "stupidly
at the last words he has written," knowing he will never
finish his task, never advance, never get anywhere. Farrington
is paralyzed by his alienation. He feels his only recourse is
sneaking out to drink, which only exacerbates his poverty and
powerlessness. When he attempts to cover up his inability to
concentrate and finish copying letters for Mr. Alleyne, he is
caught and confronted. Instead of acknowledging his under-
ling position, he attempts a witticism which, of course,
backfires. Even though he is forced to apologize, his job now
seems in jeopardy. Mr. Alleyne humiliates him by calling him
an "impertinent ruffian," a status that seems to him the most
he can hope for. As a colonial subject, Farrington is plagued
by a double consciousness. He longs for the masculine status
his physical strength should give him in his working-class
culture, but he must suffer indignities at the hands of
Mr. Alleyne because of his inability to perform a simple task a
competent child could do. Farrington should probably be
working in construction as a laborer, not an office worker
where discipline, patience, and mental concentration are
necessary.

Uses postcolonial ideas to explain Farrington's behavior.

When Farrington finally leaves work, he expects to find
some solace in the Dublin pubs. He has hocked his watch for

Transition to second example of Farrington as colonized.

drinking money, a clear indication of how desperate he is to escape the confines of regimented office work. The camaraderie of Paddy Leonard and Nosey Flynn is temporary, and Farrington is not at home in these public spaces either. He runs out of money he would have spent drinking and womanizing, and he is finally humiliated by another small British man. Called on to "uphold the national honor," Farrington's loss in an arm-wrestling contest with Weathers leaves him "full of smouldering anger and revengefulness. He is humiliated and discontented . . . His heart swelled with fury. . . ." His longing for escape from the confinement and disappointment of work has taken a disastrous turn. Farrington's already damaged self-esteem is degraded, and his repressed anger at his oppressor is near the breaking point. Perhaps his self-destructive behavior can be redirected at his home, his last possibility for comfort and acceptance.

Transition to last example.

For the unhomed colonized, however, this is not to be. Farrington enters the kitchen to find it symbolically empty, "the fire nearly out." His wife is at chapel, his five children in bed, and his dinner is cold. His agonies continue. Having internalized the humiliations suffered at work and in the pubs, Farrington has no resources left. And so in a bitter irony, he beats his son for not attending to the fire, "striking at him viciously with a stick. 'Take that, you little whelp!'" Farrington the oppressed becomes Farrington the oppressor. His role as provider and protector is cruelly turned upside-down. Farrington compensates for his defeats at the hands of Mr. Alleyne and Weathers by beating his son, and in doing so, mimics the cycle of oppression prevalent in countries dominated by the empire. Farrington is not only a cog in the bureaucratic wheel at work; he is also a pathetic, but understandable cog crushed by the wheel of power even in his own home.

Uses all three examples in concluding.

≡ FOR THINKING AND WRITING

1. Using a feminist critique of Joyce, one student claimed that "Joyce's text indulges dominance over submission." Do you think there is textual evidence to support this assertion?

2. How might various critics (postcolonial, feminist, Marxist, psychoanalytical) interpret these lines from "Counterparts":

   - "The man passed through the crowd, looking on the spectacle generally with proud satisfaction and staring masterfully at the office-girls" (para. 42).

- ■ "His heart swelled with fury and, when he thought of the woman in the big hat who had brushed against him and said *Pardon!* his fury nearly choked him" (para. 57).
- ■ "What's for my dinner?" (para. 71).

3. Influenced by New Critical ideas, one student wrote, "'Counterparts' is filled with parallel scenes and emotions that reflect one another." What textual evidence would help support this notion?

4. Engaging in a Marxist critique, one student wrote, "His unfair work conditions so distract him that he does not even know the names of his children." What is the warrant behind such an assertion? What work conditions might the student think "fair"?

5. Using a New Historicist approach, what might you learn about this story from doing research on the elementary-school curriculum in Dublin, the pay scale in a law office, the legal rights of women, the laws on domestic violence, the unemployment rate? What other practices and texts do you think would illuminate the story?

≡ A WRITING EXERCISE

Now you try. After reading the following story, construct an argument influenced by one or more of the following critical approaches: postcolonial, Marxist, reader-response, or feminist.

JAMES JOYCE
Eveline

Like "Counterparts," "Eveline" is from Dubliners *(1914).*

She sat at the window watching the evening invade the avenue. Her head was leaned against the window curtains and in her nostrils was the odor of dusty cretonne. She was tired.

Few people passed. The man out of the last house passed on his way home; she heard his footsteps clacking along the concrete pavement and afterwards crunching on the cinder path before the new red houses. One time there used to be a field there in which they used to play every evening with other people's children. Then a man from Belfast bought the field and built houses in it — not like their little brown houses but bright brick houses with shining roofs. The children of the avenue used to play together in that field — the Devines, the Waters, the Dunns, little Keogh the cripple, she and her brothers and sisters. Ernest, however, never played: he was too grown up. Her father used often to hunt them in out of the field with his blackthorn stick; but usually little Keogh used to keep *nix* and call out when he saw her father coming. Still they seemed to have been rather happy then. Her father was not so bad then; and besides, her mother was alive. That was a long time ago; she and her brothers and sisters were all grown up; her mother was dead. Tizzie Dunn was dead, too, and the Waters had gone back to England. Everything changes. Now she was going to go away like the others, to leave her home.

Home! She looked round the room, reviewing all its familiar objects which she had dusted once a week for so many years, wondering where on earth all the dust came from. Perhaps she would never see again those familiar objects from which she had never dreamed of being divided. And yet during all those years she had never found out the name of the priest whose yellowing photograph hung on the wall above the broken harmonium beside the colored print of the promises made to Blessed Margaret Mary Alacoque. He had been a school friend of her father. Whenever he showed the photograph to a visitor her father used to pass it with a casual word:

—He is in Melbourne now.

She had consented to go away, to leave her home. Was that wise? She tried to weigh each side of the question. In her home anyway she had shelter and food; she had those whom she had known all her life about her. Of course she had to work hard both in the house and at business. What would they say of her in the Stores when they found out that she had run away with a fellow? Say she was a fool, perhaps; and her place would be filled up by advertisement. Miss Gavan would be glad. She had always had an edge on her, especially whenever there were people listening.

—Miss Hill, don't you see these ladies are waiting?

—Look lively, Miss Hill, please.

She would not cry many tears at leaving the Stores.

But in her new home, in a distant unknown country, it would not be like that. Then she would be married—she, Eveline. People would treat her with respect then. She would not be treated as her mother had been. Even now, though she was over nineteen, she sometimes felt herself in danger of her father's violence. She knew it was that that had given her the palpitations. When they were growing up he had never gone for her, like he used to go for Harry and Ernest, because she was a girl; but latterly he had begun to threaten her and say what he would do to her only for her dead mother's sake. And now she had nobody to protect her. Ernest was dead and Harry, who was in the church decorating business, was nearly always down somewhere in the country. Besides, the invariable squabble for money on Saturday nights had begun to weary her unspeakably. She always gave her entire wages—seven shillings—and Harry always sent up what he could but the trouble was to get any money from her father. He said she used to squander the money, that she had no head, that he wasn't going to give her his hard-earned money to throw about the streets, and much more, for he was usually fairly bad of a Saturday night. In the end he would give her the money and ask her had she any intention of buying Sunday's dinner. Then she had to rush out as quickly as she could and do her marketing, holding her black leather purse tightly in her hand as she elbowed

5

her way through the crowds and returning home late under her load of provisions. She had hard work to keep the house together and to see that the two young children who had been left to her charge went to school regularly and got their meals regularly. It was hard work — a hard life — but now that she was about to leave it she did not find it a wholly undesirable life.

She was about to explore another life with Frank. Frank was very kind, manly, open-hearted. She was to go away with him by the night-boat to be his wife and to live with him in Buenos Aires where he had a home waiting for her. How well she remembered the first time she had seen him; he was lodging in a house on the main road where she used to visit. It seemed a few weeks ago. He was standing at the gate, his peaked cap pushed back on his head and his hair tumbled forward over a face of bronze. Then they had come to know each other. He used to meet her outside the Stores every evening and see her home. He took her to see *The Bohemian Girl* and she felt elated as she sat in an unaccustomed part of the theater with him. He was awfully fond of music and sang a little. People knew that they were courting and, when he sang about the lass that loves a sailor, she always felt pleasantly confused. He used to call her Poppens out of fun. First of all it had been an excitement for her to have a fellow and then she had begun to like him. He had tales of distant countries. He had started as a deck boy at a pound a month on a ship of the Allan Line going out to Canada. He told her the names of the ships he had been on and the names of the different services. He had sailed through the Straits of Magellan and he told her stories of the terrible Patagonians. He had fallen on his feet in Buenos Aires, he said, and had come over to the old country just for a holiday. Of course, her father had found out the affair and had forbidden her to have anything to say to him.

—I know these sailor chaps, he said.

One day he had quarreled with Frank and after that she had to meet her lover secretly.

The evening deepened in the avenue. The white of two letters in her lap grew indistinct. One was to Harry; the other was to her father. Ernest had been her favorite but she liked Harry too. Her father was becoming old lately, she noticed; he would miss her. Sometimes he could be very nice. Not long before, when she had been laid up for a day, he had read her out a ghost story and made toast for her at the fire. Another day, when their mother was alive, they had all gone for a picnic to the Hill of Howth. She remembered her father putting on her mother's bonnet to make the children laugh.

Her time was running out but she continued to sit by the window, leaning her head against the window curtain, inhaling the odor of dusty cretonne. Down far in the avenue she could hear a street organ playing. She knew the air. Strange that it should come that very night to remind her of the promise to her mother, her promise to keep the home together as long as she could. She remembered the last night of her mother's illness; she was again in the close dark room at the other side of the hall and outside she heard a melancholy air of Italy. The organ-player had been ordered to go away and given sixpence. She remembered her father strutting back into the sickroom saying:

10

—Damned Italians! coming over here!   15

As she mused the pitiful vision of her mother's life laid its spell on the very quick of her being — that life of commonplace sacrifices closing in final craziness. She trembled as she heard again her mother's voice saying constantly with foolish insistence:

—Derevaun Seraun! Derevaun Seraun!°

She stood up in a sudden impulse of terror. Escape! She must escape! Frank would save her. He would give her life, perhaps love, too. But she wanted to live. Why should she be unhappy? She had a right to happiness. Frank would take her in his arms, fold her in his arms. He would save her.

She stood among the swaying crowd in the station at the North Wall. He held her hand and she knew that he was speaking to her, saying something about the passage over and over again. The station was full of soldiers with brown baggages. Through the wide doors of the sheds she caught a glimpse of the black mass of the boat, lying in beside the quay wall, with illumined portholes. She answered nothing. She felt her cheek pale and cold and, out of a maze of distress, she prayed to God to direct her, to show her what was her duty. The boat blew a long mournful whistle into the mist. If she went, tomorrow she would be on the sea with Frank, steaming toward Buenos Aires. Their passage had been booked. Could she still draw back after all he had done for her? Her distress awoke a nausea in her body and she kept moving her lips in silent fervent prayer.

A bell clanged upon her heart. She felt him seize her hand: 20
—Come!

All the seas of the world tumbled about her heart. He was drawing her into them: he would drown her. She gripped with both hands at the iron railing.
—Come!

No! No! No! It was impossible. Her hands clutched the iron in frenzy. Amid the seas she sent a cry of anguish!
—Eveline! Evvy!   25

He rushed beyond the barrier and called to her to follow. He was shouted at to go on but he still called to her. She set her white face to him, passive, like a helpless animal. Her eyes gave him no sign of love or farewell or recognition.

[1914]

≣ FOR THINKING AND WRITING

1. There is a French expression that says to understand all is to forgive all. Given the ending of "Eveline," argue for or against this idea.

2. Compare "Counterparts" and "Eveline" (see "Strategies for Writing a Comparative Paper," p. 140), arguing that Joyce has or has not prepared us for the endings.

Derevaun Seraun!: Gaelic for "The end of pleasure is pain."

Acknowledgments *(continued from page vi)*

Allison Alsup, "Old Houses," *New Orleans Review,* issue 38.1. Copyright © Allison Alsup. Reprinted with permission.

David Barno. "A New Moral Compact." *Foreign Policy,* November 9, 2012. © 2012 Foreign Policy. Republished with permission conveyed through Copyright Clearance Center, Inc.

T. S. Eliot, "The Love Song of J. Alfred Prufrock." *Collected Poems 1909–1962.* Copyright © 1963 by T. S. Eliot. Used with permission from Faber and Faber Ltd.

"Stopping by Woods on a Snowy Evening" from THE POETRY OF ROBERT FROST edited by Edward Connery Lathem. Copyright 1923, 1928, 1969 by Henry Holt and Company. Copyright 1944, 1951, 1956 by Robert Frost. Reprinted by permission of Henry Holt and Company, LLC.

Rivka Galchen, "Usl at the Stadium." *The New Yorker,* October 12, 2015. © 2015 by Rivka Galchen. Used with permission, All rights not specifically granted herein are hereby reserved to the Licensor.

Paul Goldberger. "Disconnected Urbanism." Reprinted by permission of the author.

Edward Hirsch, "Execution" from THE NIGHT PARADE by Edward Hirsch, copyright © 1989 by Edward Hirsch. Used by permission of Alfred A. Knopf, an imprint of the Knopf Doubleday Publishing Group, a division of Penguin Random House LLC. All rights reserved.

Lynda Hull. "Night Waitress" from *Collected Poems.* Copyright © 1986 by Lynda Hull. Reprinted by permission of The Permissions Company, Inc., on behalf of Graywolf Press, Minneapolis, Minnesota, www.graywolfpress.org.

Luisa Igloria. "Regarding History" by Luisa Igloria from *Trill & Mordent,* © 2005 WorldTech Communications, Cincinnati, Ohio. Used with permission.

Jennifer Jacquet "The Seven Habits of Highly Effective Shaming" from IS SHAME NECESSARY?: NEW USES FOR AN OLD TOOL by Jennifer Jacquet, copyright © 2015 by Jennifer Jacquet. Used by permission of Pantheon Books, an imprint of the Knopf Doubleday Publishing Group, a division of Penguin Random House LLC. All rights reserved.

X. J. Kennedy. "Death of a Window Washer." *In a Prominent Bar in Secaucus: New and Selected Poems, 1955–2007,* page 168. © 2007 X. J. Kennedy. Reprinted with permission of The Johns Hopkins University Press; permission conveyed through Copyright Clearance Center, Inc.

Jamaica Kincaid. "Girl" from *At the Bottom of the River* by Jamaica Kincaid. Copyright © 1983 by Jamaica Kincaid. Reprinted by permission of Farrar, Straus & Giroux, LLC.

Yusef Komunyakaa. "Blackberries" from *Pleasure Dome: New and Collected Poems,* © 2001 by Yusef Komunyakaa. Published by Wesleyan University Press, Middletown, CT. Used by permission.

Sophia McDougall, "All Princesses Know Kung Fu [I Hate Strong Female Characters]." *New Statesman.* August 15, 2013. Copyright © 2013 New Statesman. Used with permission.

Sharon Olds. "Summer Solstice, New York City" from THE GOLD CELL by Sharon Olds, copyright © 1987 by Sharon Olds. Used by permission of Alfred A. Knopf, an imprint of the Knopf Doubleday Publishing Group, a division of Penguin Random House LLC. All rights reserved.

Mary Oliver. "Singapore" from *House of Light* by Mary Oliver, published by Beacon Press, Boston. Copyright © 1990 by Mary Oliver. Reprinted by permission of The Charlotte Sheedy Literary Agency Inc.

Daniel Orozco. "Orientation" from *Orientation and Other Stories* by Daniel Orozco. Copyright © 2011 by Daniel Orozco. Reprinted by permission of Farrar, Straus and Giroux, LLC.

Rolando Perez. "Office at Night" from *The Lining of Our Souls: Excursion into Selected Paintings of Edward Hopper* by Rolando Perez. Copyright © Cool Grove Press. Used with permission.

Regina Rini, "Should We Rename Institutions that Honour Dead Racists?" This article was originally published by Aeon Media (http://www.aeon.co, Twitter: @aeonmag). Used with permission.

Ronson, Jon. "How One Stupid Tweet Blew Up Justine Sacco's Life," *New York Times,* February 12, 2016. Copyright © 2016 Jon Ronson. Used with permission.

Index of Authors, Titles, First Lines, and Key Terms

Key term page numbers are in bold.